THE OFFICIAL

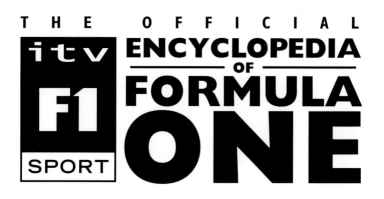

itv F1 SPORT

ENCYCLOPEDIA OF FORMULA ONE

THE ESSENTIAL GUIDE TO GRAND PRIX RACING

BRUCE JONES

CARLTON
BOOKS

Contents

The Teams 252

The Circuits 324

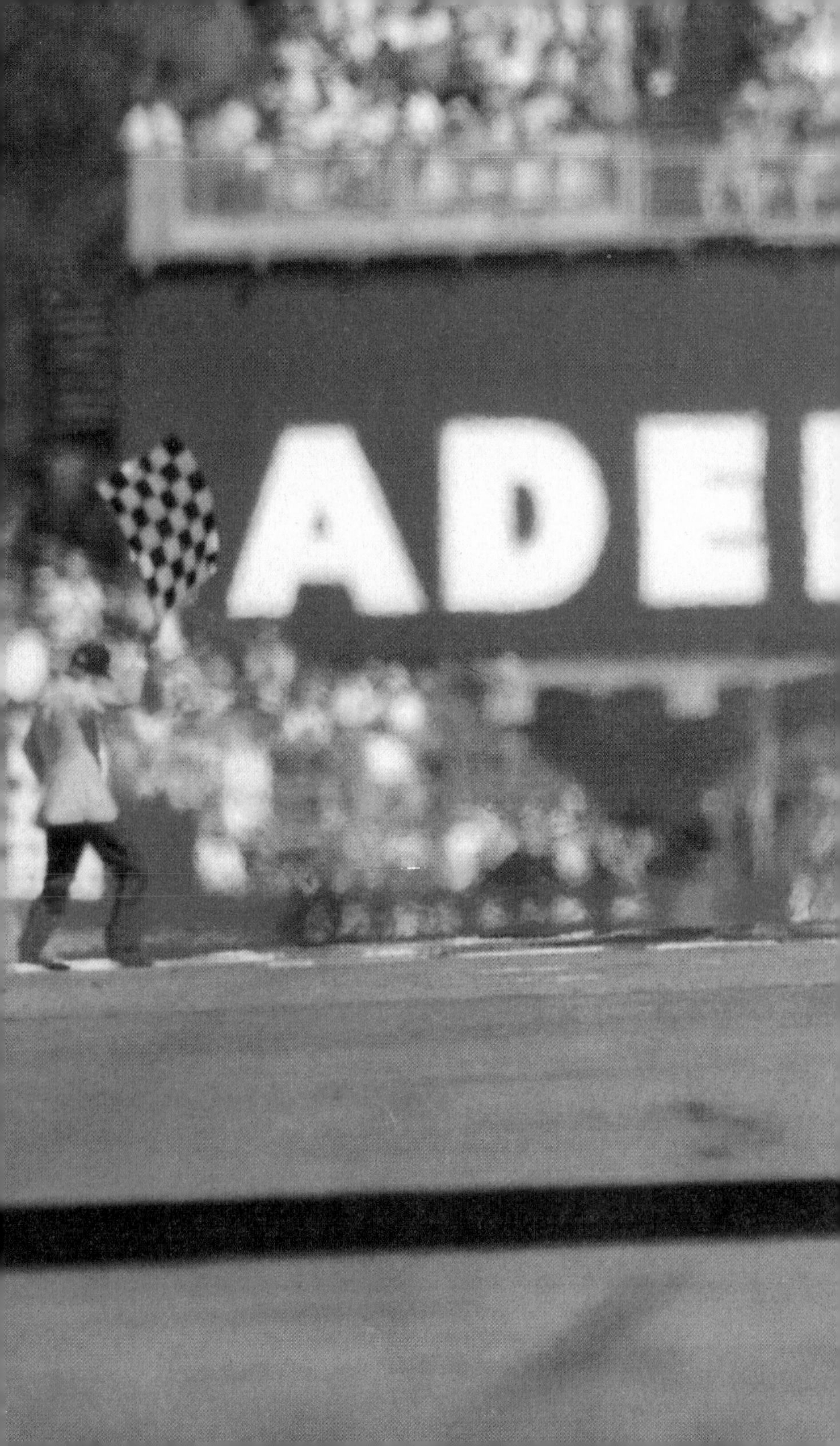
ADE

THE WORLD CHAMPIONSHIP

FORMULA ONE HAS MOVED AHEAD WITH GIGANTIC STRIDES SINCE THE WORLD Championship began in 1950. Not only have the cars changed out of all recognition, but the circuits, too, largely at the behest of Stewart in the 1970s, who had tired of seeing his contemporaries crashing with fatal consequences. Senna's death in 1994 accelerated a second wave of driver-led safety consciousness.

However, for all the changes, there is one thing that has not altered: the will to win and the fierce competition that surrounds it. Whether it was Juan Manuel

Fangio and Stirling Moss in the 1950s, Jim Clark and Jack Brabham in the 1960s, Jackie Stewart and Niki Lauda in the 1970s, Nelson Piquet or Alain Prost in the 1980s, or Ayrton Senna and Michael Schumacher in the 1990s, the epic battles to come out on top have made for compelling viewing over the last half a century and have propelled the sport into the global business that it is today.

This chapter deals, in chronological order, with each of the 51 World Championship seasons, since it all began in front of the Royal Family at Silverstone in 1950, right through to Michael Schumacher's return to title glory in the 2000 season.

KICKING UP THE SPARKS *Michael Schumacher splits Mika Hakkinen and Jean Alesi on his way to victory in the 1992 Belgian Grand Prix.*

1950

THE WORLD CHAMPIONSHIP WAS HELD FOR THE FIRST TIME IN 1950, linking the established Grands Prix of just six countries, Alfa Romeo and its drivers, Farina, Fangio and Fangioli dominated proceedings, but Ferrari was waiting for the opportunity to pounce.

In the years after the end of the Second World War it did not take long for motor racing to re-establish itself, and by 1950 the governing body had decided that the time was right to launch a World Championship. There was plenty of pre-war equipment available and also no shortage of drivers who had raced in the 1930s. True, they had lost some of the best years of their careers, but, despite the enforced break, were at the top of their game.

Alfa Romeo out in front

Alfa Romeo's superb squad comprised the legendary "three Fs": Dr Giuseppe "Nino" Farina (then aged 44), Juan Manuel Fangio (38) and Luigi Fagioli (53). Equipped with an update of the pre-war Tipo 158, they steamrollered the opposi-

tion, which was led by Ferrari.

Ferrari had been disappointing in 1949 and the team was absent from the very first race of the new series, held at a bleak Silverstone on May 13 in the presence of the royal family. There were 21 cars in the field for this first race, and Farina had the honour of taking the first pole position. Old stager Fagioli led initially, but dropped to third behind Farina and Fangio. When the latter's engine failed, Fagioli took second, ahead of local star Reg Parnell.

A week later at Monaco Farina's luck changed when he triggered a nine-car pile-up, which also took out Fagioli. Fangio was ahead of the carnage, and somehow survived when he came across it on the next lap. He went on to score a memorable win. Ferrari entered the championship for the first time, and 31-year-old Alberto Ascari was rewarded with second place, one lap down. Farina and Fagioli scored a one-two in the Swiss Grand Prix at the tricky Bremgarten road circuit, and once again Fangio suffered an engine failure – as did all three works Ferraris. At Spa Fangio fought back with his second win of the year, ahead of Fagioli. Variety was provided by Raymond Sommer, who led in his Talbot before blowing up.

DRIVERS' WORLD CHAMPIONSHIP

Pos	Driver	Nat.	Make	Pts
1	Giuseppe Farina	It	Alfa Romeo	30
2	Juan Manuel Fangio	Arg	Alfa Romeo	27
3	Luigi Fagioli	It	Alfa Romeo	24
4	Louis Rosier	Fr	Talbot	13
5	Alberto Ascari	It	Ferrari	11
6	Johnnie Parsons*	USA	Kurtis Kraft	8
7	Bill Holland*	USA	Kurtis Kraft	6
8	Prince Bira	Thai	Maserati	5
9	Reg Parnell	GB	Alfa Romeo	4
=	Louis Chiron	Mon	Maserati	4
=	Peter Whitehead	GB	Ferrari	4
=	Mauri Rose*	USA	Deidt Offenhauser	4

Best four scores from seven races to count *denotes points scored in Indy 500

Farina's laurels

The first championship, like so many to follow, came to a head in the final round at Monza. Fangio had 26 points to the 24 of the consistent Fagioli, and the 22 of Farina. Fangio and Farina had the new and more powerful 159 model, but the title was settled when Fangio retired with a seized gearbox. Farina won the race, and with it the championship. Ferrari had been working hard on a new unsupercharged engine during the sea-son, showing well in non-championship races, and Ascari was on the pace with the latest model. When his car retired, he took over the machine of team-mate Dorino Serafini and finished second, ahead of Fagioli. The most talked about car never appeared at a Grand Prix race. The much-vaunted V16 BRM made an ignominious debut in the International Trophy at Silverstone in August, retiring on the line with drive-shaft failure.

FIRST-TIME WINNER

Giuseppe Farina set the ball rolling with victory in both the first Grand Prix at Silverstone and the 1950 World Championship.

1951

ALFA ROMEO CONTINUED TO SET THE PACE, BUT FERRARI CAME CLOSE to toppling the champions. Mechanical problems had robbed him the previous year, but now Juan Manuel Fangio was dominant and claimed his first title.

For 1951 Alfa Romeo broke up the "three Fs" team, replacing Fagioli with 48-year-old Felice Bonetto. Froilan Gonzalez, who had previously driven a Maserati, joined Ascari and Luigi Villoresi at Ferrari. The stocky young Argentinian, known as the "Pampas Bull", was to become a major force during the season.

The championship was expanded to a total of seven races, with Monaco missing and events in Germany and Spain added. This time the series began in Switzerland, and in soaking conditions Fangio scored a fine win.

THE START OF SOMETHING GOOD
Juan Manuel Fangio en route to his first World Championship title at the French Grand Prix at Reims.

Moss makes his mark

Meanwhile, a promising young Englishman made his debut in a British HWM, qualifying 14th and finishing eighth. His name was Stirling Moss.

Farina and Fangio dominated the Belgian Grand Prix at

Spa, but when Fangio pitted, problems removing a rear wheel ruined his race. Farina won from the Ferraris of Ascari and Villoresi, while a fired-up Fangio set the fastest lap – but finished ninth.

Fagioli was back in an Alfa at Reims, and went on to score his first victory – but only after Fangio took over his car when his own mount had retired in a race of high attrition. Another shared car, the Ferrari of Gonzalez and Ascari, took second, ahead of Villoresi. After tyre troubles, Farina was a distant fifth.

A Ferrari win seemed on the cards, and the first finally came at Silverstone where Gonzalez put in a fine performance to take the lead from countryman Fangio when the Alfa driver pitted and stalled when he tried to rejoin. The BRM made its first championship appearance, with Reg Parnell taking a promising fifth and Peter Walker seventh.

Success for Ferrari

Ferrari proved the dominant force at the Nurburgring, the first championship race held on the long, tortuous circuit. Ascari notched up his first win, despite a late stop for rear tyres. Fangio, who required an extra scheduled fuel stop, took second for Alfa. Third to sixth places were filled with Ferraris, while Farina retired with gearbox trouble.

Monza was the penultimate round this year, and Ascari and Gonzalez celebrated a fine one-two for Ferrari in front of the

DRIVERS' WORLD CHAMPIONSHIP

Pos.	Driver	Nat.	Make	Pts
1	Juan Manuel Fangio	Arg	Alfa	31
2	Alberto Ascari	It	Ferrari	25
3	Froilan Gonzalez	Arg	Ferrari	24
4	Giuseppe Farina	It	Alfa	19
5	Luigi Villoresi	It	Ferrari	15
6	Piero Taruffi	It	Ferrari	10
7	Lee Wallard*	USA	Belanger	8
8	Felice Bonetto	It	Alfa	7
9	Mike Nazaruk*	USA	Jim Robbins	6
10	Reg Parnell	GB	Ferrari/BRM	5

Best four scores from eight races to count *denotes points scored in Indy 500

home crowd. Alfa had a much-modified car, the 159M, and Fangio was battling for the lead until a tyre failed. His storming recovery drive ended with engine failure. Farina retired early, but took over Bonetto's car and eventually earned third place.

The final race at Pedrables in Spain proved to be Alfa's swansong. Despite his Monza retirement, Fangio led Ascari by 28 points to 25 going into the race, and a dominant win secured Juan Manuel's first crown. The Ferraris suffered tyre troubles, with Gonzalez and pole man Ascari taking second and fourth, split by Farina's Alfa.

At the end of the year Alfa withdrew from Grand Prix racing, unable to finance a new car to challenge Ferrari in 1952.

Partly in response to Alfa's departure, the Fédération Internationale de l'Automobile announced that, for 1952, the World Championship would run to less powerful Formula Two rules. It was hoped that this would encourage a wider variety of cars and avoid a Ferrari walkover.

1952

FERRARI RESPONDED TO THE FORMULA TWO RULES CHANGES BY dominating the season. Alberto Ascari won every race he entered to became world champion. An injured Fangio could only watch these events from the sidelines.

Despite the change of regulations, Ferrari entered 1952 as the major force. The marque had already been highly successful in Formula Two, and had a first-class driver squad. Ascari, Villoresi and Piero Taruffi were joined by Farina – on the market after Alfa's withdrawal. The main opposition should have come from reigning champion Fangio, who had switched from Alfa Romeo to Maserati to drive the new A6GCM. However, he was forced to miss the entire season after breaking his neck in a crash during a non-championship race at Monza.

New faces

The rule change achieved its aim of attracting a variety of cars to take on the red machines. From France came the Gordinis of Jean Behra and Robert Manzon, while in Britain there was a host of projects under way, including the Cooper-Bristol, Connaught, HWM, Alta, Frazer Nash and ERA.

The most successful of these would prove to be the Cooper-Bristol, an underpowered but superb-handling machine. Its young driver was the flamboyant Englishman, Mike Hawthorn, who was the find of the year.

The championship began with the Swiss Grand Prix, notable for the absence of Ascari, who was busy with Ferrari commitments at Indianapolis. Taruffi scored an easy win, well ahead of local Ferrari privateer Rudi Fischer. The Gordini showed promise, with Behra taking third. That place was held by Moss in the HWM, but his car was withdrawn after two of its sister entries suffered hub failures.

Ascari returned at Spa, and scored his first win of the new Formula Two era in soaking conditions, ahead of team-mate Farina. Manzon gave Gordini another third, but all eyes were on Hawthorn, making his championship debut. He ran third and, after a fuel leak delayed him, finished a fine fourth. It was the highest place to date for a British car, and the first sign of great things to come from John Cooper's small company.

Pos.	Driver	Nat.	Make	Pts
DRIVERS' WORLD CHAMPIONSHIP				
1	Alberto Ascari	It	Ferrari	36
2	Giuseppe Farina	It	Ferrari	24
3	Piero Taruffi	It	Ferrari	22
4	Rudi Fischer	Swi	Ferrari	10
=	Mike Hawthorn	GB	Cooper-Bristol	10
6	Robert Manzon	Fr	Gordini	9
7	Troy Ruttman*	USA	Agajanian	8
=	Luigi Villoresi	It	Ferrari	8
9	Froilan Gonzalez	Arg	Maserati	6.5
10	Jim Rathmann*	USA	Grancor-Wynn	6
=	Jean Behra	Fr	Gordini	6

Best four scores from eight races to count *denotes points scored in Indy 500

Behra's Gordini beat the Ferraris at Reims but, unfortunately for him in this particular year, it was a non-championship race.

Ferrari triumphs again

The French Grand Prix moved to Rouen a week later, and Ascari, Farina and Taruffi finished one-two-three, with Manzon fourth. At Silverstone, Ascari and Taruffi were one-two, but Hawthorn was the darling of the crowd, rising to the challenge and finishing third. Dennis Poore also impressed with his Connaught, leading Hawthorn until a long fuel stop, before coming fourth.

The German Grand Prix at the Nurburgring was a complete Ferrari whitewash, with Ascari heading Farina, Fischer and Taruffi. Ascari had to work hard for his win: a late pit stop for oil dropped him to second and forced him to catch and repass Farina. The new Dutch event at Zandvoort saw Ascari heading home Farina and Villoresi, with Hawthorn again leading the challenge in a gallant fourth with his Cooper-Bristol.

Ascari had clinched the title before the finale at Monza, where he scored his sixth win from six starts.

RUNAWAY CHAMPION
Alberto Ascari takes the chequered flag at Silverstone for his third win in succession for Ferrari. He would also win the other three races he entered in 1952.

1953

ALBERTO ASCARI CLAIMED HIS SECOND CROWN AS FERRARI WERE again supreme in the second and final year of the Formula Two category. Fangio struck back for Maserati signalling the start of four years of domination by the maestro.

TWO OUT OF TWO
Alberto Ascari on course for his eighth win in a row at the Dutch Grand Prix at Zandvoort.

Fangio was fit and back at the start of 1953, and heading a Maserati outfit which looked as if it might upset the Ferrari bandwagon. Joining him in a strong Argentinian line-up were Gonzalez and Onofre Marimon.

Meanwhile, Hawthorn's performances with the Cooper team had not gone unnoticed, and he had earned a seat with Ferrari, alongside Ascari,

Farina and Villoresi. With Hawthorn gone, Cooper lacked a driver of substance, and Gordini provided the only real opposition to the Italian cars.

Tragedy at Buenos Aires
For the first time the World Championship tag was justified by a race outside Europe, with the series kicking off at Buenos Aires. Unfortunately, the race was marred by undis-

ciplined spectators, and Farina was involved in a tragic incident when he hit a boy who crossed the track. Nine people were killed in the mayhem that followed. It was the first fatality in a championship race.

Meanwhile, Ascari and Villoresi scored a Ferrari one-two, ahead of debutant Marimon. Hawthorn had a steady race to fourth, while local hero Fangio ran second, before retiring.

Maserati's new car arrived for Zandvoort. It showed promise, but Ascari and Farina took the usual Ferrari one-two, with the best Maserati – shared by Bonetto and Gonzalez – in third. Fangio broke a rear axle. At Spa the Maseratis were the cars to beat. Gonzalez and Fangio led the field until retiring. Inevitably Ascari was there to pick up the pieces, scoring his ninth consecutive win.

The French race was back at Reims, and proved to be a classic encounter which saw Hawthorn come of age. After taking two fourths and a sixth in the opening races, he emerged as a front-runner, getting the better of a sensational duel with Fangio to score his first win – and the first for any British driver. Strangely, Hawthorn could not repeat his French form at Silverstone, where Ascari was utterly dominant. Fangio chased hard, and finished ahead of Farina, Gonzalez and Hawthorn.

At the Nurburgring Ascari was again the man to beat, but

DRIVERS' WORLD CHAMPIONSHIP

Pos.	Driver	Nat.	Make	Pts
1	Alberto Ascari	It	Ferrari	34.5
2	Juan Manuel Fangio	Arg	Maserati	27.5
3	Giuseppe Farina	It	Ferrari	26
4	Mike Hawthorn	GB	Ferrari	19
5	Luigi Villoresi	It	Ferrari	17
6	Froilan Gonzalez	Arg	Maserati	13.5
7	Bill Vukovich*	USA	Fuel Injection Special	8
8	Emmanuel de Graffenried	Swi	Maserati	7
9	Felice Bonetto	It	Maserati	6.5
10	Art Cross*	USA	Springfield Welding	6

Best four scores from nine races to count *denotes points scored in Indy 500

he lost a front wheel early on. He made it back to the pits, and later took over Villoresi's fourth-placed car. Farina maintained Ferrari's record, winning ahead of Fangio and Hawthorn. In his new car Ascari was closing in on the British driver when the engine blew.

Ascari's year

Ascari clinched his second title at the penultimate race in Switzerland, yet it was anything but easy. Fangio led Ascari initially until gearbox and engine troubles intervened, and then Ascari lost the lead with a plug change. He dropped to fourth, but worked his way back to the lead, heading home Farina and Hawthorn.

Maserati had threatened to win all year, and it eventually happened in the finale at Monza – in bizarre circumstances. After a great slipstreaming battle Ascari looked set to win, but on the last lap he spun and forced Farina wide. The lapped Marimon also got involved, and through the dust cloud emerged Fangio, to score his first win since 1951.

1954

MERCEDES FINALLY RETURNED TO RACING AND THE "BLANK CHEQUE" operation set new standards. Juan Manuel Fangio and his wonderful W196 Silver Arrow were unstoppable. But Britain found a new star in Stirling Moss.

After two years of Formula Two it was all change for 1954, with the introduction of new 2.5-litre regulations. The big story was the decision by Mercedes-Benz to return to Grand Prix racing for the first time since the Second World War. The legendary Alfred Neubauer was still at the helm, and he snapped up Fangio to join Hans Herrmann and Karl Kling. The new W196 was a technical marvel, but was not ready until the third race of the year.

Also on the way was Lancia's new D50. The marque hired Ascari and Villoresi to drive it, but it was ready even later than the Mercedes. After two consecutive titles, Ascari effectively wasted the season. Fangio was luckier, for he was allowed to start the year in the new Maserati, the 250F. An attractive and effective car, it would be one of the mainstays of Grand Prix racing for the next few seasons. Ferrari had lost Ascari and Villoresi, but Hawthorn, Farina, Gonzalez and Frenchman Maurice Trintignant were on hand to drive the latest model.

Fangio leads the field

Fangio's decision to start the year in a Maserati was a wise one, for he duly won the opening events in Argentina and Belgium. The first race was a chaotic, rain-hit affair with the track changing several times. Quick in the wet, Fangio won through ahead of the Ferraris of Farina, Gonzalez and

FLYING START

Juan Manuel Fangio gave the all-new Mercedes W196 a winning debut at Reims on his way to a second world title.

Trintignant. Farina led the early laps in Belgium, but when he hit trouble Fangio went by, and headed home Trintignant. Moss showed he would be a force to be reckoned with by taking third.

Mercedes finally appeared at Reims with three of the magnificent W196s in streamlined, full-bodied form. The cars were perfectly suited to the fast track, and Fangio and Kling finished one-two, with Herrmann setting the fastest lap. Robert Manzon came home third for Ferrari. However, Mercedes came down to earth with a bang at Silverstone, for the streamlined bodies did not like the airfield circuit. Fangio finished fourth in his battered car, while Gonzalez scored his second British Grand Prix win.

Death at the Nurburgring

Tragedy struck at the Nurburgring when Marimon was killed in practice; he was

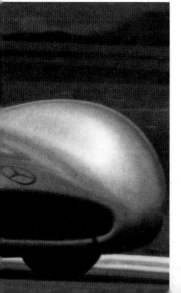

the first driver to die at a World Championship event. Countrymen Fangio and Gonzalez were distraught. but to his credit Fangio got on with the job and won the race, his Mercedes now using the new open-wheel body.

In Switzerland Fangio led from start to finish. Moss pursued him until retiring, and then Gonzalez took up the challenge and came home second. Monza established Moss as a star of the future. His performances had earned him a works Maserati seat, and he led until nine laps from the end when the oil tank split. He would eventually push the car over the line in 11th. Meanwhile, Fangio swept by to win in the streamlined Mercedes from Hawthorn. The Lancia team was finally ready for the last race in Spain. The car showed promise, for Ascari led for ten laps before retiring, and set the fastest lap. Hawthorn went on to score his second win, ahead of Maserati's young find, Luigi Musso. Mercedes had a bad day, and Fangio finished only third. But his second title was in the bag.

DRIVERS' WORLD CHAMPIONSHIP				
Pos.	Driver	Nat.	Make	Pts
1	Juan Manuel Fangio	Arg	Maserati/Mercedes	42
2	Froilan Gonzalez	Arg	Ferrari	25.14
3	Mike Hawthorn	GB	Ferrari	24.64
4	Maurice Trintignant	Fr	Ferrari	17
5	Karl Kling	Ger	Mercedes	12
6	Bill Vukovich*	USA	Fuel Injection Special	8
=	Hans Herrmann	Ger	Mercedes	8
8	Jimmy Bryan*	USA	Dean Van Lines	6
=	Giuseppe Farina	It	Ferrari	6
=	Luigi Musso	It	Maserati	6
=	Robert Mieres	Arg	Maserati	6

Best five scores from nine races to count *denotes points scored in Indy 500

1955

MERCEDES, FANGIO AND MOSS DOMINATED THE SEASON, BUT THE appalling tragedy at Le Mans, which cost over 80 lives, overshadowed everything. Mercedes later announced that it was withdrawing from Grand Prix racing.

June 11, 1955, is perhaps the blackest day in motor racing history. More than 80 people were killed when Pierre Levegh's Mercedes crashed into the crowd during the early laps at Le Mans. Grand Prix stars Fangio and Hawthorn were both peripherally involved in the incident, which had major repercussions for the sport. The Grands Prix in France, Germany, Switzerland and Spain were all cancelled, and, in fact, motor racing would never return to Switzerland.

German confidence

The German team went into the season with morale high. Neubauer had signed up Moss to partner Fangio, and now had two top-level drivers in his Silver Arrows. Maserati signed up Jean Behra to replace Moss, while Mike Hawthorn left Ferrari to drive the patriotic Vanwall. The season opener in Argentina was run in swelteringly hot conditions which saw Fangio score a comfortable victory. He was one of only two drivers able to go the full distance solo, as each of the three pursuing cars were shared by three drivers apiece as the energy-sapping heat took its toll.

At Monaco Ascari was really in the headlines, for he managed to flip his car into the harbour. He escaped this alarming incident with minor injuries. At the time he was leading, for Fangio and Moss had both retired their Mercedes. Trintignant proved a popular and surprise winner, ahead of the Lancia of Eugenio Castellotti.

Four days later Ascari was killed in a bizarre accident at Monza, while testing a Ferrari sports car. Already struggling for finance, Lancia announced its withdrawal from the sport, regrettably before the D50 had been able to fulfil its initial promise. Mercedes bounced back at Spa, where Fangio and Moss ran one-two with ease. Castellotti was allowed a final fling in a Lancia – as a privateer – and ran third before retiring from racing.

The following weekend came the Le Mans tragedy and, despite the outcry, the Grand Prix circus reconvened at Zandvoort just a week later.

Pos.	Driver	Nat.	Make	Pts
1	Juan Manuel Fangio	Arg	Mercedes	40
2	Stirling Moss	GB	Mercedes	23
3	Eugenio Castellotti	It	Lancia	12
4	Maurice Trintignant	Fr	Ferrari	11.33
5	Giuseppe Farina	It	Ferrari	10.33
6	Piero Taruffi	It	Mercedes	9
7	Bob Sweikert*	USA	John Zink Special	8
8	Robert Mieres	Arg	Maserati	7
9	Jean Behra	Fr	Maserati	6
=	Luigi Musso	It	Maserati	6

DRIVERS' WORLD CHAMPIONSHIP

Best five scores from seven races to count *denotes points scored in Indy 500

Fangio and Moss scored another Mercedes one-two, chased by Musso's Maserati. By now Hawthorn had given up on the Vanwall project, and his return to Ferrari was rewarded with a creditable seventh place.

Racing at Aintree

The British Grand Prix moved to Aintree for the first time, and Mercedes scored a crushing one-two-three-four. This time Moss headed home Fangio, with Kling and Taruffi following on. It was Stirling's first win, but for years people wondered if Fangio had allowed him to take the glory at home. At the back of the grid in a little Cooper was a rookie called Jack Brabham...

With all the cancellations, only the Monza race remained to be run, this time on the banked circuit. After Moss retired, Fangio headed Taruffi in another Mercedes one-two finish, with Castellotti third in a Ferrari. Fangio's third title was already secure, with Moss a distant second. But both men would be hit hard when Mercedes announced its withdrawal.

A hugely significant result came in a non-championship race held at the end of the season, when Tony Brooks took his Connaught to victory at Syracuse on Sicily. This famous victory was the first major British win of the World Championship era.

TOTAL CONTROL
Juan Manuel Fangio was streets ahead of his rivals throughout the 1955 season.

1956

FOLLOWING THE WITHDRAWAL OF MERCEDES, FANGIO SWITCHED TO Ferrari and won his fourth World Championship. But the Argentinian needed some luck — and the incredible generosity of his sensational new team-mate, Peter Collins.

The two Mercedes stars did not spend much time contemplating unemployment. Fangio joined Ferrari, where another fresh face was talented British youngster Collins, along with Musso and Castellotti. The promising Lancias had also found a new home at Ferrari. They had, in fact, been entered by the Scuderia at Monza the previous year, but had non-started owing to tyre troubles. Modified over the winter, they became Lancia-Ferraris.

Meanwhile, Moss returned to Maserati to race the still competitive 250F alongside Behra. Prospects looked good for the British teams. Hawthorn and Tony Brooks joined BRM, while Vanwall had modified cars for Trintignant and Harry Schell.

STAYING AHEAD
Juan Manuel Fangio leads Stirling Moss in the title-deciding 1956 Italian Grand Prix at Monza.

Connaught hoped to build on the Syracuse success.

Moss wins with Maserati

Fangio won the opener in Argentina, but he had to take over Musso's car after his own retired. The Maseratis struggled, although Behra took second place. Maserati hit back at Monaco, where Moss scored a fine second Grand Prix victory. A seemingly very off-form Fangio damaged his own car and this time took over the sister machine of Collins, which he maintained in second place.

At Spa, Fangio and Moss both hit trouble, and Collins scored a famous victory in his Lancia-Ferrari. He became the third British race winner in as many seasons. Local star Paul Frère earned a fine second

place, while Moss took over another car and recovered to third. Collins scored his second win at Reims a month later, heading home Castellotti, Behra and Fangio, the champion delayed by a pit stop. Surprise of the race was Harry Schell, who flew in the Vanwall after an early delay.

Collins went into the British Grand Prix leading the championship from the consistent Behra and Fangio. His thunder was stolen by Hawthorn and Brooks, who led the field on the return of BRM. Both hit trouble early on, however. Moss and Roy Salvadori each led until retiring, which allowed Fangio to take the honours. Collins took over the car of Alfonso de Portago and was runner-up, ahead of Behra. Fangio was an easy winner at the Nurburgring, while Collins was out of luck. His own car retired, and when he took over de Portago's machine, he crashed out of the race.

DRIVERS' WORLD CHAMPIONSHIP

Pos.	Driver	Nat.	Make	Pts
1	Juan Manuel Fangio	Arg	Ferrari	30
2	Stirling Moss	GB	Maserati	27
3	Peter Collins	GB	Ferrari	25
4	Jean Behra	Fr	Maserati	22
5	Pat Flaherty*	USA	Zinc Special	8
6	Eugenio Castellotti	It	Ferrari	7.5
7	Sam Hanks*	USA	Maley Special	6
=	Paul Frère	Bel	Ferrari	6
=	Francesco Godia	Sp	Maserati	6
=	Jack Fairman	GB	Connaught	6

Best five scores from eight races to count *denotes points scored in Indy 500

The struggle for the title

For the first time in several seasons the title fight went down to the wire at Monza. Fangio was well placed on 30 points, but Collins and Behra were eight behind – and could take the title by winning the race and setting the fastest lap. Schell again surprised everyone by running at the front in the Vanwall and, when he retired, Moss, Fangio and Collins were left to fight it out. Fangio's hopes faded with steering trouble, but he was saved when Collins – who could still have won the title – stopped and handed his car over. It was a remarkable gesture, which Fangio would never forget.

Despite a scare when he ran out of fuel, Moss just held on from Collins/Fangio in an exciting finish. With BRM and Vanwall having already shown well during the year, it was Connaught's turn to earn some success as Ron Flockhart took advantage of a high attrition rate to come in third. Further British success seemed just around the corner.

1957

FANGIO ACQUIRED HIS FIFTH AND LAST TITLE FOR MASERATI, BUT Stirling Moss and Vanwall were the true stars of a year in which the all-British team won a remarkable three races. Ferrari was struggling desperately to keep up.

There was plenty of activity during the winter, the most notable news being Fangio's switch from Ferrari to Maserati. It was quite a coup for Maserati to entice the reigning champion back to drive its latest 250F, and it proved to be a wise choice for Juan Manuel.

Meanwhile, Moss, always keen to drive British cars wherever possible, headed to Vanwall. He had already won the previous year's International Trophy for Tony Vandervell's promising concern. Hawthorn continued to hop back and forth across the English Channel, rejoining Ferrari for a third spell after a bad time with BRM. He teamed up with his great buddy Collins, plus Musso and Castellotti.

Once again Fangio won his home race in Argentina, heading home a Maserati one-two-three-four as the Ferrari challenge fell apart. Vanwall did not enter the race, and Moss had trouble at the start in his borrowed Maserati. He set the fastest lap as he recovered to seventh. After the Argentine race the talented Castellotti lost his life in a testing crash at Modena, and he was replaced by Trintignant. Then the enigmatic Alfonso de Portago was killed in the Mille Miglia. It was a bleak period indeed for Enzo Ferrari.

Monaco saw a spectacular pile-up at the start which eliminated Moss, Collins and Hawthorn. Fangio scored an easy win, while Brooks took his Vanwall to second after extricating it from the mess. Star of the race was Jack Brabham, who got his underpowered Cooper up to third before the fuel pump failed. The plucky Australian pushed it home sixth.

A British triumph

The French Grand Prix returned to Rouen and Fangio stormed to victory ahead of the Ferraris of Musso, Collins and Hawthorn. The next race was at Aintree and it proved to be a memorable day for Britain. After Moss retired his leading Vanwall, he took over the sixth-placed car of team-mate Brooks. The opposition wilted, and when Behra blew his engine – and Hawthorn punctured on

DRIVERS' WORLD CHAMPIONSHIP

Pos.	Driver	Nat.	Make	Pts
1	Juan Manuel Fangio	Arg	Maserati	40
2	Stirling Moss	GB	Vanwall	25
3	Luigi Musso	It	Ferrari	16
4	Mike Hawthorn	GB	Ferrari	13
5	Tony Brooks	GB	Vanwall	11
6	Harry Schell	USA	Maserati	10
=	Masten Gregory	USA	Maserati	10
8	Peter Collins	GB	Ferrari	8
=	Sam Hanks*	USA	Belond Exhaust	8
10	Jean Behra	Fr	Maserati	6
=	Jim Rathmann*	USA	Chiropractic	6

Best five scores from eight races to count *denotes points scored in Indy 500

the debris – Moss swept home to a wonderful victory.

Vanwall was out of luck at the Nurburgring, with both cars suffering suspension problems. But the race is remembered as one of the all-time classics, as Fangio came storming back to win after a fuel stop, leaving Collins and Hawthorn in his wake. Fangio would always regard this race in Germany as his greatest ever.

Because Spa and Zandvoort had been cancelled, an extra Italian race, the tortuous Pescara Grand Prix, was added to the series. Enzo Ferrari, supposedly opposed to Italian road circuits, did not enter Hawthorn and Collins, but loaned a "private" car to

Musso. He was in front for the first couple of laps before Moss took the lead and scored his second win of the year. Fangio finished second, and sealed his fifth and final title.

The Monza finale, no longer using the banking, saw a spectacular fight between Vanwall and Maserati. Moss headed Fangio home, with the promising German, Wolfgang von Trips, upholding Ferrari honour in third. It was a lame year for the Prancing Horse. Ferrari had not won a race all year, and clearly needed to resolve that situation in 1958. The job was made easier when Maserati withdrew its works team at the end of the season, owing to lack of funds.

THE MAIN RIVALS
Friends and former colleagues Juan Manuel Fangio and Stirling Moss in animated discussion. Fangio had the final word by winning his fifth and final World Championship.

1958

MIKE HAWTHORN PIPPED STIRLING MOSS TO THE TITLE, BUT HIS success was overshadowed by the death of his team-mate and friend, Peter Collins. Mike retired at the top, only to lose his life in a road accident soon after.

The departure of Maserati was a major blow to the sport, although the cars survived in the hands of privateers. The marque's withdrawal coincided with that of Fangio. He would run just two races in 1958, before calling it a day.

Ferrari abandoned the old Lancia-based cars, and had a new model, the 246 Dino, with Hawthorn, Collins and Musso the star drivers. Moss, Brooks and Stuart Lewis-Evans stayed with Vanwall, while John Cooper mounted a serious effort with Brabham and Roy Salvadori. Rob Walker entered a private Cooper-Climax for Trintignant, and Behra and Schell headed a revived BRM effort.

BRITISH BREAKTHROUGH
Mike Hawthorn came out on top of a three-way fight for the title with fellow Britons Stirling Moss and Tony Brooks.

British successes

The season started off with a surprise in Argentina. Most of the British teams were absent, including Vanwall, so Moss was free to replace Trintignant in Walker's Cooper. He duly won the race in a canny display, although his tyres were worn out by the end. At Monaco Trintignant was in Walker's car and, amazingly, he scored his second success in the street race. Once again, the faster cars hit trouble, including Moss's Vanwall.

The British success continued at Zandvoort, where Vanwall swept the front row. Moss won, while the BRMs of Schell and Behra finished second and third after the other

Vanwalls retired. Salvadori's Cooper was fourth, and even the best Ferrari had a British driver – that of fifth-placed Hawthorn.

Ferrari had been without a win since 1956, but the waiting ended at Reims where Hawthorn scored what would be his only victory of the season. However, there was no celebrating. Team-mate Musso, who had qualified second, was killed in the race. Fangio finished fourth in his last race.

Triumph and tragedy

At Silverstone it was the turn of Collins to win for Ferrari, with Hawthorn taking second. But a fortnight later tragedy struck again when Collins lost his life in the German Grand Prix. Brooks went on to score a hollow victory.

Moss had retired while leading in Germany, and he gained some revenge at the new event

Drivers' World Championship

Pos.	Driver	Nat.	Make	Pts
1	Mike Hawthorn	GB	Ferrari	42
2	Stirling Moss	GB	Cooper/Vanwall	41
3	Tony Brooks	GB	Vanwall	24
4	Roy Salvadori	GB	Cooper-Climax	15
5	Harry Schell	USA	BRM	14
=	Peter Collins	GB	Ferrari	14
7	Luigi Musso	It	Ferrari	12
=	Maurice Trintignant	Fr	Cooper-Climax	12
9	Stuart Lewis-Evans	GB	Vanwall	11
10	Phil Hill	USA	Ferrari	9
=	Wolfgang von Trips	Ger	Ferrari	9
=	Jean Behra	Fr	BRM	9

Best six scores from 11 races to count

Constructors' Cup

Pos.	Make	Pts
1	Vanwall	48
2	Ferrari	40
3	Cooper-Climax	31
4	BRM	18
5	Maserati	6
6	Lotus-Climax	3

in Portugal, winning from pole position with Hawthorn second. In one of the closest points battles ever, Moss led all the way and set the fastest lap in the final race in Casablanca. But, with Brooks blowing up, Hawthorn eased into second, which was all he required to take the crown. It was a terrible day for both Vanwall and Stirling, made worse when Lewis-Evans crashed and later succumbed to his injuries. The only consolation for Vanwall was the inaugural constructors' title.

Then, after quitting the sport while at his peak, Hawthorn was killed in a road accident in January. He was just 29 years old.

1959

THE OLD ORDER CHANGED FOR EVER WHEN JACK BRABHAM TOOK HIS Cooper-Climax to the 1959 championship. It was the first title for a rear-engined car, marking a triumph of handling over power. The revolution started here.

The big news of the winter was the surprise withdrawal of the Vanwall team, just as it had reached full competitiveness. But Cooper, BRM and Lotus upheld British honour. After the previous year's tragedies there were big changes at Ferrari. Brooks joined from Vanwall and Behra from BRM, while Phil Hill – an occasional Ferrari driver in 1958 – went full time. Moss kept his options open, and would appear in both Walker's Cooper-Climax, and a BRM in the colours of the British Racing Partnership.

Success for Cooper-Climax

In previous years Climax had given away a few cubic centimetres, but the latest engine was a full 2.5-litre unit. Although still a little down on power compared with its rivals, the Cooper's handling was superior.

With Argentina cancelled, the series opened at Monaco. Behra's Ferrari led until retiring, and then Moss's nimble Cooper expired, leaving Brabham to score his first win in the works Cooper. Zandvoort saw a major surprise, as Jo Bonnier notched up BRM's first victory, nine years after the marque made its first, stumbling steps. The bearded Swede had to work hard to hold off the Coopers, and was helped when Moss retired. Ferrari fought back with a fine win for Brooks at Reims, teammate Hill following him home. Moss was in the BRP BRM on this occasion, and was battling for second when he went off the road. Three marques had won the first three races, but Cooper was back in the frame at Aintree as Brabham scored his second win, ahead of Moss's BRM. Stirling just held off young Kiwi Bruce McLaren – the second works Cooper driver was starting to make a name for himself. Ferrari did not turn up, blaming Italian industrial action.

For the first and only time the German Grand Prix was

CONSTRUCTORS' CUP		
Pos.	Make	Pts
1	Cooper-Climax	40
2	Ferrari	32
3	BRM	18
4	Lotus-Climax	5

DRIVERS' WORLD CHAMPIONSHIP				
Pos.	Driver	Nat.	Make	Pts
1	Jack Brabham	Aus	Cooper-Climax	31
2	Tony Brooks	GB	Ferrari	27
3	Stirling Moss	GB	BRM/Cooper-Climax	25.5
4	Phil Hill	USA	Ferrari	20
5	Maurice Trintignant	Fr	Cooper-Climax	19
6	Bruce McLaren	NZ	Cooper-Climax	16.5
7	Dan Gurney	USA	Ferrari	13
8	Jo Bonnier	Swe	BRM	10
=	Masten Gregory	USA	Cooper-Climax	10
10	Rodger Ward*	USA	Leader Cards	8

Best five scores from nine races to count *denotes points scored in Indy 500

held on the daunting, banked Avus circuit in Berlin and, uniquely, the result was an aggregate of two 30-lap heats. Missing Aintree had obviously done Ferrari some good, for Brooks dominated the event. But, as at Reims the year before, Ferrari's celebration was muted by tragedy. Veteran Behra, who had been a mainstay of the championship since its inception, died after a crash in the sports car support race.

Brabham in command

Moss had to wait until the Portuguese race to pick up his first win of the year in Walker's Cooper. Brabham crashed out, but still led the championship as the circus moved to the penultimate race at Monza. Moss won again, ahead of Hill, while third place for Brabham kept his title challenge alive.

It was a full three months before the final race, the first ever US Grand Prix, and the only one to be held on the Sebring airfield track in Florida, home of the famous 12 hours sports car race. Moss could still lift the crown and, after taking pole, he was leading comfortably when his gearbox failed.

Brabham ran out of fuel and had to push his car home in fourth place, but the title was his come what may. A surprise win went to his team-mate McLaren, who, at 22, became the youngest Grand Prix winner – a record which still stands. Trintignant was second in another Cooper, ahead of Brooks.

MONACO MAGIC
Success in the season-opener at Monaco gave Jack Brabham a perfect start to the season.

1960

JACK BRABHAM SCORED HIS SECOND CONSECUTIVE TITLE WIN FOR Cooper, with Lotus emerging as a major force. But for a mid-season accident putting him out for several races, Stirling Moss might have won that elusive title.

By 1960 the rear-engined machines were completely dominant. For the time being Ferrari stuck with its old car and won at Monza – but only because the British teams boycotted the event. Colin Chapman's Lotus team had been in Grand Prix racing for two years with very little success, but all that was to change with the new 18, the first rear-engined model.

BRM also had a new rear-engined car, which had debuted at Monza the previous year.

Bonnier stayed on, joined by Graham Hill from Lotus and American Dan Gurney from Ferrari. Phil Hill and von Trips stayed with the Italian team, while Brabham and McLaren maintained their successful partnership at Cooper.

McLaren won the opening race in Argentina and Cliff Allison did well to get his Ferrari home second. Bonnier and Moss (still in Walker's old Cooper) had both led before retiring. Allison was seriously

SMILES ALL ROUND
Jack Brabham had every reason to smile in 1960 as he took five wins on his way to back-to-back titles.

injured in practice at Monaco. Meanwhile, Moss got his hands on the new Lotus, and won in fine style in the rain, ahead of McLaren and Phil Hill. Once again, Bonnier's BRM led before retiring, while a notable newcomer was motorbike star John Surtees in a works Lotus.

Brabham had failed to score in either race, but bounced back by winning at Zandvoort. Innes Ireland took his Lotus to second, ahead of Graham Hill. For the second consecutive race Chapman gave a first chance to a future world champion. At Monaco it was Surtees and in Holland it was a young Scot called Jim Clark. He was battling for fourth when the gearbox broke.

Tragedy at Spa

Spa was one of the blackest weekends in Grand Prix history. During practice Moss crashed heavily, breaking his legs. Then two young Britons, Chris Bristow and Alan Stacey, were killed in separate accidents. Brabham and McLaren went on to score a Cooper one-two, but only after Hill's BRM blew up while running second.

At Reims, Brabham took a third consecutive win, and on this fast track the front-engined Ferraris of Phil Hill and von Trips gave him a hard time until they broke. Graham Hill was the star at Silverstone. He stalled on the line, and drove superbly through to the lead before spinning off. Brabham came through to score his fourth straight win, followed by

the very impressive Surtees and Ireland.

Victory for Brabham

Brabham scored a fifth win in Portugal and with it clinched the title with two races still to run. After missing two races Moss was back, and ran second before he had problems.

Monza was a disappointment. The race was on the banked track once again, and the British teams boycotted it on safety grounds. Ferrari turned up in force, and Phil Hill scored a hollow victory.

The US Grand Prix moved from Sebring to Riverside, and Moss won. The race marked the demise of the 2.5-litre formula which had seen the transfer of power from Mercedes to the British rear-engined machines.

DRIVERS' WORLD CHAMPIONSHIP

Pos.	Driver	Nat.	Make	Pts
1	Jack Brabham	Aus	Cooper-Climax	43
2	Bruce McLaren	NZ	Cooper-Climax	34
3	Stirling Moss	GB	Cooper/Lotus-Climax	19
4	Innes Ireland	GB	Lotus-Climax	18
5	Phil Hill	USA	Ferrari	16
6	Wolfgang von Trips	Ger	Ferrari	10
=	Olivier Gendebien	Bel	Cooper-Climax	10
8	Richie Ginther	USA	Ferrari	8
=	Jim Clark	GB	Lotus-Climax	8
=	Jim Rathmann*	USA	Ken-Paul	8

Best six scores from ten races to count *denotes points scored in Indy 500

CONSTRUCTORS' CUP

Pos.	Make	Pts
1	Cooper-Climax	48
2	Lotus-Climax	34
3	Ferrari	26
4	BRM	8
5	Cooper-Castellotti	3
=	Cooper-Maserati	3

1961

FERRARI WAS BETTER PREPARED THAN ANYBODY ELSE FOR THE NEW formula, and dominated the season. Phil Hill took the title, but in the most tragic circumstances, after his team-mate, Wolfgang von Trips, lost his life at Monza.

It was all change for 1961 with the introduction of a 1.5-litre formula. The British manufacturers had been slow to respond, but not so Ferrari. Effectively sacrificing the previous season, the Italian team developed a rear-engined car, dubbed the "sharknose" – and a new V6 engine. Climax and BRM lagged behind, so much so that the only engine available for the British teams was the four-year-old 1475cc Climax F2.

Arrival of Porsche

Von Trips, Phil Hill and American Richie Ginther were in the lucky position of having works Ferrari seats. Welcome variety was provided by Porsche. Already successful in Formula Two, the German marque signed Gurney and Bonnier from BRM. Lotus had an excellent new chassis, the 21, and the promising Jim Clark and Ireland to drive it. BRM and Cooper used developments of their old cars. Graham Hill and Brooks led the BRM attack, while once again Brabham and McLaren teamed up at Cooper.

More than ever before, Moss had underdog status. Walker was not allowed to buy a new Lotus 21, and had to make do with the old 18 model. And yet Moss turned in one of the drives of his career in Monaco, to brilliantly beat the Ferraris of Ginther and Hill.

Ferrari took its revenge when von Trips scored his first win at Zandvoort, with Hill in second. The result was reversed at Spa, where Ferrari finished one-two-three-four and Hill took his first win against a representative field, following that boycotted Monza race the previous year. Reims was a sensational race. Hill, Ginther and von Trips retired, and Giancarlo Baghetti – making his first start in a private Ferrari – just pipped Gurney's Porsche to the line. Baghetti remains the only driver to have won on his Grand Prix debut.

CONSTRUCTORS' CUP

Pos.	Make	Pts
1	Ferrari	40
2	Lotus-Climax	32
3	Porsche	22
4	Cooper-Climax	14
5	BRM-Climax	7

DRIVERS' WORLD CHAMPIONSHIP

Pos.	Driver	Nat.	Make	Pts
1	Phil Hill	USA	Ferrari	34
2	Wolfgang von Trips	Ger	Ferrari	33
3	Stirling Moss	GB	Lotus-Climax	21
=	Dan Gurney	USA	Porsche	21
5	Richie Ginther	USA	Ferrari	16
6	Innes Ireland	GB	Lotus-Climax	12
7	Jim Clark	GB	Lotus-Climax	11
=	Bruce McLaren	NZ	Cooper-Climax	11
9	Giancarlo Baghetti	It	Ferrari	9
10	Tony Brooks	GB	BRM-Climax	6

Best five scores from eight races to count

It was back to normal at Aintree as von Trips, Hill and Ginther finished one-two-three in the rain. Moss had tried to mix it with the Italian cars before his brakes failed, but then struck back at the Nurburgring. As at Monaco, he overcame the power deficiency to beat Ferrari, heading home Hill and von Trips. The new Climax V8 engine was finally ready.

Ferrari's revenge

Nobody objected to the banks at Monza this time. Ironically the race, which should have seen the title fight between von Trips and Hill reach a crucial stage, turned to tragedy. Clark and von Trips tangled early on, and the German star was killed, along with 12 spectators. Phil Hill won the race, and with it the title.

The US Grand Prix moved to a third new venue in as many years in the form of Watkins Glen. With Ferrari not entering, Moss and Brabham battled for the lead. When they both retired, Ireland came through to score his first (and only) win, and the first for the works Lotus team. Gurney was again second, ahead of the BRM of Brooks. At the end of the year Brooks announced his retirement, after a distinguished career which was often over-shadowed by the heroic exploits of Moss and Hawthorn.

FERRARI TO THE FORE
Phil Hill leads team-mate Wolfgang von Trips during a thrilling Belgian Grand Prix. The year would end in tragedy for the Ferrari team.

1962

FERRARI'S STAR FADED IN THE MOST DRAMATIC FASHION, AS BRM AND Lotus battled it out for the championship. Graham Hill beat Jim Clark to score his first title win at the beginning of another golden era for the British teams.

The biggest story of the 1962 season occurred in a non-championship race at Goodwood on Easter Monday. Stirling Moss suffered multiple injuries when he crashed his Lotus, and he was never to race at the top level again. Moss had not won a title, and yet had been at the top of the sport for a decade. Ferrari self-destructed over the winter, as some of the top staff walked out. The team carried on with virtually unchanged cars and drivers Phil Hill and Baghetti. Promising new boys Mexican Ricardo Rodriguez and Lorenzo Bandini were also in the squad.

Ferrari in trouble

BRM had a powerful new V8 engine, and Graham Hill was joined by Ginther, who had left Ferrari at the end of 1961. Meanwhile, the Climax V8 looked good and was the choice of many top teams. Brabham quit Cooper to design his own car – although he would start the year with a Lotus – so McLaren became the team leader.

Lotus had another new car, the 25, which featured a revolutionary monocoque chassis. Clark and Trevor Taylor were the works drivers. An interesting newcomer was the Lola, entered by the Bowmaker team for John Surtees and Roy Salvadori, while Porsche had a new flat-eight engine for Gurney and Bonnier.

Unusually, the season opened at Zandvoort in May. Graham Hill scored his first win, and the first for BRM since Bonnier's victory at the same track three years earlier. Taylor finished second in only his second Grand Prix, ahead of Phil Hill. McLaren won at Monaco, chased home by Phil Hill in the Ferrari driver's best race of the year.

Spa was a historic occasion, as it marked the first win for Jim Clark, the Lotus driver

Constructors' Cup

Pos.	Make	Pts
1	BRM	42
2	Lotus-Climax	36
3	Cooper-Climax	29
4	Lola-Climax	19
5	Porsche	18
=	Ferrari	18
7	Brabham-Climax	6

Drivers' World Championship

Pos.	Driver	Nat.	Make	Pts
1	Graham Hill	GB	BRM	42
2	Jim Clark	GB	Lotus-Climax	30
3	Bruce McLaren	NZ	Cooper-Climax	27
4	John Surtees	GB	Lola-Climax	19
5	Dan Gurney	USA	Porsche	15
6	Phil Hill	USA	Ferrari	14
7	Tony Maggs	SAf	Cooper-Climax	13
8	Richie Ginther	USA	BRM	10
9	Jack Brabham	Aus	Lotus/Brabham-Climax	9
10	Trevor Taylor	GB	Lotus-Climax	6

Best five scores from nine races to count

coming home ahead of Graham and Phil Hill. Three marques had won the first three races, and it became four when Gurney gave Porsche its maiden victory at Rouen – but only after three leaders, Clark, Surtees and Graham Hill, had all retired.

Clark became the first repeat winner, dominating the British Grand Prix at Aintree ahead of Surtees and McLaren. Surtees continued his good form at the Nurburgring, finishing in second place behind Graham Hill's BRM, and just ahead of Gurney's Porsche.

Triumph for Graham Hill

Monza was the turning point in the title battle, for Graham Hill and Ginther gave BRM a one-two after a thrilling race, and Clark failed to finish. Clark fought back at Watkins Glen, heading Graham Hill home.

For the first time the finale was held at East London in South Africa, on the amazingly late date of December 29. Clark took pole position, and was leading the race until his engine failed.

Graham Hill took the win and the championship crown. It was to be BRM's only success. McLaren finished second, and took third in the points after a consistent season as Cooper's top man.

It had been a poor year for Ferrari, and the team did not even enter the two final races. To make matters worse, up-and-coming star driver Rodriguez, who had finished fourth at Spa, was killed in practice for the non-championship Mexican Grand Prix. He was just 20.

Off to a Flyer
Graham Hill won first time out at the Dutch Grand Prix and went on to take the title in the final round.

1963

THE YEAR PROVED TO BE A MEMORABLE ONE FOR JIM CLARK AND Lotus. Clark won seven races in all. It was the most devastating display of craftmanship by a single driver since the great triumph of Alberto Ascari 11 years previously.

The Porsche team withdrew in 1963 to concentrate on sports car racing. The line-ups at Lotus, BRM and Cooper were unchanged but the off-season had been busy. Having lost his Porsche ride, Dan Gurney teamed up with Jack Brabham to drive the double champion's own cars. Bowmaker/Lola withdrew, and the cars were bought by Reg Parnell for Chris Amon.

Surtees went to Ferrari, joining Belgian Willy Mairesse. The Ferrari breakaway had spawned a new team, ATS, and a pair of works Ferrari drivers, Phil Hill and Baghetti, both jumped ship.

AT A CANTER
Jim Clark won seven times in 1963 and claimed the World Championship with three races still to go.

Clark's great year

Clark led the opener at Monaco, but retired when his gearbox broke. It was to be his only retirement in an exceptionally reliable year for Lotus. With Clark out, Graham Hill and Ginther scored a one-two – it was the first of five successes in the principality for Graham.

Clark's luck changed at Spa, and he drove to a memorable victory in the rain, ahead of Bruce McLaren and Gurney (scoring the Brabham team's first top-three finish). He then led all the way at Zandvoort to win from Gurney and Surtees,

and at Reims, where even a misfire could not stop him. Clark scored his fourth win in a row at Silverstone, with Surtees in second. Another motorcycle star trying four wheels was Mike Hailwood, who finished eighth. Surtees had threatened to win for a couple of years, and he finally came good at the Nurburgring, scoring Ferrari's first success since Monza in 1961. Clark took second.

At Monza Ferrari had a new chassis, which owed a lot to Lotus's thinking and was designed to accept the forthcoming 1964 spec V8 engine. Surees battled with Clark for the lead until the overworked V6 gave up. Clark headed home Ginther and McLaren, and clinched the championship – with three races still to run.

| **Drivers' World Championship** | | | | |
Pos.	Driver	Nat.	Make	Pts
1	Jim Clark	GB	Lotus-Climax	54
2	Graham Hill	GB	BRM	29
=	Richie Ginther	USA	BRM	29
4	John Surtees	GB	Ferrari	22
5	Dan Gurney	USA	Brabham-Climax	19
6	Bruce McLaren	NZ	Cooper-Climax	17
7	Jack Brabham	Aus	Brabham-Climax	14
8	Tony Maggs	SAf	Cooper-Climax	9
9	Innes Ireland	GB	BRP-BRM	6
=	Lorenzo Bandini	It	Ferrari	6
=	Jo Bonnier	Swe	Cooper-Climax	6

Best six scores from ten races to count

| **Constructors' Cup** | |
Pos.	Make	Pts
1	Lotus-Climax	54
2	BRM	36
3	Brabham-Climax	28
4	Ferrari	26
5	Cooper-Climax	25
6	BRP-BRM	6

Hill's mixed fortunes

Graham Hill had suffered from unreliability and sheer bad luck all year, but struck back as he headed Ginther and Clark home at Watkins Glen. Mexican Pedro Rodriguez, brother of the late Ricardo, made his debut in a Lotus.

The Mexican Grand Prix was in the championship for the first time, and Clark scored his sixth win of the year. He added a record seventh in South Africa in December to cap an amazing season. Before dropped scores were taken into account, he had amassed 73 points. Brabham finished second in Mexico and then team-mate Gurney repeated the feat in South Africa, showing that "Black Jack" had got his sums right, and would be a force to reckon with.

1964

JOHN SURTEES MADE RACING HISTORY WHEN HE BECAME THE FIRST man to win a World Championship on both two wheels and four. In a thrilling finale, Surtees, in his Ferrari, just outscored Graham Hill and Jim Clark.

Ferrari had higher hopes for 1964 as the new V8 engine was mated to the chassis which had shown promise at Monza the previous year. Surtees stayed on to lead the team alongside Lorenzo Bandini. Lotus produced an updated car for Clark, the 33. Peter Arundell was the team's new number two. Hill and Ginther stayed at BRM, and had a revised car, while Cooper tried to keep up with the new monocoque technology, updating a Formula Three chassis by welding on panels.

A JOB WELL DONE

John Surtees with the chequered flag after taking second place to come out on top of a three-way battle for the title.

Fluctuating fortunes for Clark

Clark started on a high by leading at Monaco, but he had to pit when his rear roll-bar broke. Hill and Ginther scored another one-two for BRM and a late engine failure for Clark handed third place to team-mate Arundell. Clark made amends with a demonstration run to victory at Zandvoort, while Surtees gave notice of Ferrari's

championship intentions with second place, ahead of the newcomer Arundell.

The Brabham team did not fare well in the early races, but at Spa Gurney led comfortably – until running out of fuel with two laps to go. In a farcical turn of events, Hill took the lead and suffered fuel pump failure; then McLaren also ran out of gas. This allowed a surprised Clark – who had made an early stop – to take victory. At least McLaren was able to coast home in second.

Gurney made amends at Rouen, by scoring a fine first victory for the Brabham team. Graham Hill pipped Brabham for third, while once again Clark led the early stages, before his engine failed.

For the first time the British Grand Prix moved to Brands Hatch, and Clark kept up his tradition of winning at home. Hill was second and Surtees was happy to get third after two consecutive retirements. Surtees then began his surge towards the title by winning ahead of Hill and Bandini at the Nurburgring.

Success for Surtees

The first Austrian Grand Prix was held at Zeltweg, and took a high toll on machinery. Hill, Surtees, Clark, McLaren and Gurney were among the retirements, leaving Bandini to score his first Grand Prix win, ahead of Ginther. Jochen Rindt made a quiet debut in a Brabham-BRM.

Ferrari's run of success continued at Monza, where Surtees

DRIVERS' WORLD CHAMPIONSHIP				
Pos.	Driver	Nat.	Make	Pts
1	John Surtees	GB	Ferrari	40
2	Graham Hill	GB	BRM	39
3	Jim Clark	GB	Lotus-Climax	32
4	Lorenzo Bandini	It	Ferrari	23
=	Richie Ginther	USA	BRM	23
6	Dan Gurney	USA	Brabham-Climax	19
7	Bruce McLaren	NZ	Cooper-Climax	13
8	Jack Brabham	Aus	Brabham-Climax	11
=	Peter Arundell	GB	Lotus-Climax	11
10	Jo Siffert	Swi	Brabham-BRM	7

Best six scores from ten races to count

CONSTRUCTORS' CUP		
Pos.	Make	Pts
1	Ferrari	45
2	BRM	42
3	Lotus-Climax	37
4	Brabham-Climax	30
5	Cooper-Climax	16

scored his second win of the year. It was a typically exciting slipstreamer and, after Clark and Gurney fell out, McLaren and Bandini completed the top three. Hill broke his clutch on the line in Italy, but kept his title challenge afloat by winning at Watkins Glen after Clark suffered engine problems. Surtees was second, ahead of an impressive Jo Siffert.

Three drivers went to the finale in Mexico City with a crack at the title. Hill led on 39 points, Surtees had 34 and outsider Clark 30. Hill was soon out of contention for points, and Clark looked set for the title. But with just two laps to go, he struck engine trouble. Surtees had worked his way up, and was waved into second behind Gurney by team-mate Bandini – it was enough to take the title from Hill.

1965

AFTER RETIREMENTS HAD ROBBED HIM DURING 1964, JIM CLARK
bounced back to win the 1965 title — and the Indy 500 — for Lotus.
Once again a change of engine regulations at the end of the year
was the signal of the passing of an era.

The British teams struck back against Ferrari in 1965, with Lotus and Brabham using a new, 32-valve version of the Climax V8. Clark was joined by another new team-mate in the form of Mike Spence, who had driven at Monza for the team the previous year. Brabham and Gurney were joined by a newcomer from New Zealand called Denny Hulme, while Rob Walker entered Brabhams for Bonnier and Siffert.

Ferrari continued with Surtees and Bandini, and there was new competition, too, from Honda, who launched a full effort with Ginther and the lit- tle-known Ronnie Bucknum. Ginther's departure from BRM left a seat open alongside Graham Hill, and it was very ably filled by a promising young Scot who had not even driven in a Grand Prix – his name was Jackie Stewart. Talented Austrian, Jochen Rindt, joined McLaren at Cooper.

South Africa became the first race of the season for the first time, and Clark, still using the older Climax engine, scored a runaway win. Surtees continued his championship form with second, ahead of Hill. Debutant Stewart finished sixth.

Lotus at Indianapolis

Lotus was missing from the second race at Monaco. The team

CONSTRUCTORS' CUP		
Pos.	Make	Pts
I	Lotus-Climax	54
2	BRM	45
3	Brabham-Climax	27
4	Ferrari	26
5	Cooper-Climax	14
6	Honda	11

DRIVERS' WORLD CHAMPIONSHIP				
Pos.	Driver	Nat.	Make	Pts
I	Jim Clark	GB	Lotus-Climax	54
2	Graham Hill	GB	BRM	40
3	Jackie Stewart	GB	BRM	33
4	Dan Gurney	USA	Brabham-Climax	25
5	John Surtees	GB	Ferrari	17
6	Lorenzo Bandini	It	Ferrari	13
7	Richie Ginther	USA	Honda	11
8	Bruce McLaren	NZ	Cooper-Climax	10
=	Mike Spence	GB	Lotus-Climax	10
10	Jack Brabham	Aus	Brabham-Climax	9

was competing instead at Indianapolis, where Clark notched up a historic first win for a rear-engined car. In his absence Hill scored a wonderful victory in the street classic, recovering from an early incident to pass Surtees and Bandini. Clark came back with a win at Spa in the wet, ahead of Stewart and McLaren, while Ginther picked up a point in the improving Honda. Clark and Stewart then repeated their double act in the French Grand Prix, held this year on the mountainous Clermont-Ferrand track.

Clark won the British Grand Prix, back at Silverstone, for the fourth consecutive time. Clark continued his winning ways at Zandvoort, and for the third time countryman Stewart followed him home. The big surprise was the performance of Ginther, who led for two laps in the Honda.

Clark triumphant

At the Nurburgring Clark scored his sixth win of the year and his first on the daunting German track. With only six scores counting, he had reached maximum points, and the championship was his. He was in the lead pack at Monza and, after he retired with fuel pump trouble, Stewart scored a marvellous maiden win, fractionally ahead of Hill and Gurney. However, with the title sewn up, Clark's luck seemed to have deserted him. At Watkins Glen he retired with engine problems, and Hill scored BRM's third win of the year.

The season had a twist in the tail. In Mexico City Ginther gave Honda (and tyre maker Goodyear) a first win, leading from start to finish. It was the Californian's only win. The race also marked the end of the 1.5-litre formula after four seasons.

POETRY IN MOTION
Jim Clark powers through the puddles on his way to victory at the Belgian Grand Prix at Spa.

1966

IT WAS ALL CHANGE IN 1966 AS THE 3-LITRE FORMULA WAS introduced and there was a race to get new engines ready in time. Jack Brabham was better prepared than most and earned a deserved third Championship in his own car.

Both teams and engine builders were busy through the winter as they prepared for the new formula. There was no pukka new engine from Climax, so existing customers had to find their own solutions.

HISTORY MAKER
Jack Brabham won three times to become the first driver to win the title in a car bearing his own name.

Brabham's technical success

The man who did the best job was undoubtedly Jack Brabham. He announced that he was using a new V8 from the Australian Repco company.

The engine was not the most powerful, but it was reliable, light and compact, and mated well with an updated version of Brabham's existing chassis. Jack had not won a race himself since 1960, and the package was to give his career a new lease of life. With Dan Gurney moving on, Denny Hulme became his number two. Cooper had a more exotic solution, mating a Maserati V12 to a new chassis. Richie Ginther

and Jochen Rindt were the works drivers, and Rob Walker bought one for Siffert.

Ex-Cooper driver Bruce McLaren followed Brabham's example and set up his own team, initially using a Ford engine sourced from Indy Car racing. Another driver to copy the Brabham example was Gurney, whose All-American Racers concern built the neat Eagle.

It was no surprise to see Ferrari follow the V12 route, and the Scuderia produced a promising new car for John Surtees. Lorenzo Bandini stayed on as his team-mate. Both BRM and Lotus were forced to use uprated 2-litre versions of their V8 and Climax engines. BRM had an unusual H16 under development, but it did not race until late in the year.

That said, it started very well at Monaco, where less powerful cars proved a match for the new machinery. Clark took pole but had an unlucky race, while Stewart won for BRM after Surtees had led with the Ferrari.

Spa turned to chaos when eight cars retired on the wet first lap, among them Stewart, who had the worst crash of his Formula One career. Surtees won after overcoming a challenge from Rindt's Cooper-Maserati. But a few weeks later John fell out with the Italian team and left to join Cooper.

A good year for Brabham

The new Brabham-Repco came good at Reims, Jack winning after Bandini had retired. Parkes

DRIVERS' WORLD CHAMPIONSHIP

Pos.	Driver	Nat.	Make	Pts
1	Jack Brabham	Aus	Brabham-Repco	42
2	John Surtees	GB	Ferrari/Cooper-Maserati	28
3	Jochen Rindt	A	Cooper-Maserati	22
4	Denny Hulme	NZ	Brabham-Repco	18
5	Graham Hill	GB	BRM	17
6	Jim Clark	GB	Lotus-Climax/BRM	16
7	Jackie Stewart	GB	BRM	14
8	Lorenzo Bandini	It	Ferrari	12
=	Mike Parkes	GB	Ferrari	12
10	Ludovico Scarfiotti	It	Ferrari	9
11	Richie Ginther	USA	Cooper/Honda	5
12	Dan Gurney	USA	Eagle	4

Best five scores to count

CONSTRUCTORS' CUP

Pos.	Make	Pts
1	Brabham-Repco	42
2	Ferrari	31
3	Cooper-Maserati	28
4	BRM	22
5	Lotus-BRM	13
6	Lotus-Climax	8

finished a promising second. Brabham won again at Brands Hatch, with team-mate Hulme coming in second. Jack picked up a third win at Zandvoort.

Brabham's winning streak continued at the Nurburgring, where he held off the Coopers of Surtees and Rindt. His luck ran out at Monza, where he retired, along with nearly all the top runners. Ferrari newcomer Ludovico Scarfiotti won.

Despite retiring in Italy, Brabham had clinched his third title. He was on pole at Watkins Glen, but retired. Clark won the race with Cooper-Maseratis finishing second, third and fourth. Their good form continued in the finale in Mexico, which was won by Surtees.

1967

BRABHAM AND REPCO SCORED A SECOND SUCCESSIVE TITLE THROUGH the efforts of Denny Hulme, but the story of the year was the arrival of the new Cosworth DFV engine. Packaged with the Lotus 49, it marked the beginning of a new era.

Lotus had struggled through 1966, but in March that year Colin Chapman had persuaded Ford to invest in a new engine, to be built by Cosworth. The British firm embarked on an all-new V8 design for 1967, which would initially be for the exclusive use of Lotus. Chapman drew a simple but effective car to exploit it, the 49. He further strengthened his package by bringing Graham Hill back to join Clark.

That elevated Stewart to team-leader status at BRM, where he was joined by Spence. Chris Amon joined Bandini at Ferrari. Ex-Ferrari star Surtees was signed to lead Honda's effort, while Pedro Rodriguez joined Rindt at Cooper.

The season opened at the new Kyalami track in South Africa, and the race nearly saw a sensational win for privateer John Love in an old Cooper-Climax. A late stop for fuel dropped him to second, behind the Cooper-Maserati of Rodriguez.

Tragedy at Monaco

Grand Prix racing had been through a safe – or lucky – couple of seasons, but Ferrari ace Lorenzo Bandini was to lose his life at Monaco. He was leading when he crashed, and the car caught fire. Hulme won for Brabham, ahead of Hill and Amon.

Zandvoort saw the long-awaited debut of the Ford Cosworth and the Lotus 49. It was a historic day, for Clark took the win after poleman Hill's engine failed. At Spa Hill retired; then leader Clark had to pit for a plug change. Gurney took the often unreliable Eagle-Weslake to a memorable first (and only) win.

For one time only the French Grand Prix was staged at the Bugatti circuit at Le Mans. Both Lotuses broke their transmissions. It was obvious that their reliability could not back up their pace. That left Brabham

Constructors' Cup

Pos.	Make	Pts
1	Brabham	63
2	Lotus	44
3	Cooper	28
4	Ferrari	20
=	Honda	20

Drivers' World Championship

Pos.	Driver	Nat.	Make	Pts
1	Denny Hulme	NZ	Brabham-Repco	51
2	Jack Brabham	Aus	Brabham-Repco	46
3	Jim Clark	GB	Lotus-BRM/Climax/Ford	41
4	John Surtees	GB	Honda	20
=	Chris Amon	NZ	Ferrari	20
6	Pedro Rodriguez	Mex	Cooper-Maserati	15
=	Graham Hill	GB	Lotus-BRM/Ford	15
8	Dan Gurney	USA	Eagle-Weslake	13
9	Jackie Stewart	GB	BRM	10
10	Mike Spence	GB	BRM	9

Best nine scores from 11 races to count

and Hulme to finish one-two, ahead of Stewart. Lotus fortunes looked up at Silverstone, where Clark won the British Grand Prix for the fifth time in six years. Hill led for much of the race, but had suspension problems before his engine blew. Kiwis Hulme and Amon finished second and third.

Mixed fortunes for Lotus

Lotus gremlins struck again at the Nurburgring, where Clark and Hill were both sidelined by suspension failures. Gurney looked set to win, but when the Weslake blew Hulme and Brabham scored a one-two.

For the first time the circus moved to the scenic Mosport track in Canada. Ignition problems put Clark out and – surprise, surprise – Brabham and Hulme were there to take another one-two, with Hill a distant fourth. Clark was the hero at Monza, coming back from early problems to lead until he ran out of fuel. In a typically exciting finish, Surtees pipped Brabham to give Honda its first win of the 3-litre age. Luck swung to Lotus once again in Watkins Glen, where Clark and Hill managed a one-two.

Hulme had been a steady performer all year, and he just pipped his boss to the title in Mexico. Clark won from Brabham, but third was enough to keep Denny ahead.

UP AND RUNNING
Victory first time out at Monaco set Denny Hulme on the road to a first World Championship – the second in a row for the Brabham team.

1968

SPONSORSHIP AND WINGS ARRIVED ON THE FORMULA ONE SCENE, BUT the new developments were overshadowed by the death of Jim Clark. In the sad aftermath, Graham Hill bravely won his second title for the grieving Lotus team.

NEW COLOURS
Graham Hill shows off the revolutionary Gold Leaf livery of his Lotus.

Several things happened in 1968 which were to have long-term effects on Formula One, but nothing shook the racing world quite as much as Jim Clark's death in a Formula Two race at Hockenheim. The season was perhaps most notable for the introduction of overt commercial sponsorship. The previously green and yellow Lotuses were now red, white and gold, thanks to backing from Gold Leaf cigarettes.

Ford DFVs for all
Early in the year Lotus, Brabham and Ferrari began to experiment with downforce-enhancing wings, which soon became standard equipment. The DFV was made available to all comers, and for the next 15 years the engine would be both an affordable and competitive choice for anyone who wanted it.

Other big news was the arrival of Ken Tyrrell to run Matra-Fords. He scooped up Stewart as his driver, and the partnership would blossom for the next six seasons. Meanwhile, Matra's own team, with Henri Pescarolo and Jean-Pierre Beltoise, became a serious force.

Talented Belgian youngster Jacky Ickx joined Amon at Ferrari, while Hulme moved to join Bruce McLaren.

Clark and Hill continued to lead the Lotus challenge, with Siffert in a private Rob Walker car. A sign of what might have been came at Kyalami, when Clark dominated the race, ahead of team-mate Hill. By the next race, at the new Jarama track in Spain, Clark was gone. Jackie Oliver replaced him, and Hill revived Lotus morale with his first win with the 49, ahead of Hulme's McLaren. Graham then scored another victory at Monaco, where Richard Attwood finished a fine second in a BRM.

At Spa, McLaren gave his marque its first victory after Stewart ran out of fuel. It was also the first win for a DFV in something other than a Lotus 49. The next was not long in coming, for Stewart gave Tyrrell's Matra-Ford its first win at Zandvoort. There was another different winner at Rouen, where young Ickx gave Ferrari its only win of the year in pouring rain. Surtees was second for Honda, but veteran team-mate Jo Schlesser was killed.

At Brands Hatch the popular Siffert gave Walker his first win in seven years with the private 49, heading home the Ferraris of Amon and Ickx after early leaders Hill and Oliver retired.

Stewart in fine form

The Nurburgring saw one of the greatest drives of all time, with

DRIVERS' WORLD CHAMPIONSHIP				
Pos.	Driver	Nat.	Make	Pts
1	Graham Hill	GB	Lotus-Ford	48
2	Jackie Stewart	GB	Matra-Ford	36
3	Denny Hulme	NZ	McLaren-Ford	33
4	Jacky Ickx	Bel	Ferrari	27
5	Bruce McLaren	NZ	McLaren-Ford	22
6	Pedro Rodriguez	Mex	BRM	18
7	Jo Siffert	Swi	Lotus-Ford	12
=	John Surtees	GB	Honda	12
9	Jean-Pierre Beltoise	Fr	Matra	11
10	Chris Amon	NZ	Ferrari	10
All scores counted				

CONSTRUCTORS' CUP		
Pos.	Make	Pts
1	Lotus	62
2	McLaren	49
3	Matra	45
4	Ferrari	32
5	BRM	28
6	Cooper	14
=	Honda	14
8	Brabham	10

Stewart winning with a virtuoso performance in atrocious conditions. Hulme showed that his 1967 crown was deserved by winning the next two events at Monza and the Mont Tremblant circuit in Canada. At Watkins Glen newcomer Mario Andretti earned a sensational pole for Lotus, but Stewart took his third win of the year. In the Mexico City finale Stewart and Hill battled for the lead until Stewart fell back with handling problems, leaving Graham to score his third win of the year.

If the losses of Clark and Schlesser were not enough, BRM's Mike Spence was killed in a Lotus during practice at Indianapolis, and former Italian Grand Prix winner Ludovico Scarfiotti died in a hillclimb.

1969

JACKIE STEWART MARCHED FORWARD TO TAKE THE TITLE WITH KEN Tyrrell's Matra-Ford, since there was virtually no one else who could offer a consistent challenge. It looked certain that now Stewart would be the man to beat.

Jackie Stewart had come close to the title the previous year, and in 1969 everything went his way. With Matra withdrawing its own team, all efforts were concentrated on Tyrrell's outfit. Stewart and team-mate Johnny Servoz-Gavin – who had impressed in 1968 – were joined by Jean-Pierre Beltoise. Rindt took up a golden opportunity to join Hill at Lotus, while Ickx left Ferrari to replace him at

Brabham. Jack had finally given up on Repco and joined the DFV bandwagon. Surtees was available because Honda had withdrawn at the end of 1968. The DFV supremacy had taken its toll. Also gone from the scene were Eagle-Weslake and Cooper-Maserati.

Four-wheel drive fiasco

The big development of the year was four-wheel drive. Matra,

FLYING START
Jackie Stewart won five of the first six races to storm to his first title.

McLaren and Lotus all tried it, but it was a white elephant and none of the cars really worked. Stewart started the season in fine form, dominating the opening race at Kyalami. Andretti, who would have occasional drives in a third Lotus, gave him a hard time early on. Stewart won again at Montjuich Park circuit near Barcelona, but this time he was helped by retirements ahead. Amon's Ferrari broke when leading, while Lotus had a bad break. First Hill and then Rindt had huge crashes after their wings failed.

Rindt would have to miss Monaco, where the FIA announced an immediate ban on the high-mounted aerofoils which had proliferated. They soon crept back in, but in a new and less outrageous form, attached to the bodywork. Stewart and Amon both led but retired, allowing Hill to score a historic fifth win. Piers Courage finished second in a Brabham entered by Frank Williams – the first significant result for the British team owner.

The race at Spa was cancelled, and Rindt was fit enough to return at Zandvoort. He took pole and led until retiring, so Stewart scored another win. Jackie's fourth victory came at Clermont-Ferrand in France, where team-mate Beltoise did a good job to finish second.

Jackie's winning streak

Stewart won once more at Silverstone, where he battled hard with Rindt until the Austrian had to pit with a loose

DRIVERS' WORLD CHAMPIONSHIP

Pos.	Driver	Nat.	Make	Pts
1	Jackie Stewart	GB	Matra-Ford	63
2	Jacky Ickx	Bel	Brabham-Ford	37
3	Bruce McLaren	NZ	McLaren-Ford	26
4	Jochen Rindt	A	Lotus-Ford	22
5	Jean-Pierre Beltoise	Fr	Matra-Ford	21
6	Denny Hulme	NZ	McLaren-Ford	20
7	Graham Hill	GB	Lotus-Ford	19
8	Piers Courage	GB	Brabham-Ford	16
9	Jo Siffert	Swi	Lotus-Ford	15
10	Jack Brabham	Aus	Brabham-Ford	14

All scores counted

CONSTRUCTORS' CUP

Pos	Make	Pts
1	Matra-Ford	66
2	Brabham-Ford	49
3	Lotus-Ford	47
4	McLaren-Ford	38
5	BRM	7
=	Ferrari	7

wing. Ickx had a good run to second with the Brabham, and two weeks later he went one better at the Nurburgring, giving the team its first win since 1967.

The Scot clinched the title with a sixth win in an epic, slipstreaming battle at Monza, where he headed home Rindt, Beltoise and McLaren. But, after such a run of success, Stewart failed to win any of the last three races. Ickx triumphed in Canada, Rindt scored his first success at Watkins Glen and Hulme provided more variety with a win for McLaren in Mexico. Missing from the Mexican race was Graham Hill, who had broken his legs in a massive accident at Watkins Glen. He was fit for the following season, but would never win a Grand Prix again.

1970

JOCHEN RINDT WAS LEADING THE CHAMPIONSHIP FOR LOTUS WHEN he lost his life at Monza, but the popular Austrian became the Formula One's first posthumous champion. In a dark year for the sport, Bruce McLaren and Piers Courage were also killed.

DRINKS ALL ROUND
Jochen Rindt celebrates securing pole position at Brands Hatch, but the smiles would turn to tears for his wife later in the year.

The big story of the winter was the arrival of March Engineering. Seemingly out of nowhere, the British company appeared at the first race with no fewer than five DFV-powered cars. March scored a coup by getting Ken Tyrrell's nod after Matra decided to come back with its own team and V12-powered cars. The works March team had strong drivers in Amon and Siffert. Ferrari looked well placed with the all-

new 312B, and Ickx returned to drive it. BRM attracted backing from Yardley, and produced the much-improved P153.

Brabham had not won since the 1967 Canadian Grand Prix, but he started the year with a fine win in South Africa with his new BT33. Stewart led before dropping to third behind Hulme's McLaren.

Early success for March

At Jarama, Stewart gave March

a win in the marque's second-ever race. He was hounded by the rejuvenated Brabham, until Jack's engine broke. Brabham came to the fore at Monaco, holding off Rindt in a fine battle for the lead. But the Aussie slid off at the last corner, allowing Rindt to win. Tragedy struck before the next race in Belgium when Bruce McLaren was killed while testing a CanAm car at Goodwood. He had been a mainstay of Formula One since 1959.

BRM had not won since Monaco in 1966, but at Spa Rodriguez gave the team a sensational victory after holding off Amon's March. Zandvoort saw the delayed appearance of Chapman's slick new Lotus 72, and it scored a debut win in the hands of Rindt. Alas, Piers Courage perished when the De Tomaso crashed and caught fire. Another new face was dashing young Frenchman, François Cevert, who joined Tyrrell when Servoz-Gavin abruptly retired. Rindt and the 72 won at Clermont-Ferrand, and then again at Brands Hatch after Brabham ran out of fuel, while leading rookie, Brazilian Emerson Fittipaldi, drove a works Lotus 49C to eighth.

Ickx was having a bad season, with just four points on the board. He fought back with second place in the German Grand Prix, held at Hockenheim, while Rindt took his fifth win of the season. In Austria Ickx gave Ferrari a much-needed victory, heading home new team-mate Clay Regazzoni.

DRIVERS' WORLD CHAMPIONSHIP

Pos.	Driver	Nat.	Make	Pts
1	Jochen Rindt	A	Lotus-Ford	45
2	Jacky Ickx	Bel	Ferrari	40
3	Clay Regazzoni	Swi	Ferrari	33
4	Denny Hulme	NZ	McLaren-Ford	27
5	Jack Brabham	Aus	Brabham-Ford	25
=	Jackie Stewart	GB	March/Tyrrell-Ford	25
7	Chris Amon	NZ	March-Ford	23
=	Pedro Rodriguez	Mex	BRM	23
9	Jean-Pierre Beltoise	Fr	Matra	16
10	Emerson Fittipaldi	Bra	Lotus-Ford	12

All scores counted

CONSTRUCTORS' CUP

Pos.	Make	Pts
1	Lotus-Ford	59
2	Ferrari	52
3	March-Ford	48
4	Brabham-Ford	35
=	McLaren-Ford	35
6	BRM	23
=	Matra	23
8	Surtees-Ford	3

Death at Monza

Tragedy struck again in practice at Monza when Rindt crashed fatally after a mechanical failure; he was just 28 years old. The race went ahead without Lotus, and Regazzoni scored a fine win in only his fifth start. Rindt had led the title race comfortably, and the only man who could usurp him was Ickx. He led Regazzoni in a Ferrari one-two in Canada, finished fourth in Watkins Glen and then won in Mexico. It was not enough, but even he really did not want to win by default.

Canada saw the first appearance of another new marque – the Tyrrell. It showed promise in Stewart's hands, but would have to wait until 1971 for its first success.

1971

JACKIE STEWART EARNED HIS SECOND TITLE WITH A DOMINANT performance for Tyrrell. But once again, the year was tinged with sadness as racing recorded the deaths of two of the fastest and most popular stars on the circuits.

Jack Brabham was missing from the grids, having retired at the end of the previous year after 126 starts and three championships to his name. He settled into life as a team owner, and Graham Hill signed up to drive.

The works March team had had a poor first season, and the star drivers left. Siffert joined Porsche sports car colleague Rodriguez at BRM, while Amon went to the promising Matra-Simca outfit. The third

Constructors' Cup		
Pos.	Driver	Pts
1	Tyrrell-Ford	73
2	BRM	36
3	Ferrari	33
=	March-Ford	33
5	Lotus-Ford	21
6	McLaren-Ford	10
7	Matra	9
8	Surtees-Ford	8

Drivers' World Championship				
Pos.	Driver	Nat.	Make	Pts
1	Jackie Stewart	GB	Tyrrell-Ford	62
2	Ronnie Peterson	Swe	March-Ford	33
3	François Cevert	Fr	Tyrrell-Ford	26
4	Jacky Ickx	Bel	Ferrari	19
=	Jo Siffert	Swi	BRM	19
6	Emerson Fittipaldi	Bra	Lotus-Ford	16
7	Clay Regazzoni	Swi	Ferrari	13
8	Mario Andretti	USA	Ferrari	12
9	Chris Amon	NZ	Matra-Simca	9
=	Peter Gethin	GB	BRM	9
=	Denny Hulme	NZ	BRM	9
=	Pedro Rodriguez	Mex	BRM	9
=	Reine Wisell	Swe	Lotus-Ford	9
All scores counted				

STP March driver, Mario Andretti, joined Ickx and Regazzoni to become Ferrari's third driver. Early in the year the Italian team lost Ignazio Giunti in a terrible sports car crash in Argentina.

To lead its challenge March signed up Ronnie Peterson, who had done a solid job in a private car the year before. The Swede soon emerged as a leading contender, although he would never actually win a race. Ferrari drew first blood in South Africa when Andretti scored his maiden triumph, although Hulme had looked set to win for McLaren. Stewart finished second and followed it up with wins in Barcelona and Monaco. Peterson scored a fine second in the latter event.

Stewart struggled at a wet Zandvoort, finishing a disappointing 11th, while Ickx won for Ferrari. The French Grand Prix moved to the modern Paul Ricard facility, where Stewart and Cevert scored a fine one-two. Not long afterward BRM star Rodriguez, who had finished second in Holland, was killed in a minor sports car race at the Norisring.

Stewart won again at Silverstone, followed home by Peterson and then, at the Nurburgring, he and Cevert picked up their second one-two; it was a repeat of the Scot's

1969 form. BRM bounced back in fine style with a sensational win for Siffert in Austria and an even more spectacular one for Peter Gethin at Monza. In Austria few noticed the low-key debut of Niki Lauda in a rented March, while at Monza, Amon looked set to finally score his first win in the Matra-Simca – until he accidentally ripped off his visor in the closing laps and finished sixth.

A good year for Jackie

Stewart's engine had broken in Italy, but he bounced back with a win in Canada, Peterson again finishing second. In the finale at Watkins Glen it was the turn of Cevert to score his maiden win, after Stewart slipped to fifth with tyre troubles. The title was long since in his pocket, although Peterson was the big find of the year, finishing second in the championship thanks to his consistent results. Cevert, another brilliant youngster, took third.

Lotus had a disappointing year, the marque failing to win a race for the first time since 1960. A lot of effort was wasted with an Indy-derived gas turbine car, which never lived up to expectations. In October tragedy struck again: Siffert was killed when his BRM crashed and caught fire in a non-championship race at Brands Hatch. It was a sad end to the season.

VICTORY CHARGE
Jackie Stewart roars towards victory at the French Grand Prix.

1972

LOTUS RETURNED ONCE AGAIN TO THE TOP OF THE PODIUM. ITS rising star, Emerson Fittipaldi, who had shown much promise the previous year, became the youngest-ever champion at 25. There was no one else able to offer a season-long challenge.

Lotus went into 1972 armed with an updated version of the rather appropriately named 72 chassis, plus a dramatic new colour scheme. Gold Leaf had been replaced by the black and gold hues of John Player Special. The cigarette brand would become completely synonymous with the car, which would soon be known purely as a JPS. Other sponsors had been in the news as well. Yardley left BRM to join a revitalized McLaren effort, in which Hulme was partnered by Peter Revson, returning some eight years after a shaky debut in the mid-1960s.

Meanwhile BRM found major backing from Marlboro and, in what proved to be an over-ambitious plan, ran up to five cars per race. There were some changes at Brabham, which was acquired by busi-

EMMO TAKES OVER
Brazilian Emerson Fittipaldi confirmed his promise of the previous season by storming to the 1972 title, winning five times along the way.

nessman Bernie Ecclestone. Hill was joined by Argentina's Carlos Reutemann, the first talent to emerge from that country since the 1950s.

Newcomer Reutemann stunned the field when he took pole for his debut race at Buenos Aires, but it was back to normal in the race when he had to pit for tyres and Stewart won from Hulme. The Kiwi went one better in South Africa, giving McLaren its first win since the 1969 Mexican Grand Prix.

Fittipaldi gave JPS its first win in the non-championship event at Brands Hatch, and then dominated the Spanish Grand Prix. Monaco brought a total surprise when, in wet conditions, Beltoise drove a fine race for BRM. It was to be the marque's last-ever win.

Fittipaldi won at the new, and boring, Nivelles track in Belgium, and Stewart triumphed at Clermont-Ferrand after Amon again lost a race in the latter stages – this time with a puncture. Ickx's Ferrari led the British Grand Prix until the Belgian was stricken with an oil leak, allowing Fittipaldi to win. Ickx fought back with victory at the Nurburgring, ahead of team-mate Regazzoni. Fittipaldi won the next race in Austria and then triumphed again at Monza to clinch the title.

Mixed fortunes for Stewart

Stewart had not had much luck, but a new car, introduced in Austria, improved his form. He finished the season with wins at Mosport and Watkins Glen,

DRIVERS' WORLD CHAMPIONSHIP

Pos.	Driver	Nat.	Make	Pts
1	Emerson Fittipaldi	Bra	Lotus-Ford	61
2	Jackie Stewart	GB	Tyrrell-Ford	45
3	Denny Hulme	NZ	McLaren-Ford	39
4	Jacky Ickx	Bel	Ferrari	27
5	Pete Revson	USA	McLaren-Ford	23
6	François Cevert	Fr	Tyrrell-Ford	15
=	Clay Regazzoni	Swi	Ferrari	15
8	Mike Hailwood	GB	Surtees-Ford	13
9	Chris Amon	NZ	Matra	12
=	Ronnie Peterson	Swe	March-Ford	12

All scores counted

CONSTRUCTORS' CUP

Pos.	Make	Pts
1	Lotus-Ford	61
2	Tyrrell-Ford	51
3	McLaren-Ford	47
4	Ferrari	33
5	Surtees-Ford	18
6	March-Ford	15
7	BRM	14
8	Matra	12
9	Brabham-Ford	7

heading home Revson in the first race and Cevert in the latter. It was enough for Jackie to make a late run to second place in the championship, ahead of Hulme. The previous year's runner-up, Peterson, had a poor season. March's new car failed and a slightly more successful replacement was hastily built. However, Peterson had impressed the right people: for 1973 he earned himself a Lotus ride, alongside champion Fittipaldi.

But there was sad news for Ronnie's country as well. In June, veteran Jo Bonnier was killed when his Lola crashed at Le Mans. He had raced from 1957 to 1971, but never matched the form which had given him BRM's first win in 1959.

1973

JACKIE STEWART ACQUIRED HIS THIRD TITLE AFTER A HARD BATTLE with Lotus and decided to quit while he was at the top. Once again the season was blighted, this time with the deaths of François Cevert and newcomer Roger Williamson.

Colin Chapman's fortunes certainly looked good. Fittipaldi and Peterson represented a Lotus team of two top drivers, but some people remembered the previous time the team tried that with Rindt and Hill in 1969 – and Stewart won the championship.

Stewart and Cevert had developed into a fine partnership, and Hulme and Revson looked good at McLaren. Ickx was joined at Ferrari by little Arturo Merzario, who had run a few races in 1972, while Regazzoni left to join Marlboro BRM. An intriguing new marque was the American-financed Shadow. The sinister black cars were handled by Jackie Oliver and George Follmer, an American veteran with no Formula One experience. Graham Hill quit Brabham to set up his own team.

Fittipaldi begins well

Fittipaldi had a dream start to his title defence by winning in both Argentina and his native Brazil. The first was by no means easy, since Regazzoni and Cevert both led before having problems. In South Africa McLaren introduced the sleek and very modern-looking M23, which would ultimately have a lifetime of six seasons. Hulme put it on pole, but fell to fifth as Stewart scored a fine win after a heavy practice crash. Hailwood became a hero in the race as he rescued Regazzoni from his burning car.

Fittipaldi scored a third win in Spain, and then Stewart added a second in Belgium, where the track broke up and many cars skated off. Jackie won again in Monaco to make it three each for the main contenders. The race saw the debut of Briton James Hunt, in a March run by aristocrat Lord Hesketh.

CONSTRUCTORS' CUP

Pos.	Make	Pts
1	Lotus-Ford	92
2	Tyrrell-Ford	82
3	McLaren-Ford	58
4	Brabham-Ford	22
5	March-Ford	14
6	BRM	12
=	Ferrari	12
8	Shadow-Ford	9
9	Surtees-Ford	7
10	Iso-Marlboro	2

DRIVERS' WORLD CHAMPIONSHIP

Pos.	Driver	Nat.	Make	Pts
1	Jackie Stewart	GB	Tyrrell-Ford	71
2	Emerson Fittipaldi	Bra	Lotus-Ford	55
3	Ronnie Peterson	Swe	Lotus-Ford	52
4	François Cevert	Fr	Tyrrell-Ford	47
5	Pete Revson	USA	McLaren-Ford	38
6	Denny Hulme	NZ	McLaren-Ford	26
7	Carlos Reutemann	Arg	Brabham-Ford	16
8	James Hunt	GB	March-Ford	14
9	Jacky Ickx	Bel	Ferrari	12
10	Jean-Pierre Beltoise	Fr	BRM	9

All scores counted

For the first time Sweden hosted a race at the Anderstorp circuit and, although local hero Peterson was on pole, Hulme gave the M23 its maiden victory. Ronnie got his revenge in France, though, finally scoring his first win after suffering appalling luck in the early races. It did not help him much at Silverstone, where the race was stopped after a multi-car pile-up triggered by Jody Scheckter. Revson won the restarted race after Stewart spun out.

Death at Zandvoort
Tragedy returned to Zandvoort, when Roger Williamson – in only his second race – was killed in a fiery crash. Stewart and Cevert scored a one-two, a feat they repeated in Germany. In Austria, Peterson waved Fittipaldi through, but won anyway when Emerson retired. At Monza Peterson and Fittipaldi finished one-two, but the title went to Stewart. After an early stop he charged through the field to an amazing fourth place.

Revson won the chaotic, rain-hit Canadian race, which saw the first use of a pace car in Formula One. The circus moved to Watkins Glen where Stewart planned to have his 100th and last Grand Prix. But Cevert was killed in practice, and Tyrrell withdrew. It was a bitter end to a fantastic farewell season for JYS. In the race Peterson picked up a fourth win, but he was pushed hard by the fast-improving Hunt.

JACKIE STRIKES BACK
The Tyrrell's of Jackie Stewart and Francois Cevert lead the way in what would turn out to be the Scot's last German Grand Prix.

1974

THIS WAS ONE OF THE CLOSEST CHAMPIONSHIPS FOR YEARS, IN WHICH Fittipaldi and Regazzoni battled for top position. In a dramatic finale Fittipaldi claimed his second title — a first for the McLaren marque. At the year's end Denny Hulme retired.

TOP OF THE TREE
Fourth in the final round was good enough for Emerson Fittipaldi to claim his second world title.

The winter of 1973–74 was one of the busiest in memory. The big news was that Fittipaldi quit Lotus to join McLaren, along with substantial new backing from Texaco and Marlboro. Hulme stayed on as his teammate, while a third car – in Yardley colours – was entered for Hailwood.

Ickx left Ferrari to join Peterson at Lotus, while Tyrrell found himself needing two new drivers. He hired Scheckter from McLaren and French newcomer Patrick Depailler. Revson also left McLaren, join-ing French youngster Jean-Pierre Jarier at Shadow. Hill's team swapped from Shadow to Lola chassis, while Hesketh built its own car for Hunt. BRM had new French sponsors, and Beltoise led a squad of three French drivers. Amon's career took another dive as he tried to run his own team.

Shake-up at Ferrari

At Ferrari personnel changed and a completely new car was produced. Regazzoni rejoined after a year at BRM, and brought Lauda with him, who had shown some promise. From the start the revised Ferrari line-up was competitive. Hulme won the first race in Argentina, but Regazzoni qualified on the front row and Lauda took second in the race.

In Brazil, Peterson and Fittipaldi duelled for the lead until the Swede punctured, leaving Emerson to score McLaren's second win. Reutemann led that race, too, and finally came good by winning in Kyalami – Brabham's first success for exactly four years. Sadly, in pre-race testing Revson was killed when he crashed his Shadow.

At Jarama Ferrari's promise produced results when Lauda won. Fittipaldi scored a second win in Nivelles, and then Peterson triumphed at Monaco. Two weeks later Tyrrell new boys, Scheckter and Depailler, scored a brilliant one-two in Sweden.

Lauda and Regazzoni scored a Ferrari one-two in the French Grand Prix at the new Dijon track, and then Scheckter took his second win at Brands Hatch. Lauda led until puncturing near the end, and his exit from the pit lane was controversially blocked by hangers-on and an official car. He was eventually awarded fifth. At the Nurburgring Lauda threw it away on the first lap, leaving it to Regazzoni to save face for Ferrari. Reutemann won in Austria, and then Peterson was on top at Monza after both of the Ferraris failed, for his third victory of the season.

Fittipaldi stakes claim

Fittipaldi made his claim in the penultimate race at Mosport, winning ahead of Regazzoni. Incredibly, they went into the final race on equal points. In the end a fourth place was enough for Emmo, with neither of his rivals scoring. McLaren also beat Ferrari to the constructors' title, but the race was marred by the death of Austrian rookie, Helmuth Koinigg. The North American events saw the debut of two intriguing new marques from the USA, which had long been without representation in Formula One. Penske and Parnelli had plans to compete in Europe.

Constructors' Cup

Pos.	Make	Pts
1	McLaren-Ford	73
2	Ferrari	65
3	Tyrrell-Ford	52
4	Lotus-Ford	42
5	Brabham-Ford	35
6	Hesketh-Ford	15
7	BRM	10
8	Shadow-Ford	7
9	March-Ford	6
10	Williams-Ford	4

Drivers' World Championship

Pos.	Driver	Nat.	Make	Pts
1	Emerson Fittipaldi	Bra	McLaren-Ford	55
2	Clay Regazzoni	Swi	Ferrari	52
3	Jody Scheckter	SAf	Tyrrell-Ford	45
4	Niki Lauda	A	Ferrari	38
5	Ronnie Peterson	Swe	Lotus-Ford	35
6	Carlos Reutemann	Arg	Brabham-Ford	32
7	Denny Hulme	NZ	McLaren-Ford	20
8	James Hunt	GB	Hesketh-Ford	15
9	Patrick Depailler	Fr	Tyrrell-Ford	14
10	Mike Hailwood	GB	McLaren-Ford	12
=	Jacky Ickx	Bel	Lotus-Ford	12

All scores counted

1975

NIKI LAUDA DOMINATED THE SEASON IN BRILLIANT STYLE. AMAZING TO record, it was Ferrari's first championship since Surtees had triumphed 11 years earlier. Graham Hill's death in a plane crash brought a tragic end to the year.

The winter season saw few changes among the front-runners. Graham Hill planned a switch from Lola to his own Hill team. Following the first two races, he announced his retirement after an incredible 176 starts.

Jean-Pierre Jarier had shown flair on occasions, but no one expected him to start the new season in the way he did. He gave Shadow its first pole in Argentina, but non-started when the transmission broke on the warm-up lap. Fittipaldi won for McLaren, ahead of Hunt's Hesketh after the Englishman lost the lead with a mistake.

In Brazil, Jarier again took pole, and led for 28 laps before retiring. Pace scored a popular first win in his home country, ahead of local hero Fittipaldi. Pace and Reutemann shared the front row in South Africa, but Scheckter scored a home win for Tyrrell.

Disaster at Montjuich

At the Spanish race the Ferraris were the pacesetters, with Lauda and Regazzoni on the front row. But the event was beset by a dispute over safety standards at the Montjuich Park track. Eventually a boycott was avoided, but the race turned to chaos. Half the field crashed, including the Ferraris. Rolf Stommelen led in the Hill, but crashed when the rear wing broke, killing several onlookers. The race was stopped early with Mass leading.

In a soaking wet race at Monaco Lauda and the 312T came good, winning from Fittipaldi. Lauda followed that with wins at Zolder and Anderstorp.

Zandvoort brought a popular first win for Hunt and the Hesketh team. Neither had been taken seriously when they started two years earlier, but

Constructors' Cup

Pos.	Make	Pts
1	Ferrari	72.5
2	Brabham-Ford	54
3	McLaren-Ford	53
4	Hesketh-Ford	33
5	Tyrrell-Ford	25
6	Shadow-Ford	9.5
7	Lotus-Ford	9
8	March-Ford	7.5
9	Williams-Ford	6
10	Parnelli-Ford	5

Drivers' World Championship

Pos.	Driver	Nat.	Make	Pts
1	Niki Lauda	A	Ferrari	64.5
2	Emerson Fittipaldi	Bra	McLaren-Ford	45
3	Carlos Reutemann	Arg	Brabham-Ford	37
4	James Hunt	GB	Hesketh-Ford	33
5	Clay Regazzoni	Swi	Ferrari	25
6	Carlos Pace	Bra	Brabham-Ford	24
7	Jochen Mass	Ger	McLaren-Ford	20
=	Jody Scheckter	SAf	Tyrrell-Ford	20
9	Patrick Depailler	Fr	Tyrrell-Ford	12
10	Tom Pryce	GB	Shadow-Ford	8

All scores counted

James had developed into a top-rank driver, and beat Lauda in Holland in a dramatic wet/dry fight. The result was reversed when Lauda won at sunny Paul Ricard.

Silverstone chaos

The rain returned at Silverstone – for another dramatic weekend which saw 15 cars crash. Pryce stunned everyone with pole and he, Pace, Regazzoni, Jarier and Hunt all took turns in the lead. When the crashes finally forced a red flag, Fittipaldi was ahead. Surprisingly, it was to prove his last-ever Formula One victory.

In Germany, Reutemann survived as most of the front-runners had punctures, and then in Austria rain and confusion struck once more. The popular Brambilla was ahead when the race was curtailed to give the works March team its first win – and the first for any March since 1970. Tragically, however, American driver Mark Donohue crashed his Penske-entered March in the warm-up and subsequently succumbed to head injuries.

Lauda had been quietly racking up the points, and clinched his first title with a third at Monza, as team-mate Regazzoni won. Just Watkins Glen remained, and Lauda added yet another win. Lotus had its worst season to date, Peterson and Ickx wasting their time with the ancient 72.

November brought a tragedy which shocked the racing world. On the way back from a test session at Paul Ricard, Hill crashed his light plane. The double world champion and several of his team were killed.

A Fresh Face

Four mid-season victories were enough for Austrian Niki Lauda to clinch his first world title.

1976

THIS SEASON WILL GO DOWN AS ONE OF THE MOST DRAMATIC IN THE history of Formula One. Niki Lauda survived a terrible accident in Germany and was quickly back in harness, but James Hunt beat him to the title in the Japanese finale.

DOWN TO THE WIRE
James Hunt, in action at the controversial British Grand Prix, won six times, but only clinched the title in the final round.

As in 1974, Emerson Fittipaldi was at the centre of the news. After two years he quit McLaren and join his brother's team, Copersucar. McLaren was left stranded without a number one driver, but for one driver the timing was perfect.

Lord Hesketh had decided to pull the plug on his very competitive team, and Hunt was unemployed. It did not take long for him to find his way to McLaren. Ferrari, Shadow, Brabham and Tyrrell continued as before, but there were a couple of novelties on the car front.

Brabham secured Alfa engines, while Tyrrell stunned everyone by announcing a six-wheeled car, the P34. There was confusion at Lotus. Chapman designed a new car, the 77. Ickx

left for Wolf-Williams, and Peterson was joined at the first race by Andretti, a Lotus driver back in 1968–69. Neither was certain to stay, and matters were not helped when they collided in the first race in Brazil.

Once again Jarier shone in Interlagos, while Hunt repaid McLaren's faith with pole. But Lauda started, as he had finished the previous season, with a win. Hunt was on pole in Kyalami, but again Lauda won. Peterson had quit Lotus to rejoin March. An exciting addition to the calendar was a street race at Long Beach in California, dubbed the US Grand Prix West. Regazzoni led from start to finish to win.

The European season began at Jarama. All the cars were dif-

ferent since new rules banned tall air boxes, and the race saw the debut of the six-wheeler. Hunt beat Lauda, but was disqualified when the car was found to be fractionally too wide. Lauda won in Belgium and Monaco, and at neither race did Hunt score.

Sweden saw a fabulous one-two for the six-wheelers, Scheckter heading home Depailler. Hunt's luck turned at Paul Ricard, when the Ferrari broke and he won easily. The same week he was reinstated as Spanish winner, but at Brands Hatch fortune did not favour him. Lauda and Regazzoni collided at the first corner, Hunt became involved and the race was stopped. He won the restart in brilliant style, but was disqualified because he had not been running at the time of the red flag. It gave Lauda another win.

In Germany disaster struck when Lauda crashed heavily

DRIVERS' WORLD CHAMPIONSHIP				
Pos.	Driver	Nat.	Make	Pts
1	James Hunt	GB	McLaren-Ford	69
2	Niki Lauda	A	Ferrari	68
3	Jody Scheckter	SAf	Tyrrell-Ford	49
4	Patrick Depailler	Fr	Tyrrell-Ford	39
5	Clay Regazzoni	Swi	Ferrari	31
6	Mario Andretti	USA	Parnelli/Lotus-Ford	22
7	Jacques Laffite	Fr	Ligier-Matra	20
=	John Watson	GB	Penske-Ford	20
9	Jochen Mass	Ger	McLaren-Ford	19
10	Gunnar Nilsson	Swe	Lotus-Ford	11
All scores counted				

CONSTRUCTORS' CUP		
Pos.	Make	Pts
1	Ferrari	83
2	McLaren-Ford	74
3	Tyrrell-Ford	71
4	Lotus-Ford	29
5	Ligier-Ford	20
=	Penske-Ford	20
7	March-Ford	19
8	Shadow-Ford	10
9	Brabham-Alfa Romeo	9
10	Surtees-Ford	7

and was badly burned. Hunt won the race, but the world waited for news on Lauda. Somehow he pulled through and began a remarkable recovery. Unbelievably, he was back in Monza, where Peterson won for March and Niki finished fourth. Hunt failed to score, but struck back with wins at Mosport and Watkins Glen. That put him to within three points of Lauda as the circus moved to Fuji for the first Japanese Grand Prix. The weather was atrocious, and Lauda immediately pulled out. In a thrilling chase, Hunt came storming back from a tyre stop to take the third place he required for his first world title.

1977

NIKI LAUDA WAS MOST CERTAINLY NOT THE FASTEST DRIVER IN THE championship, but he was the most consistent and the Ferrari proved to be extremely reliable. He succeeded in beating off strong challenges from Andretti, Hunt and Scheckter to win his second world title.

After three seasons Scheckter quit Tyrrell to join an intriguing new team, Walter Wolf Racing. Hunt and Mass stayed at McLaren to drive the new M26, the replacement for the ageing M23 and, even before the end of 1976, Reutemann left Brabham to join Ferrari. Peterson replaced Scheckter at Tyrrell, and Watson left the now defunct Penske team to replace Reutemann at Brabham.

THE MAJOR PLAYERS
Jody Scheckter (right) takes the cheers at Hockenheim, but it was Lauda who won both the race and the title.

Debut of the 78

Chapman had pulled off another surprise, providing Andretti and his new team-mate, Gunnar Nilsson, with the stunning 78, the first "ground-effects" car. It had prominent side pods with sliding skirts which produced masses of downforce. The latest Brabham-Alfa was quick, with Watson leading the opening race in Argentina until it broke. Team-mate Carlos Pace and Hunt also led, but victory went to Scheckter and the new Wolf. Ferrari was also competitive. Reutemann won in Brazil, and then, at Kyalami, Lauda scored his first success since his accident. The race was marred by the death of Tom Pryce, with the Welshman hitting a marshal who ran across the track.

Before the next race Pace also lost his life in a plane crash.

Scheckter led for most of the way at Long Beach but, when he punctured, Andretti went ahead to give the Lotus 78 its first win. He quickly added a second in Spain.

Scheckter took his second win of the season in Monaco, which marked the 100th win for the Cosworth DFV. In Belgium there was a typically confusing wet race and it resulted in a fine win for Nilsson in the second Lotus. Hunt had had no luck in his title defence, but at Silverstone he beat Watson in a splendid duel. The race also saw the debut of Jean-Pierre Jabouille's Renault and its V6 turbocharged engine.

Success for Lauda

Lauda scored Goodyear's 100th win in Hockenheim, and once again Austria produced an unusual result, Alan Jones giving Shadow its first win in another damp encounter.

The summer witnessed a spate of Cosworth engine failures. Andretti had four in a row, while Hunt and Scheckter also suffered. Meanwhile, Lauda quietly racked up the points, scoring another win in Holland. Andretti's car held together long enough for him to win in Monza. At a wet Watkins Glen Hunt won after Stuck crashed, but Lauda's fourth place clinched the title. With that, he upped and left Ferrari.

There were still two races left. Scheckter won in Canada, after Mass tipped team-mate

Hunt off. James ended on a high note with a win in Japan, where this time the sun shone. But the race was marred by the deaths of two spectators after Ferrari new boy, Gilles Villeneuve, tangled with Peterson and the car flipped over the barrier.

Fittipaldi had another bad season with his own car, although he occasionally broke into the top six, while Peterson and Depailler struggled all year with the latest six-wheeler. At the end of the year Tyrrell ditched the concept. In contrast, fellow veteran Regazzoni did great things with the little Ensign team, picking up a few points along the way.

CONSTRUCTORS' CUP

Pos.	Make	Pts
1	Ferrari	95
2	Lotus-Ford	62
3	McLaren-Ford	60
4	Wolf-Ford	55
5	Brabham-Alfa Romeo	27
=	Tyrrell-Ford	27
7	Shadow-Ford	23
8	Ligier-Matra	18
9	Fittipaldi-Ford	11
10	Ensign-Ford	10

DRIVERS' WORLD CHAMPIONSHIP

Pos.	Driver	Nat.	Make	Pts
1	Niki Lauda	A	Ferrari	72
2	Jody Scheckter	SAf	Wolf-Ford	55
3	Mario Andretti	USA	Lotus-Ford	47
4	Carlos Reutemann	Arg	Ferrari	42
5	James Hunt	GB	McLaren-Ford	40
6	Jochen Mass	Ger	McLaren-Ford	25
7	Alan Jones	Aus	Shadow-Ford	22
8	Patrick Depailler	Fr	Tyrrell-Ford	20
=	Gunnar Nilsson	Swe	Lotus-Ford	20
10	Jacques Laffite	Fr	Ligier-Matra	18

All scores counted

1978

MARIO ANDRETTI WON THE TITLE AFTER A BRILLIANT RUN WITH Chapman's wonderful Lotus 79. But it was a year of mixed feelings for Mario, as team-mate Ronnie Peterson died as a result of injuries received in a first-lap pile-up at Monza.

Nobody seemed to cotton on to the secrets of the Lotus 78, and rival teams were in for a shock when Colin Chapman introduced the beautiful 79. He had a new second driver, too: Peterson was back at Lotus, eager to restore his name. Meanwhile, Nilsson left to join Arrows, a team formed by a breakaway group from Shadow, but he never got to drive as cancer set in, leaving the team to sign up Riccardo Patrese. Another former Shadow driver, Alan Jones, also linked up with what was effectively a new team: Williams.

Newcomer Didier Pironi joined Depailler in the four-wheel Tyrrell 008, while Patrick Tambay replaced Mass at McLaren. Villeneuve landed a full-time seat at Ferrari, alongside Reutemann. The new 312T3 was a superb machine, and the team changed to Michelin.

Andretti's year

Starting the season with the old 78, Andretti won in Argentina, with Lauda coming second. In Brazil, Reutemann won for Ferrari, and Fittipaldi finally came good with second in the "family car". Kyalami was a classic. Patrese led in the new Arrows, and the race culminated in a fabulous duel between Peterson and Depailler, Ronnie just winning. Villeneuve starred at Long Beach, leading until he hit back marker Regazzoni and allowed Reutemann to score. Monaco saw Depailler finally earn his first win. In Belgium, Mario debuted the 79, and gave notice of his intentions by disappearing into the distance, with Peterson taking second in the 78. They scored another one-two in Jarama.

By now the others were reacting. Scheckter had a prop-

CONSTRUCTORS' CUP

Pos.	Make	Pts
1	Lotus-Ford	86
2	Ferrari	58
3	Brabham-Alfa Romeo	53
4	Tyrrell-Ford	38
5	Wolf-Ford	24
6	Ligier-Matra	19
7	Fittipaldi-Ford	17
8	McLaren-Ford	15
9	Arrows-Ford	11
=	Williams-Ford	11

DRIVERS' WORLD CHAMPIONSHIP

Pos.	Driver	Nat.	Make	Pts
1	Mario Andretti	USA	Lotus-Ford	64
2	Ronnie Peterson	Swe	Lotus-Ford	51
3	Carlos Reutemann	Arg	Ferrari	48
4	Niki Lauda	A	Brabham-Alfa Romeo	44
5	Patrick Depailler	Fr	Tyrrell-Ford	34
6	John Watson	GB	Brabham-Alfa Romeo	25
7	Jody Scheckter	SAf	Wolf-Ford	24
8	Jacques Laffite	Fr	Ligier-Matra	19
9	Emerson Fittipaldi	Bra	Fittipaldi-Ford	17
=	Gilles Villeneuve	Can	Ferrari	17

All scores counted

er ground-effect Wolf, and Brabham responded with the amazing "fan car". Lauda dominated in its only race at Anderstorp before it was abruptly banned. Andretti and Peterson scored a one-two in France. At Brands Hatch they both retired, and Reutemann passed Lauda to take his third win of the year.

Tragedy at Monza

Rain struck in Austria, and Peterson drove brilliantly to win the red-flagged race. At Monza, only Peterson could now beat Mario to the title, but he was happy to obey orders. He had to take the start in the old 78, and became entangled in a massive pile-up. After a long delay the race was restarted. Andretti won from Villeneuve, but both were penalized for jumped starts. Lauda took the honours. Peterson died the following morning, and the racing world was stunned.

Jean-Pierre Jarier replaced him, and was the star of the last two races, although he retired in both events. Reutemann held off Jones in Watkins Glen, while Villeneuve won on a new track in Montreal.

There was more sadness when Nilsson succumbed to cancer 12 days after the Canadian race. He was just 29 years old.

LOTUS DOMINATION
Mario Andretti made the most of a wonderful car as he powered towards his first title. Here he celebrates victory at the French Grand Prix.

1979

GROUND-EFFECT CARS TOOK OVER THE FORMULA ONE SCENE, although some worked better than others. In a very competitive season the reliability of the Ferraris gave them top place and helped Jody Scheckter to scoop the title.

Things looked good at Lotus as Ferrari ace Reutemann joined Andretti, Martini replaced JPS as title sponsor and Chapman still had the inside line on new technology. Or did he? The wingless Lotus 80 was supposed to be a leap forward, but it did not work.

Problems with cars

Williams was also spot on with its new car, the FW07. It was not ready at the start of the season, so Jones and new teammate Regazzoni started out in the old machine. Ferrari was also late with the 312T4. It did not prove to be as a good a ground-effect car as the aforementioned machines, but it was both powerful and reliable. Scheckter quit Wolf to join Villeneuve. After 18 months in the background, Renault

expanded to a second entry for René Arnoux and built the effective RS10.

Ligier started the season with a bang, and Laffite won the races in Argentina and Brazil. The new Ferrari arrived at Kyalami, and Villeneuve and Scheckter finished one-two. Significantly, Jabouille's Renault took its first pole. Villeneuve and Scheckter repeated the result at Long Beach, where they were chased by Jones in the old Williams. Ligier bounced back in Spain, sweeping the front row and Depailler led throughout. Lotus had a rare good day with Reutemann and Andretti taking second and third. Zolder saw the debut of the Williams FW07, and the goalposts suddenly moved. Jones led easily until retiring, leaving victory to

FORZA FERRARI
Jody Scheckter was triumphant in Belgium on his way to pipping team-mate Villeneuve to the title.

Scheckter. Jody won again in Monaco, chased home by Regazzoni's FW07. After retiring in this race, Hunt decided that he had had enough and hung up his helmet. Wolf signed fiery Finn KekeRosberg to replace him.

Renault's achievement

In France, Renault's dreams came true when Jabouille gave the team its first win. And, in a thrilling finale, Villeneuve just edged Arnoux out of second after the pair banged wheels and swapped places all the way around the last lap. Then luck went the way of Williams. Regazzoni gave the team a fabulous first win at Silverstone, which was followed by successes for Jones at Hockenheim, the Osterreichring and Zandvoort. In Holland, Villeneuve dragged his three-wheeled wreckage back to the pits after he had blown a tyre while leading.

Scheckter kept collecting points, and by winning at Monza he had amassed enough

CONSTRUCTORS' CUP		
Pos.	Make	Pts
1	Ferrari	113
2	Williams-Ford	75
3	Ligier-Ford	61
4	Lotus-Ford	39
5	Tyrrell-Ford	28
6	Renault	26
7	McLaren-Ford	15
8	Brabham-Alfa Romeo	7
9	Arrows-Ford	5
10	Shadow-Ford	3

DRIVERS' WORLD CHAMPIONSHIP				
Pos.	Driver	Nat.	Make	Pts
1	Jody Scheckter	SAf	Ferrari	51
2	Gilles Villeneuve	Can	Ferrari	47
3	Alan Jones	Aus	Williams-Ford	40
4	Jacques Laffite	Fr	Ligier-Ford	36
5	Clay Regazzoni	Swi	Williams-Ford	29
6	Carlos Reutemann	Arg	Lotus-Ford	20
=	Patrick Depailler	Fr	Ligier-Ford	20
8	René Arnoux	Fr	Renault	17
9	John Watson	GB	McLaren-Ford	15
10	Mario Andretti	USA	Lotus-Ford	14
=	Jean-Pierre Jarier	Fr	Tyrrell-Ford	14
=	Didier Pironi	Fr	Tyrrell-Ford	14
Best eight scores from 15 races to count				

to claim the title with two races to go. Villeneuve, under orders, followed in his wheel tracks. By Montreal, Brabham had abandoned the awful BT48 and replaced it with the neat DFV-powered BT49. It did not interest Lauda, though, who announced that he was quitting.

The race saw a fine battle between Jones and Villeneuve, which went the way of the Williams driver as he took his fourth win of the year. The pair fought again at a wet Watkins Glen, but Jones lost a wheel after a pit stop, and the gutsy little Canadian won with another display of Ferrari reliability.

1980

ALAN JONES TRIUMPHED IN THE 1980 WORLD CHAMPIONSHIP DESPITE a strong challenge from Nelson Piquet. However, for the first time in its history, Formula One politics began to attract almost as much attention as the sport itself.

Just as Colin Chapman failed to follow up his 1978 success, so Enzo Ferrari's team lost its way in 1980. The new 312T5 was not a very efficient ground-effect car.

Another merger
The Wolf and Fittipaldi teams merged, but retained their respective drivers. Rosberg and Emerson started the season in the rebadged 1979 Wolfs, while a new F8 came on stream later. Alfa-Romeo now returned with two Marlboro-backed machines for Bruno Giacomelli and Depailler. Jones began the season much as he finished 1979. He dominated in Argentina, despite spinning three times. Piquet scored his best result to date with second, while Rosberg gave some hint of his

potential with third. Long Beach saw the end of Clay Regazzoni's career. He crashed heavily and was paralysed.

Meanwhile, Piquet took pole and scored his first win, ahead of Patrese and Fittipaldi. Most of the big names retired, including Depailler, who had held a fine second with the new Alfa. The FW07B made its bow at Zolder and, although it was quick, Jones and Reutemann were led home by Pironi, another first-time winner. Didier was on form again at Monaco, but, after he hit the barrier, the steady Reutemann took victory.

At Jarama politics and racing collided head on, as FOCA was in dispute with FISA. A confusing weekend ended with a "Formula DFV" race going ahead without Ferrari, Alfa and Renault. The Renaults were quick but fragile in Germany and, when leader Jones had a puncture, Laffite took the victo-

DRIVERS' WORLD CHAMPIONSHIP

Pos.	Driver	Nat.	Make	Pts
1	Alan Jones	Aus	Williams-Ford	67
2	Nelson Piquet	Bra	Brabham-Ford	54
3	Carlos Reutemann	Arg	Williams-Ford	42
4	Jacques Laffite	Fr	Ligier-Ford	34
5	Didier Pironi	Fr	Ligier-Ford	32
6	René Arnoux	Fr	Renault	29
7	Elio de Angelis	It	Lotus-Ford	13
8	Jean-Pierre Jabouille	Fr	Renault	9
9	Riccardo Patrese	It	Arrows-Ford	7
10	Derek Daly	Ire	Tyrrell-Ford	6
=	Jean-Pierre Jarier	Fr	Tyrrell-Ford	6
=	Keke Rosberg	Fin	Fittipaldi-Ford	6
=	Gilles Villeneuve	Can	Ferrari	6
=	John Watson	GB	McLaren-Ford	6

CONSTRUCTORS' CUP

Pos.	Make	Pts
1	Williams-Ford	120
2	Ligier-Ford	66
3	Brabham-Ford	55
4	Renault	38
5	Lotus-Ford	14
6	Tyrrell-Ford	12
7	Arrows-Ford	11
=	Fittipaldi-Ford	11
=	McLaren-Ford	11
10	Ferrari	8

ry. Sadly, in pre-race testing Depailler crashed fatally in the Alfa.

France took another win in Austria, Jabouille scoring his second success as he held off the determined Jones. Lotus test driver Nigel Mansell was finally given his chance in a third car, only to have to start the race in a fuel-soaked race suit. In Holland, Jones threw it away by damaging a skirt on a kerb. Piquet, who was developing into a deadly rival, took the win, ahead of Arnoux.

The Italian Grand Prix moved to Imola for the first time, and Piquet scored another win from a brake-troubled Jones.

Duel at the top

The situation was tense going to Montreal, and it blew up when Piquet and Jones tangled on the first lap and caused a huge pile-up. For the restart, Piquet had to ride in the spare, and his qualifying engine duly failed. Pironi led all the way, but was penalized for a jumped start. Jones sat in second and took maximum points, and the title.

Two big names drove their final races at the Glen. Having failed to qualify the dreadful Ferrari in Canada, Scheckter finished 11th and last. Meanwhile, Fittipaldi broke his suspension on lap 15, ending another trying season with his own team.

WINNING FOR WILLIAMS
Alan Jones won five times to claim the World Championship for both himself and the Williams team.

1981

NELSON PIQUET SUCCESSFULLY TURNED THE TABLES ON ALAN JONES IN 1981, winning his first World Championship and the first for Brabham since Bernie Ecclestone had taken control. Unfortunately, off-track disputes and not the racing dominated the headlines.

BY A HAIR'S BREADTH
Nelson Piquet won the title by just one point to become the second Brazilian World Champion.

After the disaster of 1980, Ferrari switched to a new V6 turbo engine, the Italian team becoming the first to follow Renault's pioneering route.

The other big news of the winter was the takeover of McLaren by Ron Dennis. John Barnard set to work on a revolutionary carbon-fibre chassis and Prost left and replaced Jabouille at Renault.

The championship began at Long Beach and with sliding skirts officially banned. Patrese took a surprise pole with the Arrows, but victory went to champion Jones, ahead of Reutemann and Piquet. The Ferraris were quick, but fragile. In Brazil, the new rules turned to farce. Brabham had perfected a hydro-pneumatic suspension system – the car was legal in the pits, but on the track it sat down and the skirts touched the ground. Piquet took pole, started the wet race on slicks and blew it. Reutemann led Jones home controverisally, because he was supposed to let Jones past.

In Argentina, Piquet made no mistake, winning easily, while unrated team-mate Hector Rebaque ran second until his car broke.

The European season started at Imola with the newly invented San Marino Grand Prix – an excuse to have two races in Italy. Villeneuve and Pironi both led the wet race early on, but Piquet came through to win from Patrese and Reutemann.

Disaster at Zolder

At Zolder, a mechanic from the small Osella team died after being struck by a car in practice, and an Arrows mechanic suffered broken legs when hit attending Patrese's stalled car on the grid – just as the race started. Pironi led until his brakes went, Jones crashed out after earlier knocking Piquet off and the win went to Reutemann.

Mansell was in great form at Monaco, qualifying third behind Piquet and Villeneuve. Nelson led, but Jones put him under pressure and the Brazilian crashed out. Jones suffered a fuel pick-up problem and Villeneuve sped by to score a superb win in the unwieldy Ferrari. Amazingly, he repeated that success at Jarama. After Jones fell off, Gilles led a train comprising Laffite, Watson, Reutemann and de Angelis.

Dijon was another odd race. Rain split the event into two parts, and Prost scored his first win in the Renault. Watson and Piquet completed the top three.

Triumph for Watson

Wattie's big day came at Silverstone. Prost and Arnoux both took turns in the lead, but when they failed John was in the right place. It was his first win since Austria in 1976.

Villeneuve, Prost and Arnoux all took turns in the lead in Germany. Jones and Reutemann both had engine problems of varying degrees. Piquet took a canny win, with Prost second. Austria brought a popular win for Laffite.

At Zandvoort, Prost and Jones fought hard in the early stages, until Jones's tyres went off. Prost pulled away to win from Piquet, with Jones third. Reutemann tangled with

CONSTRUCTORS' CUP		
Pos.	Make	Pts
1	Williams-Ford	95
2	Brabham-Ford	61
3	Renault	54
4	Ligier-Matra	44
5	Ferrari	34
6	McLaren-Ford	28
7	Lotus-Ford	22
8	Alfa Romeo	10
=	Arrows-Ford	10
=	Tyrrell-Ford	10

DRIVERS' WORLD CHAMPIONSHIP				
Pos.	Driver	Nat.	Make	Pts
1	Nelson Piquet	Bra	Brabham-Ford	50
2	Carlos Reutemann	Arg	Williams-Ford	49
3	Alan Jones	Aus	Williams-Ford	46
4	Jacques Laffite	Fr	Ligier-Matra	44
5	Alain Prost	Fr	Renault	43
6	John Watson	GB	McLaren-Ford	27
7	Gilles Villeneuve	Can	Ferrari	25
8	Elio de Angelis	It	Lotus-Ford	14
9	Rene Arnoux	Fr	Renault	11
=	Hector Rebaque	Mex	Brabham-Ford	11
All scores counted				

Laffite, so Piquet took the title lead. Prost led all the way at Monza, winning from Jones and Reutemann. Piquet looked set for third until his engine went on the last lap.

The Canadian Grand Prix was an exciting, wet event. Jones spun off while leading, Prost took over, then Laffite got to the front and held on to win. So they headed for the finale with Reutemann on 49, Piquet on 48, and Laffite on 43.

The race was held in a car park in Las Vegas. Reutemann took pole, but faded away in the race. Jones won with Piquet fifth and Laffite sixth – which gave Piquet the title by just a single point.

1982

THE 1982 SEASON PROVED TO BE ONE OF THE MOST TURBULENT — and tragic — in the history of Formula One. Keke Rosberg became the first man since 1964 to secure the world championship with just a single victory to his name.

Lauda was back after two years, joining John Watson at McLaren. Williams replaced Jones with Keke Rosberg, and Brabham looked better than for a long time, with Riccardo Patrese as Piquet's team-mate.

Piquet crashed in the opening race at Kyalami, and the Renaults dominated until Prost had a puncture. But he charged back from eighth to win from Reutemann and Arnoux.

Lauda won at Long Beach from Rosberg. The disqualifica-tions of the first and second in Brazil, Piquet and Rosberg, over water tanks for brake cooling, had led FOCA teams to boycott San Marino, and it was a half-hearted event with just 14 cars entering. Tyrrell, bound by Italian sponsors, broke ranks to join the manufacturer outfits. Pironi and Villeneuve dominated and traded places in what many thought was a show for the fans. Pironi passed the Canadian on the last lap, to take the victory and so, a deadly feud began.

Another black day at Zolder

The feud rumbled on to Zolder where, in final qualifying, desperate to outgun Pironi, tragedy struck. Villeneuve hit the back of Jochen Mass's March and was launched into a frightening roll. The most entertaining driver of the era was killed. The race went ahead without Ferrari, and Watson won.

Monaco was dramatic: Arnoux led until spinning; Prost took over until crashing heavily with three laps to go; Patrese then led, but spun; and Pironi and de Cesaris went by. With one lap to go, Pironi stopped with electrical problems, de Cesaris ran out of fuel and Williams replacement Derek Daly, retired after clouting the barrier. Patrese duly recovered to win.

CONSTRUCTORS' CUP

Pos.	Make	Pts
1	Ferrari	74
2	McLaren-Ford	69
3	Renault	62
4	Williams-Ford	58
5	Brabham-Ford/BMW	41
6	Lotus-Ford	30
7	Tyrrell-Ford	25
8	Ligier-Matra	20
9	Alfa Romeo	7
10	Arrows-Ford	5

DRIVERS' WORLD CHAMPIONSHIP

Pos.	Driver	Nat.	Make	Pts
1	Keke Rosberg	Fin	Williams-Ford	44
2	Didier Pironi	Fr	Ferrari	39
=	John Watson	GB	McLaren-Ford	39
4	Alain Prost	Fr	Renault	34
5	Niki Lauda	A	McLaren-Ford	30
6	Rene Arnoux	Fr	Renault	28
7	Michele Alboreto	It	Tyrrell-Ford	25
=	Patrick Tambay	Fr	Ferrari	25
9	Elio de Angelis	It	Lotus-Ford	23
10	Riccardo Patrese	It	Brabham-Ford	21

All scores counted

In Montreal, now named the Circuit Gilles Villeneuve. Pironi stalled from pole and was hit by Riccardo Paletti, who was killed. Piquet won the race and Patrese came in second. At Zandvoort, Ferrari finally had some good news, with Pironi winning in fine style as new second driver Patrick Tambay settled in well.

Brands Hatch saw Lauda win, but the star of the race was Warwick, who got the tank-like Toleman up to second before retiring. Pironi went to Hockenheim leading by nine points. But in wet practice struck the back of Prost's Renault and was launched into a career-ending accident that broke his legs. In the race Tambay scored his first win in the second Ferrari, ahead of Arnoux and Rosberg.

In the Swiss Grand Prix, held at Dijon-Prenois in France(!), the Renaults led, but Rosberg came through to win from Prost. After Arnoux won at Monza, from Tambay, Watson then had to win the final race, at Las Vegas, to deprive Rosberg of the title. Arnoux and Prost both led, but a shock victory went to Alboreto. Watson was second, but it was not enough and fifth-placed Rosberg took the honours.

ONCE WAS ENOUGH
Keke Rosberg won just once, at Dijon, but still claimed the title.

1983

NELSON PIQUET NOTCHED UP HIS SECOND WORLD TITLE AS ALAIN Prost and Renault threw away their chances during what was a safe season, with neither strikes nor technical squabbles. The action on the track was all that mattered.

New flat-bottom regulations cut downforce and got rid of sidepods, while turbos (and pit stops) became essential. And Williams, for whom champion Keke Rosberg was joined by Jacques Laffite, wasn't ready and would have to spend another year with DFV power until its Honda-powered car was ready. The Japanese manufacturer was back after a 15-year break making a low-key start with the small Spirit team. McLaren, too, had to be patient. It had arranged for sponsor TAG to pay for Porsche's V6 and, until that was ready, Lauda and Watson were stuck with the DFV.

Colin Chapman had scored a coup by securing Renault engines for Lotus. Though he died suddenly, Lotus carried on: de Angelis had the new car for race two, while Mansell used DFV power until mid-season.

Of those with turbo experience, Brabham's Piquet and Patrese had stuck with BMW engines, while Arnoux left Renault to join Tambay at Ferrari. Toleman had a much-improved car for Warwick and Giacomelli. The other leading teams were stuck with DFV power, these including Ligier, Arrows and Tyrrell.

Piquet begins well

Piquet won in impressive style in Rio, but Rosberg drew all the attention. He led, had a fire at his pit stop, recovered to second and was then excluded for a push start.

Long Beach was a rare opportunity for the DFV cars to shine. Watson and Lauda qualified 22nd and 23rd, but they got the race set-up right and came charging through to finish one-two, with Arnoux third.

Unusually, the European season kicked off at Paul Ricard, and Renault continued its habit

Constructors' Cup

Pos.	Make	Pts
1	Ferrari	89
2	Renault	79
3	Brabham-BMW	72
4	Williams-Ford/Honda	36
5	McLaren-Ford/Porsche	34
6	Alfa Romeo	18
7	Lotus-Ford/Renault	12
=	Tyrrell-Ford	12
9	Toleman-Hart	10
10	Arrows-Ford	4

Drivers' World Championship

Pos.	Driver	Nat.	Make	Pts
1	Nelson Piquet	Bra	Brabham-BMW	59
2	Alain Prost	Fr	Renault	57
3	René Arnoux	Fr	Ferrari	49
4	Patrick Tambay	Fr	Ferrari	40
5	Keke Rosberg	Fin	Williams-Ford	27
6	Eddie Cheever	USA	Renault	22
=	John Watson	GB	McLaren-Ford	22
8	Andrea de Cesaris	It	Alfa Romeo	15
9	Riccardo Patrese	It	Brabham-BMW	13
10	Niki Lauda	A	McLaren-Ford	12

All scores counted

of winning at home, with Prost coming first. Tambay then scored an emotional win for Ferrari at Imola.

Monaco was another chance for the DFVs to shine. Rosberg qualified sixth behind the turbos, but it rained and he chose to start on slicks. He was in the lead by the lap two and pulled away as the others pitted.

After a 13-year break, the Belgian Grand Prix returned to Spa. It was rebuilt and much shorter than the original, but it was instantly regarded as the best on the calendar. De Cesaris took the lead, but retired with engine problems. Prost took over and held on to the flag.

Detroit gave the DFV runners another chance and Alboreto scored his second win for Tyrrell. This was the 155th victory for the Ford Cosworth DFV, and also the last. In Canada Arnoux dominated for Ferrari, ahead of Cheever and Tambay.

Prost scored a brilliant win at Silverstone. The Ferraris led, but Prost pushed them as they used up their tyres. Piquet came through to take second place.

Arnoux scored another win at Hockenheim and de Cesaris took a lucky second.

Prost had to work hard to win in Austria, passing Arnoux with six laps to go. Piquet kept his title hopes alive with third, and Prost's lead was now 14 points. He got it wrong in Holland, sliding into Piquet, putting them both out. Arnoux drove a good race to win from tenth.

Monza brought the worst possible result for Prost: retirement, while Piquet won and Arnoux was second.

Britain hosted the Grand Prix of Europe, at Brands Hatch. Piquet won again, but Prost kept his hopes alive with second.

Just South Africa remained, and Piquet was quick in the first half, while Arnoux stopped early and Prost became stuck in a battle for third. His turbo was failing, though, and he retired. Piquet dropped to third, as Patrese won from de Cesaris, but had ensured that he scored the vital points needed for the title.

DOUBLE CHAMPION
Piquet found BMW power more to his liking and won three races en route to the title.

1984

NIKI LAUDA ONCE AGAIN TOOK ADVANTAGE OF THE OPPORTUNITY TO display his judgement and guile when he beat his faster and younger team-mate, Alain Prost, to take the title. This was to be the first of many great years for McLaren.

Alain Prost stunned the Formula One world when he upped and joined McLaren, after falling out with Renault's management. With the TAG/ Porsche engine up to speed, McLaren looked the best bet.

There was a clean sweep at Renault, with Tambay and Warwick joining as Cheever found a new home at Alfa, where he was joined by Patrese.

Ligier had sourced Renault and attracted de Cesaris from Alfa. He joined French new-comer François Hesnault. Arrows had two good drivers in Boutsen and Surer, although they would start the year with DFVs. Tyrrell produced a nimble car and was blessed with two great rookies, Stefan Bellof and Martin Brundle.

Alboreto led in Brazil, but spun out, letting Lauda and Warwick take turns in front. Prost came through to win, though, while Rosberg showed Honda's potential with second.

McLaren was dominant in South Africa. Piquet led until encountering problems, and Lauda won. Prost had to start in the spare, and stormed through from the back to take second. Toleman's Ayrton Senna scored his first point.

The European season kicked off in Belgium and a return to Zolder. Alboreto led all the way for his first win in a Ferrari, with Warwick second.

McLaren was on form at Imola, as Prost led all the way, despite a spin. Lauda retired with engine failure and Piquet held second until a turbo failed, so Arnoux inherited the place.

Renault desperately wanted to win in France, and Tambay led for most of the race, but had both brake and clutch problems, letting Lauda by to win.

Trouble at Monaco

Monaco was wet, and Renault's

CONSTRUCTORS' CUP		
Pos.	Make	Pts
1	McLaren-Porsche	143.5
2	Ferrari	57.5
3	Lotus-Renault	47
4	Brabham-BMW	38
5	Renault	34
6	Williams-Honda	25.5
7	Toleman-Hart	16
8	Alfa Romeo	11
9	Arrows-Ford/BMW	6
10	Ligier-Renault	3

DRIVERS' WORLD CHAMPIONSHIP				
Pos.	Driver	Nat.	Make	Pts
1	Niki Lauda	A	McLaren-Porsche	72
2	Alain Prost	Fr	McLaren-Porsche	71.5
3	Elio de Angelis	It	Lotus-Renault	34
4	Michele Alboreto	It	Ferrari	30.5
5	Nelson Piquet	Bra	Brabham-BMW	29
6	René Arnoux	Fr	Ferrari	27
7	Derek Warwick	GB	Renault	23
8	Keke Rosberg	Fin	Williams-Honda	20.5
9	Nigel Mansell	GB	Lotus-Renault	13
=	Ayrton Senna	Bra	Toleman-Hart	13
All scores counted				

Tambay and Warwick crashed at the first corner, while Prost led Mansell. Mansell took the lead only to crash. Prost regained the lead and was still in front when the race was red-flagged, and half points were awarded.

At Montreal, Piquet was back. The Brabham had a new oil cooler in the front, intended to help with weight distribution, but the side effect was that Piquet burned his feet while leading from start to finish!

Detroit started with a shunt between Piquet, Prost and Mansell. All three were back for the restart, and Piquet led all the way.

Next was Dallas. It was ragingly hot, the track broke up, many crashed and the circus never went back. Rosberg won in style. Mansell led, but his gearbox broke and he collapsed while pushing the car to the line.

Sanity returned when the circus returned to Europe for Brands Hatch, though the race was stopped after Jonathan Palmer crashed his RAM. Prost led until his gearbox failed, leaving Lauda to win.

De Angelis and Piquet retired while leading at Hockenheim, and Prost won from Lauda. Lauda gained revenge by winning in Austria. Piquet led early on in Holland, until he suffered an oil leak, so Prost and Lauda completed another demo run. By now the McLaren stars had a lock on the title: Lauda 54, Prost 52.5.

Prost's engine blew in Monza, and Lauda cantered to victory ahead of Alboreto.

By now Tyrrell had been banned for irregularities found in Detroit, losing their points. Many saw sinister undertones in the way the sole "atmo" runner was thrown out.

For the first time Formula One went to the new Nürburgring for the European GP. Prost led all the way, while Alboreto and Piquet – both out of fuel – were second and third. Lauda finished fourth after a spin, making it Lauda 66, Prost 62.5.

The finale was at Estoril, and Prost won, while Lauda did all he needed to do and came second to secure the title by the closest-ever margin.

MAGNIFICENT McLAREN
Only half a point seperated team-mates Niki Lauda and Alain Prost after the final round. Lauda took the title, with Prost 36½ points ahead of the third-placed driver.

1985

ALAIN PROST FINALLY MADE IT TO THE TOP IN 1985. AFTER BEING squeezed out in the previous two years, the Frenchman secured his first World Championship at the end of a highly competitive year in the McLaren-TAG. Nothing could stop him now.

THE FIRST OF FOUR
Alain Prost was so dominant that he wrapped up the title at Brands Hatch with two races to go.

Two future World Champions made big career moves for 1985. Nigel Mansell left Lotus to join Williams. While Ayrton Senna quit Toleman for Lotus.

Jacques Laffite returned to Ligier from Williams, while Arrows signed Gerhard Berger, who had shone for ATS, and Teo Fabi led a reorganised Toleman from the Monaco race on. Tyrrell finally joined the turbo club, landing Renaults his Brundle and Bellof.

Alboreto began in fine form, taking pole for Ferrari in Rio. Rosberg was alongside him, and both led, but victory went to Prost, while Alboreto took second, ahead of de Angelis. Arnoux finished fourth in the

second Ferrari, but fell out with Enzo and was replaced by Stefan Johansson.

Senna put his Lotus on pole in Portugal. The race was soaking wet, but the weather only emphasised his skills as he stormed to his first win. Alboreto was a distant second.

Senna was again on pole at Imola, and led for 56 laps before running out of fuel. Johansson took over, but he too ran dry. So Prost was first home, only to be disqualified for being underweight. Thus victory went to de Angelis with the rest a lap behind...

Senna took pole in Monaco. And he and Alboreto took turns in the lead, but Prost came through for his second win of the year. Alboreto kept up his scoring rate with second.

Lotus swept the front row in Canada, with de Angelis ahead of Senna. Elio led for 15 laps before Alboreto took over and won, while Johansson made it a Ferrari one-two.

Senna was back on pole in Detroit, but he was one of many to crash, along with Mansell and Prost. Rosberg took the lead early on to give Williams its first win of the year.

Rosberg took pole at Paul Ricard, but it was Brabham's day as Piquet won and gave Pirelli its first success since 1957! Rosberg led for ten laps and took second, ahead of Prost.

Rosberg shines at Silverstone

Silverstone saw the most impressive qualifying lap of the year as Rosberg stormed to pole at over 160mph. Yet Senna led for 58 laps until he ran out of fuel. Prost took over and won by a lap from Alboreto.

The all-new Nurburgring played host to the German Grand Prix for the first time, and Toleman's Teo Fabi took a surprise pole. Ferrari men, Alboreto and Johansson, tangled at the first corner, but Alboreto fought back to win after Rosberg and Senna had spells in front. Prost continued to pile up points with second place.

The Austrian Grand Prix had to be restarted after a first lap crash. Lauda led for the first time this year but retired and Prost went on to win. Senna and Alboreto were next up.

Zandvoort hosted a Grand Prix for the final time, and Piquet took pole, but Rosberg led early on. Prost took over when Rosberg retired yet again, but Lauda came through for his first win of the year – and what turned out to be the last of his career.

Monza was a familiar story, with Senna on pole and Rosberg leading early on. But Prost won from Piquet and Senna. Prost was on pole at Spa, but Senna won from Mansell.

As in 1983, Brands Hatch hosted the European Grand Prix. And Mansell came good in front of his home crowd, scor-

DRIVERS' WORLD CHAMPIONSHIP

Pos.	Driver	Nat.	Make	Pts
1	Alain Prost	Fr	McLaren-Porsche	73
2	Michele Alboreto	It	Ferrari	53
3	Keke Rosberg	Fin	Williams-Honda	40
4	Ayrton Senna	Bra	Lotus-Renault	38
5	Elio de Angelis	It	Lotus-Renault	33
6	Nigel Mansell	GB	Williams-Honda	31
7	Stefan Johansson	Swe	Ferrari	26
8	Nelson Piquet	Bra	Brabham-BMW	21
9	Jacques Laffite	Fr	Ligier-Renault	16
10	Niki Lauda	A	McLaren-Porsche	14

Best 11 scores from 16 races to count

CONSTRUCTORS' CUP

Pos.	Make	Pts
1	McLaren-Porsche	90
2	Ferrari	82
3	Lotus-Renault	71
=	Williams-Honda	71
5	Brabham-BMW	26
6	Ligier-Renault	23
7	Renault	16
8	Arrows-BMW	14
9	Tyrrell-Ford/Renault	7

ing his first win ahead of Senna and Rosberg. Meanwhile, fourth place clinched the title for a cautious Prost.

Mansell was on top form now, and at Kyalami he took pole and led Rosberg home, with Prost third.

The season ended with a new race at Adelaide. Senna took pole, but Prost won, while Ligier ended the season on a high note, with Laffite and Streiff taking second and third. Lauda led a couple of laps, but crashed.

Although Formula One had enjoyed a relatively safe season, two talented drivers lost their lives in sports cars: Manfred Winkelhock, of ATS, died at Mosport Park, while Tyrrell's Bellof was killed at Spa.

1986

THIS SAW ONE OF THE MOST DRAMATIC CONCLUSIONS OF RECENT years. Mansell and Piquet had fought hard all year, but in the final race Nigel blew a tyre, Piquet made a precautionary stop, and a disbelieving Prost sped through to take the title.

Having lost Lauda to retirement, McLaren replaced him with another former champion: Keke Rosberg. The Finn was also replaced by a champion with Piquet moving across from Brabham. Lotus wanted to hire Warwick, but Senna did not want a top name alongside him, so they chose Johnny Dumfries. Meanwhile, de Angelis left Lotus for Brabham. Over the winter Toleman turned into Benetton, and the talented Berger joined Fabi, with BMW engines perhaps the most powerful in the field.

Piquet got off to the best possible start, winning his home Grand Prix at Rio. Senna took pole, and he and Prost led before Piquet took over.

Spain had a Grand Prix again, on the twisty Jerez track. And it produced a thrilling race, with Senna holding off Mansell by a mere 0.014 seconds.

Senna was on pole at Imola, but a jammed wheel bearing forced him out, while Rosberg fell from second to fifth, his tank dry of fuel. Piquet and Rosberg led, but the reliable Prost was there to win from Piquet.

Prost broke Senna's string of poles at Monaco, and led Rosberg home. Senna led briefly, but fell to third.

Tragedy struck when de Angelis was killed in testing at Paul Ricard.

Piquet took pole at Spa, but Mansell came through to win from Senna and Johansson.

In a black weekend in June, former Osella driver Jo Gartner was killed at Le Mans, while Arrows star Marc Surer was injured in a rally.

Brabham was back up to strength in Canada, Warwick returning from the Jaguar sports car team. Mansell took pole and won from Prost.

Senna won from pole in

CONSTRUCTORS' CUP

Pos.	Make	Pts
1	Williams-Honda	141
2	McLaren-Porsche	96
3	Lotus-Renault	58
4	Ferrari	37
5	Ligier-Renault	29
6	Benetton-BMW	19
7	Tyrrell-Renault	11
8	Lola-Ford	6
9	Brabham-BMW	2

DRIVERS' WORLD CHAMPIONSHIP

Pos.	Driver	Nat.	Make	Pts
1	Alain Prost	Fr	McLaren-Porsche	72
2	Nigel Mansell	GB	Williams-Honda	70
3	Nelson Piquet	Bra	Williams-Honda	69
4	Ayrton Senna	Bra	Lotus-Renault	55
5	Stefan Johansson	Swe	Ferrari	23
6	Keke Rosberg	Fin	McLaren-Porsche	22
7	Gerhard Berger	A	Benetton-BMW	17
8	Michele Alboreto	It	Ferrari	14
=	René Arnoux	Fr	Ligier-Renault	14
=	Jacques Laffite	Fr	Ligier-Renault	14

Best 11 scores from 16 races to count

Detroit, but both Ligiers took a turn in the lead, with Laffite finishing second.

Mansell won at Paul Ricard, ahead of Prost, Piquet and Rosberg. And nobody was going to stop him at home, although Piquet pipped him for pole at Brands Hatch. Nigel had a drive shaft break, but his day was saved by a red flag as Johansson and Laffite collided and Laffite hit a barrier, breaking his legs. Mansell won the restart after a tussle with Piquet.

The German Grand Prix returned to Hockenheim. On this power track it was a surprise to see Rosberg and Prost on the front row, but Keke led before Piquet took over and won to keep his title challenge alive.

Behind the Iron Curtain

The twisty and slow Hungaroring circuit made its debut, as Formula One made its first visit to the Eastern bloc and Piquet outran Senna to win.

BMW power ruled in Austria as Fabi and Berger grabbed the front row for Benetton. Berger led until his turbo blew, and in a race of high attrition it was inevitably Prost who kept it flowing to win from Alboreto.

Fabi took pole at Monza with what was possibly the most powerful car ever seen in Formula One. He shared the front row with Prost, but Piquet led Mansell to a Williams one-two.

Senna was on pole in Portugal, but Mansell led all the way to win from Prost and Piquet.

The campaign's third new track was, in fact, an old one – but the circus had not visited Mexico City since 1970. Benetton finally came good and Berger scored his first win.

In a dramatic finale in Adelaide, with both Williams drivers and Prost up for the title, Mansell was perfectly placed to take the title when a rear tyre blew. Williams made Piquet pit for a precautionary change, and he fell to second behind Prost. Victory gave the Frenchman his second title.

OUT WITH A BANG
A blow-out for Nigel Mansell in the dramatic final round at Adelaide handed the title to Alain Prost.

1987

TEAM-MATES NELSON PIQUET AND NIGEL MANSELL FOUGHT FOR THE title, and the Englishman was a strong contender until an accident sidelined him in Japan. Piquet accepted the laurels for the third time, even before the final race had started.

With the FIA considering turbos now too powerful and engine development too expensive, a new formula was announced: from 1989, Formula One would return to atmospheric engines. There would be two interim years, and to encourage teams to change the Jim Clark Cup was introduced for drivers of "atmo" cars.

In response, Cosworth produced the "atmo" DFZ which was used by Tyrrell, March, AGS and Larrousse. Elsewhere, Renault had withdrawn and Lotus had attracted Honda, with Satoru Nakajima as part of the package. Ford moved to Benetton, with Boutsen joining Fabi in the team as Berger had moved on to Ferrari to partner Alboreto after Johansson had joined Prost at McLaren. Williams continued with Mansell and double World Champion Piquet.

Mansell and Piquet shared the front row in Rio, and although Piquet led early on, Prost won with Piquet second and Johansson third. In Imola luck went against Piquet when he crashed and was unable to start. Mansell powered past poleman Senna to win the race.

Mansell and Piquet shared the front row at Spa. The race was stopped after Tyrrell's Streiff and Palmer crashed. So did Mansell and Senna later on, leading to a confrontation. Prost won after Piquet retired, with Johansson second and de Cesaris a surprise third for Brabham.

Mansell led at Monaco until his turbo broke, leaving Senna to score the first of his many wins there. Piquet was second ahead of Alboreto and Berger. In Detroit, Mansell led from pole, but Senna took over as he was hit by cramp and won from Piquet and Prost.

CONSTRUCTORS' CUP		
Pos.	Make	Pts
1	Williams	137
2	McLaren	76
3	Lotus	64
4	Ferrari	53
5	Benetton	28
6	Arrows	11
=	Tyrrell	11
8	Brabham	10
9	Lola	3
10	Zakspeed	2

DRIVERS' WORLD CHAMPIONSHIP				
Pos.	Driver	Nat.	Make	Pts
1	Nelson Piquet	Bra	Williams-Honda	73
2	Nigel Mansell	GB	Williams-Honda	61
3	Ayrton Senna	Bra	Lotus-Honda	57
4	Alain Prost	Fr	McLaren-Porsche	46
5	Gerhard Berger	A	Ferrari	36
6	Stefan Johansson	Swe	McLaren-Porsche	30
7	Michele Alboreto	It	Ferrari	17
8	Thierry Boutsen	Bel	Benetton-Ford	16
9	Teo Fabi	It	Benetton-Ford	12
10	Eddie Cheever	USA	Arrows-Megatron	8
Best 11 scores from 16 races to count				

Two in a row for Mansell

Mansell won at Paul Ricard. Then, after a late tyre stop at Silverstone, Mansell beat Piquet in an inspired charge that culminated in victory. Senna and Nakajima followed the Williams pair home for a Honda top-four.

Mansell's engine failed in Germany and Piquet won while Johansson came second with a flat tyre, as just seven cars finished. Then Mansell took pole in Hungary, but failed to finish when he lost a wheel nut, and Piquet won from Senna and Prost. The Austrian Grand Prix was stopped twice by crashes on the pit straight before Mansell won easily from Piquet.

Piquet pipped Mansell to pole at Monza, and then won the race with Mansell third, the pair split by Senna. Berger led most of the way in Portugal but Prost won with Piquet third, while Mansell retired.

Mansell won at Jerez ahead of Prost, Johansson and Piquet. Then he won in Mexico, in a race interrupted by an accident from which Warwick emerged unscathed. Piquet was second.

For the first time since 1976 Japan had a Grand Prix, this time at Suzuka. Mansell crashed in practice and hurt his back. Piquet celebrated, for Mansell was out for the weekend, and was to miss the final race, too, making Piquet champion. Ironically, Piquet didn't score in either. Instead, Berger won both. Senna and Johansson followed him home in Japan, then Berger led all the way in Australia from Senna. However, the Lotus was disqualified for having illegal brakes, and it cost Senna second place in the championship.

Palmer won the Jim Clark Cup, while Tyrrell won the constructors' version. Not that many people noticed, with Palmer 11th overall.

1988

ALAIN PROST SCORED MORE POINTS THAN McLAREN TEAM-MATE
Ayrton Senna, but the Brazilian claimed the title because he could count his best 11 results from the 16 rounds and, moreover, had eight wins to Prost's seven.

SUPER SENNA
The Brazilian won eight races en route to his first World Championship title.

Senna qualified on pole from Mansell's Williams in Brazil, with Prost third, but had to start from the pits. Prost passed Mansell. So did Ferrari's Berger. And no one headed Prost again. Senna reached second, but was disqualified for using the spare car. Thus Berger was promoted to second and Nelson Piquet to third for Lotus.

Senna led all the way at Imola, helped by Prost being slow off the line and being forced to be his shadow. Senna was almost a minute up on Prost with 12 laps to go at Monaco, when he grazed the barriers. It was several hours before he re-emerged from his apartment, by which time Prost

had won from Berger and Alboreto.

Prost beat Senna in Mexico with only Berger on the same lap. In Canada, it was another McLaren one-two, although this time Senna won from Prost.

Senna and Prost finished in the same order in Detroit, while Mansell retired for the sixth race in a row. In France, anxious that Senna was eroding his lead, Prost won with Senna a distant second, suffering from gearbox problems.

So difficult were the wet conditions at Silverstone that few will recall that Senna passed the Ferraris to win. What people will recall is that Prost pulled off, saying the conditions were

too dangerous. Mansell was second and Nannini third.

Senna won in Germany with Prost second. Then Senna led in Hungary, but hit traffic on the straight. Prost dived inside him, but Senna let him slide by and regained the lead. Senna won again in Belgium, where he overcame a poor start to move into the points lead. Prost was second with Benetton's Boutsen and Nannini third and fourth.

Breakthrough for Ferrari

Berger broke McLaren's run, and to make matters better, it was a Ferrari one-two, with Alboreto half a second behind. Better still, the race was in Italy... But what of McLaren? Prost retired when second with engine failure, while Senna was leading on the penultimate lap, but struggling with fuel consumption. Then he found Williams replacement driver Jean-Louis Schlesser at the chicane. They touched, sending Senna into retirement and the crowd wild. Eddie Cheever and Derek Warwick were third and fourth for Arrows.

McLaren won in Portugal, with Prost taking the spoils. The race had to be restarted and Senna led the first lap then swerved at Prost when he pulled alongside as they passed the pits. Prost didn't back down and took the lead. Senna fell back with handling problems and Ivan Capelli became Prost's challenger. Driving his March like never before, the Italian was the star of the race, but had to settle for second.

Pos.	Driver	Nat.	Make	Pts
DRIVERS' WORLD CHAMPIONSHIP				
1	Ayrton Senna	Bra	McLaren-Honda	90
2	Alain Prost	Fr	McLaren-Honda	87
3	Gerhard Berger	A	Ferrari	41
4	Thierry Boutsen	Bel	Benetton-Ford	27
5	Michele Alboreto	It	Ferrari	24
6	Nelson Piquet	Bra	Lotus-Honda	22
7	Ivan Capelli	It	March-Judd	17
=	Derek Warwick	GB	Arrows-Megatron	17
9	Nigel Mansell	GB	Williams-Judd	12
=	Alessandro Nannini	It	Benetton-Ford	12

Best 11 scores from 16 races to count

Pos.	Make	Pts
CONSTRUCTORS' CUP		
1	McLaren-Honda	199
2	Ferrari	65
3	Benetton-Ford	39
4	Arrows-Megatron BMW	23
=	Lotus-Honda	23
6	March-Judd	22
7	Williams-Judd	20
8	Tyrrell-Ford	5
9	Rial-Ford	3
10	Minardi	1

Prost won again in Spain with Senna struggling home fourth, troubled by a computer that gave confusing readings about his fuel consumption. Mansell was a distant second with Nannini third.

Senna stalled in Japan and was in 14th going into the first corner. Prost thus found himself in the lead, but he had to contend with Capelli, who led briefly before his electrics failed. Senna then caught and passed Prost for his eighth win to wrap up the title. Prost was second, with Boutsen third yet again. Prost gained a little compensation by winning the last race of the turbo era in Australia from Senna and Piquet.

1989

THE MCLAREN STEAMROLLER ROLLED ON INEXORABLY. THIS TIME IT was the turn of Alain Prost to take the world title, and join the serried ranks of three-time winners. The only trouble was that he was no longer on speaking terms with Senna...

The battle between Prost and Senna raged on, with the rest of the field reduced to a supporting role. Mansell had quit Williams for Ferrari to drive alongside Berger, while Williams had got rid of its Judd engines and signed with Renault.

Senna claimed pole from Patrese in Brazil, but he went off at the first corner and Patrese took an early lead, although Mansell was able to control the race and take the win as Prost hit trouble.

Senna led at Imola, but the race was stopped when Berger crashed at Tamburello. Prost

got away better at the restart, but Senna overturned a pre-race deal and snatched the lead.

Senna and Prost started from the front row in Monaco and Senna led all the way to win easily from Prost, while Brundle was denied third by electrical failure that let Brabham team-mate Modena through.

Senna then dominated in Mexico, while Prost chose the wrong tyres and fell to fifth. Mansell ran second, but his gearbox failed and this promoted Patrese and Tyrrell's Alboreto to complete the rostrum.

Prost won on the streets of

CLASH OF THE TITANS
Prost and Senna clashed at Suzuka, and although Senna crossed the line first, he was disqualified to hand Prost his third world title.

CONSTRUCTORS' CUP

Pos.	Make	Pts
1	McLaren-Honda	141
2	Williams-Renault	77
3	Ferrari	59
4	Benetton-Ford	39
5	Tyrrell-Ford	16
6	Lotus-Judd	15
7	Arrows-Ford	13
8	Brabham-Judd	8
=	Dallara-Ford	8
10	Minardi-Ford	6
=	Onyx-Ford	6

DRIVERS' WORLD CHAMPIONSHIP

Pos.	Driver	Nat.	Make	Pts
1	Alain Prost	Fr	McLaren-Honda	76
2	Ayrton Senna	Bra	McLaren-Honda	60
3	Riccardo Patrese	It	Williams-Renault	40
4	Nigel Mansell	GB	Ferrari	38
5	Thierry Boutsen	Bel	Williams-Renault	37
6	Alessandro Nannini	It	Benetton-Ford	32
7	Gerhard Berger	A	Ferrari	21
8	Nelson Piquet	Bra	Lotus-Judd	12
9	Jean Alesi	Fr	Tyrrell-Ford	8
10	Derek Warwick	GB	Arrows-Ford	7

Best 11 scores from 16 races to count

Phoenix as Senna's electrics failed, leaving Prost free to beat Patrese.

McLaren domination was broken in Canada when Boutsen scored his first win after the McLarens retired. Patrese made it a Williams one-two.

Prost moves ahead

Prost led all the way in France as Senna retired on lap one. The first lap of the restart that is, as Gugelmin caused the race to be stopped when he flipped his Leyton House into the first corner. Mansell was second despite starting from the pits after his car was damaged at the first start.

Senna failed to score at the British Grand Prix, spinning out of the lead to let Prost through to win again. Mansell delighted the crowd with second, despite delays with a puncture.

Senna struck back in Germany, recovering from a slower pitstop to retake the lead when Prost's gearbox started balking. Mansell was third.

Mansell proved his worth he tigered his way from 12th to win in Hungary, while Senna came second with Boutsen third.

It was wet at Spa, and Senna led all the way. The sun was out at Monza – well, for Prost at least, as he won from Berger and Boutsen.

In Portugal, Berger won from Prost and Johansson. Mansell missed his pit, reversed and was black flagged. This he ignored and then spun out with Senna, later being given a one-race ban, so he took no part in Spain. This left Senna to win with Berger second and Prost third.

Prost and Senna clashed in Japan and settled the title race in Prost's favour. Senna dived up the inside into the chicane, but Prost refused to cede and they spun. Prost retired on the spot, but Senna was push-started before pitting for a new nose and still was first to the finish, before he was disqualified for receiving external assistance, and that handed Nannini his first win.

Boutsen won again in Adelaide in the wet after Senna had stormed clear, but ploughed into Brundle's spray-hidden Brabham.

1990

IT WAS AYRTON SENNA VERSUS ALAIN PROST FOR THE THIRD SEASON in a row. As in 1988, the Brazilian took the spoils, with no-one else in sight. But at one time it looked as though he wasn't going to be allowed to start the championship at all.

The trouble between Senna and the authorities stemmed from his clash with Prost in Japan in 1989, and the fact that he then accused FISA president Jean-Marie Balestre of manipulating the title and was subsequently refused entry for 1990. It was only with the first race in sight that Senna was readmitted.

Senna tracked down Alesi's Tyrrell at Phoenix, took the lead, was re-passed but then pulled clear. Boutsen was third in his Williams. While Prost, now with Ferrari, climbed to fourth before retiring.

Senna was set for victory in Brazil when Satoru Nakajima forced him to pit for a new nose, confining him to third behind Prost and Berger.

Williams driver Patrese ended a seven-year drought to win at Imola. Senna led from pole, but a stone jammed in his brakes and he spun off, while Prost came fourth behind Berger and Benetton's Nannini. Then Senna dominated at Monaco, chased by Alesi's nimble Tyrrell.

Berger jumped the start in Canada and was penalized a

SENNA PLAYS ROUGH
Senna's McLaren and Prost's Ferrari lie trackside after their coming together at Suzuka (right), but as they walk away (below) Senna knows that he is the World Champion for the second time.

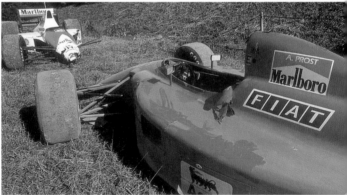

minute. With time to make up, Senna waved Berger by. Yet, though finishing 45 seconds clear, he was classified only fourth, as Senna won.

Prost forges ahead

Prost qualified 13th in Mexico, but he drove a patient race to win on a track that ate tyres. Senna led for 60 laps, but had a puncture, with Mansell completing a Ferrari one-two.

Prost won at Paul Ricard after Capelli had led for Leyton House, a team that had never scored a point, taking the lead with three laps to go.

Mansell announced at Silverstone that he would retire at the end of the year, while Prost won after Mansell had retired with gearbox problems and Boutsen took second with Senna coming back from a spin for third.

Hockenheim was next, and it was Senna's turn to win after struggling to re-pass Nannini who ran non-stop to the Brazilian's one planned stop.

Senna was pipped by Boutsen in Hungary, having taken off Nannini shortly before the flag.

Warwick's Lotus was destroyed at Monza. Amazingly, he ran back to the pits and took the spare car for the restart, which Senna won from Prost. Senna then beat Prost in Belgium.

Mansell left his mark in Portugal by chopping Prost at the start, causing him to lift off and fall to fifth. This left Mansell to motor to victory, from Senna

DRIVERS' WORLD CHAMPIONSHIP				
Pos.	Driver	Nat.	Make	Pts
1	Ayrton Senna	Bra	McLaren-Honda	78
2	Alain Prost	Fr	Ferrari	71
3	Nelson Piquet	Bra	Benetton-Ford	43
4	Gerhard Berger	A	McLaren-Honda	43
5	Nigel Mansell	GB	Ferrari	37
6	Thierry Boutsen	Bel	Williams-Renault	34
7	Riccardo Patrese	It	Williams-Renault	23
8	Alessandro Nannini	It	Benetton-Ford	21
9	Jean Alesi	Fr	Tyrrell-Ford	13
10	Ivan Capelli	It	Leyton House-Judd	6
=	Roberto Moreno	Bra	Benetton-Ford	6
=	Aguri Suzuki	Jap	Lola-Lamborghini	6

Best 11 scores from 16 races to count

CONSTRUCTORS' CUP		
Pos.	Make	Pts
1	McLaren-Honda	121
2	Ferrari	110
3	Benetton-Ford	71
4	Williams-Renault	57
5	Tyrrell-Ford	16
6	Leyton House-Judd	11
=	Lola-Lambourghini	11
8	Lotus-Lambourghini	3
9	Arrows-Ford	2
=	Brabham-Judd	2

with Prost fighting back to third.

Prost then won at Jerez, gaining valuable points as Senna retired.

Senna and Prost clashed again at Suzuka, this time on the first lap. Both were out on the spot, giving Senna the title. Then the quarrels began. Almost obscured by this drama, Piquet led home a Benetton one-two ahead of Moreno who had replaced Nannini who had severed one of his hands in a helicopter crash.

Piquet won in Australia. Mansell and Prost were second and third, Senna having crashed from the lead.

1991

AYRTON SENNA AND McLAREN MADE IT TWO WORLD CHAMPIONSHIP titles in succession, while Nigel Mansell elected not to quit Formula One, but to race for Williams, who were in strong form. He would challenge Senna, but would fall short yet again.

Senna left his opposition standing by winning the first four races. The first, the US Grand Prix at Phoenix, was won by 16 seconds from Alain Prost's Ferrari and Nelson Piquet's Benetton. It was closer in Brazil, as Senna pipped the Williams of a fast-closing Riccardo Patrese with his own team-mate Gerhard Berger close behind. However, only one thing mattered to Senna: he had won his home race at his eighth attempt.

The San Marino Grand Prix was easier, with only Berger finishing on the same lap. Patrese became the first driver to lead Senna, but his Williams suffered engine problems. Mansell went off on the first lap after colliding with Martin Brundle. So to Senna's stamping ground: Monaco. He duly won. The closest anyone got to him was Stefano Modena. But his Tyrrell's engine blew, taking

out Patrese who went off on its oil slick.

Mansell had the Canadian Grand Prix in his pocket, but his engine died when he waved to the crowds on the final lap, letting Piquet by for victory.

Patrese hit the top in Mexico after a late-race challenge from Mansell. Senna followed them home, then attacked Honda for not having an engine able to match the Renaults.

Boost for Mansell

Mansell took his first win of the year when Magny-Cours held the French Grand Prix for the first time, having swapped the lead with Prost. Senna resisted a challenge from Alesi for third. Mansell then repeated his success at Silverstone. Senna should have been second, but he ran out of fuel on the last lap, letting Berger and Prost past. Mansell made it three in a row

DRIVERS' WORLD CHAMPIONSHIP				
Pos.	Driver	Nat.	Make	Pts
1	Ayrton Senna	Bra	McLaren-Honda	96
2	Nigel Mansell	GB	Williams-Renault	72
3	Riccardo Patrese	It	Williams-Renault	53
4	Gerhard Berger	A	McLaren-Honda	43
5	Alain Prost	Fr	Ferrari	34
6	Nelson Piquet	Bra	Benetton-Ford	26.5
7	Jean Alesi	Fr	Ferrari	21
8	Stefano Modena	It	Tyrrell-Honda	10
9	Andrea de Cesaris	It	Jordan-Ford	9
10	Roberto Moreno	Bra	Benetton-Ford	8
All scores counted				

CONSTRUCTORS' CUP		
Pos.	Make	Pts
1	McLaren-Honda	139
2	Williams-Renault	125
3	Ferrari	55.5
4	Benetton-Ford	38.5
5	Jordan-Ford	13
6	Tyrrell-Honda	12
7	Minardi-Ferrari	6
8	Dallara-Judd	5
9	Brabham-Yamaha	3
=	Lotus-Judd	3

at Hockenheim. Amazingly, Senna ran out of fuel on the last lap again, this time losing fourth place.

Senna won in Hungary. With the power circuits to come, it was to be his last likely victory until a return to the twistier tracks. Spa favours those with power, so it was a surprise to see Senna win. He had been outpaced by Mansell and Alesi, but both retired. Jordan's Andrea de Cesaris was set for second, but his engine failed. His team-mate was debutant Michael Schumacher, who outqualified him, but was out on lap one. By the next race he was driving for Benetton in place of Roberto Moreno. Senna led for many laps at Monza, but was eating his tyres so fell to second place behind

Mansell. Schumacher scored his first points, coming fifth.

Patrese won in Portugal, but this was handed to him when Mansell lost a wheel leaving the pits. The wheel was reapplied, but in an illegal place, so Mansell was kicked out. Senna grabbed second. Mansell won at Barcelona from Prost and Patrese with Senna fifth. It was Berger's turn to win in Japan, albeit only after Senna slowed to let him by. By then, the title was already his, having seen Mansell crash out of the race.

The season closed in Adelaide where Senna dominated in torrential conditions in a race that was halted after 14 laps. The race took place without Prost, who'd been fired by Ferrari. He was leaving the team anyway, tired of the politics.

IN A CLASS OF HIS OWN
Ayrton Senna started his title defence with four straight wins, including this one for McLaren at his home track Interlagos.

1992

THIS WAS THE YEAR WHEN NIGEL MANSELL FINALLY SHOWED THE racing world he could be a World Champion, not just a melodramatic bit-player. Seldom has any driver dominated the Formula One championship to such an extent as he did.

It was the sixth race before Nigel Mansell was beaten and his tally stood at eight wins after the first ten. He wrapped up the title at the next race, with five still to run. By year's end, he had almost double the score of the second-placed driver, Williams team-mate Riccardo Patrese. Nigel's driving was from the top drawer, but he was given a huge help by Williams with its fabulous chassis and world-beating Renault engine.

The season started in South Africa and Mansell enjoyed his reacquaintance with Kyalami, for he won by 24 seconds from Patrese. Mexico was next.

And it was the same story, with Mansell heading a Williams one-two. Schumacher made his first podium visit, finishing third for Benetton. At Interlagos, Williams were first and second again, Mansell winning by 30 seconds.

With Mansell dominant in Spain, the major surprise was that it was Schumacher not Patrese who came second after Patrese spun. Mansell took his fifth win at Imola, with Patrese second again. Senna fought to third, but his input had been so great that it was 20 minutes before he was able to climb from his McLaren.

STREETS AHEAD
Nigel Mansell romped to glory in both the World Championship and here at the British Grand Prix.

Senna's narrow Monaco win

Mansell's run came to an end at Monaco, losing to Senna. But only just, with Mansell only 0.2 seconds away after a struggle to re-pass Senna after he'd pitted to replace a puncture.

Senna had led past half-distance in Montreal, but his electrics failed, by which time Mansell had spun and Berger came through to win. The French Grand Prix should have been Patrese's. But the race was halted by rain and he lost out on the restart as team orders forced him to wave Mansell past. Patrese was not happy.

There was only going to be one winner at Silverstone: Mansell. Pole, fastest lap and victory by 40 seconds was proof of that. Patrese was second, with Brundle taking third when Senna pulled off. Mansell won again at Hockenheim, this time ahead of Senna, with Schumacher coming in third.

Mansell hoped to wrap up the title with a win at the Hungaroring, but had to play second fiddle to Senna. However, that was enough for him to claim the coveted crown.

Schumacher scored his first win at Spa. Despite light rain, everyone started on slicks. But the rain grew worse and only Senna stuck with slicks. If the rain had stopped, it would have been a masterstroke, but it didn't and Senna would finish fifth. Schumacher judged the conditions best to win from Mansell and Patrese.

DRIVERS' WORLD CHAMPIONSHIP

Pos.	Driver	Nat.	Make	Pts
1	Nigel Mansell	GB	Williams-Renault	108
2	Riccardo Patrese	It	Williams-Honda	56
3	Michael Schumacher	Ger	Benetton-Ford	53
4	Ayrton Senna	Bra	McLaren-Honda	50
5	Gerhard Berger	A	McLaren-Honda	49
6	Martin Brundle	GB	Benetton-Ford	38
7	Jean Alesi	Fr	Ferrari	18
8	Mika Hakkinen	Fin	Lotus-Ford	11
9	Andrea de Cesaris	It	Tyrrell-Ilmor	8
10	Michael Alboreto	It	Footwork-Honda	6

All scores counted

CONSTRUCTORS' CUP

Pos.	Make	Pts
1	Williams-Renault	164
2	McLaren-Honda	99
3	Benetton-Ford	91
4	Ferrari	21
5	Lotus-Ford	13
6	Tyrrell-Ilmor	8
7	Footwork-Mugen	6
=	Ligier-Renault	6
9	March-Ilmor	3
10	Dallara-Ferrari	2

Mansell ceded the lead at Monza so that Patrese could win, but both hit gearbox problems, with Patrese limping home fifth as Senna came through to win. Mansell was back to winning form at Estoril, but he was nearly caught out by wreckage from Patrese's car after the Italian had flipped after clipping Berger.

Mansell waved Patrese into the lead at Suzuka, but the favour led to nothing as his engine blew. Then the season came to an end in Adelaide, with Berger grabbing his second win of the year, finishing ahead of Schumacher in a race that lost Mansell and Senna in a shunt when contesting the lead.

1993

DOMINATION BY ONE DRIVER WAS THE NAME OF THE GAME. AND again the driver was in a Williams, but this time it was Alain Prost, who had been helped by a year away from the cockpit to regain both his composure and passion for racing.

GLORIOUS SWANSONG
After watching from the sidelines, Alain Prost returned to the fast lane in some style, winning seven times and claiming a fourth world title.

It was known early in 1992 that Frank Williams was anxious to have Prost or Ayrton Senna in place of Mansell, triggering his departure to Indycars. So Williams began 1993 with Prost in the lead car and Damon Hill upgraded from the test team.

Senna made the early running for McLaren at Kyalami, but Prost hit the front and stayed there to beat Senna by 20 seconds, with Ligier's Mark Blundell a surprise third.

Prost was leading in Brazil when rain started and he hit a car that had spun. This put Hill in front, but he became Senna's prey and lost out to finish sec-

ond. Rain hit the European Grand Prix at Donington Park, but Senna starred as he forced his way from fourth into the lead by the end of a stunning first lap and roared away as his rivals tiptoed in his wake.

Hill led the early laps at Imola but spun off, leaving Prost to triumph. Hill led from the start at Barcelona, dropped behind Prost but reapplied the pressure and was looking good until his engine blew, leaving Prost to win from Senna and Schumacher. Indycar star Michael Andretti finally finished a race for McLaren, doing so in fifth. Prost led at Monaco,

DRIVERS' WORLD CHAMPIONSHIP

Pos.	Driver	Nat.	Make	Pts
I	Alain Prost	Fr	Williams-Renault	99
2	Ayrton Senna	Bra	McLaren-Ford	73
3	Damon Hill	GB	Williams-Renault	69
4	Michael Schumacher	Ger	Benetton-Ford	52
5	Riccardo Patrese	It	Benetton-Ford	20
6	Jean Alesi	Fr	Ferrari	16
7	Martin Brundle	GB	Ligier-Renault	13
8	Gerhard Berger	A	Ferrari	12
9	Johnny Herbert	GB	Lotus-Ford	11
10	Mark Blundell	GB	Ligier-Renault	10

All scores counted

CONSTRUCTORS' CUP

Pos.	Make	Pts
I	Williams-Renault	168
2	McLaren-Ford	84
3	Benetton-Ford	72
4	Ferrari	28
5	Ligier-Renault	23
6	Lotus-Ford	12
=	Sauber-Ilmor	12
8	Minardi-Ford	7
9	Footwork-Mugen	4
10	Jordan-Hart	3
=	Larrousse-Lambourghini	3

but was given a stop-and-go and magnified this by stalling. This put Schumacher in front, but his hydraulics failed and so Senna took over for his sixth win in the principality. Hill came second, with Jean Alesi third for Ferrari.

The Canadian Grand Prix marked the start of a four-race streak for Prost. Considering the superiority of Williams, it was surprising that it took until round eight before they scored a one-two. Fittingly, it was on Renault's home patch in France. Hill led from pole, but was delayed in the pits and was demoted by Prost.

Hill led at Silverstone until two-thirds distance when his engine blew. So Prost motored on for his 50th win. Schumacher and Riccardo Patrese finished second and third.

Hill's winning streak

Hill was set for victory in Germany until a tyre blew two laps from home. Prost, 10 seconds behind after a stop-and-go, flew past as Hill tried to struggle back to the pits, with Schumacher and Blundell second and third. Hill finally won at the Hungaroring, leading throughout after Prost was forced to start from the rear of the grid after stalling on the parade lap. Senna shadowed Hill, but then retired.

Schumacher and Prost trailed Hill at Spa, while Alesi and Andretti were second and third behind Hill at Monza. Prost should have won to clinch his fourth world title, but his engine blew five laps from home.

Schumacher won at Estoril, but he really had to work for it, as Prost was on his tail. Second was enough for Prost to claim the title and he duly announced his retirement.

Senna won in Japan, but he then punched debutant Eddie Irvine who, he felt, had blocked him en route to sixth. Prost and Mika Hakkinen – in at McLaren in place of Andretti – ran second and third all race. The season ended in Adelaide, and a win for Senna. Prost was second, Hill third, with the rest a lap adrift.

1994

IT WAS A MEMORABLY BAD YEAR, A CHAMPIONSHIP MARRED BY Senna's death and further spoiled by controversy. The title race went down to the wire in Adelaide and then Michael Schumacher clinched the crown — in questionable fashion.

Ayrton Senna seemed sure to win the title now that he'd joined Williams. But this is not how it worked out. Indeed, by the time of his death, the Brazilian had scored no points from the first two races, while Michael Schumacher had two wins to his credit for Benetton.

With driver aids such as traction control banned and refuelling now a prerequisite, Senna led in Brazil, but Benetton were kings of the pit stop and had Schumacher back out in the lead. Senna spun into retirement in his efforts to keep up, letting team-mate Damon Hill through to finish second.

The all-new TI Circuit in Japan was next, but Senna was tipped into the gravel at the first corner by former team-mate Mika Hakkinen. This left Schumacher clear to win from Gerhard Berger's Ferrari and an ecstatic Rubens Barrichello secured Jordan's first poduim.

Then came Imola. Roland Ratzenberger hit a wall at 190mph in his Simtek during qualifying and died. Then Senna crashed out of the lead at the Tamburello kink during the early stages of the race, suffering fatal injuries, that left Schumacher to score a cheerless win.

Schumacher made it four from four, with Martin Brundle 37 seconds behind for McLaren and Berger third.

Schumacher became stuck in fifth at Barcelona. Hill went by, but the German hung on to finish second, with Mark Blundell third for Tyrrell.

Schumacher then beat Hill by 40 seconds in Montreal, where Senna's replacement David Coulthard scored his first points, even leading early on.

Renault paid for Nigel Mansell to make a one-off return at Magny-Cours. Despite

DRIVERS' WORLD CHAMPIONSHIP

Pos.	Driver	Nat.	Make	Pts
1	Michael Schumacher	Ger	Benetton-Ford	92
2	Damon Hill	GB	Williams-Renault	91
3	Gerhard Berger	A	Ferrari	41
4	Mika Hakkinen	Fin	McLaren-Peugeot	26
5	Jean Alesi	Fr	Ferrari	24
6	Rubens Barrichello	Bra	Jordan-Hart	19
7	Martin Brundle	GB	McLaren-Peugeot	16
8	David Coulthard	GB	Williams-Renault	14
9	Nigel Mansell	GB	Williams-Renault	13
10	Jos Verstappen	Neth	Benetton-Ford	10

All scores counted

CONSTRUCTORS' CUP

Pos.	Make	Pts
1	Williams-Renault	118
2	Benetton-Ford	103
3	Ferrari	71
4	McLaren-Peugeot	42
5	Jordan-Hart	28
6	Ligier-Renault	13
=	Tyrrell-Yamaha	13
8	Sauber-Mercedes	12
9	Footwork-Ford	9
10	Minardi-Ford	5

qualifying on the front row with Hill, Schumacher blasted past both at the start to win.

Fun and games

Schumacher broke grid order at Silverstone, passing poleman Hill on the parade lap. He was shown the black flag, but ignored it, earning a two- race suspension. Eventually, he came in for his stop-and-go penalty, so Hill won.

His suspension was deferred, but victory at Hockenheim went to Berger, breaking a 58-race victory drought for Ferrari. The race is recalled more for a pit fire that engulfed Jos Verstappen's Benetton. Incredibly, he escaped with only minor burns.

Schumacher and Verstappen sandwiched Hill in first and third in Hungary. Then Schumacher won from Hill and Hakkinen at Spa, but he'd ground away too much of his "plank" (a strip on the underside of the car), and was disqualified.

Schumacher missed both Monza and Estoril as a result of the ban and Hill won both.

Then Schumacher beat Hill

at Jerez when the Williams wouldn't take on its fuel. Schumacher led at Suzuka, but the wet race turned when he chose to pit twice, Hill just once. It was a vital win, as Schumacher's points lead was cut to one going in to the final round.

Just before mid-distance in the Adelaide shoot-out, Schumacher grazed a wall. Hill dived for a gap and the German, knowing that his car was damaged, drove into him. This made Schumacher champion, as Hill's car was also too damaged to go on, leaving Mansell to win from Berger.

FOUR IN A ROW

Michael Schumacher blasts through the tunnel at Monaco on his way to a fourth successive victory for Benetton.

THE KING IS DEAD

The wreckage of Ayrton Senna's car lies trackside at Tamburello after his fatal accident in the opening lap of the San Marino Grand Prix.

1995

WILLIAMS VERSUS BENETTON. DAMON HILL AGAINST MICHAEL Schumacher. Top qualifier vying with the world's best racer. There was lots of action, but it was all over with a race to spare as the German claimed his second straight world title.

TWO IN A ROW
Michael Schumacher won his second successive title with two races still to go.

On pole at Brazil, Hill was leading from Schumacher when his suspension collapsed, allowing the German to win from Hill's team-mate David Coulthard.

Argentina was next and Hill dominated from Jean Alesi's Ferrari. Then came a poignant return to Imola. This time, all went well, and Hill won from the Ferraris, Alesi beating Berger into second. As for Schumacher? Well, he made a mistake and thumped his car into the barriers.

It all came right for Benetton in Spain, with Schumacher heading Herbert home.

One-stop wonders
Hill took pole convincingly at Monaco. In the race, though, Benetton's one-stop tactics helped Schumacher beat the

twice-stopping Hill by 35 seconds.

In Canada, Alesi nipped through for his first Grand Prix win after 91 attempts with Schuamcher coming in second.

Schumacher beat Hill to win in France, taking control with his pitstop strategy rather than with a piece of overtaking on the track.

The British Grand Prix saw Hill and Schumacher come together at Priory and both were taken out. Coulthard thus looked set for his first win, but was called in for a ten-second penalty for speeding in the pit-lane and thus Herbert came through to win from Alesi.

Schumacher won from Coulthard at Hockenheim to open up a 21-point lead. Hill crashed out of the lead on the second lap, but made amends in Hungary with the perfect performance: pole, fastest lap and victory.

Hill and Schumacher were invloved in a fierce battle for the lead in Belgium, and although Schumacher won, he was given a one-race ban suspended for four races for his robust tactics.

Schumacher and Hill collided again in Italy and Herbert came through to win.

Estoril belongs to Coulthard

Coulthard finally got his reward in Portugal, with Schumacher demoting Hill to third in the dying laps.

The Grand Prix of Europe, at the Nurburgring, was a belter with Schumacher catching Alesi

DRIVERS' WORLD CHAMPIONSHIP

Pos.	Driver	Nat.	Make	Pts
1	Michael Schumacher	Ger	Benetton-Renault	102
2	Damon Hill	GB	Williams-Renault	69
3	David Coulthard	GB	Williams-Renault	49
4	Johnny Herbert	GB	Benetton-Renault	45
5	Jean Alesi	Fr	Ferrari	42
6	Gerhard Berger	A	Ferrari	31
7	Mika Hakkinen	Fin	McLaren-Mercedes	17
8	Olivier Panis	Fr	Ligier-Mugen Honda	16
9	Heinz-Harald Frentzen	Ger	Sauber-Ford	15
10	Mark Blundell	GB	McLaren-Mercedes	13

All scores counted

CONSTRUCTORS' CUP

Pos.	Make	Pts
1	Benetton-Renault	137
2	Williams-Renault	112
3	Ferrari	73
4	McLaren-Mercedes	30
5	Ligier-Mugen	24
6	Jordan-Peugeot	21
7	Sauber-Ford	18
8	Footwork-Hart	5
=	Tyrrell-Yamaha	5
10	Minardi-Ford	1

with three laps to run to seal victory and all but wrap up the title.

The Pacific Grand Prix at the TI Circuit was won by Schumacher and thus he claimed his second world title in a row and the new champion really rubbed it in at Suzuka, taking his ninth win of the year, which also gave Benetton its first Constructors' Cup.

Coulthard wanted to end his time with Williams with a victory at Adelaide, but Hill gained some consolation as he dominated the race to win by two laps from Olivier Panis's Ligier and Gianni Morbidelli's Arrows after all of the frontrunners had been forced to retire.

1996

IT WAS A CASE OF MISSION ACCOMPLISHED FOR DAMON HILL. FOR, IN 1996, he finally landed the World Championship that Michael Schumacher had kept out of his grasp for the previous two seasons. He had finally made the might of Williams pay.

The 1996 season was the one in which Damon Hill was going to put the record straight. With 1994 and 1995 World Champion Michael Schumacher moving to Ferrari, the idea was that there would be no-one who could stop the Englishman from emulating his late father, Graham Hill, by becoming World Champion.

Four wins from the first five races gave lie to this as the Williams team flexed its muscles. But then the fates struck and deprived Hill of a clear victory at the Monaco Grand Prix. On that strange day, just three cars finished, with Olivier Panis a surprise winner for Ligier. Then retirement in the Spanish Grand Prix also meant no points for Hill, and a full-house for Schumacher who put on a masterful display in the wet.

It should be pointed out, though, that from the very first race in Australia, Hill found there was a threat from within, new Williams team-mate, Indycar Champion Jacques Villeneuve, having made the most of a comprehensive winter of testing to get to grips with Formula One. Villeneuve had to wait only until the fourth race, the Grand Prix of Europe at the Nurburgring, to hit the big time, winning a great chase to the line ahead of Schumacher.

Bad news follows good

Victories in Canada and France put Hill back on track, but there was no such luck on home ground at Silverstone where he crashed and Villeneuve won. Hill's world appeared to cave in at the next race, in Hockenheim, when a story broke that he was to lose his ride at Williams to Heinz-Harald Frentzen. He was able to leave Germany wearing a smile, though, as he picked up a fortunate win when Benetton's Gerhard Berger had his Renault

DRIVERS' WORLD CHAMPIONSHIP

Pos.	Driver	Nat.	Make	Pts
1	Damon Hill	GB	Williams-Renault	97
2	Jacques Villeneuve	Can	Williams-Renault	78
3	Michael Schumacher	Ger	Ferrari	59
4	Jean Alesi	Fr	Benetton-Renault	47
5	Mika Hakkinen	Fin	McLaren-Mercedes	31
6	Gerhard Berger	A	Benetton-Renault	21
7	David Coulthard	GB	McLaren-Mercedes	18
8	Rubens Barrichello	Bra	Jordan-Peugeot	14
9	Olivier Panis	Fr	Ligier-Mugen	13
10	Eddie Irvine	GB	Ferrari	11

All scores counted

CONSTRUCTORS' CUP

Pos.	Make	Pts
1	Williams-Renault	175
2	Ferrari	70
3	Benetton-Renault	68
4	McLaren-Mercedes	49
5	Jordan-Peugeot	22
6	Ligier-Mugen	15
7	Sauber-Ford	11
8	Tyrrell-Yamaha	5
9	Footwork-Hart	1

engine blow up with just three laps to go, giving Hill a 21-point lead over Villeneuve who was third that day.

This was soon whittled down, however, as Villeneuve won in Hungary by a short head from Hill, then reduced Hill's advantage to 13 at the Belgian Grand Prix as he was placed second behind Schumacher with Hill only fifth. A few days later, Frank Williams announced that Frentzen would be replacing Hill. Even if Hill landed the world title, he would be looking elsewhere for his employment for 1997. And all the top drives were now filled.

When Hill crashed out of the lead in Italy, matters looked serious. But Villeneuve also failed to score, so Hill was in a position to wrap it all up in Portugal, and he led, bar pit-stops, until lap 48 of the 70-lap race distance. But then Villeneuve motored past him after a fabulous drive that saw him pass Schumacher around the outside of the fearsome last corner, and this took the title race down to the wire at the final round in Japan, albeit with Hill needing just one point to clinch the coveted prize.

Hill and British racing fans will all remember the outcome of that one, as Damon stamped his authority on proceedings at Suzuka and led all the way to sign out in style with a win. He had become the first-ever second generation World Champion as Villeneuve had lost a wheel and crashed out 15 laps from the finish. For Hill, this was a life's goal reached at last. For Villeneuve, you could sense that it was just the beginning of a great Formula One career.

ON THE ROAD TO GLORY
Damon Hill gets the vital break in the title-deciding race at Suzuka.

1997

CHAMPION IN 1994 AND 1995, SCHUMACHER CAME CLOSE TO A THIRD title in 1997, but he failed to land the one Ferrari craved by clashing with Jacques Villeneuve at the final round, leaving the Canadian to win for Williams.

Ferrari spent the bulk of the 1990s chasing the World Championship, but between Schumacher and the crown lay Williams with its strong Renault engines and Jacques Villeneuve – runner-up to Damon Hill in 1996 – joined by Heinz-Harald Frentzen.

So, it was a mighty shock at the opening race in Melbourne when David Coulthard took McLaren back to the winner's circle for the first time since

Ayrton Senna won at Adelaide at the end of 1993, with Schumacher second. That Villeneuve had qualified on pole by over over a second from Frentzen with Schumacher a further third of a second back was a pointer. Shame then that he was tipped off by Schumacher's team-mate Eddie Irvine at the first corner.

Villeneuve won the next two races in Brazil and Argentina. Frentzen dispelled the pressure of having gone pointless to date by winning ahead of the Ferraris at Imola. Villeneuve led early on, but lost out at the first stops and lost third when his gearbox failed.

Monaco was next and Michael Schumacher got the jump on polesitter Frentzen to lead all the way in the wet. Rubens Barrichello claimed an emotional second place for the new Stewart team.

DRIVERS' WORLD CHAMPIONSHIP

Pos.	Driver	Nat.	Make	Pts
1	Jacques Villeneuve	Can	Williams-Renault	81
2	Michael Schumacher	Ger	Ferrari	78
3	Heinz-Harald Frentzen	Ger	Williams-Renault	42
4	Jean Alesi	Fr	Benetton-Renault	36
=	David Coulthard	GB	McLaren-Mercedes	36
6	Gerhard Berger	A	Benetton-Renault	27
=	Mika Hakkinen	Fin	McLaren-Mercedes	27
8	Eddie Irvine	GB	Ferrari	24
9	Giancarlo Fisichella	It	Jordan-Peugeot	20
10	Olivier Panis	Fr	Prost-Mugen Honda	16

All scores counted

CONSTRUCTORS' CUP

Pos.	Make	Pts
1	Williams-Renault	123
2	Ferrari	102
3	Benetton-Renault	67
4	McLaren-Mercedes	63
5	Jordan-Peugeot	33
6	Prost-Mugen	21
7	Sauber-Petronas	16
8	Arrows-Yamaha	9
9	Stewart-Ford	6
10	Tyrrell-Ford	2

Villeneuve showed his guile in Spain, winning ahead of Panis and Benetton's Jean Alesi.

The Canadian Grand Prix will be recalled for two events: firstly Panis breaking his legs in a high-speed collision with the barriers, and secondly for Coulthard dominating until his engine fluffed at a pit stop when leading on the very same lap, thus handing the race to Michael Schumacher.

Schumacher won again at Magny-Cours with Frentzen coming in second.

Villeneuve collected a lucky ten points at Silverstone after Hakkinen's engine blew en route to his first win. Alesi was second, with Alexander Wurz third on only his third appearance as a stand-in for Berger who had sinus problems.

Berger returned at Hockenheim. And what a return! He not only claimed pole, but also set fastest lap and led almost every lap to win... with Michael Schumacher and Hakkinen completing the podium. Villeneuve finished fifth.

In Hungary, Damon Hill qualified the unimpressive Arrows third and passed Michael Schumacher for the lead and then led until halfway around the final lap when Villeneuve swept past his ailing Arrows to win.

Michael Schumacher won at Spa with Fisichella second and Frentzen third. The Italian Grand Prix was won in the pits, as Coulthard used his only stop to find a way past long-time leader Alesi and Villeneuve won at both the A1 Ring and the Nurburgring to open up a nine-point lead over Schumacher.

Ferrari had to fight back at Suzuka, and Schumacher won-with Villeneuve fifth and was now only one point behind. And so to Jerez, where Schumacher famously pulled across on Villeneuve, and was left in both the gravel trap and in disgrace. Villeneuve was able to bring his slightly damaged car home, ceding the lead only on the final lap when he let Hakkinen and Coulthard through, as third place gave him the points needed for the title.

CHAMPIONSHIP CLINCHER
Michael Schumacher pulls across on Jacques Villeneuve at Jerez in the final race. The German retired, his Canadian rival became champion for the first time.

1998

THE FORMULA ONE WORLD CHAMPIONSHIP HAS ALWAYS BEEN ABOUT a clash of individuals, and 1998 will go down as one of the epic encounters as it was Mika Hakkinen versus Michael Schumacher and McLaren versus Ferrari. And no quarter was given.

JOB WELL DONE
David Coulthard congratulates McLaren team-mate Mika Hakkinen after he clinched his first title in the final round at Suzuka.

It didn't look as though there would be a season-long battle for the championship after the opening race in Melbourne when the McLarens creamed the opposition, lapping the entire field, but there was controversy after Coulthard let Hakkinen through for the win, honouring a pre-race agreement. Those extra four points would turn out to be crucial come the end of the season.

The Brazilian Grand Prix came and went with Hakkinen followed home by Coulthard, with Schumacher in third place.

Schumacher then fought back in Argentina after muscling Coulthard out of the lead. Hakkinen could only trail home second with Eddie Irvine

making it a doubly good day for Ferrari by finishing third.

This appeared to have been something of a false dawn, however, when McLaren dominated at Imola. Hakkinen may have dropped out, but Coulthard cruised to the finish-line ahead of Schumacher.

Hakkinen then bounced back, dominating the Spanish Grand Prix, with team-mate Coulthard second, and going on to take victory at Monaco with Giancarlo Fisichella surviving a spin to come home in second place ahead of Irvine.

Three in a row

It all changed in Canada. McLaren had looked set for another maximum haul of points, but then Hakkinen found himself without a drive at the second start, after Wurz had triggered a restart after an impressively aerobatic moment. Then Coulthard dropped out of the lead when his car failed, leaving the way open for Schumacher to win.

Victory followed for Schumacher in both the French and the British Grands Prix (although he should not have been allowed to keep his win after taking a stop-go penalty in the pits after passing the chequered flag) to close the gap. McLaren bounced back with Hakkinen and Coulthard finishing first and second in both Austria and Germany. They should have repeated this in Hungary, too, but Ferrari tactician Ross Brawn put Schumacher on a three-stop strategy that worked a treat for a famous win.

Damon Hill recorded Jordan's first win at Spa with team-mate Ralf Schumacher second. Brother Michael was then gifted a win on home ground at Monza to bring him level on points with Hakkinen and although he led at the Nurburgring, Hakkinen came from behind to win and thus headed into the last round four points ahead with important momentum behind him.

Last round shoot-out

Yes, those four gifted points from Australia had come home to roost. And this put the pressure on Schumacher, knowing that he had to win to become champion. And, even if he did, Hakkinen was going to have to finish third or lower. So he was relying heavily on team-mate Eddie Irvine. Then Schumacher stalled at the start and was forced to start the race from the back of the grid. The battle was over and Hakkinen raced off to his eighth win and the World Championship that had looked his right from his early days in racing.

McLaren took the Constructors' Cup for the first time since 1991, 22 points ahead of Ferrari. Williams, the dominant team of the previous two seasons, won the battle of the best of the rest, ahead of the fast-improving Jordan team and Benetton.

Drivers' World Championship

Pos.	Driver	Nat.	Make	Pts
1	Mika Hakkinen	Fin	McLaren-Mercedes	100
2	Michael Schumacher	Ger	Ferrari	86
3	David Coulthard	GB	McLaren-Mercedes	56
4	Eddie Irvine	GB	Ferrari	47
5	Jacques Villeneuve	Can	Williams-Mecachrome	21
6	Damon Hill	GB	Jordan-Mugen Honda	20
7	Heinz-Harald Frentzen	Ger	Williams-Mecachrome	17
8	Alexander Wurz	A	Benetton-Mecachrome	17
9	Giancarlo Fisichella	It	Benetton-Mecachrome	16
10	Ralf Schumacher	Ger	Jordan-Mugen Honda	14

Constructors' Cup

Pos.	Make	Pts
1	McLaren-Mercedes	156
2	Ferrari	133
3	Williams-Mecachrome	38
4	Jordan-Mugen Honda	34
5	Benetton-Playlife	33
6	Sauber-Petronas	10
7	Arrows	6
8	Stewart-Ford	5
9	Prost-Peugeot	1

1999

THIS WAS 1998 ALL OVER AGAIN: MIKA HAKKINEN VERSUS MICHAEL Schumacher. But then the German broke a leg at the British Grand Prix and Hakkinen faced a new challenge from Eddie Irvine, a challenge that raged all the way to the final round.

All the cars had to race on tyres with an extra groove in them, but this failed to shuffle the order, with Jordan, Williams and Benetton still fighting to be the best of the rest. The major novelty was the arrival of a new team: BAR. Jacques Villeneuve had moved from Williams to join his friend Craig Pollock, with Ricardo Zonta in the number two seat.

Both McLaren's retired at Melbourne and it was Eddie Irvine, and not Schumacher, who benefitted, to come away with his first-ever win.

Hakkinen overcame a gearbox problem to overhaul Schumacher for victory at Interlagos.

It was an all-McLaren front row at Imola, but the Ferraris were right with them. This pressure paid in the race, when Hakkinen pressed too hard in his attempts to build up a lead, running over the kerbs out of the Traguardo chicane and clouting the wall. The crowd became even more excited when Schumacher outran David Coulthard to win. Ferrari's improving form was emphasised when Ferrari finished first and second at Monaco.

McLaren meted out its traditional one-two in Spain, and then Schumacher stuck his Ferrari into the wall when leading to give Hakkinen maximum points in Canada, with Fisichella second.

Frentzen won at Magny-Cours, thanks to a clever refuelling tactics when the team put in sufficient fuel to see him home. Hakkinen came home second to go eight points clear.

The title battle was to change at Silverstone as Schumacher crashed on the first lap and broke his right leg. Hakkinen was unable to benefit and Coulthard came through to win. Irvine won at the A1-Ring

DRIVERS' WORLD CHAMPIONSHIP

Pos.	Driver	Nat.	Make	Pts
1	Mika Hakkinen	Fin	McLaren-Mercedes	76
2	Eddie Irvine	GB	Ferrari	74
3	Heinz-Harald Frentzen	Ger	Jordan-Mugen Honda	54
4	David Coulthard	GB	McLaren-Mercedes	48
5	Michael Schumacher	Ger	Ferrari	44
6	Ralf Schumacher	Ger	Williams-Supertec	35
7	Rubens Barrichello	Bra	Stewart-Ford	21
8	Johnny Herbert	GB	Stewart-Ford	15
9	Giancarlo Fisichella	It	Benetton-Playlife	13
10	Mika Salo	Fin	BAR-Supertec/Ferrari	10

All scores counted

CONSTRUCTORS' CUP

Pos.	Make	Pts
1	Ferrari	128
2	McLaren-Mercedes	124
3	Jordan-Mugen Honda	61
4	Stewart-Ford	36
5	Williams-Supertec	35
6	Benetton-Playlife	16
7	Prost-Peugeot	9
8	Sauber-Petronas	5
9	Arrows	1
	Minardi-Ford	1

after Coulthard had tipped Hakkinen into a spin on the first lap. With Hakkinen finishing third, Irvine who was now just two points down. This became even more of a nightmare for Hakkinen at Hockenheim when he had a blow-out and crashed coming into the stadium. Again Irvine won, this time courtesy of Schumacher's stand-in, Mika Salo, who let him through.

It was a Hakkinen-Coulthard one-two in Hungary and then Coulthard won ahead of Hakkinen at Spa, with Frentzen keeping Irvine back in fourth.

The pressure was on at Monza and again Hakkinen cracked when leading, spinning out. Frentzen drove a great race to win at Monza with Ralf Schumacher second and Irvine finishing sixth.

Victory for Stewart

Rain shuffled the order at the European GP at the Nurburgring and after a series of leaders dropped out, Johnny Herbert profited to hand the Stewart team its first victory. Hakkinen was fifth, with Irvine seventh.

Schumacher delayed his comeback until F1's first visit to Malaysia. And there he dutifully held back Hakkinen so that Irvine could win.

Arriving at Suzuka with a four-point deficit, Hakkinen knew that the best way of claiming his second title on the trot was to win. And this he did, leading all the way from Schumacher, with Irvine third. Even if Irvine had been let through to second and ended the year equal on points, Hakkinen would have taken the title by dint of having five wins to Irvine's four.

TWO OUT OF TWO
A start-to-finish win for Hakkinen at Suzuka brought him his second successive championship.

2000

SO, FERRARI CAN REST AT LAST, ITS COUNTLESS MILLIONS HAVE yielded the drivers' title for the first time since 1979 when Jody Scheckter claimed the crown. And who more fitting to bring them the glory they have sought so passionately than Michael Schumacher.

Schumacher was brought in to Ferrari in 1996 on the sport's largest retainer with one aim: to give the team its tenth drivers' title. However, it was no easy matter, even though Schumacher wrapped it up with one round to go. Fighting him all the way was McLaren's Mika Hakkinen, with their respective team-mates Rubens Barrichello and David Coulthard both in the hunt at the season's mid-point.

Apart from Barrichello swapping rides with Eddie Irvine, the top two teams had remarkable stability in personnel. Indeed, Benetton aside, every other team had undergone some change. Williams had signed 20-year-old Jenson Button and changed its Supertec engines for ones from the returning BMW. BAR, were back for a second year this time with Honda engines.

Ferrari's dream start

The season kicked off at Melbourne, and both McLarens broke allowing Schumacher to lead Barrichello home for a Ferrari one-two. Third place went to Ralf Schumacher, the BMW in his Williams stronger than people had been led to believe.

Ferrari's dream start continued when Hakkinen retired from the lead at Interlagos, with Coulthard disqualified from second due to his front wing. Schumacher then beat the McLarens fair and square at Imola. So, three races in, and Schumacher had 30 points to Hakkinen's six.

Barrichello led the British Grand Prix to mid-distance, but Coulthard was right on his tail and took over with a great move around the outside at Stowe and went on to win.

Reigning champion Hakkinen got his show on the road with

DRIVERS' WORLD CHAMPIONSHIP

Pos.	Driver	Nat.	Make	Pts
1	Michael Schumacher	Ger	Ferrari	108
2	Mika Hakkinen	Fin	McLaren-Mercedes	89
3	David Coulthard	GB	McLaren-Mercedes	73
4	Rubens Barrichello	Bra	Ferrari	62
5	Ralf Schumacher	Ger	Williams-BMW	24
6	Giancarlo Fisichella	Ita	Benetton-Playlife	18
7	Jacques Villeneuve	Can	BAR-Honda	17
8	Jenson Button	GB	Williams-BMW	12
9	Heinz-Harald Frentzen	Ger	Jordan-Mugen Honda	11
10	Jarno Trulli	Ita	Jordan-Mugen Honda	6

All scores counted

CONSTRUCTORS' CUP

Pos.	Make	Pts
1	Ferrari	170
2	McLaren-Mercedes	152
3	Williams-BMW	36
4	Benetton-Playlife	20
5	BAR-Honda	20
6	Jordan-Mugen Honda	17
7	Arrows-Supertec	7
8	Sauber-Petronas	6
9	Jaguar	4
10	Minardi-Fondmetal	0
	Prost-Peugeot	0

victory in Spain. Coulthard was fortunate to be there at all, having survived a plane crash that killed his pilot and co-pilot, and showed great bravery in racing with cracked ribs.

The pendulum swung Ferrari's way at the Nurburgring when Schumacher showed his wet-weather skills to take his fourth win and looked set to make that five at Monaco, before his suspension collapsed. Coulthard was left clear to win.

Schumacher won from Barrichello in Canada, before Coulthard outraced the German at Magny-Cours.

Hakkinen bounced back at the A1-Ring by leading from start to finish after Schumacher had been involved in an incident at the first corner, and he suffered the same fate at Hockenheim, before team-mate Barrichello notched his first-ever Grand Prix win.

Hakkinen won at the Hungaroring and performed the best overtaking manoeuvre of the season at Spa when he slip-streamed Schumacher at Les Combes – his reward was victory. The Italian Grand Prix was marred by the death of a marshal following a huge accident on the opening lap, but Schumacher came through to win from Hakkinen.

Reborn in the USA

Formula One and the United States were reacquainted after a nine-year break when the circus moved to the Indianapolis Motor Speedway and Schumacher won easily after Hakkinen's engine failed.

Hakkinen got the jump at Suzuka, but slick tactics, traffic and a brief shower put Schumacher in front where he stayed to the finish to secure his third World Championship and Ferrari's first since Jody Scheckter in 1979. The party continued at Sepang, Malaysia, when he made it four wins in succession after pipping Coulthard to the line.

MISSION ACCOMPLISHED
Michael Schumacher pumps the air with delight after securing the drivers' title at Suzuka, the first for Ferrari since 1979.

THE GREAT DRIVERS

ALL THE DRIVERS WHO HAVE REACHED FORMULA ONE OVER THE YEARS ARE A little bit special, however much we like to think we could do the same from the comfort and safety of our armchairs. Nevertheless, certain drivers stand out as being a little bit more special than the others. There are a myriad of drivers who have won races, lost races, starred and disappointed in Formula One since its inception in 1950. Here is a selection of those drivers, ranging from the all-time greats to those who shone but failed in their quest to climb to the top of

the Formula One tree and then there are those who simply have a story to tell. After all, Eddie Irvine may well be recalled in years to come as the driver who was bopped on the chin by Ayrton Senna on his Grand Prix debut rather than for his exploits over the years with Ferrari and Jaguar. Everyone listed here had a dream. Some achieved it, whereas others did not. Indeed, looking through the following list, it is immensely sad to see how may were killed in their bid for glory. Thankfully, racing is far safer today than when drivers used to take their positions on the starting grid clad in cotton shirts and flat caps.

All statistics are correct to the end of the 2000 World Championship.

FLYING FINN *World Champion in 1998 and 1999, Mika Hakkinen is one of the modern-day major title contenders.*

A

MICHELE ALBORETO
Nationality: **Italian**
Born: **1956**

This dignified Italian had a long and frustrating Formula One career that petered out in 1994 and he followed a phalanx of his former rivals into the world of touring car racing. Second in the 1979 Italian Formula Three series, Michele won the European crown in 1980. Formula Two beckoned for 1981, but Michele so impressed Tyrrell with a one-off drive at the San Marino Grand Prix that they gave him a contract until the end of 1983. During the next three years he won twice, both times on North American

MICHELE ALBORETO
Two wins in 1985 left him as runner-up to Prost in the championship.

soil. His second win – at Detroit in 1983 – was a landmark, for it was the last win for a normally-aspirated engine before the turbocharged cars completed their stranglehold. Ferrari followed from 1984 to 1988, and he won on his third outing, at Zolder, helping him to fourth place overall. Two wins assisted Michele to second overall in 1985, but thereafter his career tailed off. He returned to Tyrrell in 1989, then crossed to Larrousse in mid-season. Three years with Footwork, with little or no reward, followed before his worst year: 1993, with the new Scuderia Italia team. The car was a beast, and Michele failed to qualify it five times. A year with Minardi restored his pride, but he now accepted that his best days were over and headed off to join the German Touring Car Championship at the controls of a works Alfa Romeo.

Career Record
- *194 Grands Prix, 5 wins (Caesars Palace GP 1982, US GP 1983, Belgian GP 1984, Canadian GP 1985, German GP 1985)*
- *No championship title (best result – 2nd overall 1985)*

JEAN ALESI
Nationality: **French**
Born: **1964**

Born in France of Sicilian parents, Jean was viewed as an outsider until he started to shine in the junior formulae, and only then was he considered a Frenchman. Running with next to no sponsorship, he starred in the 1986 French Formula Three Championship, finishing second to Yannick Dalmas. He went one better in 1987 before moving up to Formula 3000 in 1988. Halfway through his second year in this category, a vacancy came up at Tyrrell for the French Grand Prix and his team boss, Eddie Jordan, propelled Jean into the seat. Jean responded in style, taking fourth place. In the first race of 1990, Jean swapped the lead with Ayrton Senna's McLaren, finishing second. Another second came at Monaco. Jean joined Ferrari in 1991, and despite endless promise it wasn't until the 1995 Canadian Grand Prix that he won. He should also have won in Italy, and drove a belter in the wet at the Nurburgring. Jean went to Benetton in 1996 and had his best-ever season finishing fourth overall despite not winning a race, then stayed on for 1997 before moving on to Sauber for 1998 and then Prost in 2000 as his career tailed off.

Career Record

- 184 Grands Prix, 1 win (Canadian GP 1995)
- No championship title (best result – 4th overall 1996)

PHILIPPE ALLIOT
Nationality: **French**
Born: **1954**

Philippe began his racing career with three years in the French Formule Renault series, claiming the title in 1978. Formula Three proved an even harder nut to crack, and it took him four years before he moved on to Formula Two in 1983. Then followed two years with the unsuccessful RAM team in Formula One. He then moved to Ligier for the second half of 1986, before joining the Larrousse Lola team, for whom he raced for three seasons, scoring points on four occasions. A return to Ligier was fruitless in 1990 and curtailed his Formula One career. However, he bounced back with Larrousse in 1993 and scored his only fifth place, at the San Marino Grand Prix. Hopes of a Grand Prix swansong with McLaren in 1994, thanks to French engine supplier Peugeot, were disappointed when team boss Ron Dennis chose Martin Brundle instead, even though Philippe had a run-out in place of the suspended Mika Hakkinen in Hungary.

Career Record

- 109 Grands Prix, no wins (best result – 5th, San Marino GP 1993)
- No championship title (best result – 16th overall 1987)

CHRIS AMON
Nationality: **New Zealander**
Born: **1943**

This affable Kiwi did everything in Formula One except win a race, or a World Championship one at least. Chris was spotted by team owner Reg Parnell and invited to contest the 1963 Formula One season, arriving in Europe while still a baby-faced 19-year-old and claiming his first points before his 21st birthday. Parnell's death left Chris in limbo in 1965 and 1966, but Ferrari signed him for 1967 and he came third in his first race at Monaco. A win would surely follow. Wrong. Second at Brands Hatch in 1968 was the best he could do. A move to the fledgling March team for 1970 enabled Chris to win a Formula One race – the International Trophy at Silverstone – but, sadly, this was a non-championship affair. His championship season saw him twice second to finish seventh overall. A two-year spell at Matra was next and produced victory first time out, in the Argentinian Grand Prix. But this was another non-championship affair. It almost went right at Clermont-Ferrand in 1972. The race was his for the taking when he suffered a puncture. A season with Tecno in 1973 produced nothing and his move to run his own car in 1974 was even less successful. A few races for the under-financed Ensign team in 1975–76 reminded people of his undoubted speed, but it all came to little despite flashes of genius. Truly this was a talent wasted.

Career Record

■ *96 Grands Prix, no wins (best result – 2nd, British GP 1968, Belgian GP 1970, French GP 1970)*

■ *No championship title (best result – 4th overall 1967)*

MARIO ANDRETTI
Nationality: **American**
Born: **1940**

Here is a man who wanted to race more than almost any man before him – or since. And this will to race stayed with Mario until his retirement at the end of 1994, and helped him to achieve one of the most comprehensive career tallies of all time. Starting in sprint cars on the local dirt ovals, "Super Wop", as he was known, graduated to Indy Car racing in 1964 and amazed the establishment by winning the title in 1965. Another title followed in 1966 and a third in 1969, but, by the time of his third crown, he had already achieved an ambition by making his Formula One debut (for Lotus) at the end of 1968. Again Mario upset the establishment, for he qualified on pole first time out at Watkins Glen. A mixed Formula One programme followed from 1969 to 1974 with Lotus, March, Ferrari – including victory in the 1971 South African Grand Prix – and Parnelli, as he split his time with Indy Car and sports car racing before joined the Grand Prix circus full-time with Parnelli in 1975. Parnelli folded and Mario joined the team that gave him his Formula One break: Lotus. It was in a poor state, but he and boss Colin Chapman rebuilt it, winning the 1976

Japanese Grand Prix. More progress was made in 1977 and Mario was crowned World Champion in 1978 after winning six races. Two more years followed with Lotus before he raced for Alfa Romeo in 1981. Then it was back to Indy Cars and a full-time diet of American racing from 1982. He won the Indy Car title for the fourth time in 1984 and was on the pace right until his final few years when he raced alongside Nigel Mansell for the Newman-Haas team in the early 1990s.

Career Record

■ 128 Grands Prix, 12 wins (South African GP 1971, Japanese GP 1976, US West GP 1977, Spanish GP 1977, French GP 1977, Italian GP 1977, Argentinian GP 1978, Belgian GP 1978, Spanish GP 1978, French GP 1978, German GP 1978, Dutch GP 1978)
■ World Champion 1978

MICHAEL ANDRETTI
Nationality: **American**
Born: **1962**

Michael, son of Mario, ripped through the junior ranks of American racing, winning the Formula Super Vee and Formula Atlantic titles en route to graduating to the Indy Car scene in 1984. He was second in 1986, 1987 and 1990, before he claimed the Indy Car title in 1991. Egged on by his father, Michael tried Formula One with McLaren in 1993. What a

MARIO ANDRETTI
His joy for racing saw him take the world title in 1978.

disaster! It seemed that if there was an accident he was in it. But this is unfair, for he had the mighty Ayrton Senna as a team-mate and a McLaren chassis that did not want to play the game. Perhaps one of his biggest mistakes was attempting to commute from the USA, since the team never really felt that he was part of the outfit and he was replaced after peaking with a third in the Italian Grand Prix. Winning ways soon came back on his return to Indy Cars, giving Reynard victory on its first race in the formula, then doing the same for Swift in 1998.

Career Record

■ 13 Grands Prix, no wins (best result – 3rd, Italian GP 1993)

■ No championship title (best result – 11th overall 1993)

RENÉ ARNOUX
Nationality: **French**
Born: **1948**

One of the fruits of a government-backed scheme to unearth French talent in the 1970s, René did all the right things as he rocketed into Formula One. It was only when he reached the highest echelon that he started to run off the rails. His speed was never in question, simply his application. He beat future Formula One rival, Patrick Tambay, to take the French Formule Renault title in 1973. An abortive move to the European Formula 5000 Championship in 1974 was followed by a return to the French ladder to stardom in Formule Super Renault in 1975. He duly won the title and progressed to Formula Two in 1976, being pipped to the title in the final round by Jean-Pierre Jabouille. He went one better in 1977. Then came Formula One, albeit with a slow start, in 1978 with the fledgling Martini team. It folded mid-season and René had a couple of runs for Surtees. However, for 1979 it all came right and he joined Jabouille in the Renault works team. A brace of wins at the start of 1980 pushed him into the limelight, but his form faded until he won the 1982 French Grand Prix against team orders ahead of team favourite Alain Prost. For 1983, René moved to Ferrari, winning three times as he was placed third overall behind Nelson Piquet and Prost. These were to be his last wins, though, and he was shown the door after the first race of 1985. In 1986 he was back, this time with Ligier, with whom he raced for four seasons, but produced next to no results after the first of these. Since retiring from Formula One, René has been involved with the DAMS (Driot Arnoux Motor Sport) Formula 3000 team, the most successful in the history of the formula.

Career Record

■ 149 Grands Prix, 7 wins (Brazilian GP 1980, South African GP 1980, French GP 1982, Italian GP 1982, Canadian GP 1983, German GP 1983, Dutch GP 1983)

■ *No championship title (best result – 3rd overall 1983)*

PETER ARUNDELL
Nationality: **British**
Born: **1933**

Peter Arundell shone like a star, but his career became unstuck when he had a major accident in a Formula Two race at Reims and he was never as quick again. Strong form in the junior categories earned Peter the attention of Lotus boss, Colin Chapman, who snapped him up for Formula Junior where he won the 1962 British title. Although anxious to move into Formula One, he waited to make his break with Lotus, and thus had to spend 1963 contesting non-championship Formula One races in addition to Formula Junior. For 1964, though, Peter was in Formula One with Lotus. Third in his first two races, at Monaco and then at Zandvoort, he had driven in only four races when he spun in his concurrent Formula Two race at Reims and was T-boned by Richie Ginther. Thrown from the cockpit, he suffered numerous broken bones and it was two years before he was fit enough to race in Formula One again. However, his return season with Lotus yielded just one sixth place and his career fizzled out.

Career Record
■ *11 Grands Prix, no wins (best result – 3rd, Monaco GP 1964, Dutch GP 1964)*
■ *No championship title (best result – 8th overall 1964)*

ALBERTO ASCARI
Nationality: **Italian**
Born: **1918**
Died: **1955**

He was Mr Superstition – a great racing driver, a double World Champion, but also a man ruled by lucky charms and coincidence. Born into a motor racing family – his Grand Prix racer father Antonio died in an accident at the Montlhery track near Paris when Alberto was seven – he soon turned to

ALBERTO ASCARI
As a double World Champion in 1952 and 1953 he was Ferrari's first big star.

motorized competition, starting with motorcycles. He progressed to cars in 1940, competing in the mighty Mille Miglia road race for Ferrari. His deal was clinched, as team patron Enzo Ferrari was a former team-mate of Alberto's father. Alberto had his first taste of Grand Prix racing in 1947. Between then and the start of modern-day Formula One in 1950, he won several Grands Prix and was thus an obvious choice to lead the Ferrari team in the 1950 Formula One World Championship, in which he was placed fifth. His form was better in 1951 and he won twice to finish the year as runner-up to Juan Manuel Fangio. A change in the rules meant that Formula One was run to 2-litre regulations in 1952 and this played into Alberto's hands, for Ferrari had a good engine ready. He missed the first race, in which team-mate Piero Taruffi was victorious, but duly won six races and the title. Indeed, he kept this winning streak going into 1953, taking the first three races as he motored to his second consecutive title. A change to Maserati in 1954, while waiting for the Lancias to be ready, proved little. Indeed, it was not until the start of 1955 that the Lancias were up to speed. However, Alberto was soon to perish in a freak accident when testing a sports car at Monza for protégé Eugenio Castellotti. Acknowledging Alberto's attention to numbers and dates, it is uncanny to note

that, like his father, he had died on the 26th of a month, at the age of 36, at the exit of a fast left-hander, four days after walking away from an accident.

Career Record

■ *31 Grands Prix, 13 wins (German GP 1951, Italian GP 1951, Belgian GP 1952, French GP 1952, British GP 1952, German GP 1952, Dutch GP 1952, Italian GP 1952, Argentinian GP 1953, Dutch GP 1953, Belgian GP 1953, British GP 1953, Swiss GP 1953)*

■ *World Champion 1952 and 1953*

RICHARD ATTWOOD
Nationality: **British**
Born: **1940**

After an apprenticeship in Formula Junior, during which he won the Monaco support race in 1963, followed by an unhappy period with a limited Formula One programme with BRM in 1964, Dickie went on to enjoy a shot at the big time with a Reg Parnell Racing Lotus-BRM in 1965, collecting a couple of sixth places. However, he raced sports cars for the next two seasons before joining BRM to replace Mike Spence. His second place, first time out at Monaco, amazed all and sundry. Sadly, this form was never repeated and he was to race sports cars from then on, winning the Le Mans 24 Hours for Porsche in 1970. Today, Dickie stars on the historic racing scene.

Career Record

- ■ *17 Grands Prix, no wins (best result – 2nd, Monaco GP 1968)*
- ■ *No championship title (best result – 13th overall 1968 and 1969)*

LUCA BADOER

Nationality: **Italian**

Born: **1971**

Luca starred in Italian Formula Three. He then won the Formula 3000 title at his first attempt and made his Formula One debut with the uncompetitive Scuderia Italia team in 1993, though he often outpaced his team-mate Michele Alboreto. Luca sat on the sidelines in 1994, but was back with Minardi in 1995 and was equal to both team-mates, Pierluigi Martini and Pedro Lamy. He drove for Forti in 1996 until the team collapsed. Luca became Ferrari's test driver, then returned to racing with Minardi in 1999, breaking down when he retired from fourth place at the Nurburgring.

Career Record

- ■ *44 Grands Prix, no wins (best result – 7th, San Marino GP 1993)*
- ■ *No championship title*

GIANCARLO BAGHETTI

Nationality: **Italian**

Born: **1934**

It is unlikely that anyone will ever match his feat of winning on his Grand Prix debut. Yet this is what happened when he joined Ferrari for the 1961 French Grand Prix at Reims. He had raced sports cars before Formula Junior attracted Giancarlo to try single-seaters in 1958. Success in this propelled him to Ferrari in 1961, when he won the non-championship Syracuse and Naples Grands Prix. Then came his big day at Reims where Giancarlo resisted everything that Porsche's Dan Gurney could throw at him. A limited season with Ferrari in 1962 was followed by a spell with the Italian ATS team in 1963 and another racing a Centro Sud BRM in 1964.

Career Record

- ■ *21 Grands Prix, 1 win (French GP 1961)*
- ■ *No championship title (best result – 9th overall 1961)*

JULIAN BAILEY

Nationality: **British**

Born: **1961**

One of the quickest of the quick in British club racing in the early 1980s, Julian overcame a huge shunt to win the Formula Ford Festival in 1982. A lack of cash restricted his subsequent movement up the hierarchy, but he made it to Formula Three by 1985 and on to Formula 3000 by 1987, where he won once, at Brands Hatch. Julian finally, made it to Formula One in 1988, racing for Tyrrell, but he chose a year when Tyrrell was not competitive; he often failed to qualify and collected no points. It looked as though he had had his shot and missed. Ever resourceful, Julian raised the money to buy a seat at Lotus in 1991 and scored his best finish, a sixth place at the San Marino Grand Prix, before his money ran out after four races. Since then he has raced sports cars and touring cars.

Career Record

■ *7 Grands Prix, no wins (best result – 6th, San Marino GP 1991)*

■ *No championship title (best result – 18th overall 1991)*

MAURA BALDI
Nationality: **Italian**
Born: **1954**

Several seasons at the front end of the grid in the European Formula Three Championship in the late 1970s saw Mauro come on strong to win the prestigious Monaco Formula Three race in 1980. Electing to stay on for a fourth year of Formula Three in 1981, he won the European title and then bypassed Formula Two to join the Arrows Formula One team for 1982. His first point came at the Dutch Grand Prix. A move to the works Alfa Romeo team for 1983 was not a success and Mauro was not invited to stay on for 1994 so found himself with the new Spirit team. This was floundering by early 1985, and since then Mauro has raced with great success in sports cars, winning the 1990 world title.

Career Record

■ *36 Grands Prix, no wins (best result – 5th, Dutch GP 1983)*

■ *No championship title (best result – 16th overall 1983)*

LORENZO BANDINI
Nationality: **Italian**
Born: **1935**
Died: **1967**

Lorenzo's racing career started in saloon cars loaned to him by the owner of the garage at which he was a mechanic. By 1959, he was on the grid for the new Formula Junior category, and his form over the next two seasons was enough to attract the attention of Ferrari. He was pipped for a vacant seat early in 1961 by compatriot Giancarlo Baghetti. Scuderia Centro Sud gave him his Formula One debut in a Cooper-Maserati and he drove well enough to join Ferrari for 1962. Lorenzo was third at his first attempt, at Monaco. Despite being selected only occasionally by the team, he also won the non-championship Mediterranean Grand Prix. Dropped in 1963, he was soon back at Ferrari after Willy Mairesse was injured. He even won the Le Mans 24 Hours for the marque. Lorenzo's only Grand Prix triumph came in 1964 when he won the Austrian Grand Prix at Zeltweg, and he ranked fourth overall at the end of the season, three places behind team-mate John Surtees. Monaco was to prove his happiest hunting ground in 1965 and 1966, with second place each time. And it was in the second

half of 1966 that he finally became Ferrari's number one driver. However, it was Monaco that was to prove his undoing. Running second behind Denny Hulme's Brabham at Monaco in 1967, Lorenzo's Ferrari clipped the barriers at the chicane and flipped. It caught fire instantly and Lorenzo was terribly burned while an inadequately equipped crew of marshals extricated him. He died of his burns within a week.

Career Record

- ■ *42 Grands Prix, 1 win (Austrian GP 1964)*
- ■ *No championship title (best result – 4th overall 1964)*

RUBENS BARRICHELLO

Nationality: **Brazilian**
Born: **1972**

Rubens had one of the fastest-ever climbs from karting to Formula One. The key to this was the long-term backing of Brazilian sponsor Arsico. Like Ayrton Senna, Rubens came from São Paulo, his home overlooking Interlagos. After collecting five karting titles, Rubens arrived in Europe at 17 and won the GM Euroseries. He then pipped David Coulthard to the 1991 British Formula Three title. Rubens had less success in Formula 3000 with the Il Barone Rampante team in 1992, but was still third overall and was ready for Formula One before his 21st birthday. Jordan snapped him up and Rubens was nearly second on his third outing, the European Grand Prix, before fuel feed problems scuppered that. Rubens was third at the TI Circuit in 1994, claimed pole in the wet at Spa and finished fourth five times. Sadly, 1995 featured many mechanical failures. Usually outpaced in qualifying by teammate Eddie Irvine, Rubens peaked with second in Canada. The 1996 season saw little progress, so he turned to Stewart for 1997, coming sec-

LORENZO BANDINI
Won the Le Mans 24 Hours for Ferrari and played second fiddle to John Surtees for the marque in 1964.

ond at Monaco and staying on for a second season in 1998, but this yielded little. His third year with Stewart was better as he led in Brazil and claimed pole at Magny-Cours. Third places at Imola and the Nurburgring helped him to seventh overall. But then he swapped rides with Irvine and went to Ferrari for 2000, scoring his first win at Hockenheim to rank fourth overall.

Career Record
- ■ *130 Grands Prix, 1 wins (German GP 2000)*
- ■ *No championship title (best result – 4th 2000)*

JEAN BEHRA
Nationality: French
Born: 1921
Died: 1959

After a career racing motorcycles, "Jeannot" switched to four-wheeled competition in 1949 and graduated to Formula One with Gordini in 1952, a year in which, amazingly, he won the non-championship Reims Grand Prix ahead of the best of the Ferraris, earning him the undying devotion of his home fans. Tenth overall in his first season, he stayed on with Gordini for two more years, but became frustrated by mechanical breakages and moved to the works Maserati team for 1955. He kicked off with non-championship wins at Pau and Bordeaux and backed this up many sports car wins, but success eluded him when it counted in the World Championship.

Fourth overall in 1956, a year during which he crashed in the Tourist Trophy and sliced off one of his ears, Jean scored his best-ever Grand Prix result in Argentina in 1957 when he finished second to team-mate Juan Manuel Fangio. Heading for victory in that year's British Grand Prix, he was thwarted by clutch failure and his career dipped from then on. A drive for BRM in 1958 yielded nothing and so the offer to join Ferrari was eagerly accepted. Sadly, he was killed in a sports car race at Avus.

Career Record
- ■ *52 Grands Prix, no wins (best result – 2nd, Argentinian GP 1956, Argentinian GP 1957)*
- ■ *No championship title (best result – 4th overall 1956)*

DEREK BELL
Nationality: British
Born: 1941

Very few British drivers have driven in Formula One for Ferrari. However, of those who have, few have failed to make their mark in the sport's top category. Derek was, however, one of the unlucky ones. Propelled through the junior formulae, first by his charismatic stepfather and then by Peter Westbury, Derek starred in Formula Two, catching the eye of Enzo Ferrari who signed him up for the last few Grands Prix of 1968. However, no regular drives followed, and the next three years saw him turn out for three different teams in only four Grands Prix, peaking with sixth at the 1970 US Grand Prix for Surtees. Things looked better for 1972 when he managed five races for the Martini team. But again he had no joy, so he rejoined Surtees for 1974, qualifying only once. He now looked to sports cars for his glory and has won the Le Mans 24 Hours five times.

Career Record
- 9 Grands Prix, no wins (best result – 6th, US GP 1970)
- No championship title (best result – 22nd overall 1970)

STEFAN BELLOF
Nationality: German
Born: 1957
Died: 1985

Germany had long been aware of its failure to win the World Championship and, if Stefan Bellof had not been killed in a sports car race in 1985, it could all have been very different. Exciting is a description that does not really do justice to Stefan's driving: it was electrifying. He was, in short, a joy to watch – on the ragged edge of control where others would long previously have lost it. Fresh out of karting, he won the German Formula Ford Championship, vaulted to Formula Three for 1981 and was third overall. In Formula Two, in 1982, he drove with great success for the Maurer team, winning the first two races. However, results tailed off, with retirements blunting

his achievement. So a second Formula Two season became essential, dovetailed with sports car races for the works Porsche team. He made it to Formula One in 1984 with Tyrrell and was challenging for victory at Monaco, but heavy rain stopped play when he was third, thwarting both he and Ayrton Senna as they closed on Alain Prost. However, the Tyrrell team was found to have committed a technical irregularity and all his points were removed for the 1984 season. At least Stefan was able to enjoy winning six times for Porsche en route to claiming the world title. For 1985 he found the Tyrrell to be less competitive, and had only a fourth and a sixth to his name when he overstepped the mark in a sports car race at Spa, failing in a crazy attempt to overtake in the daunting Eau Rouge corner. He died instantly.

Career Record
- 20 Grands Prix, no wins (best result – 4th, US East GP 1985)
- No championship title (best result – 15th overall 1985)

JEAN-PIERRE BELTOISE
Nationality: French
Born: 1937

Hugely successful as a motorcycle racer, Jean-Pierre first raced a car in 1963, and indeed his early sports car races nearly cost him movement in one of his arms after a crash at Reims in 1964. However, he fought back to win the French Formula

Three title in 1965 for Matra, embellishing this with victory in the Monaco Formula Three race in 1966, and several months later made his Grand Prix debut, winning the Formula Two class in the German Grand Prix. It was not until 1968 that he was given his first run in a Grand Prix in a Formula One car, still with Matra. However, this produced fifth place and he was allowed to continue, soon exceeding this result with second at the Dutch Grand Prix. His progress continued into 1969 and a further second place helped him to fifth overall. He stayed on with Matra for 1970 and 1971, but things turned sour when he was threatened with the suspension of his licence following the death of Ignazio Giunti after an incident involving Jean-Pierre in a sports car race in Argentina. Then, in 1972, it all came right – at Monaco at least, when he won in torrential conditions for BRM. That was his only ever win, however, and he faded from Formula One after two further seasons with BRM.

Career Record
- 86 *Grands Prix, 1 win (Monaco GP 1972)*
- No *championship title (best result – 5th overall 1969)*

GERHARD BERGER
Nationality: Austrian

Born: 1959

Gerhard started racing Alfasuds, but Formula Three soon followed and at this he was very successful, chasing Ivan Capelli for the European title in 1984. At the end of that year, he had a shot at Formula One with ATS, finishing sixth on his second outing, even though he was not eligible for points. Things looked good for 1985, but Gerhard broke his neck in a road accident. Defying doctors' orders, he was up and about far ahead of their predictions and joined Arrows for 1985, scoring points in the final two races. A move to the new Benetton team in 1986 produced his first win, in Mexico, and helped Gerhard land a ride with Ferrari for 1987. Again he peaked at the end of the year, this time with two wins. Another win and more consistent scoring saw him finish third overall in 1988, but his final season with Ferrari saw him fail to finish a race until September. Angered by this lack of mechanical fortitude, Gerhard moved to McLaren for 1990 to drive alongside Ayrton Senna. Seldom as quick as Senna, at least he taught the Brazilian to smile and Gerhard was a regular front-runner until the end of 1992 when he returned to Ferrari. The pressures of leading Ferrari through its longest non-winning streak was huge, but he brought this to a close at the 1994 German Grand Prix. He should have added to this in the Australian Grand Prix, but he ran wide, letting Nigel Mansell through, yet finished second to ensure he ended up third overall. Unable to live with Williams and Benetton in 1995,

Career Record

Gerhard brought his Ferrari home third six times. Electing not to stay on, he headed back to Benetton in 1996, but the wins didn't come, as shown when his engine blew when leading in Germany. A strong second in Brazil was a false dawn in 1997, but he sprung back from missing three races with sinus trouble to win from pole in Germany before announcing his retirement. He is now in charge of BMW's Formula One programme.

- 210 Grands Prix, 10 wins (Mexican GP 1986, Japanese GP 1987, Australian GP 1987, Italian GP 1988, Portuguese GP 1989, Japanese GP 1991, Canadian GP 1992, Australian GP 1992, German GP 1994, German GP 1997)
- No championship title (best result – 3rd overall 1988 and 1994)

GERHARD BERGER

Continues in Formula One after a long and successful career overseeing BMW's programme in the sport.

ERIC BERNARD

Nationality: **French**

Born: **1964**

After victory in the national kart series, Eric beat Jean Alesi to win the prestigious Winfield school scholarship in 1983, and that launched him into Formule Renault. A strong run in this was followed by title success in 1985 that boosted him into Formula Three, in which he finished second to Alesi in 1987. Formula 3000 was another category that took two bites, with Eric finishing third overall for DAMS in 1989. His two Formula One outings that year for Larrousse were backed up with a full-time ride for 1990, with Eric claiming fourth at the British Grand Prix. A weak 1991 season followed, and it was curtailed when he broke a leg in Japan. To many this would have been the end, but Eric fought back bravely and returned to the Ligier team in 1994, peaking with third place at the extraordinary German Grand Prix (won by Gerhard Berger), his only scoring drive of the year. However, as rookie team-mate and fellow country-man Olivier Panis outpaced him more often than not, it spelt the end of Eric's Formula One career.

Career Record

■ 45 Grands Prix, no wins (best result – 3rd, German GP 1994)

■ No championship title (best result – 13th overall 1990)

LUCIEN BIANCHI

Nationality: **Belgian**

Born: **1934**

Died: **1969**

Born into an Italian family that was tempted to Belgium to work for racing driver Johnny Claes, Lucien cut his teeth in sports cars and rallying before moving on to racing single-seaters for 1959. The first Grand Prix for which he quali-fied was, fittingly, the Belgian GP in 1960 and he drove his Cooper into the points, finishing sixth. However, he dropped back to sports cars, and it was not until 1968 that Lucien had a decent crack at Formula One, albeit with the little-fancied BRM-powered Cooper. That year, his highlight was winning the Le Mans 24 Hours. And it was to sports cars that he turned in 1969, but they later claimed his life at Le Mans.

Career Record

■ 17 Grands Prix, no wins (best result – 3rd Monaco GP 1968)

■ No championship title (best result – 17th overall 1968)

"B BIRA"

Nationality: **Thai**

Born: **1914**

Died: **1985**

Prince Birabongse Bhanuban, a colourful figure on the European social scene in the mid-1930s, was also a car fanatic from an early age and, when at school in England, made it his ambition to become a racing driver. He eventually graduated to a mighty ERA, but his career was interrupted by the Second World War, after which he won various Formula Two races before making his Formula One debut in 1950 for Maserati, for whom he finished fifth at Monaco and then fourth in the Swiss Grand Prix. Running for Maserati, then Gordini, then Connaught, then Maserati again, "B Bira" raced on until the start of 1955 when he decided to retire.

Career Record
■ *19 Grands Prix, no wins (best result – 4th, Swiss GP 1950, French GP 1954)*
■ *No championship title (best result – 8th overall 1950)*

MARK BLUNDELL
Nationality: **British**
Born: **1966**

Mark arrived in Formula Ford aged 17 as a seasoned competitor after many years of racing in moto-cross. Armed with family wealth and the "will to win", he contested 70 races that year. This propelled him into Formula Ford 2000 for the next two seasons, racing with – and often beating – rivals such as Damon Hill, Johnny Herbert and Bertrand Gachot. Most people would then have gone to Formula Three in 1987, but not Mark, who leapt directly to Formula 3000. A chance to drive for the works Lola team came his way in 1988, but this bombed after he had achieved second place in the first round. Staying on for 1989, he had an even worse season. But sports cars came to his rescue and he drove with great speed for the works Nissan team. A test-driving contract for Williams followed in 1990, and Mark made his Formula One racing debut with Brabham in 1991. He dropped to sports cars again in 1992, but was back in Formula One with Ligier in 1993 and scored third place first time out, ending up tenth overall. A move to Tyrrell in 1994 saw Mark suffer at the hands of Japanese team-mate Ukyo Katayama, raising cries of unfair treatment, but, either way, it cost him the chance to stay on for 1995. Drafted into the McLaren line-up when Mansell couldn't fit into the car, he got the drive for keeps when Mansell quit. Mark brought the tricky car home in the points six times, but lost out in the chase for a Sauber ride in 1996, and moved on to become a race-winner in Indycars in 1997.

Career Record
■ *61 Grands Prix, no wins (best result – 3rd, South African GP 1993, German GP 1993, Spanish GP 1994)*
■ *No championship title (best result – 10th overall 1993 and 1995)*

RAUL BOESEL
Nationality: **Brazilian**
Born: **1957**

Raul came second in the British Formula Ford series in 1980. Making sure that he scored points rather than threw them away in a win-or-bust approach, Raul finished third in the British Formula Three championship and leapt into Formula One for 1982. But the March team was not the one to be with that year and his best result was eighth at the Belgian Grand Prix. Frustrated, he moved to Ligier for 1983 and went one better with seventh place in the US Grand Prix West. However, no points came his way and Raul headed to Indycars. A period racing for the Jaguar sports car team netted Raul the 1987 world title, but he returned to Indycars in the 1990s.

Career Record
- 23 Grands Prix, no wins (best result – 7th, US West GP 1983)
- No championship title

FELICE BONETTO
Nationality: **Italian**
Born: **1903**
Died: **1953**

The average age of drivers in the inaugural Formula One World Championship race in 1950, held at Silverstone, was almost double the age of today's grid and when Felice made his debut in the Swiss Grand Prix that year, he was five days short of his 47th birthday. A star in the lengthy and heroic Italian road races of the 1930s, his move to Formula One came with Ferrari for whom he had shone in several non-championship races. He entered his own Maserati in

several Grands Prix in 1950 and was signed to drive a works Alfa Romeo in 1951, finishing third in the Italian Grand Prix. A move to sports cars followed, but he returned to Formula One at the end of 1952 and was going well in the works Maserati in 1953 before being killed on the Carrera Panamericana road race through Mexico.

Career Record
- 15 Grands Prix, no wins (best result – 3rd, Italian GP 1951, Dutch GP 1953)
- No championship title (best result – 8th overall 1951)

JOAKIM BONNIER
Nationality: **Swedish**
Born: **1930**
Died: **1972**

Having begun his career in rallying and after honing his skills in ice races, Jo was awarded the Swedish Alfa Romeo franchise and used its Disco Volante in sports car races. He bought a Maserati 250F with which to race in Formula One, starting at the 1956 Italian Grand Prix. Jo's first full season was 1958 and his results improved when he moved to BRM, taking fourth in the Moroccan Grand Prix. However, his victory at Zandvoort in 1959 marked the end of BRM's long wait for a Grand Prix win. That was his golden moment, and the following year and a half produced only three fifth places. He raced a Porsche in 1961–62, but was overshadowed by team-mate

Dan Gurney. Jo was held in high esteem by the drivers, and he founded the Grand Prix Drivers' Association which fought to make circuits safer. Three years with Rob Walker's team, driving Coopers and Brabhams saw many fifth and sixth places and, though Joakim chipped away with his own privately entered Coopers and McLarens until 1971 that was his lot. He was killed at Le Mans in 1972.

Career Record
■ 102 Grands Prix, 1 win (Dutch GP 1959)
■ No championship title (best result – 8th overall 1959)

and he finished third overall in 1979, a year when Alain Prost was champion. The whole of 1980 was spent trying to raise the cash to race in Formula One, and so he made his debut in 1981 with ATS, scoring his solitary point for sixth place in the British Grand Prix. His money ran out after only three races with Tyrrell in 1982 and Slim's greatest success since has been in truck racing.

Career Record
■ 10 Grands Prix, no wins (best result – 6th, British GP 1981)
■ No championship title (best result – 18th overall 1981)

JOAKIM BONNIER
Tasted success at the Dutch GP in 1959 and led the fight to make the sport safer by founding the Grand Prix Drivers' Association.

SLIM BORGUDD
Nationality: Swedish
Born: 1946

Slim used the money gained from his musical exploits as Abba's drummer to go racing. He contested the 1978 European Formula Three series,

JEAN-CHRISTOPHE BOULLION
Nationality: French
Born: 1969

Jean-Christophe flew in Formula Ford, then showed great pace in French Formula Three and won the Formula

3000 title in 1994 for the DAMS team. He matched the pace of Hill and Coulthard as Williams test driver, but was given a chance to race at Sauber when Karl Wendlinger was dropped before Monaco in 1995. Occasionally quick, often erratic, he was dropped before the year was out, but he had further seasons as Williams test driver.

Career Record
- 11 Grands Prix, no wins (best result – 5th, German GP 1995)
- No championship title (best result – 16th overall 1995)

THIERRY BOUTSEN
Nationality: Belgian
Born: 1957

Thierry rocketed through Formula Ford. His maiden year in Formula Three in 1979 was not so sweet, but he came good and landed a works ride for 1980, finishing second overall to Michele Alboreto. Formula Two followed and he was second again, this time to Geoff Lees. But he had done enough to impress. And so Thierry made it to Formula One for 1983 with Arrows, with whom he stayed until 1986, peaking with second at Imola in 1985. He moved to Benetton in 1987 and five third places in 1988 helped Thierry to fourth overall. A move to Williams in 1989 yielded two wins, both in the wet. Although he won again in 1990, holding off massive pressure from Ayrton Senna in Hungary, his contract with

Williams was not renewed. He moved to Ligier for 1991 and 1992, which proved a mistake, as the team were well off the pace even with Renault engines. When Ivan Capelli was sacked by Jordan in 1993, Thierry moved there, but he did not last the season. He has since raced in touring cars and sports cars.

Career Record
- 163 Grands Prix, 3 wins (Canadian GP 1989, Australian GP 1989, Hungarian GP 1990)
- No championship title (best result – 4th overall 1988)

DAVID BRABHAM
Nationality: Australian
Born: 1965

Youngest of Sir Jack Brabham's three sons, David considered racing only after spending a summer watching his brother Geoff race in the USA. As soon as he returned to Australia he started in single-seaters, then joined his parents in England and was an instant hit in Formula Three. He won a long, hard fight with Allan McNish for the 1989 title and backed this up by winning the Macau Grand Prix, the unofficial world final for Formula Three. David made his Formula One debut in 1990 when Middlebridge, the team that was set to run him in Formula 3000, bought the Brabham Grand Prix team, an outfit that had been sold off by his father when he retired from racing in 1970. However, the car was not a gem and David was dropped at the end of the year, turning successfully to sports cars. After a spell with Jaguar and then Toyota, he made it back to Formula One with the formation of the Simtek team in 1994. It was a ghastly year, for team-mate Roland Ratzenberger was killed at Imola and the taciturn David showed great inner strength to remotivate the team. Fighting from the back of the grid, he gave it his all, with a best finish of tenth, but he could not find the money to continue and became a works BMW touring car driver, before moving to sports cars.

Career Record

■ *24 Grands Prix, no wins (best result – 10th, Spanish GP 1994)*
■ *No championship title*

JACK BRABHAM

Nationality: Australian

Born: 1926

Jack started in midget racing at the age of 20 and then moved to hill climbs, but when the organisers objected to advertising on his car, he turned his attention to the Kiwi scene and impressed in the 1954 New Zealand Grand Prix. He was persuaded to make the trip to Europe, became associated with John Cooper and made his World Championship debut in the 1955 British Grand Prix. Sticking with Cooper, Jack drove the marque's sports car and Formula Two car over the next few seasons, enjoying an

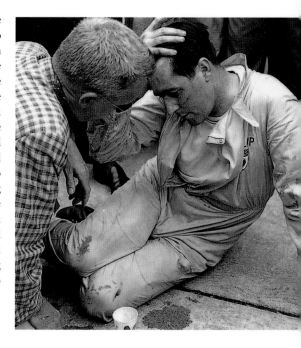

increasing number of World Championship outings. His first points came with fourth place in the 1958 Monaco Grand Prix. By 1959, however, the Coopers were a real force in Formula One, driven by Brabham, Stirling Moss, Maurice Trintignant, Bruce McLaren and Masten Gregory. Although Moss led for much of the season opener at Monte Carlo, it was Brabham who won the race. He won again at Aintree, was second at Zandvoort and third at Monza and Reims, then sealed the championship at Sebring by pushing his car to the finish in fourth place after running out of fuel. If anybody felt that his title had been fortunate, their doubts were quashed in 1960 when he won his second successive title with five straight wins – at Zandvoort, Spa, Reims,

JACK BRABHAM
The three-time World Champion lies exhausted after having to push his car over the line at the 1959 US GP to clinch his first title.

Silverstone and Oporto. For 1961 there was a new 1.5-litre engine formula and Ferrari leapt to the fore. Ever shrewd, Brabham saw the potential for a production racing car company and with his old acquaintance, Ron Tauranac, formed Motor Racing Developments. The first Brabham made its debut in 1962, and a fourth place by Brabham at the US Grand Prix brought the first points ever scored by a driver in a car of his own manufacture. Dan Gurney joined him, and although they won non-championship races at Solitude and Zeltweg, they did not win a Grand Prix until the French Grand Prix of 1964. Business demands sent Brabham into semi-retirement in 1965, but he decided to come back full-time alongside Denny Hulme for 1966, when he clinched his third championship – winning at Reims, Silverstone, Zandvoort and the Nurburgring. Hulme brought another championship for Brabham in 1967, beating the boss into second place. Hulme then moved to McLaren and Jack signed Jochen Rindt. All but unbeatable in Formula Two, Rindt had problems with the unreliable new Repco engine and left for Lotus for 1969 and Brabham was joined by Jacky Ickx. While Brabham's season was hampered by a broken ankle, Ickx finished second overall to Jackie Stewart's dominant Matra-Ford and was snapped up by Ferrari. Brabham was determined that 1970 would be his final year, as it

was, after all, his 23rd season behind the wheel. It started well, with Jack overhauling reigning World Champion Stewart in the new March and winning at Kyalami, but the pair would finish the year joint fifth, as Rindt became the sport's only posthumous World Champion. He hung up his hat after the Mexican Grand Prix and after running cars for Graham Hill and Tim Schenken in 1971, sold the team to Bernie Ecclestone. He has since watched from the sidelines as the racing careers of his sons, Geoff, Gary and David have shaped up, being involved in finding the funding to launch the Simtek team in 1994 with David as the team leader.

Career Record

■ *126 Grands Prix, 14 wins (Monaco GP 1959, British GP 1959, Dutch GP 1960, Belgian GP 1960, French GP 1960, British GP 1960, Portuguese GP 1960, French GP 1961, British GP 1961, Dutch GP 1961, German GP 1961, French GP 1967, Canadian GP 1967, South African GP 1970)*
■ *World Champion 1959, 1960 and 1966*

VITTORIO BRAMBILLA
Nationality: Italian
Born: 1937

Born in Monza, he raced motorcycles, then karts, before joining his brother Tino in Formula Three in 1968. Despite not doing all the rounds, Vittorio finished second overall. He went one better in 1969. The brothers teamed up in Formula Two in 1970, but Vittorio spent much of the year blowing engines in his efforts to keep up with drivers in newer machinery. Occasional quick drives were not enough, especially with Vittorio junking several chassis, and money was too tight for success to follow. Only when Beta Tools agreed to finance him in 1973 did he make progress. He took Beta Tools to Formula One in 1974 with March and he scored his first point before the year was out. His second season promised so much, with pole in Sweden, but offered frequent retirements until he held it all together to win the Austrian Grand Prix after a downpour. Seconds after crossing the finish line, Vittorio punched the air with delight and crashed. He moved to Surtees in 1977 and did poorly, with the exception of a fourth place in Belgium. Then came disaster in the 1978 Italian Grand Prix when he was struck on the head in the accident that was to inflict fatal injuries on Ronnie Peterson. It was not until a year later that Vittorio was back in the cockpit, returning at Monza for Alfa Romeo. However, the old speed was not there and he retired from Formula One after a handful more Grands Prix.

Career Record
■ *74 Grands Prix, 1 win (Austrian GP 1975)*
■ *No championship title (best result – 11th overall 1975)*

TONY BRISE
Nationality: British
Born: 1952
Died: 1975

Tony could have been a World Champion, but he died in the same light aircraft accident that claimed the life of Graham Hill. Encouraged into the sport by his father, a former racer, Tony started in karts at the age of ten and shone in Formula Ford, finishing second in the 1971 British series. Moving up to Formula Three in 1972 was not a great success, since he had the wrong car. However, he picked up a drive with the GRD team for 1973 and won the British title ahead of Alan Jones and Jacques Laffite. For 1974 Tony tried Formula Atlantic with a works Modus and finished third overall. Hill signed him up for F1 for 1975, and Tony did great things with what was clearly not a very quick car, getting it into the points in Sweden, but that plane crash denied us the knowledge of just how far he would have gone.

Career Record
■ *10 Grands Prix, no wins (best result – 6th, Swedish GP 1975)*
■ *No championship title (best result – 19th overall 1975)*

CHRIS BRISTOW
Nationality: British
Born: 1937
Died: 1960

After starting in an MG special, Chris was helped into more competitive equipment by his

TONY BROOKS

One of Britian's earliest Formula One stars celebrates victory at the 1958 Italian Grand Prix.

father in 1957, and his form in 1958 led him to be signed up by the British Racing Partnership for 1959. This offered him the chance to race single-seaters as well as sports cars, and he made his Grand Prix debut in the British Grand Prix, albeit in Formula Two equipment. The death of team-mate Harry Schell pitched Chris into the role of team leader shortly after BRP put him into Formula One with a Yeoman Credit Racing Cooper. Sadly, he suffered a fatal accident in the Belgian Grand Prix on a dark day at Spa that also claimed the life of his compatriot Alan Stacey.

Career Record

- 4 Grands Prix, no wins (best result – 10th British GP 1959)
- No championship title

TONY BROOKS

Nationality: British

Born: 1932

Tony Brooks was a driver of consummate skill. If he had not been bitten by the racing bug he would have gone on to become a dentist, dabbling in sports cars as a pleasant distraction from his studies. However, in 1955 he went abroad and raced a Connaught. In only his second race, the non-championship but nevertheless well-attended Syracuse Grand Prix, he thrashed all comers. It was the first win by a British driver in a British car since 1924... World Championship Formula One followed in 1956 with BRM, but his season was foreshortened when he was thrown from his car at Silverstone and broke his jaw. Vanwall signed him up for 1957. Second place first time out, at Monaco, was followed by victory at the British Grand Prix, an event in which he started but handed over his car in mid-race to Stirling Moss as he himself was suffering from leg injuries inflicted during the Le Mans 24 Hours. Staying with Vanwall for 1958, he was tipped by the retiring Juan Manuel Fangio as the likely World Champion, but though Tony won three times – each time on the real drivers' circuits – he wound up third overall. Ferrari signed him for 1959 and Tony won twice more, ending the year second to Jack Brabham. The following two seasons saw him drive a Cooper for Yeoman Credit Racing and then a works BRM, but he was no longer prepared to take what he now considered to be unnecessary risks. Thus he retired at the end of 1961 to run a motor business.

Career Record

■ *38 Grands Prix, 6 wins (British GP 1957, Belgian GP 1958, German GP 1958, Italian GP 1958, French GP 1959, German GP 1959)*
■ *No championship title (best result – 2nd overall 1959)*

MARTIN BRUNDLE

Nationality: **British**

Born: **1959**

How a driver who made Ayrton Senna work so hard for the British Formula Three title could race in Formula One for a decade and not score a win is a mystery. Senna had whipped all comers in the first half of 1983, but Martin became the quicker of the two in his Eddie Jordan Racing Ralt and took the title down to the wire. Ken Tyrrell was not slow to identify this talent and signed Martin for 1984. He was fifth in his first Grand Prix, in Brazil. Coming second in Detroit behind Nelson Piquet propelled Martin to the brink. But a race later he broke his ankles at Dallas. To add insult to injury, Tyrrell was adjudged to be running illegal cars, and the team's results were scrapped. In 1986 he had four points-scoring drives, but his career took a dive when he chose to join the German Zakspeed team in 1987. It was hopeless and Martin was left without a drive in 1988. Fortunately, he raced for Jaguar and won the World Sports Car Championship, also having a one-off drive for Williams at Spa. For 1989 he drove for Brabham, but this was not the team it had been and he went back to sports car racing for 1990, winning the Le Mans 24 Hours. A return to Brabham for 1991 was not a success, since the Yamaha engines were no match for the opposition. Then came his big break, a ride at Benetton. The trouble was that he was alongside Michael Schumacher who soon proved himself team leader as Martin struggled to finish races. From San Marino on, though, he scored points in all but one race to claim sixth overall, usually racing better than Schumacher. But what hurt Martin was his inability to put in a flier in qualifying. A move to Ligier in 1993 brought more regular points scores and seventh overall. Then it looked as though he was out of a top ride for 1994, but he hung in there for a McLaren seat and claimed it at the last minute. Again no wins came, but Martin was twice on the rostrum and was seventh overall. He had to share the second Ligier with Aguri Suzuki in 1995 and his best drive was when he chased David Coulthard for third at Magny-Cours. A ride with Jordan for 1996 promised more than it delivered. Martin has built a new career as a much-respected co-commentator with Murray Walker on ITV.

Career Record
- *158 Grands Prix, no wins (best result – 2nd, Italian GP 1992, Monaco GP 1994)*
- *No championship title (best result – 6th overall 1992)*

JENSON BUTTON
Nationality: **British**
Born: **1980**
Jenson won his first karting title at 11 and was European Super A champion in 1997. Moving into Formula Ford as soon as he was old enough, he won the British Championship and the Formula Ford Festival. On pole for his first Formula Three race in 1999, he suffered from having the less competitive Renault engine and ended the year third overall. However, he was invited to test for Prost. He impressed, but then was snapped up by Williams after a

shoot-out for its second seat. Jenson outqualified his teammate Ralf Schumacher at his second race, going on to finish fifth. He added five more point-scoring drives, but lost his ride for 2001, heading to Benetton for two years before Williams wants him back.

Career Record
- *17 Grands Prix, no wins (best result – 4th, German GP 2000)*
- *No championship title (best result – 8th overall 2000)*

C

ALEX CAFFI
Nationality: **Italian**
Born: **1964**
Ever the bridesmaid, Alex was second in the Italian Formula Three series in 1984 and 1985, then third in 1986. His Formula One break came in 1987 when he drove the unwieldy Osella. His fortune was better in 1988 with a Scuderia Italia Dallara. Staying on for 1989, he took fourth place at Monaco and was then running fifth at Phoenix (having been second earlier on) when team-mate Andrea de Cesaris tipped him into the wall. Alex moved to Arrows in 1990, but it was not a success. Staying with the team, now renamed Footwork, he found his chances were hampered by heavy and uncompetitive Porsche engines and then by a jaw-breaking road acci-

dent. He qualified only twice on his return. Just when he thought it could get no worse, it did: he joined the new Andrea Moda team for 1992. He quit after two races and elected to race in touring cars in Italy and Spain.

Career Record

- *56 Grands Prix, no wins (best result – 4th, Monaco GP 1989)*
- *No championship title (best result – 16th overall 1989 and 1990)*

IVAN CAPELLI

Nationality: **Italian**

Born: **1963**

Hot from karting, Ivan went direct to Formula Three and dominated the Italian series at his second attempt, in 1983. Staying with Enzo Coloni's team for 1984, he won the Monaco race and later the European Championship ahead of Gerhard Berger and Johnny Dumfries. A limited Formula 3000 campaign in 1985 produced a win at the Osterreichring and promoted Ivan to the Tyrrell Formula One team for a couple of races. Amazingly, he was fourth on his second outing, in Australia, yet no offer for 1986 was forthcoming. So Ivan returned to Formula 3000, winning the title for Genoa Racing. He joined March for 1987 and claimed a point at Monaco, but 1988 was better, as he was in the points six times, chasing Alain Prost's McLaren in Portugal before settling for second. The 1989 sea-

son was an unmitigated disaster, the March chassis handling like a pig. But 1990 was much better and Ivan led the French Grand Prix for 46 laps before Alain Prost pushed his Ferrari ahead with just three laps to go. Third place at the following race looked to be his reward, but a fuel pipe frayed and he was out. After a troubled season in 1991 he was signed for Ferrari for 1992. But points were few and far between, and after two races for Jordan in 1993, he was fired.

Career Record

- *92 Grands Prix, no wins (best result – 2nd, Portuguese GP 1988, French GP 1990)*
- *No championship title (best result – 7th overall 1988)*

EUGENIO CASTELLOTTI

Nationality: **Italian**

Born: **1930**

Died: **1957**

Eugenio cut a swathe through European sports car racing in the early 1950s and made his Formula One debut at the 1955 Argentinian Grand Prix with Lancia and swept to second place on his second outing, at Monaco. On the death of teammate Alberto Ascari, he became team leader and scored three more times to be third overall. Continuing with the Lancia-Ferrari set-up in 1956, Eugenio was second in the French Grand Prix and finished sixth overall in the championship. He won the legendary Mille Miglia road race to make up for his disappointment with his Formula

One. Eugenio was only to race in one more Grand Prix, however, being killed when testing for Ferrari at its Modena testing circuit in early 1957.

Career Record
- 14 Grands Prix, no wins (best result – 2nd, Monaco GP 1955, French GP 1956)
- No championship title (best result – 3rd overall 1955)

JOHNNY CECOTTO
Nationality: **Venezuelan**
Born: **1956**

After becoming the youngest-ever 350cc motorcycle world champion, Johnny swapped across to four wheels with a drive in Formula Two in 1980. By 1982 he was a front-runner, only losing out on the title to works March team-mate Corrado Fabi when dropped scores were taken into consideration. His Formula One debut came in 1983 when he joined the little Theodore team, amazingly finishing in sixth place in his second race, at Long Beach. No more points followed and he moved to Toleman for 1984, but his single-seater career was cut short with a leg-breaking shunt at Brands Hatch. Subsequently, Johnny has won numerous titles in touring car racing in Italy and Germany.

Career Record
- 18 Grands Prix, no wins (best result – 6th, US West GP 1983)
- No championship title (best result – 19th overall 1983)

FRANÇOIS CEVERT
Nationality: **French**
Born: **1944**
Died: **1973**

Fate struck a cruel blow when it claimed the life of this talented Frenchman at the 1973 US Grand Prix, for he was poised to assume Jackie Stewart's role as Tyrrell team leader and thus make a bid to become the first French World Champion. French Formula Three champion in 1968, François was promoted by Tecno to its Formula Two squad and finished third overall in 1969. Tyrrell snapped him up for 1970 and put him under the tutelage of Stewart. François was second twice in 1971 before winning the final race of the season, at Watkins Glen, the track that would later claim his life. This helped him to third overall behind Stewart and Ferrari's Jacky Ickx. The 1972 season was not such a success, with two more second places, yet François made up for this by finishing second in the Le Mans 24 Hours. In 1973 he was second six times, three times behind Stewart. Then then came that fateful day in upper New York State...

Career Record
- 47 Grands Prix, 1 win (US GP 1971)
- No championship title (best result – 3rd overall 1971)

EDDIE CHEEVER
Nationality: **American**
Born: **1958**
Eddie shone in Formula Three

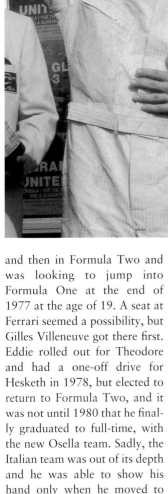

FRANÇOIS CEVERT
The Frenchman is all smiles after securing his first (and only) win at the 1971 US Grand Prix at the track that would later claim his life.

and then in Formula Two and was looking to jump into Formula One at the end of 1977 at the age of 19. A seat at Ferrari seemed a possibility, but Gilles Villeneuve got there first. Eddie rolled out for Theodore and had a one-off drive for Hesketh in 1978, but elected to return to Formula Two, and it was not until 1980 that he finally graduated to full-time, with the new Osella team. Sadly, the Italian team was out of its depth and he was able to show his hand only when he moved to Tyrrell in 1981, putting in five points-scoring drives. He hit the rostrum in 1982 with Ligier, peaking with second place at Detroit. This helped him to land a ride for 1983, but this was alongside Alain Prost at Renault and Eddie could not live with the comparison, even though his sixth overall marked his best year to date. Two years with the Benetton-Alfa Romeo team and three with Arrows came next, but the star was fading and Eddie headed to Indy Cars, winning the 1998 Indy 500.

Career Record
■ *132 Grands Prix, no wins (best result – 2nd US GP 1982, Canadian GP 1983)*
■ *No championship title (best result – 6th overall 1983)*

LOUIS CHIRON

Nationality: **Monegasque**
Born: **1899**
Died: **1979**

Louis scored more than a dozen Grands Prix wins before the Second World War and several more after it. Nicknamed "the Old Fox" in deference to his advanced age and wily tactics, he was on the grid for the first World Championship race in 1950, driving a works Maserati. Third place at his native Monte Carlo was his best result that year, and indeed his championship career. The unreliability of the Lago-Talbot he raced in 1951 wasted the year and it signalled the end of his serious bid for Formula One glory, although he turned out for assorted Grands Prix until 1956.

Career Record

- 15 Grands Prix, no wins (best result – 3rd, Monaco GP 1950)
- No championship title (best result – 9th overall 1950)

JIM CLARK

Nationality: **British**
Born: **1936**
Died: **1968**

The son of a Scottish farmer from the border country, Jim was entered in an autotest by local garage owner Jock McBain. Not only did Jim enjoy the experience, but he won. After a few local rallies, close friend Ian Scott-Watson lent Clark a DKW for his first race in 1956, a Porsche followed, and for 1958 McBain reformed the Border Reivers team and bought a D-type Jaguar with which Jim scored 12 wins from 20 starts. Scott-Watson then bought a Lotus Elite for Clark to drive, and Jim had a scrap with Lotus boss Colin Chapman on his first visit to Brands Hatch. Chapman's company was in the embryonic stages and, when a Formula One deal that Clark had been promised with Aston Martin failed to materialize, he joined Lotus to drive in Formula Two and Formula Junior in 1960. He started winning immediately and Chapman entered him in the Dutch Grand Prix, where he ran fifth before retiring. Jim became a full-time Grand Prix driver in 1961, but was involved in the accident that killed Wolfgang von Trips and 13 spectators in the Italian Grand Prix at Monza. He scored his first Grand Prix win at Spa-Francorchamps – a circuit he loathed – in 1962 and fought with Graham Hill for the title before losing out at the final round in South Africa, when the car broke while he was leading. Clark was untouchable in 1963, taking seven wins from ten starts. He also was second on his first appearance in the Indianapolis 500, a race that saw local hero Parnelli Jones controversially allowed to continue to victory in a car that was leaking oil. Whatever, Clark and Lotus and shocked the establishment and sent a clear message that the days of the traditional, front-

engined roadsters were numbered. Then, after finishing third overall behind John Surtees and Hill in 1964, wins in the South African, Belgian, French, British, Dutch and German Grands Prix in 1965 gave him a second world title. He also won the Indianapolis 500. With the 3-litre formula introduced for 1966, Lotus didn't have the engines to mount a title bid and it wasn't until the Cosworth DFV was introduced in 1967 that Clark bounced back. He gave the engine a debut win at Zandvoort and pushed Denny Hulme hard for the title. Clark started 1968 by winning the South African Grand Prix, to break Fangio's record of 24 Grand Prix victories. Then, driving in a Formula Two race at Hockenheim, he inexplicably crashed into a tree and was killed instantly. Even though driver fatalities were relatively common in the 1960s,

Jim's death rocked the establishment, as everyone had considered him as the best, above the accidents that afflicted other drivers.

Career Record
- 72 *Grands Prix, 25 wins (Belgian GP 1962, British GP 1962, US GP 1962, Belgian GP 1963, Dutch GP 1963, French GP 1963, British GP 1963, Italian GP 1963, Mexican GP 1963, South African GP 1963, Dutch GP 1964, Belgian GP 1964, British GP 1964, South African GP 1965, Belgian GP 1965, French GP 1965, British GP 1965, Dutch GP 1965, German GP 1965, US GP 1966, Dutch GP 1967, British GP 1967, US GP 1967, Mexican GP 1967, South African GP 1968)*
- *World Champion 1963 and 1965*

JIM CLARK
Britain's greatest-ever Formula One driver on the way to his final Grand Prix victory, in 1968 at South Africa.

PETER COLLINS

Nationality: **British**

Born: **1931**

Died: **1958**

The tricks learned in three years of Formula 500 racing were to stand Peter in good stead throughout his career, and he made a big impression when he moved up to Formula Two with HWM in 1952. Sadly, the cars were not reliable, but Aston Martin was sufficiently impressed to sign him for its sports car team. A ride with BRM in 1955 was limited by the late arrival of its new car. However, Ferrari signed Peter for 1956 and two wins, in Belgium and France, followed, helping Peter to finish third overall behind Juan Manuel Fangio and Stirling Moss in the championship. The following year was not so good, and he failed to win as his Lancia-Ferrari was outclassed by the rival Maseratis and Vanwalls. Peter was back on form with the advent of Ferrari's classic Dino 246 Grand Prix car in 1958. Cruelly, just a fortnight after he had stormed home ahead of Mike Hawthorn in the British Grand Prix at Silverstone, he was killed in the German Grand Prix at the Nurburgring when chasing Tony Brooks's Vanwall for the lead.

PETER COLLINS

A true gentleman who spurned personal glory to help his team-mate Juan Manuel Fangio to a fourth world title in 1956.

Career Record

■ *32 Grands Prix, 3 wins (Belgian GP 1956, French GP 1956, British GP 1958)*
■ *No championship title (best result – 3rd overall 1956)*

ERIK COMAS

Nationality: **French**

Born: **1963**

Too many talented drivers from one country arriving at the top will spoil one another's chances. Thus Erik found himself competing with Jean Alesi and Eric Bernard. Erik won the French Formule Renault title in 1986 and then suffered from being number two to Bernard in Formula Three. Thus, it was not until his second year in Formula Three, in 1988, that he won the French title. Formula 3000 saw Erik partner Bernard again. He scored more points, but lost the title to Alesi by the smallest of margins. Yet again he stayed on for a repeat, winning the 1990 crown. Two years in Formula One with Ligier were his reward, but he scored no points in 1991. He scored in Canada, France and Germany in 1992, then Erik had a huge shunt at Spa from which he was lucky to escape. Larrousse was his home for the next two years, but a trio of sixth places was his paltry recompense.

Career Record

- 59 Grands Prix, no wins (best result – 5th, French GP 1982)
- No championship title (best result – 11th 1992)

DAVID COULTHARD

Nationality: **British**

Born: **1971**

After a successful career in karts, David graduated to Formula Ford in 1989 and drove so well that he became the first winner of the McLaren/ *Autosport* Young Driver award, being granted a run in a Formula One car. He was beaten by Rubens Barrichello in both the GM Euroseries and then in the 1991 British Formula Three series. He stumbled by finishing only ninth in Formula 3000 for Paul Stewart Racing in 1992, but he was on the podium at the last two races and carried this form into 1993, when he won at Enna and finished up third. A greater success though, was his role as Williams test driver. No ride was forthcoming for 1994, so it was back to Formula 3000 and more test driving. Second in the first race was followed by Senna's death at Imola and thus David moved up to Formula One. He soon got on to Hill's pace and peaked with second in Portugal, before making way for Nigel Mansell in the final three races. David raced on at Williams in 1995, winning in Portugal. He also led in Belgium and Italy, and ended up third overall, but contractual obligations moved him to McLaren for 1996, where he and Hakkinen struggled to keep up with the Williams drivers. But David won first time out in 1997, later adding a win at Monza en route to equal third overall. Strong form at the start of 1998 laid the way open for a title battle with Hakkinen, but he slipped into a support role and finished up third overall. Winning only once dropped

PIERS COURAGE

Nationality: British

Born: 1942

Died: 1970

Heir to the Courage brewing fortunes, Piers cared little for brewing and chose to race cars instead. Since his father refused to give him financial support he had to make his own way in racing. With Jonathan Williams he formed Anglo-Swiss Racing and went after Formula Three glory across Europe. It was a hand-to-mouth existence, with both men looking to survive on their prize money. A more professional approach was employed in 1965 and Piers started to win races. However, he had a tendency to spin away good positions, and it was not until 1968 that he was given a proper crack at Formula One after shining in the Tasman series in New Zealand. Piers was given his break by Tim Parnell who asked him to drive a BRM, and was in the points before the year was out. For 1969 he teamed up with Frank Williams and was promptly second at Monaco, matching this with second in the US Grand Prix. For the following season Williams ran him in a de Tomaso, but it was not a patch on the Brabham he used in 1969. But then Piers was killed in a fiery accident in the Dutch Grand Prix.

DAVID COULTHARD

The Scotsman inches ever closer to the world title he craves.

him to fourth overall in 1999, but three wins in 2000 gave him a shot at the title before his form dipped and he ended up third again. However, he was lucky still to be racing, as he survived a plane crash that killed his pilot and co-pilot.

Career Record

■ *107 Grands Prix, 9 wins (Portuguese GP 1995, Australian GP 1997, Italian GP 1997, San Marino GP 1998, British GP 1999, Belgian GP 1999, British GP 2000, Monaco GP 2000, French GP 2000)*

■ *No championship title (best result – 3rd overall 1995, 1998 & 2000)*

Career Record

■ *28 Grands Prix, no wins (best result – 2nd, Monaco GP 1969, US GP 1969)*

■ *No championship title (best result – 8th overall 1969)*

D

YANNICK DALMAS
Nationality: **French**
Born: **1961**

Yannick was French Formule Renault champion in 1984 and landed a top drive in Formula Three for 1985 with the crack ORECA team, and ended up finishing second overall. In time-honoured fashion, he stayed on to become team leader and won the title in 1986. Formula 3000 was next and Yannick gained two victories, but poor results elsewere left him fifth overall. Before the year was out, however, he had his first taste of Formula One with the Larrousse Calmels team, scoring fifth place at his third attempt. However, he was adjudged not to have competed in enough Grands Prix to be eligible for points. Staying on with the team in 1988, he was not at his best, which he put down to ill health. Back with Larrousse in 1989, things were even worse and Yannick was forced out of the team to make way for Michele Alboreto. He picked up a ride with the tiny AGS team, but often failed to make it through pre-qualifying. The 1990 season was only slightly better. Career salvation came with a drive in the Peugeot sports car team, and Yannick won the Le Mans 24 Hours in 1992. Since 1993, Yannick's career has been sustained predominantly by a diet of touring cars.

Career Record
■ *23 Grands Prix, no wins (best result – 7th, Monaco GP 1988, US GP 1988)*
■ *No championship title*

DEREK DALY
Nationality: **Irish**
Born: **1953**

Derek was Irish Formula Ford champion in 1975, Formula Ford Festival winner in 1976 and won the BP British Formula Three crown in 1977 before kicking off his Formula One career with the Hesketh team in 1978 and led until he spun off in a very wet International Trophy at Silverstone. His form in the World Championship was not so good, as he failed to qualify on all three outings. Crossing to Ensign was an improvement, and he scored a point before the year was out. A move to Tyrrell halfway through 1979 preceded a full season with Tyrrell in 1980 and his most spectacular shunt of all on the opening lap of the Monaco Grand Prix when he became airborne and landed right on his team-mate, Jean-Pierre Jarier. His ride with March yielded not a point in 1981. A ride with Theodore in 1982 looked equally dire, but Carlos Reutemann quit suddenly, and Derek was asked to take his place at Williams alongside Keke Rosberg. The Finn went on to win the title, while the Irishman never made it to the rostrum and quit Formula One for Indycars. Despite a leg-smashing shunt in 1984, Derek went on racing in Indycars and then sports cars until 1992, and has since become a respected television commentator in the United States.

Career Record

■ *49 Grands Prix, no wins (best result – 4th, Argentinian GP 1980, British GP 1980)*

■ *No championship title (best result – 10th overall 1980)*

CHRISTIAN DANNER

Nationality: **German**

Born: **1958**

Christian first came to prominence when he raced a BMW M1 in 1980. BMW signed him on a three-year contract and placed him in the works March Formula Two team for 1981, despite his having no single-seater experience. It took him until the end of 1983 to get on to the pace. Driving for Bob Sparshott, he was the inaugural Formula 3000 champion in 1985 and was given two Formula One outings by Zakspeed. A move to Osella for 1986 produced little and Christian joined Arrows in mid-season, hitting the points in Austria. Returning to Zakspeed in 1987, he had little to cheer about. Christian's final shot at Formula One was with the new Rial team in 1989 and he came fourth at Phoenix, but only qualified once thereafter, and quit again for touring cars.

Career Record

■ *36 Grands Prix, no wins*

(best result – 4th, US GP 1989)

■ *No championship title (best result – 18th overall 1986)*

ELIO DE ANGELIS

Nationality: **Italian**

Born: **1958**

Died: **1986**

Very few drivers have reached Formula One as early in life as Elio did, for he had a full-time ride when he was only 20. Coming from a wealthy family, he cut his teeth on karts, then blasted into Formula Three, pipping Piercarlo Ghinzani to the 1977 Italian crown. He won the 1978 Monaco Formula Three race but had little to shout about in Formula Two. Family backing propelled him into Formula One for 1979 with Shadow. Elio picked up a fourth place at Watkins Glen, but the car was never really competitive. He joined Lotus for 1980 and made the most of the superior equipment to finish second in his second outing, in Brazil. The following year showed consistent points scoring, then in Austria in 1982 he had his first win, by a nose, from Keke Rosberg's Williams. A change to Renault engines scuppered 1983, but 1984 was much better and Elio ended up third overall. A second win was picked up in San Marino in 1985, and he led the title race awhile before falling back to fifth at season's end. Elio moved to Brabham for 1986 and it was while testing at Paul Ricard that he crashed and died.

Career Record

- *108 Grands Prix, 2 wins (Austrian GP 1982, San Marino GP 1985)*
- *No championship title (best result – 3rd overall 1984)*

ANDREA DE CESARIS

Nationality: **Italian**

Born: **1959**

Andrea's passage to Formula One was eased by strong Marlboro connections. However, along the way, he was world karting champion, finished second to Chico Serra in the 1979 British Formula Three series and placed fifth for Ron Dennis's Project Four Formula Two team. Before 1980 was out Andrea made his

Formula One debut with Alfa Romeo. He drove for McLaren in 1981, but was he wild! Indeed, by the season's end, he had scored but one point and junked numerous chassis. If it had not been for his powerful backers his Formula One career would have ended there, particularly if the other drivers had been given a say. He simply scared them all with unpredictable driving. However, Andrea spent 1982 and 1983 with Alfa Romeo. He came third at Monaco in 1982, but he could have won. Lying second going into the final lap behind Didier Pironi, he was gifted the lead when the Ferrari's electrics failed but, cruelly, Andrea had run out of

ELIO DE ANGELIS

Just 20 when he arrived on the Formula One stage, his career peaked with third place in the 1984 championship.

fuel. Andrea led again, at Spa in 1983, but his engine blew, and even though he scored two second places, he was on to pastures new – Ligier – for 1984. Two seasons with the French team produced little, so then Andrea went to Minardi, then Brabham, then Rial, then Dallara, then Jordan, then Tyrrell, Jordan again and finally to Sauber before his Formula One days ended in 1994 with Andrea, the second-most experienced Formula One driver ever, behind Riccardo Patrese. But still with no win ...

Career Record
- 208 Grands Prix, no wins (best result – 2nd, German GP 1983, South African GP 1983)
- No championship title (best result – 8th overall 1983)

EMMANUEL DE GRAFFENRIED
Nationality: **Swiss**
Born: **1914**

"Toulo", or Baron de Graffenried to be correct, was one of the stars in the post-war years, winning the 1949 British Grand Prix in a Maserati. He drove the same car when the World Championship began in 1950, but struggled against his rivals' newer equipment. However, Alfa Romeo gave him a run at the non-championship Geneva Grand Prix and he came second. Alfa signed him for 1951 and he had a best place finish of fifth at the Swiss GP. In 1952 and 1953, he raced

with a Maserati, coming fourth in the 1953 Belgian Grand Prix – his best result. He also won the non-championship Syracuse Grand Prix.

Career Record
- 22 Grands Prix, no wins (best result – 4th, Belgian GP 1953)
- No championship title (best result – 8th overall 1953)

PEDRO DE LA ROSA
Nationality: **Spanish**
Born: **1971**

Pedro endured a lengthy apprenticeship before breaking into Formula One in 1999. Spanish Formula Ford champion in 1990, he moved to Britain in 1991, winning the British and European Formula Renault titles the following year. A strong first year of Formula Three suggested a title bid in 1994, but weak Renault engines ruined that. He dominated Japanese Formula Three in 1995. Moving up to Formula Nippon, he was champion in 1997 and became Jordan's test driver in 1998 before landing a fulltime ride with Arrows in 1999, scoring on his debut. He ran third on two occasions in 2000, but each time mechanical failure led to his retirement.

Career Record
- 33 Grands Prix, no wins (best result – 6th, Australian GP 1999, European GP 2000, German GP 2000)
- No championship title (best result – 16th overall 2000)

PATRICK DEPAILLER

Nationality: **French**

Born: **1944**

Died: **1980**

For years it looked as though this little Frenchman would always be a bridesmaid in Formula One. Then, at the Monaco Grand Prix in 1978, after collecting eight second, frustrating, places, he finally came good to climb the top step on the rostrum. Patrick had a lengthy but muddled schooling in Formula Three and Formula Two that saw him step back down to Formula Three in 1971 and claim the French title. Armed with this, he won the Monaco Formula Three race and was rewarded with two Formula One outings by Tyrrell, finishing seventh at Watkins Glen. However, he spent the rest of the year in Formula Two, and 1973 and 1974, when he won the European title. But 1974 was also his first full season of Formula One. Patrick did well, with second place in Sweden. The next four years were spent with Tyrrell, with points scores aplenty, but only that one win at Monaco to his name. A move to Ligier in 1979 brought another win, in Spain, but then Patrick smashed up his legs in a hang-gliding accident. He joined Alfa Romeo for 1980, but when testing before that year's German Grand Prix, Patrick crashed fatally.

Career Record

■ *95 Grands Prix, 2 wins (Monaco GP 1978, Spanish GP 1979)*

■ *No championship title (best result – 4th overall 1976)*

PEDRO DINIZ

Nationality: **Brazilian**

Born: **1970**

This charming Brazilian will never be allowed to forget that he bought his way into Formula One. Formula Three was followed by two years in Formula 3000 that produced the odd flash of speed. Pedro bought his way into the Forti Corse team when it arrived in Formula One in 1995, then moved to Ligier for 1996, and then on to Arrows in 1997, sometimes outpacing team-mate Damon Hill and pushing Mika Salo hard in 1998. Moving to Sauber in 1999, Pedro was sixth three times, but he failed to score in 2000, making several notable driving mistakes that earned him the scorn of his rivals.

Career Record

■ *99 Grands Prix, no wins (best result – 5th, Luxembourg GP 1997, Belgian GP 1998)*

■ *No championship title (best result-13th overall 1998)*

MARTIN DONNELLY

Nationality: **British**

Born: **1964**

One of the bright lights of the British scene in the 1980s, this Ulsterman was quick both in Formula Ford 2000 and then in Formula Three. Halfway through 1988, he jumped up to Formula 3000, scoring two wins and two second places from four outings for Eddie

Jordan Racing to place third overall. Staying on in Formula 3000 in 1989 was not proving so successful, but Martin took the opportunity to make his Formula One debut in France for Arrows. A full-time ride with Lotus was his reward for 1990 and Martin was doing increasingly well, matching the pace of experienced team-mate Derek Warwick, when he had a huge shunt in qualifying for the Spanish Grand Prix. His car disintegrated and Martin was left in the middle of the track strapped only to his seat. His injuries were horrific but, bit by bit, he fought back to health. To see if he could still do it, he had a test run in a Formula 3000 car, but has since concentrated on managing teams on the British single-seater scene.

Career Record
- 13 Grands Prix, no wins (best result – 7th, Hungarian GP 1990)
- No championship title

MARK DONOHUE
Nationality: **American**
Born: **1937**
Died: **1975**

Mr Successful in American racing, Mark never made the grade in Formula One. His early career was financed by sports car driver, Walt Hansgen, but then Roger Penske signed Mark up. This pair won the TransAm title and the Daytona 24 Hours in 1968 and 1969, then took second place in the 1970 Indy 500, won the TransAm series

again, led the Indy 500 and won an Indycar race. Mark made his Formula One debut in a Penske-entered McLaren in the Canadian Grand Prix, finishing third. He won the Indy 500 in 1972, but was injured by crashing his CanAm Porsche. Using the same turbocharged Porsche, he stormed the 1973 CanAm series, then announced his retirement, but returned when Penske decided to go into Formula One in 1974. The Penske chassis was not a success and it was replaced with a March after Mark had scored one fifth place. He was fifth first time out in the March, but a crash in practice for the Austrian Grand Prix left him unconscious. He apppeared to recover, but died from a brain haemorrhage two days later.

Career Record
- 14 Grands Prix, no wins (best result – 3rd, Canadian GP 1971)
- No championship title (best result –15th overall 1975)

JOHNNY DUMFRIES
Nationality: **British**
Born: **1958**

Johnny tried to pass himself off as a painter and decorator when he started in Formula Ford, certain that if people discovered he was the Marquis of Bute, they would make life hard for him. He won the 1984 British Formula Three title and came third in a close-fought European series. His crack at Formula 3000 with the Onyx team in 1985 was less successful and he quit mid-season. Help was at hand, though, as Ayrton Senna did not want Derek Warwick to join him at Lotus in 1986, convinced that the team could not run cars for two topline drivers. So, amid a furore, Warwick was turned away and Dumfries found himself in Formula One. But he was very much the team's number two, and lost his drive when Lotus signed to use Honda engines in 1987 and a Japanese driver came as part of the deal. A spell in sports cars followed, and he won the 1988 Le Mans 24 Hours for Jaguar.

Career Record
- 15 *Grands Prix, no wins (best result – 5th, Hungarian GP 1986)*
- *No championship title (best result – 13th overall 1986)*

GUY EDWARDS
Nationality: **British**
Born: **1942**

Guy gained a reputation more as a sponsorship-chaser than for his driving. He scored his best results in the European 2-litre sports car series and in Formula 5000. In 1974, he got his break in Formula One with the Embassy Hill team, but it was not a front-runner. In 1976, he came back with a Penthouse-sponsored Hesketh, but found this even further off

the pace and retired to the Aurora British Formula One series in which he had far more success. Since hanging up his helmet he has worked as a sponsorship consultant, linking Silk Cut to the Jaguar sports car team before taking his portfolio to Lotus. However, this was not a success and the team folded at the end of 1994 with massive debts.

Career Record
- 11 *Grands Prix, no wins (best result – 7th, Swedish GP 1974)*
- *No championship title*

VIC ELFORD
Nationality: **British**
Born: **1935**

A winner in rallies, rallycross and sports cars, Vic was no slouch in Formula One machinery. He had a very good year in 1968, for he won the Monte Carlo Rally, the Daytona 24 Hours, the Targa Florio and the Nurburgring 1,000 kms, and he made his Formula One debut, albeit in a Cooper when Coopers were no longer the cars to have. Somehow, he carried one around to a fourth and a fifth place finish. A privately entered McLaren followed for 1969, but Vic hit some debris in the German Grand Prix, crashed and broke his arm, putting his career into a downward spiral. Since 1974 he has run a racing school in the USA.

Career Record
- 13 *Grands Prix, no wins*

(best result – 4th, French GP 1968)

■ *No championship title (best result – 13th overall 1969)*

HARALD ERTL
Nationality: **Austrian**
Born: **1948**
Died: **1982**

This bearded Austrian journalist worked his way through the German Formula Vee, Super Vee and then Formula Three series before turning to touring cars, winning the Tourist Trophy for BMW at Silverstone in 1973. His Formula One break did not come until 1975 when he landed a ride in a privately entered Hesketh. Harald plugged away for the next two seasons with Hesketh and also raced concurrently in Formula Two. Then, in 1978, he changed across to an Ensign, but had little success and elected to race in the radical Group 5 series in Germany. Sadly, Harald lost his life in a light aircraft crash in 1982.

Career Record
■ *18 Grands Prix, no wins (best result – 7th, British GP 1976)*
■ *No championship title*

PHILIPPE ETANCELIN
Nationality: **French**
Born: **1896**
Died: **1981**

"Phi Phi" was another of the over-50s gang who lined up on the grid at Silverstone in 1950 for the first-ever World Championship round. Famed for his back-to-front cloth cap, he had starred for Bugatti in the 1930s and had won the Le Mans 24 Hours for Alfa Romeo in 1934. He raced an aged Lago-Talbot in 1950, yet still scored two fifth place finishes, before retiring from the World Championship in 1952.

Career Record
■ *12 Grands Prix, no wins (best result – 5th, French GP 1950, Italian GP 1950)*
■ *No championship title (best result – 13th overall 1950)*

F

TEO FABI
Nationality: **Italian**
Born: **1955**

European karting champion in 1975, he duly graduated through Formula Three to land a ride in Formula Two for 1979. Despite a mixed season, he was signed to lead the works March squad in 1980, finishing third behind the dominant Tolemans. Set for a move with March to Formula One for 1981, he lost the drive to Derek Daly and so went to the USA and shone in the CanAm sports car series. Teo got his Formula One break in 1982, though, with Toleman. It was a wretched year and he was glad when long-time backer Robin Herd helped him land an Indy Car ride for 1983. Teo claimed pole for the Indy 500 and

notched up four wins. Back in Formula One in 1984, with Brabham, he scored his first points with third place around ths streets of Detroit. His first pole came with Toleman in 1985, at the Nurburgring, but he retired with clutch failure. Indeed, Teo retired most races. Toleman metamorphosed into the Benetton team in 1986, and Teo took two more poles near the end of the year, again without results to match this expertise in qualifying in the wild days of turbocharged engines that would hold together only for a few pumped-up laps. The 1987 season was more successful in terms of gathering points, but it was to be Teo's last in Formula One, as he moved back to Indycars. He chose to drive the Porsche project car. It did not work, so he went sports car racing and won the 1991 world title for Jaguar. Since then he has drifted back to the Indycar scene.

Career Record

■ *64 Grands Prix, no wins (best result – 3rd, US GP East 1984, Austrian GP 1987)*

■ *No championship title (best result – 9th overall 1987)*

LUIGI FAGIOLI
Nationality: Italian
Born: 1898
Died: 1952

One of the top names in Italian racing in the 1930s, Luigi was a race winner for Maserati, Alfa Romeo and then Auto Union. He was almost 52 when the World Championship began in 1950. His maturity helped him collect points aplenty, with four second places, to finish third overall. Being asked in 1951 to hand his car over to Fangio during the French Grand Prix was too much for Luigi and, even though Fangio went on to win the race, he quit Formula One that very instant. A brief career

TEO FABI
A winner on the Indycar scene, expertise in qualifying never materialized into wins for the Italian in Formula One.

in sports cars came to an end in 1952 when he crashed at Monaco and died of his injuries.

Career Record

- 7 Grands Prix, 1 win (French GP 1951, shared with Fangio)
- No championship title (best result – 3rd overall 1950)

JUAN MANUEL FANGIO

Nationality: Argentinian

Born: 1911

Died: 1995

Born in Balcarce, Juan Manuel had his first taste of racing while riding as a mechanic in a car driven by a customer of the garage where he worked. After military service, he opened his own garage and started to drive in the long and hazardous road races that were so popular in Argentina at the time. He was beginning to enjoy success when wartime restrictions intervened. He returned to racing in 1947. The Argentine Automobile Club had bought two Maseratis to be driven against visiting Italian aces Achille Varzi and Luigi Villoresi, and one was entrusted to Juan Manuel who went so well against these overseas stars that he picked up financial support to further his single-seater career. With the backing of the Perón regime and a Maserati, Juan Manuel was sent to Europe and started to win regularly in 1949, gaining a ride with Alfa Romeo for the first World Championship in 1950.

He lost out by the narrowest of margins to team-mate Nino Farina, but became World Champion in 1951. The Tipo 159 Alfa Romeo was by now past its sell-by date, and Juan Manuel moved to Maserati when Alfa Romeo dropped out of Formula One. But he broke his neck in the non-championship Monza Grand Prix, which kept him out of the cockpit until 1952. He returned in 1953 with Maserati, for whom he won the Italian Grand Prix, but Alberto Ascari's Ferrari dominated the season. Juan Manuel won the first two Grands Prix in 1954, but Mercedes poached him to head their team. He then won another four races that year to be champion, before taking a second title in 1955 with four wins. At the end of that season, Mercedes withdrew in the wake of the Le Mans disaster when 80 spectators were killed by an errant car, and Fangio rejoined Ferrari. The championship that year became a race between Juan Manuel, team-mate Peter Collins, and Stirling Moss in a Maserati. At Monza, Collins handed over his car to Fangio after the Argentinian's had failed, guaranteeing the great man a fourth world title. For 1957, Fangio returned to Maserati and won the world title for the fifth time, with four wins. In 1958, Juan Manuel was fourth in his home Grand Prix, endured being kidnapped when in Cuba for a sports car race, and then drove his last race in the French Grand Prix at

Reims, in which he also finished fourth. Then he retired to concentrate on running his garage business, although he was frequently called back to Europe in his role as one of the sport's great ambassadors. Juan Manuel died of kidney failure in 1995.

Career Record

■ 51 Grands Prix, 24 wins (Monaco GP 1950, Belgian GP 1950, French GP 1950, Swiss GP 1951, French GP 1951, shared with Fagioli, Spanish GP 1951, Italian GP 1953, Argentinian GP 1954, Belgian GP 1954, French GP 1954, German GP 1954, Swiss GP 1954, Italian GP 1954, Argentinian GP 1955, Belgian GP 1955, Dutch GP 1955, Italian GP 1955, Argentinian GP 1956, shared with Musso, British

GP 1956, German GP 1956, Argentinian GP 1957, Monaco GP 1957, French GP 1957, German GP 1957)
■ World Champion 1951, 1954, 1955, 1956 and 1957

GIUSEPPE FARINA

Nationality: **Italian**

Born: **1906**

Died: **1966**

"Nino" was the first World Champion, cleaning up for Alfa Romeo in 1950 by winning half of the six races. He started in hill climbs in the early 1930s, but progressed to circuit racing with Maserati and learned from the tutelage of the legendary Tazio Nuvolari. He won the Italian drivers' title in 1937, 1938 and 1939, putting himself into a strong position when the war ended, and was duly rewarded in 1950. A model to other colleagues with his

JUAN MANUEL FANGIO
The Argentine takes the plaudits after wrapping up his fourth world title at the 1956 Italian Grand Prix.

straight-arm driving style, "Nino" could not match team-mate Juan Manuel Fangio's pace in 1951. For 1952 he joined Ferrari, but this was not to produce a race win until the 1953 German Grand Prix as he was overshadowed by Alberto Ascari. Engulfed in flames in a sports car race at the start of 1954, "Nino" was not back in the cockpit until 1955, but he retired mid-season, unable to live with the pain of racing, even though he dosed himself with painkillers. He later dabbled with the Indy 500, but then retired, only to be killed in a road accident.

Career Record
- 33 Grands Prix, 5 wins (British GP 1950, Swiss GP 1950, Italian GP 1950, Belgian GP 1951, German GP 1953)
- World Champion 1950

GIANCARLO FISICHELLA
Nationality: Italian
Born: 1973

Italian Formula Three champion in 1994, when he also won at Monaco, Giancarlo was groomed for stardom by Alfa Romeo in 1995 and 1996 in the International Touring Car Championship. But he also got a crack at Formula One with Minardi. Moving to Jordan for 1997 saw him blossom, and after leading in Germany he came good by finishing second in the Belgian Grand Prix. Although he wanted to stay at Jordan, Benetton had his name

on a contract for the 1998 season and he collected a pair of second places for them. It was more of the same in 1999, with second at Montreal, but again the Benetton team lost ground in the second half of the year. The 2000 season saw him reach the second step on the podium yet again.

Career Record
- 74 Grands Prix, no wins (best result – 2nd, Belgian GP 1997, Monaco GP 1998, Canadian GP 1998, Canadian GP 1999, Brazilian GP 2000)
- No championship title (best result – 6th overall 2000)

CHRISTIAN FITTIPALDI
Nationality: Brazilian
Born: 1971

Son of Wilson Fittipaldi and nephew of Emerson, Christian worked his way up the Brazilian rankings, then raced in British Formula Three in 1990, peaking with victory in the final round, ahead of his team-mate Mika Hakkinen. Christian was Formula 3000 champion at his first attempt with Pacific in 1991. And so he found himself in Formula One in 1992, joining Minardi. He kicked off 1993 with fourth in Brazil, but this form was not repeated and his most famed move was his attempt to pass Pierluigi Martini on the finish line at Monza, with Christian clipping his team-mate's car and flipping before landing on his three remaining wheels. Two more fourth places followed for Footwork in 1994, but Christian became disaffected and moved to Indycars for 1995.

Career Record

■ *40 Grands Prix, no wins (best result – 4th, South African GP 1993, Pacific GP 1994, German GP 1994)*

■ *No championship title (best result – 13th overall 1993)*

EMERSON FITTIPALDI

Nationality: **Brazilian**

Born: **1946**

Few people have ever achieved as much as fast in motor racing as Emerson. Starting on 50cc motorbikes, he followed older brother Wilson into karts and both progressed to cars, racing, of all things, a Renault Gordini. Having trounced the opposition in Brazil, Emerson moved to Europe in 1969. He bought a Formula Ford car and could not stop winning. Racing school proprietor Jim Russell spotted this talent and signed Emerson to race his Formula Three Lotus. He won the Lombank Formula Three title that year and Lotus signed him for its Formula Two team for 1970 and, in mid-season, team boss Colin Chapman hurried Emerson into Formula One, partly to forestall rival team managers from signing him. Emerson won fifth time out, at Watkins Glen, giving Lotus a boost after the death of lead driver, Jochen Rindt, at the previous race. No wins followed in 1971, but Emerson claimed the 1972 title, in so doing becoming the youngest champion ever. Second to Jackie Stewart in 1973, he moved to McLaren and won the 1974 world title, and followed this by being runner-up to Niki Lauda in 1975. In 1976, he left McLaren to join brother Wilson's team, Copersucar. Emerson's brilliance coaxed the car into a top-three position twice in the next five years, but his talents were wast-

EMERSON FITTIPALDI
The 1972 champion starts his title defence with a win on home ground at the 1973 Argentinian Grand Prix. Another world title would come in 1974.

ed in generally inferior equipment and then he called it a day and moved to Indycars, becoming the champion in 1989 for Patrick Racing, having also won the Indianapolis 500. Emerson won the big race again in 1993 for Penske and remains one of the big names Stateside, continuing to outpace drivers half his age, including his nephew Christian.

Career Record
■ 144 Grands Prix, 14 wins (US GP 1970, Spanish GP 1972, Belgian GP 1972, British GP 1972, Austrian GP 1972, Italian GP 1972, Argentinian GP 1973, Brazilian GP 1973, Spanish GP 1973, Brazilian GP 1974, Belgian GP 1974, Canadian GP 1974, Argentinian GP 1975, British GP 1975)
■ World Champion 1972 and 1974

WILSON FITTIPALDI
Nationality: **Brazilian**
Born: **1943**

Wilson may have started racing first, but he was almost immediately overshadowed by his younger brother Emerson. He headed Emerson to Europe, but his foray was not so successful and he did not return there until 1970 to race in Formula Three. Formula Two followed in 1971 and Wilson was into Formula One in 1972 with Brabham. Two seasons yielded two points-scoring drives, and he lost third place in the 1973

Monaco Grand Prix when his car failed to pick up its fuel. And so Wilson quit Formula One in 1974. He was back a year later, though, with his own Brazilian-built car. It was not a success and he retired to run Emerson in the team for the next five years.

Career Record
■ 36 Grands Prix, no wins (best result – 5th, German GP 1973)
■ No championship title (best result – 15th overall 1973)

RON FLOCKHART
Nationality: **British**
Born: **1923**
Died: **1962**

Ron came to prominence on the British scene when he started racing an ERA in the early 1950s. He made his Grand Prix debut at Silverstone in 1954, then came home third in a Connaught in the 1956 Italian Grand Prix. He also won the Le Mans 24 Hours that year, and the next, before landing a full-time ride with BRM in 1959. The results he desired did not materialize and Ron went off to become a pilot. He died in 1962, crashing in Australia while practising for a record attempt on the London to Sydney route.

Career Record
■ 13 Grands Prix, no wins (best result – 3rd, French GP 1956)
■ No championship title (best result – 11th overall 1956)

GEORGE FOLLMER

Nationality: **American**

Born: **1934**

Formula One seemed a long way from George's ambitions during his lengthy spell racing sports cars in the USA. However, at the age of 39, he found himself making his Grand Prix debut, for Shadow. This came in 1973 and he ran the whole season, peaking with third place, second time out, at the Spanish Grand Prix. At the end of the year he returned to the US scene, racing again in the CanAm sportscar series and then winning the 1976 TransAm title.

Career Record

- 12 Grands Prix, no wins (best result – 3rd, Spanish GP 1973)
- No championship title (best result – 13th overall 1973)

HEINZ-HARALD FRENTZEN

Nationality: **German**

Born: **1967**

Heinz-Harald graduated from karting to Formula Ford. He raced in the 1988 GM Euroseries, giving Mika Hakkinen a hard time in the final two races. He was second in the 1989 German Formula Three series, behind Karl Wendlinger, but ahead of Michael Schumacher. A move into sports cars with the Mercedes junior team followed. He drove in Formula 3000 at the same time, but it did not propel him to Formula One, so he went to Japan to race in their Formula 3000 series. Good form saw him land a ride with Sauber for 1994 and he came fourth in the French Grand Prix. Heinz-Harald drove some storming races in 1995 against superior machinery, coming

HEINZ-HARALD FRENTZEN
After a miserable time at Williams in 1997, it all came together for the German when he moved to Jordan and two wins were the reward in 1999.

third at Monza. He replaced Damon Hill at Williams in 1997, winning at Imola, but no wins followed before the end of 1998 and he moved to Jordan for 1999. The results were almost instant as he won at both Magny-Cours and Monza to rank third overall, making his 2000 campaign less satisfactory as he had to settle for a pair of thirds.

Career Record
- *114 Grands Prix, 3 wins (San Marino GP 1997, French GP 1999, Italian GP 1999)*
- *No title (best result – 2nd overall 1997)*

PAUL FRÈRE
Nationality: Belgian
Born: 1917
A motoring journalist who came good, Paul was always eager to retain his training and race for fun. With remarkably little experience beyond racing an MG, he found himself driving an HWM in the 1952 Belgian Grand Prix. And he came fifth ... Paul was in and out of drives in the latter half of the 1950s and thus his second-place finish for Ferrari at Spa in 1956 was the utmost surprise. He also managed to win the Le Mans 24 Hours in 1960.

Career Record
- *11 Grands Prix, no wins (best result – 2nd, Belgian GP 1956)*
- *No championship title (best result – 7th overall 1956)*

BERTRAND GACHOT
Nationality: Belgian
Born: 1962
A cosmopolitan mixture of Belgian, French and Luxembourgeois, Bertrand was the first driver to race under the flag of the European Community. Trained when in karting never to cede a corner to another driver, even if it meant crashing himself, he gained the reputation of being uncompromising. Bertrand was a contemporary of Mark Blundell, Damon Hill and Johnny Herbert in British Formula Ford in the mid-1980s, and he finished as the runner-up to Herbert in the 1987 British Formula Three Championship, before graduating to Formula 3000 and then straight on to Formula One in 1989. Unfortunately, Bernard joined the Moneytron Onyx team and seldom qualified. An even worse year followed in 1990 when he drove the overweight, Subaru-powered Coloni. Salvation came in 1991, from Jordan. And all was going well, including fifth place in Canada, when Bertrand was jailed for spraying CS gas in the face of a London taxi driver. Back with Larrousse in 1992, he struggled through 1994 with Pacific, as a shareholder of the team. He was forced to stand down, however, when funds ran short in 1995, Bertrand still managed an eighth place for the dying Pacific team.

Career Record

■ *42 Grands Prix, no wins (best result – 5th, Canadian GP 1991)*

■ *No championship title (best result – 12th overall 1991)*

HOWDEN GANLEY
Nationality: **New Zealander**
Born: **1941**

Lacking racing opportunities in New Zealand, Howden came to England at the age of 19 and found employment as a mechanic. That was in 1961, and it was not until 1967 that he had earned enough for a real crack at Formula Three. Success was slow in coming, however, and only in 1970 did he enter the limelight by finishing second to Peter Gethin in the Formula 5000 Championship. This helped him land a Formula One ride with BRM for 1971. Points were scored before the end of the year, and Howden stayed with BRM for 1972, albeit with little improvement in form, although he did finish second in the Le Mans 24 Hours. Changing to Frank Williams's young team in 1973 failed to help since the Iso chassis was cerrtainly no world beater, and he quit the sport's top category after two races with March and two non-qualifiying runs with the Japanese Maki chassis in 1974. Howden joined forces with fellow Formula One racer Tim Schenken to form the Tiga (Tim/Ganley) race car manufac-turing company.

Career Record

■ *35 Grands Prix, no wins (best result – 4th, US GP 1971, German GP 1972)*

■ *No championship title (best result – 12th overall 1972)*

BERTRAND GACHOT
His career peaked with fifth place in the 1991 Canadian Grand Prix.

OLIVIER GENDEBIEN
Nationality: **Belgian**
Born: **1924**

Olivier met up with a rally driver while he was working in the Belgian Congo and agreed to try his luck as a co-driver on his return to Europe in the mid-1950s. Their performances led to the offer of a works Ferrari sports car drive, backed up with selected Formula One outings. Amazingly, Olivier placed fifth on his debut, the 1956 Argentinian Grand Prix. By and large, though, such Formula One outings were limited and his success was restricted to sports cars: indeed, he won the Le Mans 24 Hours an incredible four times between 1958 and 1962. It was not until 1960 that he got a fair run, with a Yeoman Credit Cooper. Immediately the results came, with third place in Belgium followed by second in the French Grand Prix. However, after driving for a mixture of teams in 1961, he quit for sports cars.

Career Record
- 14 Grands Prix, no wins (best result – 2nd, French GP 1960)
- No championship title (best result – 6th overall 1960)

PETER GETHIN
Nationality: **British**
Born: **1940**

A hundredth of a second was the advantage Peter had over Ronnie Peterson when he scored his one and only Grand Prix win, at Monza in 1971. It was the blink of an eye, but the moment of a lifetime. Having chosen not to follow his father and become a jockey, Peter served his apprenticeship in club racing instead, starting in 1962 in a Lotus 7. In Formula Three by 1965, he raced in Europe and graduation did not come until 1968. Minor success was achieved, but the formation of Formula 5000 in 1969 gave him the boost he needed in a semi-works McLaren. He won the title, and repeated the feat in 1970. By the time of the second title, though, he had a handful of Grands Prix under his belt, having been seconded into the McLaren line-up after Bruce McLaren's death, scoring once. He failed to score for McLaren in 1971, but changed to BRM and scored his famous win in Italy. He was only to score once more. Peter won the Pau Grand Prix for Formula Two cars and raced on in Formula 5000 until 1977.

Career Record
- 30 Grands Prix, 1 win (Italian GP 1971)
- No championship title (best result – 9th overall 1971)

PIERCARLO GHINZANI
Nationality: **Italian**
Born: **1952**

It was through the clinching of deals that Piercarlo extended his Formula One career from 1981 to 1989 with a points tally of just two... Considering he started in motor racing in

1970, his rise to Formula One was very slow. It took him until 1973 to reach Formula Three. He won the European title in 1977 and moved on to Formula Two. A Formula One ride was clinched in 1981 when he joined Osella, and he stayed with the team until mid-1985 when he crossed over to Toleman, scoring his only points at Dallas (taking fifth place) in 1984. He was back with Osella in 1986; then Ligier, Zakspeed and Osella for a third time followed before he finally called it a day.

Career Record

■ *76 Grands Prix, no wins (best result – 5th, US GP 1984)*

■ *No championship title (best result – 19th overall 1984)*

BRUNO GIACOMELLI

Nationality: **Italian**

Born: **1952**

There was something about Bruno that appealed to both team managers (his speed), the press (his approachability) and fans (he looked so cuddly). He was first seen in Britain in 1976 when he did all he could to stop Rupert Keegan from winning the Formula Three title. March showed faith in him and Bruno raced for Robin Herd's team in 1977 in Formula Two, also making his Formula One debut for McLaren at Monza. McLaren ran Bruno again in 1978, briefly, and then Bruno joined Alfa Romeo, for whom he raced until the end of 1982,

never landing the results to match the speed. A year with Toleman followed, before a six-year lay-off that was interspersed with sports car and Indycar races and then a fruitless bid to qualify the Life in 1990.

Career Record

■ *69 Grands Prix, no wins (best result – 3rd, Caesar's Palace GP 1981)*

■ *No championship title (best result – 15th overall 1981)*

RICHIE GINTHER

Nationality: **American**

Born: **1930**

Died: **1989**

With the exception of Dan Gurney and Phil Hill, Richie was the only American Formula One driver to succeed in the 1960s. He made his name racing a Porsche in the late 1950s. This earned him a works Ferrari sports car contract and brought him to Europe for 1960. He drove in only three Grands Prix that year, scoring each time, peaking with second at Monza. Another second place followed in 1961, at Monaco, and another at the same venue in 1962 when he had joined BRM. Over the next two years he was second five more times, but that win finally came, for Honda, in Mexico in 1965. He quit racing in 1967.

Career Record

■ *52 Grands Prix, 1 win Mexican GP 1965)*

■ *No championship title (best result – 2nd overall 1963)*

IGNAZIO GIUNTI

Nationality: **Italian**
Born: **1941**
Died: **1971**

Ignazio gained his competitive instinct in hill climbs in the mid-1960s and was soon elevated to racing sports cars. He joined the Ferrari Formula One line-up for 1970 alongside Jacky Ickx and Clay Regazzoni. He did enough to stay on for 1971, by finishing fourth at Spa, but he was killed in a freak accident in a sports car race at Buenos Aires when he hit Jean-Pierre Beltoise's stranded Matra.

Career Record

- *4 Grands Prix, no wins (best result – 4th, Belgian GP 1970)*
- *No championship title (best result – 17th overall 1970)*

FROILAN GONZALEZ

Nationality: **Argentinian**
Born: **1922**

The "Pampas Bull", as Froilan was known, was a real character, built more like an all-in wrestler than a jockey. He made his Formula One debut in the Monaco Grand Prix, racing a Maserati for the Scuderia Argentina team in place of compatriot Juan Manuel Fangio who had crossed over to Alfa Romeo. No results came his way in 1950, but 1951 was better, for he joined Ferrari and his exuberant, sideways-is-best style saw him on the rostrum for each of the five races he drove for the team, winning the British Grand Prix. Indeed, this was Ferrari's

first victory in a World Championship Grand Prix. He backed this up by winning the non-championship Pescara Grand Prix, but signed for Maserati for 1952. No wins followed, so he went back to Ferrari in 1954 and again won the British Grand Prix, also winning three non-championship races, the Le Mans 24 Hours and several other sports car races. Indeed, had it not been for Fangio, he would have been World Champion. Thereafter he raced mainly at home and retired to run a garage business.

Career Record

- *26 Grands Prix, 2 wins (British GP 1951, British GP 1954)*
- *No championship title (best result – 2nd overall 1954)*

MASTEN GREGORY

Nationality: **American**
Born: **1932**
Died: **1985**

Family wealth made Masten's progress easy. If he wanted to race a car, he bought it. Having raced sports cars in the mid-1950s with growing confidence, he took the plunge and went to Formula One in 1957 with a Scuderia Centro Sud Maserati, coming third on his debut at Monaco. Finishing in the points each time out, he placed sixth overall. And this was to prove his best year. Racing for Cooper in 1959 as number three to Jack Brabham and Bruce McLaren, Masten came second in the Portuguese Grand Prix, but then he crashed in a sports car race and was injured. Indeed, when Masten came to look for a Formula One ride for 1960, his reputation as a crasher went against him, and this led to him racing Cooper and then Lotus cars for four seasons with little success. He signed off with four races in a privately entered BRM in 1965, but it was in sports cars that he earned his glory, winning the Le Mans 24 Hours in 1965 with Jochen Rindt. Many other wins followed before he retired from racing altogether in 1971.

Career Record
■ *38 Grands Prix, no wins (best result – 2nd, Portuguese GP 1959)*
■ *No championship title (best result – 6th overall 1957)*

OLIVIER GROUILLARD
Nationality: **French**
Born: **1958**

After winning the French Formula Three title in 1984 at his second attempt, with the topline ORECA team, Olivier progressed with the team to Formula 3000 and showed well, but it was to be four years before he scored two wins for the GDBA team and ended up second overall to Roberto Moreno. He thus graduated from motor racing's second division, landing a ride with Ligier for 1989. Fittingly, Olivier scored his first points on home soil, but the next three seasons – spent with Osella, Fondmetal and then Tyrrell – produced nothing.

Nothing, that is, except regular fist shaking from other drivers as he wandered into their path when they were on a flier in qualifying, or obstructed the leaders as they came up to lap him. No one was sad to see Olivier go and try his luck in Indycars.

Career Record
■ *41 Grands Prix, no wins (best result – 6th, French GP 1989)*
■ *No championship title (best result – 26th overall 1989)*

ROBERTO GUERRERO
Nationality: **Colombian**
Born: **1958**

Roberto's arrival in Britain was an immediate hit in Formula Ford in 1978 and he came joint second overall in the 1980 Formula Three series behind Stefan Johansson. Formula Two was not such a hit and, despite winning at Thruxton, Roberto ended up seventh overall in a year dominated by Geoff Lees. However, he had done enough to land a Formula One ride with Ensign for 1982. This was a foot in the door, but a move to the Theodore team for 1983 proved no more successful and so Roberto headed west for Indycars, anxious simply to have a car that stood a chance of winning. Second in the 1984 Indy 500 behind Rick Mears, he won twice in 1987, but then crashed and went into a coma. Although he fought his way back to fitness, his form was never the same. But then, to everyone's delight, this charming individual stuck his car on pole for the Indy 500 in 1992, only to crash on the parade lap.

Career Record
■ *21 Grands Prix, no wins (best result – 8th, German GP 1982)*
■ No *championship title*

MAURICIO GUGELMIN
Nationality: **Brazilian**
Born: **1963**

A friend of Ayrton Senna, Mauricio followed him to Britain. Echoing Ayrton's moves, he drove for West Surrey Racing in Formula Three and won the 1985 title plus the Macau Grand Prix. West Surrey decided to move up to Formula 3000 with Mauricio in 1986, but this proved a disaster. So Mauricio transferred to the works Ralt team in 1987 and won first time out, but dropped to fourth overall by year's end. However, this was enough to earn him a Formula One drive for 1988 with the Leyton House March team. For the next four years Mauricio was synonymous with the team's aquamarine colours. Results were mixed, but highlights included third place in Brazil in 1989 and running second in France behind team-mate Ivan Capelli in 1990 before retiring. Then Capelli fell back to second right at the end. The team folded and so Mauricio moved to the new Jordan team for 1992, but the Yamaha engine was gutless and this sounded the death knell of Mauricio's Formula One career.

He is now an Indycar regular.

Career Record
■ *74 Grands Prix, no wins (best result – 3rd, Brazilian GP 1989)*
■ No *championship title (best result – 13th overall 1988)*

DAN GURNEY
Nationality: **American**
Born: **1931**

To many fans, Dan is the greatest American ever in Formula One, even though statistics tell a different story. What made Dan stand out was that he built his own car – the Eagle – and won in that. A spell in the army in Korea intervened before he bought himself a Triumph TR2 and raced it. Over the next few years the cars became more exotic and Dan more successful, earning an invitation to race in Europe for Ferrari in 1958. He landed a contract to race Formula One for the team in 1959, with Enzo no doubt aware of the sales value of having American attention focused on Ferrari. And so began a long Formula One career, and he kicked off with second place behind team-mate Tony Brooks in the German Grand Prix. However, he moved to BRM for 1960 and then on to Porsche for 1961. With reliability he had only dreamt of at BRM, he finished third overall despite not winning a race. Staying on for 1962, though, he did get to the top step of the rostrum, at the French Grand Prix. Indeed, Rouen was a happy stamping ground for Dan, for his next win came there in 1964, his second year with Brabham. And he rounded out that year with another win, in Mexico. Ironically, both 1963 and 1965 saw him in the points more often, frequently challenging Jim Clark. Then Dan bit the bullet and built his own cars for 1966. The Eagle came good in 1967 with Weslake power in place of Climax, and Dan brought this beautiful car home first in Belgium, but all too often it broke. He won the Le Mans 24 Hours for Ford with AJ Foyt. Success for Dan was later to come outside Formula One, with second in the Indy 500 in 1968 and '69. But on the death of Bruce McLaren, he returned to Formula One with McLaren's team. Then he worked on turning his Indycars and sports cars into winners.

Career Record

■ 86 Grands Prix, 4 wins (French GP 1962, French GP 1964, Mexican GP 1964, Belgian GP 1967)
■ No championship title (best result – 3rd overall 1961)

of Man's Tourist Trophy, Mike moved to four-wheeled sport in 1963 in Formula Junior. He was invited to move to Formula One in 1964, driving a Lotus for Reg Parnell. At the end of 1967 he chose to concentrate on cars, taking part in many sports car events, then winning in Formula 5000 in a car entered by another motorcycling World Champion, John Surtees. Mike returned to Formula One in 1971 with Surtees, finishing fourth at Monza after leading several times. Second place in the 1972 Italian Grand Prix was his best result and his Formula One career was brought to an end when he crashed his McLaren in the 1974 German Grand Prix, breaking a leg. He dabbled with motorcycles until 1979. Then, he and his two children were killed in a road accident in 1981.

Career Record

■ 50 Grands Prix, no wins (best result – 2nd, Italian GP 1972)
■ No championship title (best result – 8th overall 1972)

H

MIKE HAILWOOD
Nationality: **British**
Born: **1941**
Died: **1981**
Best known as a nine-time motorcycle World Champion, and 12-time winner of the Isle

MIKA HAKKINEN
Nationality: **Finnish**
Born: **1968**
After winning the Finnish karting title, Mika bought JJ Lehto's Formula Ford and broke most of his lap records en route to the 1987 Scandinavian title. He then won the GM Euroseries in 1988 and graduated to British Formula Three. He

MIKA HAKKINEN
The "Flying Finn" needed all of his powers of concentration to hold off final-race title challenges in both 1998 and 1999.

ing in Australia, but his recovery was extraordinary and he was a frontrunner in 1996 and 1997 whenever the McLaren was competitive, finally achieving his first win at Jerez after disappointments at Silverstone and the Nurburgring. The 1998 season started with victory in Australia and he then won seven more times to beat arch-rival Michael Schumacher at the final round to clinch the title. He was World Champion again in 1999, but was thwarted in 2000 as Ferrari came on strong and he won just four races for McLaren to be edged into second place by his great rival, Michael Schumacher.

Career Record
- 145 Grands Prix, 18 wins (European GP 1997, Australian GP 1998, Brazilian GP 1998, Spanish GP 1998, Monaco GP 1998, Austrian GP 1998, German GP 1998, Luxembourg GP 1998, Japanese GP 1998, Brazilian GP 1999, Spanish GP 1999, Canadian GP 1999, Hungarian GP 1999, Japanese GP 1999, Spanish GP 2000, Austrian GP 2000, Hungarian GP 2000, Belgian GP 2000)
- World Champion 1998 and 1999

joined West Surrey Racing in 1990 and cleaned up, beating fellow Finn Mika Salo. He jumped direct to Formula One, with Lotus, running with the big names until mechanical gremlins struck. In 1992, he peaked with fourth in Hungary. He was sold a dummy and signed for McLaren for 1993, then Ayrton Senna decided to race after all and Mika was left as test driver. However, he got to drive at the end of the year and outqualified Senna, landing a full-time ride for 1994. This resulted in second in Belgium and five thirds. The mid-winged MP4/10 was a beast in the first part of the 1995 season, and it was only when the MP4/10B arrived that he scored two second-place finishes. He suffered serious head injuries in qualify-

MIKE HAWTHORN
Nationality: British
Born: 1929
Died: 1959
Tall, blond, bullish and never without a cap and bow-tie, this

flamboyant man gave the British public the international success it craved in the 1950s. Being brought up on the spectator banks at Brooklands fired his enthusiasm for racing and so, with his father's assistance, Mike entered the world of competition at the 1950 Brighton speed trials. By 1952 he had graduated to single-seaters and had won his first race in a Formula Two Cooper, even beating a similarly mounted Juan Manuel Fangio later in the day. This was to be the making of Mike, and his Grand Prix debut followed, with fourth place at Spa behind the mighty Ferraris. Then he was third in the British Grand Prix and fourth overall at the year's end. Impressed by this newcomer, Enzo Ferrari offered Mike a works drive for 1953, some-

thing Mike accepted, winning the French Grand Prix as he worked his way to fourth overall again. Third overall was his reward for his performances in 1954, with victory in the Spanish Grand Prix. Mike's racing was then limited by the death of his father, but he bounced back in 1957, again proving to be a front-runner. However, 1958 was the year in which it all came right. He won only once, but consistent scoring gave him the title, making him Britain's first Formula One World Champion. He then retired, only to be killed in a car crash in 1959.

Career Record

■ *45 Grands Prix, 3 wins (French GP 1953, Spanish GP 1954, French GP 1958)*
■ *World Champion 1958*

MIKE HAWTHORN
Second place in the final race meant that he pipped Stirling Moss and Tony Brooks in 1958 to become Britain's first World Champion.

BRIAN HENTON
Nationality: **British**
Born: **1946**

He rose to Formula Three after three years in the junior formulae and won the British title at his second attempt in 1974. Formula Two followed, with three unsuccessful outings for the struggling Lotus team. But then it was back to Formula Two and Brian found himself out of a ride after just one race. He returned to Formula One in 1977 with a privately entered March, but he qualified it just once. So it was back to Formula Two again in 1978, this time with a three-year spell that culminated in Brian beating Toleman team-mate Derek Warwick to the title in 1980. Both moved up to Formula One with Toleman, but that first season was a tough one and Brian qualified the heavy "General Belgrano" just once. Finally, he got a better shot, racing for Arrows in 1982 in place of the injured Marc Surer, then moved across to Tyrrell. He never quite scored and by the middle of 1983 he had retired.

Career Record
■ 19 Grands Prix, no wins
  (best result – 7th, German
  GP 1982)
■ No championship title

JOHNNY HERBERT
Nationality: **British**
Born: **1964**

Karting hotshot Johnny starred in Formula Ford before Eddie Jordan signed him for Formula Three in 1987. Johnny promptly won the British title. He was set for the 1988 Formula 3000 title when he suffered horrendous leg injuries at Brands Hatch on the day he had signed a Benetton Formula One contract. He finished an amazing fourth on his Formula One debut in Brazil, but his shattered heels could not cope with braking on the tighter tracks and he was dropped. His fourth mentor was Peter Collins, who signed him for Lotus for 1990, and there Johnny stayed until 1994. A move to Benetton in 1995 was seen as Johnny's big chance, but the team focused solely on Michael Schumacher. Johnny inherited wins at Silverstone and Monza, though, to end up fourth overall. He raced for Sauber in 1996 and pushed team-mate Heinz-Harald Frentzen, becoming the team's number one for 1997, but a lack of testing slowed the team and Johnny did well to salvage third in Hungary. Joined by Jean Alesi in 1998, he continued to shine despite having little hope of victory, but moved on to Stewart for 1999, scoring a surprise win in a wet/dry race at the Nurburgring. After a farewell season driving for the Jaguar team in 2000, Johnny is now looking to race in ChampCars.

Career Record
■ 162 Grands Prix, 3 wins
  (British GP 1995, Italian GP
  1995, European GP 1999)
■ No championship title (best
  result – 4th overall 1995)

HANS HERRMANN

Nationality: German

Born: 1928

A sports car racer of repute, Hans was elevated to Mercedes' Formula One team in 1954. He was in the points before the year was out, but his 1955 season was interrupted by injuries. When he was fit to return, Mercedes had quit racing and so Hans drove for Maserati, Cooper, BRM, Porsche, Brabham and Lotus in the rest of his career spread thinly between 1957 and 1969. It was in sports cars that he shone in this period, though, signing off with victory at Le Mans in 1970 in a Porsche.

Career Record

- 18 Grands Prix, no wins (best result – 3rd, Swiss GP 1954)
- No championship title (best result – 6th overall 1954)

DAMON HILL

Nationality: British

Born: 1960

Fifteen when father Graham died in a light aircraft crash, Damon didn't take to cars until 1984 when he tried Formula Ford. Formula Three was next and he was third in 1988 behind JJ Lehto and Gary Brabham. Three seasons of Formula 3000 followed, with the second seeing Damon lead race after race before retiring. He made his Formula One debut for Brabham in 1992, but qualified the car just twice. Useful mileage was gained as test driver for Williams and the team signed him for 1993. Robbed of wins in Britain and Germany, he came good in Hungary and followed this with wins in Belgium and Italy to be third overall. Damon was then thrust into the role of team leader on Ayrton Senna's death in 1994 and achieved a morale-boosting win in Spain. The year became fraught with Michael Schumacher's disqualifications and Damon closed the gap by winning four more races. Victory in Japan set the stage for a final-race shoot-out, and Schumacher's chop that took Damon out in Australia was

DAMON HILL

He became the first second generation World Champion in the history of Formula One when he won the title in 1996.

seen the world over. The last thing he wanted was for Schumacher to have equal Renault power in 1995. Despite winning two of the first three races, he won only twice more, to end up second again after several shunts with Schumacher. His dream was realized in 1996, when he started with four wins from the first five races. But, a mid-season dip in fortune and the winning progress of his team-mate, Jacques Villeneuve, saw the title race go to the final round in Japan. There Damon kept his head, controlled the race for his eighth win and took the coveted crown. With all the top seats already filled, he joined Arrows for 1997. The season was going nowhere when Damon led until the final lap in Hungary, salvaging second as his gearbox failed. Wanting more, he headed for Jordan for 1998, and there he turned around a team in trouble into a winning outfit by the 13th race. His second year with Jordan was a poor one, so Damon retired from racing.

Career Record
■ *115 Grands Prix, 22 wins (Hungarian GP 1993, Belgian GP 1993, Italian GP 1993, Spanish GP 1994, British GP 1994, Belgian GP 1994, Italian GP 1994, Portuguese GP 1994, Japanese GP 1994, Argentinian GP 1995, San Marino GP 1995, Hungarian GP 1995, Australian GP 1995, Australian GP 1996, Brazilian GP 1996, Argentinian GP 1996, San Marino GP 1996, Canadian GP 1996, French GP 1996, German GP 1996, Japanese GP 1996, Belgian GP 1998)*
■ *World Champion 1996*

GRAHAM HILL
Nationality: British
Born: 1939
Died: 1975

Born in London, Graham didn't pass his driving test until he was 24. He then attended the racing school at Brands Hatch. Hooked, he gave up his job to work as a mechanic at the racing school, competing in one of the school cars in lieu of payment. Then Hill met Colin Chapman and went to work for him at Lotus. Hill built his own Lotus XI for 1956, when he almost won the *Autosport* club racing series, but suffered a mechanical failure in the final round. He drove a variety of machinery in 1957, but then went back to Chapman as a works Lotus driver in 1958. He made his Grand Prix debut at Monaco, and ran fourth before a wheel fell off. Monaco was, however, to become synonymous with Graham. Throughout a career which spanned 176 Grands Prix – a record at the time – he would win five times around the streets of the Principality, earning himself the "Mr Monaco" title. Graham became disenchanted with the Lotuses' fragility and left for BRM at the end of 1959.

Equipped with a new V8 in 1962, he became a potent force, winning the Dutch, German and Italian Grands Prix to set up a South African finale with Jim Clark. The Scot led, but when the Lotus broke Graham snatched both victory and the title. He was runner-up to Clark, John Surtees and Clark again in 1963, 1964 and 1965. Graham's defeat by Surtees was galling as he'd scored more points than the former motorcyclist, but lost out by a point when dropped scores were taken into consideration. Graham won the Indianapolis 500 in 1966, the year after Jim Clark had ruffled the establishment with a British success. He was tempted back to Lotus in 1967 as team-mate to Clark, who narrowly missed out on the title to Denny Hulme. However, all was not lost as the Lotus 49 with the new Ford Cosworth DFV engine had been a sensation when introduced mid-season, and looked promising for 1968. Clark won the season-opening South African Grand Prix, but was killed in a Formula Two race. His death devastated Chapman, but Graham put the team back on course by winning the Spanish Grand Prix. He fought a three-

GRAHAM HILL
The double World Champion on his way to the first of five wins at Monaco in 1963.

way tussle with Jackie Stewart's Matra and Hulme's McLaren, winning his second world title with victory in the Mexican Grand Prix season finale. Graham was outpaced by new team-mate Jochen Rindt in 1969. Then, at Watkins Glen, he spun and popped his seatbelt. Unable to re-fasten it, he resumed but had a puncture and crashed, and was thrown out, breaking his legs. He returned in 1971 to spend two seasons with Brabham, but was never the same driver again. After racing a Shadow, a Lola and finally a Hill for his Embassy Racing team, Graham vacated the cockpit midway through 1975 to make way for up-and-coming Briton Tony Brise. He had won the Le Mans 24 Hours in 1972 for Matra, partnered by Henri Pescarolo, ensuring himself a place in the record books as the first driver to win the Formula One World Championship, the Indianapolis 500 and the famous French enduro, and now he intended to concentrate on management. But piloting his plane returnng from a test at Paul Ricard, he hit a tree on the approach to Elstree. Brise also died in the crash, along with the team manager, designer and two mechanics.

Career Record

■ *176 Grands Prix, 14 wins (Dutch GP 1962, German GP 1962, Italian GP 1962, South African GP 1962, Monaco GP 1963, US GP 1963, Monaco GP 1964, US GP 1964, Monaco GP 1965,* *US GP 1965, Spanish GP 1968, Monaco GP 1968, Mexican GP 1968, Monaco GP 1969)*
■ *World Champion 1962 and 1968*

PHIL HILL
Nationality: **American**
Born: **1927**

The first American to make much of an impact in Formula One, Phil earned his spurs in sports car races before coming to Europe in 1954 to race at Le Mans. Driving a privately entered Ferrari in the USA in 1955, he went well enough to attract the attention of Enzo Ferrari and was signed up for a number of European races in 1956. He moved to Ferrari's Formula One squad in 1958, being given his first full season in 1959, struggling with one of the old front-engined Ferraris. The first of his three Grand Prix wins came in 1960 at Monza, but 1961 was to be his best season as he took his "Sharknose" Ferrari to two wins which was enough for the title after the death of team-mate Wolfgang von Trips in the penultimate race. He ran with Ferrari again in 1962, but moved on to less successful times at ATS and Cooper before he returned to sports cars. Ill health forced Phil to retire from racing in 1967.

Career Record

■ *48 Grands Prix, 3 wins (Italian GP 1960, Belgian GP 1961, Italian GP 1961)*
■ *World Champion 1961*

DENNY HULME

Nationality: **New Zealander**

Born: **1936**

Died: **1992**

Known as "The Bear" for his taciturn manner and fast temper, Denny was revered by those close to him. He started racing at the age of 20 in 1956, hill climbing an MG TF. Success followed and he quit New Zealand for Europe in 1960 to race in Formula Junior. He went to work at Jack Brabham's garage in 1961, and so started a long relationship with his fellow Antipodean. Denny finished second to Brabham in the 1964 Formula Two series, and he joined his boss's Formula One team for 1965. Two solid seasons were followed by his best-ever year – 1967 – in which he won twice and claimed the World Championship. He joined compatriot Bruce McLaren's team for 1968 and stayed there until he retired from Formula One seven years later, scoring six more wins. During this time Denny also raced with huge success in CanAm sports cars. He returned to racing, only for fun, in the 1990s and died of a heart attack while competing in Australia's famous Bathurst touring car race.

Career Record

- 112 Grands Prix, 8 wins (Monaco GP 1967, German GP 1967, Italian GP 1968, Canadian GP 1968, Mexican GP 1969, South African GP 1972, Swedish GP 1973, Argentinian GP 1974)
- World Champion 1967

JAMES HUNT

Nationality: **British**

Born: **1947**

Died: **1993**

James was tempestuous in his early years, leaving a trail of crashed cars behind him when he raced Minis and then in Formula Three. However, his talent was spotted and the wealthy Lord Hesketh helped

JAMES HUNT
He won five times en route to the 1976 title.

"Hunt the Shunt" into Formula Two and then into Formula One with an off-the-peg March in 1973. James soon rattled the regulars by chasing Ronnie Peterson home for second place in the US Grand Prix. That vital first win came in Holland in 1975 and James resembled a latterday Mike Hawthorn, with the newspapers following his every move, his wooing of beautiful women and his anti-establishment antics. While this irked James, it helped Formula One gain a popular image in Britain. This was rewarded in 1976 when he moved to McLaren, scored six wins and claimed the title amid a downpour in the final race, in Japan. Friend and rival Niki Lauda pulled into the pits and said it was too dangerous to race. James stayed out and clinched the third place he needed to lift the crown. He won three more times, then drove for Wolf in 1979 but became disenchanted, retiring in mid-season. He moved into the commentary box as a perfect foil for Murray Walker. His death, less than a year after Denny Hulme and also from a heart attack, shocked the racing world.

Career Record

■ 92 *Grands Prix, 10 wins (Dutch GP 1975, Spanish GP 1976, French GP 1976, German GP 1976, Dutch GP 1976, Canadian GP 1976, US GP 1976, British GP 1977, US GP 1977, Japanese GP 1977)*

■ *World Champion 1976*

JACKY ICKX
Nationality: **Belgian**
Born: **1945**

Jacky started on motorcycles then turned to saloons in 1965, twice winning the Spa 24 Hours. But he caught the eye of Formula One team boss, Ken Tyrrell, who put him into his Formula Three team. Jacky was fast straight away, but his Matra lacked reliability. Tyrrell promoted him to Formula Two for 1966. He won three races in 1967, even having the audacity to qualify third for the German Grand Prix when pitched in against more powerful Formula One cars. Running fourth in this race before his suspension broke ensured that he was promoted to Formula One for 1968, with Ferrari. He was fourth overall in his first season, winning the French Grand Prix. In 1969 he moved to Brabham and won twice more, also winning the Le Mans 24 Hours, yet there was nothing he could do to keep the title from Jackie Stewart. Back with Ferrari in 1970, he won three times, but was second again. Three more years with Ferrari became ever more frustrating as the Italian cars were no match for the cars from Tyrrell and Lotus. He joined Lotus for 1974, just as that team's fortunes started to slide, and Ferrari's improved. The twilight of his career was spent with Williams, Ensign and Ligier, leaving Jacky to draw satisfaction from his record tally of six wins in the Le Mans 24 Hours. Has since been involved with the modernization of the Spa circuit.

Career Record

- 116 Grands Prix, 8 wins (French GP 1968, German GP 1969, Canadian GP 1969, Austrian GP 1970, Canadian GP 1970, Mexican GP 1970, Dutch GP 1971, German GP 1972)
- No championship title (best result – 2nd overall 1969 and 1970)

TAKI INOUE

Nationality: Japanese

Born: 1963

Blessed with money aplenty, Inoue arrived in Formula One in 1995 with little to show for his years in the junior formulae. Two seasons of Formula 3000 had helped him grow used to the speed, but his form for Arrows was weak and he was all but invisible except when being lapped.

Career Record

- 18 Grands Prix, no wins (best result – 8th, Italian GP 1995)
- No championship title

INNES IRELAND

Nationality: British

Born: 1930

Died: 1993

One of the true characters of British motor racing, Innes was a great party-goer and racon-

teur, and the strictures of contemporary Formula One were an anathema to him. He did not start racing until he was 26 when he bought a Lotus XI sports car. Strong form led to Lotus boss, Colin Chapman, signing Innes for his 1959 Formula One line-up. But the Lotus 16 frequently broke down. In 1960, with the arrival of the Lotus 18, all looked to be going Innes's way in the Argentinian Grand Prix, but his gear linkage broke. Two second places were the best he could manage. It all came good in the last race of 1961 when Innes won at Watkins Glen. But Chapman dropped him from the team to make way for young hot-shot Jim Clark. Innes was furious. He raced a private-

JACKY ICKX

The Belgian found the ultimate accolade a tough nut to crack – he finished runner-up in both 1969 and 1970.

EDDIE IRVINE

The Ulsterman finally landed the No. 1 driver's seat he craved when he joined Jaguar in 2000 after three seasons as Michael Schumacher's No. 2 at Ferrari.

ly entered Lotus in 1962 without much success. Driving for the British Racing Partnership in 1963 and 1964, he had little chance of success in the team's own BRP chassis. His final shot was with a Reg Parnell Racing Lotus in 1965, but this came to nought. Innes died of cancer shortly after taking over the helm of the British Racing Drivers' Club.

Career Record
- *50 Grands Prix, 1 win (US GP 1961)*
- *No championship title (best result – 4th overall 1960)*

EDDIE IRVINE

Nationality: British

Born: 1965

Ayrton Senna took exception to this Ulsterman on his Grand Prix debut in Japan in 1993, punching him for having the audacity to re-pass him after being lapped. So, Eddie had made his mark. British Formula Ford champion in 1987, he shone in Formula Three in 1988 then moved up to Formula 3000 with Pacific in 1989. Signed by Eddie Jordan for 1990, he was third overall, winning at Hockenheim. With no drive in the offing, Eddie raced

and doing next to no testing hurt his chances in his first year with Ferrari in 1996, but it all came good in 1997, with second in Argentina. He was a valuable number two again in 1998, then became a winner in 1999. However, his big chance came when Schumacher broke a leg and he became team leader. Three further wins took him to the final round in front, but Hakkinen won to take the title. Eddie moved to Jaguar for 2000, this time as number one, but the team had a poor year and his best result was fourth place at Monaco.

Career Record

■ *113 Grands Prix, 4 wins (Australian GP 1999, Austrian GP 1999, German GP 1999, Malaysian GP 1999)*

■ *No championship title (best result – 2nd overall 1999)*

sports cars and Formula 3000 in Japan for the next three years, before Jordan asked him to make that Formula One debut at Suzuka, where he came sixth. He was teamed with Rubens Barrichello in 1994, but was involved in a huge accident in the first round that saw him banned for a race. His attitude at the hearing led to this being extended to three races. By 1995, Eddie's "bad boy" reputation was behind him, and although he qualified well, mechanical failures restricted his scoring, but he was third in Canada. Mechanical failures

JEAN-PIERRE JABOUILLE

Nationality: **French**

Born: **1942**

Jean-Pierre earned himself a permanent place in Formula One history when he scored the first victory for a turbocharged car, and the fact that it was at the wheel of a Renault in the French Grand Prix, in 1979, also guaranteed that the occasion was one of nationalistic fervour. That the popular Frenchman should have the honour of taking the first turbo victory was appropriate, for it was he who had had to pilot the hopelessly unreliable Renault turbo in its first steps in Formula One in 1977. After a successful career in Formula Two, he had made his Formula One debut in a one-off drive for Frank Williams in the 1974 French Grand Prix. However, he would only taste success at Renault, for whom he began his full-time Grand Prix career in 1977, after being involved in the turbo car's development from the very beginning. He won one further Grand Prix, in Austria in 1980, before breaking a leg in that year's Canadian race. He returned with Ligier in 1981, but, still not fully fit, he retired after just a few races. Jean-Pierre raced in Peugeot's sports car team in the early 1990s, before being placed in charge of the French manufacturer's motor sport programme.

Career record

■ *49 Grands Prix, 2 wins (French GP 1979, Austrian GP 1980)*

■ *No championship title (best result – 8th overall 1980)*

only when a fuel-metering unit forced him to retire. Similarly, when a chance to revive his career came with Lotus in 1978, he was dominating the Canadian Grand Prix before brake problems intervened. Early in his career he had a reputation for wildness, but he brought himself under control and won the Formula Two title for the works March-BMW team in 1973, two years after he made his Formula One debut, also for March, before moving to Shadow. After 1978 his career began slowly to go downhill. Two years with Tyrrell provided him with no breakthrough and, after a disastrous time with Osella and then Ligier in the early 1980s, Formula One left him behind at the end of 1983. He revived his fortunes in the mid-1990s, racing sports cars.

Career record

■ *134 Grands Prix. No wins (best result – 3rd, Monaco GP 1974, South African GP 1979, British GP 1979)*

■ *No championship title (best result – 10th overall 1979 and 1980)*

JEAN-PIERRE JARIER
Nationality: **French**
Born: **1946**

Jean-Pierre raced in 134 Grands Prix during 1973–83, but despite being both fast and brave, he never won one. He was at his best for the Shadow team in the mid-1970s, and lost the 1975 Brazilian Grand Prix

STEFAN JOHANSSON
Nationality: **Swedish**
Born: **1956**

After winning the British Formula Three Championship in 1980 and being a leading figure in Formula Two in the early 1980s, the genial and popular Swede clearly had Formula One potential, but it was not until

ALAN JONES
The 1980 World Champion started the defence of his title with a win at Long Beach.

mid-1983 that he made his debut with the fledgling Spirit-Honda team. Honda switched its engine to Williams in 1984, and Stefan had to put up with a few guest drives for Tyrrell and Toleman, for whom he looked set to be the number one driver in 1985 before a dispute over tyres left him without a drive. Ferrari provided him with a lifeline, hiring Stefan to replace René Arnoux. The Swede earned two second places in 1985, and impressed enough to be kept on for 1986, when a succession of mechanical problems and bad luck led to him being replaced by Gerhard Berger for 1987. Stefan went to McLaren, but he was outpaced by Alain Prost and dropped for Ayrton Senna for 1988. He moved to Indycars in 1991 and now runs a sports car team in the USA.

Career record

■ 79 *Grands Prix, no wins (best result – 2nd, Canadian GP 1985, US GP 1985,*

Belgian GP 1987, German GP 1987)

■ No *championship title (best result – 5th overall 1986)*

ALAN JONES
Nationality: **Australian**
Born: **1946**

Alan was the driver with whom the Williams team first made its breakthrough into the Formula One front line and the man who won the team its first World Championship. Ever since his father, Stan, raced in Australia in the 1950s, young Alan had decided he wanted to be World Champion. He made his Grand Prix debut in 1975 in a private Hesketh, and soon earned himself a reputation as a hard-trying charger. He scored a fine victory in the 1977 Austrian Grand Prix for Shadow, but it was at Williams where his career really took off. Some excellent showings in 1978 were the precursor to true success in 1979, when he won four Grands Prix in Patrick Head's superb ground-effect FW07, and only early-season unreliability prevented an assault on the World Championship. No such mistakes were made in 1980, though, when five wins helped him storm to a title that he might well have retained in 1981 had it not been for more unreliability. He retired at the end of 1981, made a brief return for Arrows in 1983, and a full-time one with the Haas Lola team in late 1985 and 1986. But the car was poor, and Alan retired from Formula One. He has since raced touring cars and has commentated on Australian television.

Career record

■ 116 Grands Prix, 12 wins (Austrian GP 1977, German GP 1979, Austrian GP 1979, Dutch GP 1979, Canadian GP 1979, Argentinian GP 1980, French GP 1980, British GP 1980, Canadian GP 1980, US East GP 1980, US West GP 1981, Las Vegas GP 1981)

■ World Champion 1980

UKYO KATAYAMA
Nationality: **Japanese**
Born: **1963**

The best Grand Prix driver to come out of Japan, Ukyo looked out of his depth in Formula One, but some stirring drives for Tyrrell in 1994, where he usually had the mea-

sure of his team-mate Mark Blundell, gave the lie to that. Ukyo won junior single-seater titles in Japan in 1983–84 and then came to Europe to race in Formula Renault and Formula Three in 1986 and 1987. He went back to Japan to race in Formula 3000 in 1988, and won the title in 1991. He made his Formula One debut with Larrousse in 1992, and showed well against Bertrand Gachot. A terrible year followed and many thought his tiny physique meant he would never be strong enough to drive a modern Formula One car. But in 1994 it became clear that talent and speed were also allied to his sunny personality. Ukyo had a thin season in 1995, failing to score as Tyrrell struggled to keep up with the richer teams. He also had a huge accident in Portugal. Sadly, 1996 was no better, and he moved on to Minardi for 1997 before quitting at the end of the year to go mountain climbing.

Career record

■ 95 Grands Prix, no wins (best result – 5th, Brazilian GP 1994, San Marino GP 1994)

■ No championship title (best result – 17th overall 1994)

RUPERT KEEGAN
Nationality: **British**
Born: **1955**

Rupert was a fun-loving playboy who also possessed a fair amount of talent. He won the British Formula Three

Championship in 1976 and graduated to Formula One the following year. The Hesketh he drove was one of the worst cars of the year, but to his credit Rupert managed to qualify for every race he entered. A season with the ailing Surtees team in 1978 was less successful, and he had to step back to win the British Formula One series in 1979. His return to Formula One in 1980 with a RAM Williams and briefly in 1982 with March brought little reward.

Career record

■ *25 Grands Prix, no wins (best result – 7th, Austrian GP 1977)*

■ *No championship title*

KARL KLING

Nationality: **German**

Born: **1910**

Karl raced sports cars until the 1950s, when success in Formula Two led to him being invited into the Mercedes sports car and Formula One teams. He won the Carrera Panamericana sports car race in 1952, and briefly drove for Alfa Romeo in 1953, before rejoining Mercedes when it re-entered Formula One in 1954. Kling was overshadowed by Juan Manuel Fangio and slipped back in 1955, when Stirling Moss joined the team. He took up a management position with Mercedes in 1955.

Career record

■ *11 Grands Prix, no wins*

(best result – 2nd, French GP 1954)

■ *No championship title (best result – 5th overall 1954)*

L

JACQUES LAFFITE

Nationality: **French**

Born: **1943**

Jacques' impish sense of humour and irreverence, allied to a considerable talent behind the wheel, brightened the Grand Prix scene for over ten years during the 1970s and 1980s. Having won the French Formula Three and European Formula Two titles in the early 1970s, Jacques made his Grand Prix debut for the Williams

JACQUES LAFFITE
The Frenchman started the 1979 season with victories in both Argentina and Brazil, but ended the season fourth overall.

team in 1974. He and team boss Frank Williams got on well, and Jacques helped keep the team afloat by taking a timely second place in the German Grand Prix in 1975. The following year he joined the new Ligier team and they developed well together, until finally tasting victory in 1977 in Sweden. No more wins followed until 1979 when the team switched from Matra V12 power to a Cosworth V8. Jacques and the JS11 won the first two races of the season, but he didn't win again until mid-1980. A return to Matra power in 1981 saw Jacques take two wins and make a late-season push for the title, but after a dreadful 1982 he left to drive for Williams in 1983. Usually, though, he was overshadowed in the uncompetitive cars by team-mate Keke Rosberg, and he returned to Ligier in 1985. The cars were quick, and Jacques went with them all the way, scoring a number of podium finishes and briefly leading the Detroit Grand Prix in 1986. However, an accident at the British Grand Prix ended his Formula One career.

Career record
■ 176 Grands Prix, 6 wins (Swedish GP 1977, Argentinian GP 1979, Brazilian GP 1979, German GP 1980, Austrian GP 1981, Canadian GP 1981)
■ No championship title (best result – 4th overall 1979, 1980 and 1981)

JAN LAMMERS
Nationality: **Dutch**
Born: **1956**

The diminutive Dutchman progressed through the single-seater ranks in the 1970s, after winning the Dutch Touring Car Championship in 1973, his first year in racing. He won the 1978 European Formula Three Championship, and moved into Formula One in 1979 with the Shadow team, as team-mate to Elio de Angelis. But the cars were uncompetitive, and later spells with ATS, Ensign and Theodore did little to establish him in Formula One. Through the 1980s Jan established himself as a sports car ace. He returned briefly to Grand Prix racing in a March at the end of 1992, but plans for 1993 were thwarted when the financially troubled team was forced to close its doors.

Career record
■ 23 Grands Prix, no wins (best result – 9th, Canadian GP 1979)
■ No championship title

PEDRO LAMY
Nationality: **Portuguese**
Born: **1972**

Pedro is feted in his home country as a sporting superstar, beaming from many a billboard. Fresh from karting, he swept the board in the junior formulae, winning the Formula Vauxhall Euroseries in 1991 while still a fresh-faced teenager, then the German Formula Three title in 1992 before finishing a close runner-up in Formula 3000 in 1993. Substantial backing from Portugal led to Formula One and a few outings in a Lotus at the end of 1993, when he ran close to the pace of highly rated team-mate, Johnny Herbert. A full season would have followed in 1994, but he suffered wing failure testing at Silverstone, flew into an empty spectator area and broke both legs. After a long recovery, Pedro bounced back with Minardi in 1995, scoring his first point in the final race, at Adelaide. The 1996 season was hampered by a lack of power, and he has since raced sports cars and touring cars.

Career record

■ *32 Grands Prix, no wins (best result – 6th, Australian GP 1995)*

■ *No championship title (best result – 17th overall 1995)*

NICOLA LARINI

Nationality: **Italian**

Born: **1964**

Nicola dominated the Italian junior formulae in the mid-1980s, taking the Italian Formula Three title with Coloni in 1986, before moving up to Formula One with the team at the end of 1987. He switched to Osella in 1988–89, when some brilliant drives in weak machinery earned him a seat at Ligier for 1990. Unfortunately, neither this car nor the Lamborghini he drove in 1991 were competitive, and he left Formula One for touring cars in 1992. Nicola won the Italian

title with Alfa Romeo in 1992, and then went on to dominate the highly competitive German Championship in 1993. As the Ferrari Formula One team's test driver he subbed for an injured Jean Alesi in early 1994, finishing second in the ill-fated San Marino Grand Prix, but Alesi's return saw Nicola go back to touring cars. Made Formula One comeback with Sauber in 1997, but was dropped after only five races and returned to racing touring cars.

Career record

■ *49 Grands Prix, no wins (best result – 2nd, San Marino GP 1994)*

■ *No championship title (best result– 14th overall 1994)*

NIKI LAUDA

Nationality: **Austrian**

Born: **1949**

Niki cut his teeth on hill climbs in 1968, with a Mini Cooper and then with a Porsche 908. Progressing to single-seaters in 1969, he raced in Formula Vee and in Formula Three the following season. Then Niki bought a ride with the March Formula Two team in 1971, and needed to be given the "slow" signal to prevent him beating team-mate Ronnie Peterson at Rouen. He made an inauspicious Formula One debut in the Austrian Grand Prix at the Osterreichring, but he was undeterred and bought himself into the March Formula One team for 1972. The car was a lemon and Niki had nothing to

NIKI LAUDA

As he was before the horrific accident at the Nurburgring in 1976.

show for his gamble. However, he was offered the third BRM for 1973 alongside Jean-Pierre Beltoise and Clay Regazzoni. Both were Grand Prix winners, and things looked up when he started to outpace them. He finished fifth in the Belgian Grand Prix at Zolder, and led at Silverstone. Niki led in the rain in Canada and attracted Ferrari's attention, and joined them for 1974. He scored his first win in the Spanish Grand Prix at Jarama, then backed it up with another at Zandvoort. Nine times he started from pole, and he looked favourite to win the title until Brands Hatch when a puncture forced him to pit from the lead. Because of an official's car blocking the pit lane, he was stranded as Jody Scheckter swept to victory. Anxious to make amends at the Nurburgring, he crashed on the opening lap. Then he ran off the road on a patch of oil when leading in Canada, and he ended up fourth overall as Emerson Fittipaldi won the title for McLaren. In 1975, after a winter of testing, a more reliable Niki dominated with a hat-trick of wins in the Monaco, Belgian and Swedish Grands Prix. It looked certain that he would win back-to-back world titles in 1976 as he won four of the first six races. However, he crashed on the first lap of the German Grand Prix at the Nurburgring. Niki was badly burnt and had inhaled poisonous fumes.

Incredibly, he was back, badly scarred, at Monza, where he turned in a heroic drive for fourth place. A late-season run by James Hunt threatened his lead and, in the last race at Fuji, Niki pulled off after a lap in appalling conditions. Hunt went on to finish third to take the title by a point. Ferrari had signed Carlos Reutemann to lead the team in 1977, convinced that Niki would not be the driver he had been. But, with feisty determination, Niki tested furiously and won the third race at Kyalami. Further wins in Holland and Germany gave him his second title. Angered at Ferrari politics, Niki left for Brabham in 1978, but he didn't enjoy much success. However, he did win in Sweden, beating the all-conquering Lotuses with the BT46B "fan car". Niki retired at the end of 1979, but returned in 1982, winning twice for McLaren (at the US West and the British Grands Prix). It was the beginning of the turbo era, and McLaren struggled until it got hold of TAG-Porsche turbos. In 1984, Niki used his craft to beat team-mate Alain Prost. Although Niki finished the year with five wins to Prost's seven, he was a vital half-point ahead for his third world title. Niki's final year was 1985, and he knew he wouldn't be able to hold Prost again. But he won a superb battle with the Frenchman at Zandvoort for his final triumph, and led his last race in Adelaide, too, before retiring. Niki is now an adviser at Ferrari.

Career record

■ *171 Grands Prix, 25 wins (Spanish GP 1974, Dutch GP 1974, Monaco GP 1975, Belgian GP 1975, Swedish GP 1975, French GP 1975, US GP 1975, Brazilian GP 1976, South African GP 1976, Belgian GP 1976, Monaco GP 1976, British GP 1976, South African GP 1977, German GP 1977, Dutch GP 1977, Swedish GP 1978, Italian GP 1978, US West GP 1982, British GP 1982, South African GP 1984, French GP 1984, British GP 1984, Austrian GP 1984, Italian GP 1984, Dutch GP 1985)*

■ *World Champion 1975, 1977 and 1984*

JJ LEHTO

Nationality: Finnish

Born: 1966

Great success was forecast for JJ (real name Jyrki Jarvilehto) who had won the European, Scandinavian and Finnish Formula Ford 1600 titles by 1986. When he came to Britain in 1987 he dominated the national and European Formula Ford 2000 scene before winning the closely fought British Formula Three series in 1988. Formula 3000 was a less fruitful hunting ground, but he established a respected Formula One reputation with drives at Onyx, Dallara and Sauber between 1989 and 1993 before landing a seat at Benetton in 1994. JJ broke his neck in a pre-season testing accident and, though he was close to the pace of his team-mate Michael Schumacher, on his first race back, the deaths of friend Roland Ratzenberger and Ayrton Senna affected him deeply, and when it was clear that his neck still wasn't completely healed Benetton dropped him. He then raced in the German Touring Car Championship in 1995 and 1996, then became the world's top sports car driver when leading McLaren's GT attack against the Mercedes in 1997. After a year in Indycars in 1998, he returned to sports cars with BMW in 1999.

Career record
- 60 Grands Prix, no wins (best result – 3rd, San Marino GP 1991)
- No championship title (best result –12th overall 1991)

STUART LEWIS-EVANS
Nationality: **British**
Born: **1930**
Died: **1958**

The statistics of his career do not add up to much, but that belies a rare and delicate talent. This frail man was a leading exponent of Formula Three for five years before being given his Formula One debut by Connaught at the end of 1956. After showing well in the Connaught early in 1957, he was signed by Vanwall to partner its two stars, Stirling Moss and Tony Brooks. Stuart put in some truly brilliant performances, but in World Championship races, although his flair and finesse were evident, he had only a fifth place at Pescara to show for his efforts by the end of the year. Nevertheless, he won considerable admiration from his teammates, and played a crucial role in helping Vanwall to win the first Constructors' title, in 1958. He appeared on the threshold of a splendid Formula One career, but he crashed heavily in the 1958 Moroccan Grand Prix, and suffered severe burns in the ensuing fire. He died six days later.

Career record
- 14 Grands Prix, no wins (best result – 3rd, Belgian GP 1958, Portuguese GP 1958)
- No championship title (best result – 9th overall 1958)

GUY LIGIER
Nationality: **French**
Born: **1930**

Guy did not start motor racing until he was in his 30s, having previously had a distinguished career in rugby. He had some top-six finishes in Formula Two in 1964 before moving into Formula One in 1966. However, Guy suffered a broken kneecap in mid-season, but returned in 1967, when he replaced his Cooper-Maserati with a more competitive Brabham, and he scored his only point at the Nurburgring. Guy went back to Formula Two in 1968, but after the death of his close friend, Jo Schlesser, he retired, only to return the following year. He started building sports cars in 1970, and that led to a Formula One team being set up in 1976. There have been brief periods when Ligiers have been competitive, but they have generally failed to make the most of their resources. Ligier sold most of his shareholding in the team in 1992–93.

Career record

■ *12 Grands Prix, no wins (best result – 6th, German GP 1967)*

■ *No championship title (best result – 19th overall 1967)*

LELLA LOMBARDI

Nationality: **Italian**

Born: **1943**

Died: **1992**

Lella is the only woman to date to finish in the top six in a Grand Prix, in Spain in 1975. Spells in Formula Monza and Formula Three in Italy led to a Formula 5000 programme in 1974, in which she poked her critics in the eye by finishing fourth in the championship, and that earned her a full season in Formula One in a March in 1975, when she also finished seventh in the German Grand Prix. Lella then dropped out of Formula One, but continued her career in sports cars. She died of cancer in 1992.

Career record

■ *12 Grands Prix, no wins (best result – 6th, Spanish GP 1975)*

■ *No championship title (best result – 21st overall 1975)*

JOHN LOVE

Nationality: **Rhodesian**

Born: **1924**

He never made it in Formula One in Europe. In 1964, however, he won the first of his six South African Formula One titles, and although he regularly raced in the country's World Championship Grand Prix, success eluded him. He came closest during the South African Grand Prix in 1967, when only a precautionary late pit stop for fuel lost him the race.

Career record

■ *9 Grands Prix, no wins (best result – 2nd, South African GP 1967) * No championship title (best result – 11th overall 1967)*

BRETT LUNGER

Nationality: **American**

Born: **1945**

An heir to the wealthy DuPont family, Brett's early racing career was interrupted by a spell in Vietnam in the American army. He resumed in Formula 5000 in 1971, moving up to Formula One in 1975 as James Hunt's team-mate at Hesketh (peaking with tenth in the Austrian Grand Prix). He then switched to Surtees in 1976, and drove a private McLaren in 1977–78, with minimal impact.

Career record

■ *34 Grands Prix, no wins (best result – 7th, Belgian GP 1977)*

■ *No championship title*

M

BRUCE McLAREN

Nationality: **New Zealander**
Born: **1937**
Died: **1970**

A talented driver and the man who established what is now the second most successful Grand Prix team of all time, he arrived on the Formula One scene in 1959 with a series of assured performances with Cooper before winning the final Grand Prix of the year at the US Grand Prix. After winning the first race of 1960, McLaren slipped into a supporting role to reigning champion Jack Brabham, becoming team leader in 1961 when Brabham left. But after several frustrating seasons, which had been briefly enlivened by winning the 1962 Monaco Grand Prix, Bruce formed his own team in 1964. In partnership with abrasive American Teddy Mayer, tolerant, popular McLaren built his company into a successful, professional outfit with a reputation for technical excellence. In 1968, he enticed his friend Denny Hulme, the reigning World Champion, to join and, while Hulme set the pace in Formula One, McLarens dominated the American CanAm sports car series for the rest of the decade. Bruce continued to race in Formula One, and occasionally shone, winning the 1968 Belgian Grand Prix, and dominating the Race of Champions the same year. He developed a reputation for consistency and safety, which made it ironic that he should die while testing one of his CanAm cars at Goodwood in 1970.

BRUCE McLAREN

One of four visits to the victory circle for the Kiwi, at Monaco in 1962.

Career record

- *101 Grands Prix, 4 wins (US GP 1959, Argentinian GP 1960, Monaco GP 1962, Belgian GP 1968)*
- *No championship title (best result – 2nd overall 1960)*

TONY MAGGS
Nationality: **South African**
Born: **1937**

Came to prominence in 1961 when he shared the European Formula Junior title with Jo Schlesser. He was snapped up by Cooper for 1962–63 and, although he came second in the French Grand Prix both years, he was replaced by Phil Hill and moved to drive a BRM for Scuderia Centro Sud. Drove his final Grand Prix in South Africa in 1965, then raced in sports cars until he killed a boy in a crash and quit the sport.

Career record

- *25 Grands Prix, no wins (best result – 2nd, French GP 1962, French GP 1963)*
- *No championship title (best result – 7th overall 1962)*

UMBERTO MAGLIOLI
Nationality: **Italian**
Born: **1928**

An accomplished sports car driver, Umberto only occasionally drove in Grands Prix as a junior driver for Ferrari in the mid-1950s, followed by three races for Maserati in 1956. Leg injuries interrupted his career, but he won the 1959 Sebring 12 Hours, a race he won again in

1964. He also won the 1968 Targa Florio driving a Porsche.

Career record

- *10 Grands Prix, no wins (best result – 3rd, Italian GP 1954, Argentinian GP 1955)*
- *No championship title (best result – 18th overall 1954)*

JAN MAGNUSSEN
Nationality: **Danish**
Born: **1973**

A double World Kart Champion, Jan won the Formula Ford Festival in 1992, then walked away with the 1994 British Formula Three series, with 14 wins in 18 races for Paul Stewart Racing. McLaren signed him as test driver for 1995, while Mercedes fielded him in the International Touring Car series. Jan finished as runner-up to Bernd Schneider. He got his Formula One break when he stood in at McLaren for the 1995 Pacific Grand Prix when Hakkinen had appendicitis. He then raced a Penske in several Indycar races before Jackie Stewart brought him back to Formula One when he signed him for Stewart Grand Prix for 1997, where Jan endured a run of engine failures. With sketchy form in 1998, he was replaced by Jos Verstappen and now races sports cars in the USA.

Career record

- *25 Grand Prix, no wins (best result – 6th, Canadian GP 1998)*
- *No championship title (best result – 15th overall 1998)*

WILLY MAIRESSE

Nationality: **Belgian**

Born: **1928**

Died: **1969**

Willy was famous for his lurid accidents. Ferrari signed him in 1960, and he was in and out of Formula One until he signed up as number two to John Surtees in 1963. He ended his Grand Prix career after crashing out of the German Grand Prix. Raced in sports cars until 1968, when he crashed in a Ford GT40 at Le Mans after a door flew open, and he suffered head injuries. He was ill for a year and, as he realized there was no place for him in racing, killed himself.

Career record

- *12 Grands Prix, no wins (best result – 4th, Italian GP 1962)*
- *No championship title (best result – 14th overall 1962)*

NIGEL MANSELL

Nationality: **British**

Born: **1953**

A successful run in karting and Formula Ford wasn't matched by similar glory in Formula Three and Formula Two, so Nigel had Colin Chapman to thank for giving him his Formula One break with Lotus in the 1980 Austrian Grand Prix. Soaked by petrol leaking into the cockpit, Nigel drove in increasing pain as the fuel burnt his skin. He didn't give up though, and kept going until the engine failed. This was the making of Nigel, his bulldog spirit recognized as a virtue. Gaining a full-time drive with Lotus in 1981, he made progress but did not win over the next four seasons, with his greatest disappointment being crashing out of the lead at Monaco in 1984. A move to Williams in 1985 brought Nigel the success he craved, with victory in the European Grand Prix at Brands Hatch, followed immediately by another in the next race at Kyalami to leave him sixth overall, three positions higher than his previous best ranking. The 1986 season went superbly for Nigel, with five wins, but it ended in tears in the Australian Grand Prix when his left rear tyre exploded at the end of the main straight and he was out of the race, unlucky to have lost the world title, but lucky to be alive. He had a straight fight for the title in 1987 with Williams team-mate Nelson Piquet. Heading for the penultimate race in Japan with six wins under his belt, Nigel was 12 points behind the Brazilian. But he crashed in qualifying and injured his back, which finished his season and left him as runner-up for the second season in a row. The following season was a disaster, Nigel finished only ninth overall because of Williams's uncompetitive Judd engines. Nigel joined Ferrari for 1989, earning the adoration of the Italian fans by winning first time out, in the Brazilian Grand Prix, and he finished the year fourth overall. Alain Prost joined Mansell at Ferrari in 1990, fazing the Englishman, and he won only once, after chopping across

NIGEL MANSELL

After getting so close to the sport's ultimate prize, "Our Nige" feels the years of frustration evaporate after clinching the title at the 1992 Hungarian Grand Prix.

Prost's bows on the run to the first corner at Estoril. This forced Prost to slow and he fell to fifth, losing the world title to Ayrton Senna. So it was back to Williams for 1991. Nigel won five Grands Prix, yet still he had to play second fiddle to Senna's McLaren. However, Nigel got it all right in 1992, winning a record nine Grands Prix to become World Champion. Surprisingly Williams didn't want to retain his services, so Nigel decided to have a shot at Indycars. He joined the Newman/Haas team and amazingly won the opening race of the season, then crashed heavily when he tried a banked oval for the first time. Yet he was back up to speed for the Indianapolis 500. He nearly won that, too, only dropping to third in the closing laps. Three more wins followed, and he scooped the title. But success one year doesn't guarantee it the next, and so it proved in 1994 when Penske cleaned up. Nigel returned to Formula One in mid-season to drive for Williams in four races, signing off by winning the Australian Grand Prix. In 1995, he joined McLaren, but quit after two races and retired. Well, he sort of retired, as he has since been courted for numerous drives – most recently taking part in the Chamonix 24 Hours ice race in 1998 – as touring car teams chase his services.

Career record

■ *185 Grands Prix, 31 wins (European GP 1985, South African GP 1985, Belgian GP 1986, Canadian GP 1986, French GP 1986, British GP 1986, Portuguese GP 1986, San Marino GP 1987, French GP 1987, British GP 1987, Austrian GP 1987, Spanish GP 1987, Mexican GP 1987, Brazilian GP 1989, Hungarian GP 1989, Portuguese GP 1990, French GP 1991, British GP 1991, German GP 1991, Italian GP 1991, Spanish GP 1991, South African GP 1992, Mexican GP 1992, Brazilian GP 1992, Spanish GP 1992, San Marino GP 1992, French GP 1992, British GP 1992, German GP 1992, Portuguese GP 1992, Australian GP 1994)*
■ *World Champion 1992*

ROBERT MANZON

Nationality: **French**

Born: **1917**

He was a mainstay of the Gordini team in the early 1950s, but it was an era dominated by Maserati, Ferrari and then Mercedes. However, there were excellent performances, including third places in the 1952 Belgian Grand Prix and at Reims in 1954.

Career record

■ *28 Grands Prix, no wins (best result – 3rd, Belgian GP 1952, French GP 1954)*
■ *No championship title (best result – 6th overall 1952)*

ONOFRE MARIMON

Nationality: **Argentinian**

Born: **1923**

Died: **1954**

A protégé of Fangio, Onofre joined the works Maserati team in 1953 after showing great promise. He stood in for Fangio in some early-season non-championship races, and when Fangio left to join Mercedes he found himself effectively leading the team. He finished an excellent third in the British Grand Prix, ahead of Fangio, and seemed destined for great things, but he was killed instantly in a crash at the Nurburgring during practice for the German Grand Prix.

Career record

■ *11 Grands Prix, no wins (best result – 3rd, Belgian GP 1953, British GP 1954)*
■ *No championship title (best result – 11th overall 1953)*

PIERLUIGI MARTINI

Nationality: **Italian**

Born: **1961**

Perennially underrated, Pierluigi became a respected member of the Grand Prix fraternity. After winning the European Formula Three title in 1983 and failing to qualify a Toleman at the 1984 Italian Grand Prix, the inexperienced Martini suffered an appalling debut season in Formula One with the uncompetitive Minardi-Motori Moderni team. But a step back to Formula 3000 saw him come back in 1988 a changed man, and in

Formula One in 1989 he was at his best, briefly leading the Portuguese Grand Prix and qualifying an amazing third in Australia. Since then he has been consigned to the midfield, alternating between the Minardi and Scuderia Italia teams. Pierluigi missed the first half of 1993, when dropped by Scuderia Italia, but returned with Minardi, for which he drove until a cash crisis saw him dropped in the middle of 1995, when he seemed to have lost his motivation.

Career record

- *119 Grands Prix, no wins (best result – 4th, San Marino GP 1991, Poruguese GP 1991)*
- *No championship title (best result – 11th overall 1991)*

JOCHEN MASS
Nationality: German
Born: 1946

Jochen graduated to Formula One with Surtees after strong showings in Formula Two. He was an excellent number two to Emerson Fittipaldi at McLaren in 1975, winning the Spanish Grand Prix, but dropped into a subordinate role after James Hunt arrived in 1976, when Mass could not match the Englishman's pace on the track. He moved to ATS in 1978, but broke a leg in a test at Silverstone. He drove for Arrows in 1979–80, had a year off in 1981 and returned for an uncompetitive season with March in 1982, after which he concentrated on sports cars, winning Le Mans for Mercedes in 1989. The following year he acted as tutor to the company's young stars before retiring at the end of 1991.

JOCHEN MASS
The German rounded out his career with March in 1982.

Career record
■ *105 Grands Prix, 1 win (Spanish GP 1975)*
■ *No championship title (best result –7th overall 1975)*

ARTURO MERZARIO
Nationality: **Italian**
Born: **1943**

Little Arturo made his name in sports cars, then joined Ferrari in 1970. By 1972 he had put in enough promising performances to be promoted to the Grand Prix team mid-season. His feistiness served him well through Ferrari's nadir in 1973. It also appealed to Frank Williams, who signed Arturo in 1974. He took a couple of good points finishes, but things did not go well the following year, and he quit mid-season. He drove a works March in 1976, and ran his own private March in 1977 before setting up his own team in 1978. The car, however, was a disaster, which struggled to qualify, and wound up not only his Formula One career, but most of his money.

Career record
■ *57 Grands Prix, no wins (best result – 4th, Brazilian GP 1973, South African GP 1973, Italian GP 1974)*
■ *No championship title (best result – 12th overall 1973)*

JOHN MILES
Nationality: **British**
Born: **1943**

The son of actor Sir Bernard Miles, John began his motor racing career with an extremely successful period in Lotus sports cars during 1966–68. After a brief fling with Formula Two in 1969, he was entrusted by Lotus boss, Colin Chapman, with the development of the four-wheel drive Lotus 63. He became Jochen Rindt's number two in 1970 after Graham Hill broke both his legs in an accident, but as an engineer was nervous of the fragility of the Lotus 72, and was dropped after Rindt's death in the Italian Grand Prix, signalling the end of his Formula One career.

Career record
■ *12 Grands Prix, no wins (best result – 5th, South African GP 1970)*
■ *No championship title (best result – 19th overall 1970)*

STEFANO MODENA
Nationality: **Italian**
Born: **1963**

A splendid year in Formula Three, when he impressed the Grand Prix community in the support race to the Monaco Grand Prix in 1986, marked him as a man to watch, and as he assuredly went about winning the Formula 3000 title at his first attempt in 1987, he seemed set for stardom. But his first three years in Formula One were with back-of-the-grid teams, and it was not until he joined Tyrrell-Honda in 1991 that his ability occasionally showed. However, the car was not as good as expected and, after a splendid performance at Monaco when he qualified second to Ayrton

Senna, and a superb second in the next race, at Montreal, Stefano became dispirited by the car's problems and faded badly. He was signed to drive for Jordan in 1992, but the project dramatically failed to gel, and Stefano's Formula One career came to an end. He has since shone in touring cars where he continues to show the speed people always knew he possessed.

Career record

■ 70 Grands Prix, no wins (best result – 2nd, Canadian GP 1991)

■ No championship title (best result – 8th overall 1991)

ANDREA MONTERMINI
Nationality: **Italian**
Born: **1964**

Chirpy and jockey-sized, Andrea was one of the top names in Italian Formula Three in the late 1980s, finishing second at Monaco in 1989. He flitted in and out of teams in Formula 3000, with 1992 his best year when he won a handful of races. Andrea impressed in several Indycar outings in 1993 before making it to Formula One with Simtek in 1994, but immediately broke his ankles. He returned with Pacific in 1995 and struggled with the machinery. Andrea then moved to Forti Corse and suffered...

Career record

■ 21 Grands Prix, no wins (best result – 8th, German GP 1995)

■ No championship title

GIANNI MORBIDELLI
Nationality: **Italian**
Born: **1968**

Gianni graduated from karts to Formula Three in 1987. A propensity for accidents thwarted him until 1989, when he claimed the crown and earned a testing contract with Ferrari. He made a brief Grand Prix debut in Brazil in 1990 as a stand-in for Emanuele Pirro in a Dallara, and then replaced Paolo Barilla at Minardi for the final two races after a year in Formula 3000. He stayed on at Minardi with Ferrari power in 1991 and, although the car failed to live up to expectations, he impressed enough to be drafted in to replace Alain Prost at the Australian Grand Prix, where he scored a half-point for sixth. An unsuccessful year with Minardi followed, after which Formula One left him behind for a year, and he raced in Italian touring cars before returning to put in some impressive performances with Arrows in 1994. Financial difficulties led to Gianni being dropped mid-1995, but he returned for the last three races and came third at Adelaide, two laps down. Replaced Nicola Larini at Sauber in 1997, but broke his arm and missed three races and then the final one at Suzuka.

Career record

■ 68 Grands Prix, no wins (best result – 3rd, Australian GP 1995)

■ No championship title (best result – 14th overall 1995)

ROBERTO MORENO
Nationality: **Brazilian**
Born: **1959**

Roberto's Formula One career was over almost before it started when he failed to qualify a Lotus at the 1982 Dutch Grand Prix. He was to get another chance, but that race handicapped him for a number of years. After finishing second to team-mate Mike Thackwell in the 1984 European Formula Two Championship, Roberto moved to Indycars. A return to Europe in 1987 saw him race in Formula 3000 and do a handful of Grands Prix for the fledgling AGS team. He stayed in Formula 3000 the following year and won the title impressively. Ferrari awarded him a testing contract and he joined Coloni, and then Eurobrun, before being given his big break at the end of 1990 at Benetton alongside Nelson Piquet and replacing the injured Alessandro Nannini. A second place behind Piquet at the Japanese Grand Prix ensured he was kept on for the following year, but he was kicked out of the team (just after scoring his best result of the year, a fourth at the Belgian Grand Prix), as Benetton snapped up Michael Schumacher. A year with the hapless Andrea Moda outfit in 1992 was far less than he deserved. Roberto then suffered with the hopeless Forti in 1995 (with a best result of 14th, again at the Belgian Grand Prix) and moved to Indycars for 1996, having a real shot at the title in 2000.

Career record
■ *42 Grands Prix, no wins (best result – 2nd, Japanese GP 1990)*
■ *No championship title (best result – 10th overall 1990 and 1991)*

STIRLING MOSS
Nationality: **British**
Born: **1929**

Born into a family steeped in motor sport, Stirling cut his teeth on local hill climbs. He moved on to racing in 1949 and racked up Formula Three wins before signing to drive the HWM Formula Two car in 1950, as well as taking part in every sports car race he was offered a ride in. Even rallying was considered in a quest to further his career, and Moss fin-

ished second on the Monte Carlo Rally in 1952. His Grand Prix outings stood little chance of success between 1951 and 1953, since he was behind the wheel of British cars that had no answer to the superior Italian Alfa Romeos and Maseratis. For 1954, though, Stirling approached Neubauer, boss of the Mercedes team, but he suggested Moss should spend the year showing what he could do in a competitive car, so a Maserati was bought. Third place first time out in the Belgian Grand Prix prompted Neubauer to sign him for Mercedes in 1955 to drive alongside Juan Manuel Fangio, with Stirling taking his first World Championship win when Fangio seemed to let him by in the British Grand Prix at Aintree. They ended the year with Fangio champion and Moss runner-up. But Mercedes withdrew, and he went to Maserati while Fangio joined Ferrari. Stirling won twice, once less than Fangio, and again finished as runner-up to the Argentinian. He drove a Vanwall in 1957, winning three races, but still ended the year behind Fangio. Staying with Vanwall in 1958, he won four times but was runner-up for the fourth year in succession, losing out at the final hurdle when rival Mike Hawthorn scrabbled his way past Ferrari team-mate Phil Hill in the Moroccan Grand Prix to claim the extra point he needed to pip Stirling, the race winner that day. He drove assorted cars, in 1959 and 1960, but was predominantly seen in a

STIRLING MOSS

After finishing as runner-up for four consecutive years (1955–58), he was surely the best driver never to become World Champion.

Cooper, winning twice in 1959. However, Stirling also raced a Lotus and gave the marque its first ever win at Monaco in 1960. He won again later in the year after recovering from leg and back injuries from when he was thrown out of his car while qualifying at Spa-Francorchamps. Formula One changed radically in 1961, with 2.5-litre engines being replaced by 1.5-litre engines. Ferrari was well prepared and its engine was the class of the field. Stirling raced with the less powerful Coventry Climax engine in his Lotus and still managed to win twice on circuits where there were corners aplenty. But his career came to a close in a non-championship meeting at Goodwood in 1962, as he crashed into an earth bank incurring head injuries. A belated dabble with touring cars in the late 1970s has been followed by an increasing number of sorties in historic racing.

Career record

- 66 Grands Prix, 16 wins (British GP 1955, Monaco GP 1956, Italian GP 1956, British GP 1957, shared with Brooks, Pescara GP 1957, Italian GP 1957, Argentinian GP 1958, Dutch GP 1958, Portuguese GP 1958, Moroccan GP 1958, Portuguese GP 1959, Italian GP 1959, Monaco GP 1960, US GP 1960, Monaco GP 1961, German GP 1961)
- No championship title (best result – 2nd overall 1955, 1956, 1957 and 1958)

LUIGI MUSSO

Nationality: Italian

Born: 1924

Died: 1958

Luigi dominated sports car racing in Italy in the early 1950s before buying a Maserati 250F, winning the non-championship Pescara Grand Prix and finishing second in the Spanish Grand Prix in 1954. A string of good results in 1955 saw him join Ferrari for 1956, and he won his first race, the Argentinian Grand Prix, sharing his Lancia-Ferrari with Juan Manuel Fangio. In 1957, he won the non-championship Marne Grand Prix, but was by now struggling to keep pace with team-mates Mike Hawthorn and Peter Collins. Chasing them at Reims, he ran wide on a long, fast corner, and the car flipped in a ditch. The unfortunate Luigi was killed on the spot.

Career record

- 24 Grands Prix, 1 win (Argentinian GP 1956)
- No championship title (best result – 3rd overall 1957)

SATORU NAKAJIMA

Nationality: Japanese

Born: 1953

Japan's first regular Grand Prix driver, Satoru was Honda's representative on the grid in the late 1980s. After a glittering career in Japan, he moved up to

Formula One and was made Ayrton Senna's team-mate at Lotus in 1987, when the team first ran Honda engines. Miles off Senna's pace (although he did come fourth in the British Grand Prix), Satoru ran much closer to Nelson Piquet in the team in 1988, and in 1989 he matched his best Formula One result to date, coming fourth in the torrential rains of Adelaide. Satoru raced for Tyrrell for the next two seasons, before bowing out at the end of 1991 to run teams in both Japanese Formula 3000 and Formula Three.

Career record

■ *74 Grands Prix, no wins (best result – 4th, British GP 1987, Australian GP 1989)*
■ *No championship title (best result – 11th overall 1987)*

SHINJI NAKANO
Nationality: **Japanese**
Born: **1971**

Shinji raced in British Formula Vauxhall in 1990 before moving to Japanese Formula 3000 in 1992, where he peaked with sixth in 1996. Backing from Mugen landed him a Formula One ride with Prost in 1997, and he scored a pair of sixth places before moving to Minardi.

Career record

■ *33 Grands Prix debut, no wins (best result – 6th, Canadian GP 1997, Hungarian GP 1997)*
■ *No championship title (best result – 16th overall 1997)*

ALESSANDRO NANNINI
Nationality: **Italian**
Born: **1959**

His Formula One career was cut short when an arm was severed in a helicopter accident, but microsurgery reattached the limb, and Alessandro became a race-winner in the German Touring series. Given his chance in Formula One with Minardi, he was more than a match for Andrea de Cesaris before joining Benetton in 1988, where he sometimes outpaced Thierry Boutsen. He won in Japan in 1989 when Ayrton Senna was disqualified and, after being outshone by Nelson Piquet, came of age in the second part of 1990. Was pipped by Senna in Germany after a brilliant drive, and lost in Hungary after being elbowed out of the way, again by Senna. But then, after Sandro was third in Spain, came the helicopter crash.

Career record

■ *77 Grands Prix, 1 win (Japanese GP 1989)*
■ *No championship title (best result – 6th overall 1989)*

GUNNAR NILSSON
Nationality: **Swedish**
Born: **1948**
Died: **1978**

After winning the British Formula Three title in 1975, Gunnar was drafted into the Lotus Grand Prix team for 1976. He won the wet 1977 Belgian Grand Prix, but then became increasingly inconsistent. No one knew it at the

GUNNAR NILSSON
The Swede showed great promise in his two years with Lotus, but terminal cancer prevented his move to Arrows for 1978.

time, but Gunnar was suffering from cancer and, although he signed for the fledgling Arrows team in 1978, he was never well enough to drive the car and he died that autumn.

Career record
- *31 Grands Prix, 1 win (Belgian GP 1977)*
- *No championship title (best result – 8th overall 1977)*

JACKIE OLIVER
Nationality: **British**
Born: **1942**

Better known now as the boss

of the Arrows team, Jackie had a distinguished driving career. Success with Lotus in Formula Two ensured that he was in the right place to be drafted into the Grand Prix team when Jim Clark was killed in 1968. Jackie crashed in his first two races, but led the British Grand Prix before his transmission failed and, although he rounded off the season with third place in Mexico, he was dropped in favour of Jochen Rindt for 1970. He joined BRM for a couple of years, scoring two top-six finishes. Jackie returned to Formula One with the new Shadow team in 1973 and finished third in the Canadian Grand Prix at Mosport Park, although many people think he won on a day when lap charts were thrown into confusion by a wet/dry race and the use of a pace car. He drove for Shadow in 1977, but by then was heavily involved in the management of the team, which he quit to set up Arrows in 1978, before going on to sell the team to Tom Walkinshaw in 1996.

Career record
■ 50 Grands Prix, no wins (best result – 3rd, Mexican GP 1968)
■ No championship title (best result – 13th overall 1968)

P

CARLOS PACE
Nationality: Brazilian
Born: 1944
Died: 1977

Having raced for most of the 1960s in Brazil, where his long-time friends and rivals were the Fittipaldi brothers, Carlos came to Britain in 1970. Success in Formula Three and Formula Two led to a drive with Frank Williams's Formula One team in 1972, for whom he showed well against team leader Henri Pescarolo. He left Williams at the end of the year to join Surtees, where some excellent performances were ruined by poor reliability and in mid-1974 he quit. Soon though, he was snapped up by Bernie Ecclestone's Brabham team, and in 1975 he took a fine victory in the Brazilian Grand Prix. Second in the 1977 Argentinian Grand Prix boded well, but he was killed in a light aircraft accident.

Career record
■ 72 Grands Prix, 1 win (Brazilian GP 1975)
■ No championship title (best result – 6th overall 1975)

JONATHAN PALMER
Nationality: British
Born: 1956

After dominating the British Formula Three Championship in 1981 and then Formula Two in 1984, Jonathan drove first for RAM and then Zakspeed in Formula One, although he had shown well in a one-off drive with Williams in the 1983 European Grand Prix where he finished 13th. There then started a three-year liaison with Tyrrell. In his first season, 1987, he won the Jim Clark Cup as best non-turbo driver, but 1988 was a disaster with a poor car. His career was briefly revitalized by the 018 chassis in 1989, only for him to be overshadowed by Jean Alesi in the latter half of the season. After that, Palmer, with some realistic self-appraisal, decided his career was over. He commentated for the BBC then formed his own junior formula for 1998.

Career record
■ 82 Grands Prix, no wins (best result – 4th, Australian GP 1987)
■ No championship title (best result – 11th overall 1987)

OLIVIER PANIS

Nationality: French

Born: 1966

OLIVIER PANIS

The Frenchman's career peaked with a surprise victory in the 1996 Monaco Grand Prix.

Second in the French Formula Three Championship in 1991, before graduating to Formula 3000, Olivier chose the wrong chassis in 1992. But in 1993 he took the title for the DAMS team. His debut Formula One season, with Ligier in 1994, showed admirable consistency, as he finished 15 of the 16 races. His best result was a second in Germany, when half the field was wiped out on lap one. Olivier's second season with Ligier was saved by another second in the Adelaide finale. Against the run of play, Olivier won at Monaco in the wet in 1996. He stayed on when team became Prost in 1997, shining on Bridgestones, but broke his legs in Canada. Two poor seasons followed and he was dropped. Spent 2000 as test driver for McLaren and shone to the extent that he will race for BAR in 2001.

Career record

■ *74 Grands Prix, 1 win (Monaco GP 1996)*

■ *No championship title (best result – 8th overall 1995)*

MASSIMILIANO PAPIS

Nationality: Italian

Born: 1969

"Massi" came to racing from karts. Race-winning form in Formula Three was followed by two years in Formula 3000 that produced just one win, a runaway affair at Barcelona in 1994. He joined Footwork mid-1995 when Gianni Morbidelli's money ran dry and was faster than team-mate Taki Inoue. But, so was everyone. He was dropped before the year was out, but shone in the 1996 Daytona 24 Hour sportscar race in a private Ferrari. He now races in Indycar series.

Career record

■ *7 Grands Prix, no wins (best result – 7th, Italian GP 1995)*

■ *No championship title*

MIKE PARKES

Nationality: **British**

Born: **1931**

Died: **1977**

Elevated to the Ferrari Grand Prix team in 1966 after establishing himself as one of the world's leading sports car drivers, a brief Formula One career followed, in which his best results were second to Ludovico Scarfiotti in the 1966 Italian Grand Prix, and victory in the following year's International Trophy race at Silverstone. But a huge accident in the 1967 Belgian Grand Prix left Mike lying beside his upturned Ferrari with a broken leg. Mike managed teams for Fiat and Lancia in touring cars, and was then involved in the Lancia rally team, when killed in a road crash in 1977.

Career record

- 6 *Grands Prix, no wins (best result – 2nd, French GP 1966, Italian GP 1966)*
- *No championship title (best result – 8th overall 1966)*

REG PARNELL

Nationality: **British**

Born: **1911**

Died: **1964**

Although what would have been the best years of his career were taken away by the Second World War, Reg was one of Britain's most respected professionals. Success in a Maserati in domestic events in the late 1940s meant he was invited to drive for the Maserati works team in 1950. He finished an excellent third in the first World Championship Grand Prix, at Silverstone in a works Alfa Romeo, then drove the "Thinwall Special" Ferrari to a points finish in 1951, after which he raced twice more in British Grands Prix (finishing seventh in 1952), but concentrated on national events around the world.

Career record

- 6 *Grands Prix, no wins (best result – 3rd, British GP 1950)*
- *No championship title (best result – 9th overall 1950)*

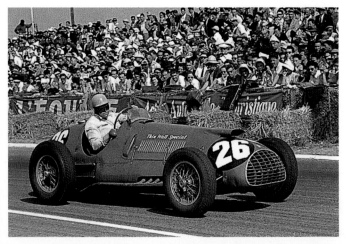

REG PARNELL
Third place in the World Championship's first-ever Grand Prix at Silverstone was his best result.

RICCARDO PATRESE

Nationality: Italian

Born: 1954

Although in the later stages of his career, Riccardo was one of the most popular personalities in Formula One, in his youth he was Grand Prix racing's "enfant terrible". The personality transformation took place over a decade at the beginning of what turned into Formula One's longest career – 256 Grand Prix starts. At the beginning he was quick but unruly and, although he led the South African Grand Prix in 1978 in the new Arrows team's second race, success eluded him until he joined Brabham in 1982, when he won the Monaco Grand Prix. But he made too many mistakes and in 1983 threw away the San Marino Grand Prix, but put in a flawless performance to win in South Africa. In the mid-1980s his career went into a downward spiral, with Alfa Romeo and then Brabham, only for him to be given a chance to revitalize it with Williams in 1988. He forged an excellent working relationship with technical director Patrick Head, and also returned to winning ways, finding a new serenity in simply being lucky enough, as he saw it, to be employed by a top team in a sport he loved. This rejuvenation was never more evident than when Nigel Mansell returned to the team in 1991, and had to play second fiddle to Riccardo through the first half of the season. In 1992, though, Riccardo was pushed into the shadows by Mansell and, after a season at Benetton when he could not match Michael Schumacher's pace, Formula One left him behind. Despite offers to return in 1994, he

RICCARDO PATRESE

The popular Italian drove in more Grands Prix than any other driver.

chose to concentrate on touring cars instead.

Career record

■ 256 Grands Prix, 6 wins (Monaco GP 1982, South African GP 1983, San Marino GP 1990, Mexican GP 1991, Portuguese GP 1991, Japanese GP 1992)

■ No championship title (best result – 2nd overall 1992)

HENRI PESCAROLO
Nationality: **French**
Born: **1942**

Henri was carried into Formula One by Matra on the strength of strong Formula Three, Formula Two and sports car performances, but not before his career had suffered a major setback when a crash at Le Mans in 1969 left him with severe burns. Nevertheless, fully recovered, Henri was drafted into the Matra Formula One team in 1970, and took an excellent third place at Monaco, followed by a fourth place at Silverstone in Frank Williams's March in 1971. Henri dropped out of Formula One and only returned occasionally, before committing to sports car racing full-time at the end of 1976, notching up the fourth of his wins in the Le Mans 24 Hours in 1984.

Career record

■ 57 Grands Prix, no wins (best result – 3rd, Monaco GP 1970)

■ No championship title (best result – 12th overall 1970)

RONNIE PETERSON
Nationality: **Swedish**
Born: **1944**
Died: **1978**

Widely regarded as the fastest driver in the world in the mid-1970s, Ronnie's seat-of-the-pants driving style and astonishing car control won him an army of fans. This gentle man made his Grand Prix debut with the March team in 1970, having scored many successes in Formula Three for the outfit. The following year it became clear that Peterson was a world-class talent when he took four second places, and was runner-up to Jackie Stewart in the World Championship. He would not win a Grand Prix, however, until he left March to join Lotus in 1973, winning the French, Austrian, Italian and US East Grands Prix in the Lotus 72, and finishing third in the World Championship. He dragged the now ageing car to three more victories in 1974, but a dreadful 1975 season with Lotus prompted a switch back to March for the following year, when he took one win, before a lucrative offer to drive Ken Tyrrell's six-wheel P34 in 1977 turned into a disaster. Questions were asked about Ronnie's ability, but he emphatically answered them after returning to Lotus in 1978 as number two to Mario Andretti. Together they dominated the season in the Lotus 79 and, as well as scoring two more superb wins, Ronnie often sat just feet from Andretti's exhausts, his integrity refusing to allow him to break his contract and pass the American. This form was enough to win him an offer to be McLaren's number one driver in 1979, but then tragedy reared its ugly head at the start of the Italian Grand Prix when a multiple shunt left him with serious leg injuries, a bone marrow embolism entered his bloodstream, and the Swede died the following morning, thus depriving Formula One of one of its most electrifying talents.

Career record
- *124 Grands Prix, 10 wins (French GP 1973, Austrian GP 1973, Italian GP 1973, US East GP 1973, Monaco GP 1974, French GP 1974, Italian GP 1974, Italian GP 1976, South African GP 1978, Austrian GP 1978)*
- *No championship title (best result – 2nd overall 1971 and 1978)*

NELSON PIQUET
Nationality: **Brazilian**
Born: **1952**

When Nelson joined Williams in 1986 it became clear that although he was one of Formula One's very top performers, his reputation had to some extent been founded on superior equipment at Brabham. Nelson shot to prominence by winning the British Formula Three title in 1978 and, after a couple of races for McLaren and Ensign that year, the irreverent Brazilian was signed full-time by Brabham for 1979. He was immediately quick, pushing team leader Niki Lauda hard all the time, and when Lauda retired suddenly towards the end of 1979, Nelson became team leader. The following year saw him win three Grands Prix and push Alan Jones for the World Championship, which he clinched the following year, overhauling Carlos Reutemann in the final race at Las Vegas. A switch to BMW turbos by Brabham in 1982 led to a season of unreliability and only one win, but in 1983 he took a second title, this time snatching it from Alain Prost at the final race, after a late-season push from BMW. In the following

years Brabham slowly drifted away from competitiveness, Nelson only taking three wins in two years, and he left at the end of 1985 to earn what he saw as his due at Williams. But a rude shock awaited him there in the form of Nigel Mansell, whom most Formula One observers had expected Piquet to outpace easily. Both Nelson and Mansell lost out on the 1986 world title to Prost, and Nelson was not amused by Williams's refusal to ask Mansell to give way to him, which in his view had allowed Prost to snatch the title. Still, he took a third title in 1987, rely-

ing on consistency and reliability after a heavy accident early in the season. There followed a disastrous two seasons with Lotus, which further damaged Nelson's reputation, although he went some way to repairing it at Benetton in 1990–91, when he won a further three races. Upon Michael Schumacher's arrival in 1991, however, Nelson became surplus to Benetton's requirements and, with no leading Formula One drives available, retired from Grand Prix racing. He entered the Indianapolis 500, but crashed heavily in qualifying, badly damaging his feet. Many

NELSON PIQUET
A long and illustrious career saw the Brazilian lift the world driver's crown three times.

DIDIER PIRONI

Nationality: French

Born: **1952**

Died: **1987**

Motivated by a burning desire to be France's first World Champion, Didier's cold, calculating, approach was disrupted for ever in August 1982 when he crashed with extreme violence in practice for the German Grand Prix, badly breaking both his legs and ending his motor racing career. An impressive debut year with Tyrrell in 1978, when his reputation was bolstered by a win at Le Mans in an Alpine-Renault, followed by marking time the following year, led him to a drive with Ligier in 1980, where he comfortably outpaced team leader Jacques Laffite. Didier scored his first Grand Prix win in Belgium that year and was extremely unlucky not to win in Britain, too, following a superb charge through the field. For 1981 he joined Gilles Villeneuve at Ferrari, and for the first time in his career was unable to get on terms with a team-mate. A sole fourth place was all he could achieve in a year when the brilliant French-Canadian took two wins. Didier was determined that the same fate should not befall him in 1982, when he was at the centre of a tragic sequence of events. He snatched victory against team orders as Villeneuve was cruising to the flag at Imola. Villeneuve was killed at the following race, and now Didier looked set on a course for the world title. He won the Dutch Grand Prix in masterful style, and comfortably

DIDIER PIRONI

The Frenchman was a winner at the 1982 Dutch Grand Prix, but an accident later in the year ended his career.

thought the accident would end his career, but he returned to Indy in 1993.

Career record

- 204 Grands Prix, 23 wins (US West GP 1980, Dutch GP 1980, Italian GP 1980, Argentinian GP 1981, San Marino GP 1981, German GP 1981, Canadian GP 1982, Brazilian GP 1983, Italian GP 1983, European GP 1983, Canadian GP 1984, Detroit GP 1984, French GP 1985, Brazilian GP 1986, German GP 1986, Hungarian GP 1986, Italian GP 1986, German GP 1987, Hungarian GP 1987, Italian GP 1987, Japanese GP 1990, Australian GP 1990, Canadian GP 1991)
- World Champion 1981, 1983 and 1987

led the championship when he arrived in Hockenheim. After the crash came dozens of operations, and although he vowed to return one day, it looked increasingly unlikely. For thrills Didier turned to powerboat racing. The Frenchman's approach had always been uncompromising and when he hit the wake of an oil tanker without easing off the throttle, his boat flipped, and Didier and his two crew members were killed instantly.

Career record
- 70 Grands Prix, 3 wins (Belgian GP 1980, San Marino GP 1982, Dutch GP 1982)
- No championship title (best result – 2nd overall 1982)

EMANUELE PIRRO
Nationality: **Italian**
Born: **1962**

A brilliant touring car driver, Emanuele never quite made the grade in Formula One. After a long apprenticeship in Formulae Three and Two, and then 3000, in all of which he took several victories, he became McLaren's test driver in 1988, before replacing Johnny Herbert at Benetton halfway through 1989. He was dropped at the end of the year, and drove for Dallara for the next two seasons, before going back to touring cars for good.

Career record
- 37 Grands Prix, no wins (best result – 5th, Australian GP 1989)

- No championship title (best result – 18th overall 1991)

ALAIN PROST
Nationality: **French**
Born: **1955**

After winning the 1973 World Karting title, Alain turned to cars. Success followed success and title followed title, in Formule Renault, Formule Super Renault and then Formula Three. There, he dominated the European championship and walked away with the Monaco Formula Three race before he reached Formula One in 1980. Alain then racked up the world-beating tally of 51 Grand Prix wins at an average of almost four points per race in the 199 Grands Prix he started, which is equivalent to third place every time he raced. Apart from Juan Manuel Fangio and Alberto Ascari in the less competitive 1950s, no one else has matched that average. Alain leapt past Formula Two to make his Formula One debut in Argentina. His car, a McLaren, wasn't one of the quick ones of the time, but he outpaced his experienced team-mate, John Watson, and hauled it to an eye-catching sixth place. Fifth place followed in the Brazilian Grand Prix, but then he broke his wrist in the South African Grand Prix. Renault was anxious to sign the best French talent, so Alain joined the team for 1981, fittingly winning the French Grand Prix at Dijon-Prenois. Two more wins followed, in the Dutch and Italian

ALAIN PROST

The Frenchman may have won more Grands Prix as a driver than anyone else, but success as a team owner has proved to be more elusive.

Grands Prix, to leave him fifth overall. In 1982, Alain went one place better. Then, in 1983, he was runner-up by just two points to Nelson Piquet. Fed up with being blamed by the French press for losing to Piquet, he returned to McLaren for 1984. Second overall to team-mate Niki Lauda by half a point at his first attempt, Alain finally, in 1985, gained the world title that he had been threatening for so long to win. He did the same again in 1986, clinching the crown in the famous three-way shoot-out in Adelaide which

Nigel Mansell lost when he had a huge blow-out. Worried the same would happen to him, Piquet pitted for fresh tyres, allowing Alain through to win the race and the title. Three more seasons with McLaren resulted in fourth overall in 1987, second to team-mate Ayrton Senna in 1988 and then first again in 1989. Their mutual antipathy was to rear its head again in 1990 when Alain had moved to Ferrari. Leading into the first corner at Suzuka, Senna clashed with him and became champion, leaving Alain as run-

ner-up. The following year produced no wins, and, disillu-
sioned with his car and with
Ferrari politics, he spoke out
once and was fired, going off to
spend a season as a commentator. Alain returned for a swansong season with Williams in
1993, a year that yielded seven
wins and his fourth world title.
However, news that Senna was
to join him in 1994 saw Alain
tender his resignation. After a
spell as adviser at McLaren, he
took over the Ligier team and
renamed it Prost for 1997.

Career record

■ *201 Grands Prix, 51 wins
(French GP 1981, Dutch GP
1981, Italian GP 1981,
South African GP 1982,
French GP 1983, Belgian GP
1983, British GP 1983,
Austrian GP 1983, Brazilian
GP 1984, San Marino GP
1984, Monaco GP 1984,
German GP 1984, Dutch GP
1984, European GP 1984,
Portuguese GP 1984,
Brazilian GP 1985, San
Marino GP 1985, Monaco
GP 1985, British GP 1985,
Austrian GP 1985, Italian
GP 1985, San Marino GP
1986, Monaco GP 1986,
Austrian GP 1986,
Australian GP 1986,
Brazilian GP 1987, Belgian
GP 1987, Portuguese GP
1987, Brazilian GP 1988,
Monaco GP 1988, Mexican
GP 1988, French GP 1988,
Portuguese GP 1988,
Spanish GP 1988, Australian
GP 1988, US GP 1989,
French GP 1989, British GP*
*1989, Italian GP 1989,
Brazilian GP 1990, Mexican
GP 1990, French GP 1990,
British GP 1990, Spanish GP
1990, South African GP
1993, San Marino GP 1993,
Spanish GP 1993, Canadian
GP 1993, French GP 1993,
British GP 1993, German
GP 1993)*
■ *World Champion 1985,
1986, 1989 and 1993*

TOM PRYCE

Nationality: British

Born: 1949

Died: 1977

Tom moved into Formula One
in 1974 with the Shadow team
after an excellent Formula
Three career, and from the
beginning showed himself to
have great natural pace, putting
the car on the second row of the
grid in only his second race. He
won the non-championship
Race of Champions at Brands
Hatch at the start of 1975, but
it was an up-and-down year,
highlighted by pole at the
British Grand Prix and great
drives in both the German and
Austrian races. Financial troubles blighted 1976, but a new
sponsor provided fresh hope for
1977. Then, in a bizarre accident, Tom hit a marshal who
was crossing the straight just
over a blind brow in the middle
of the South African Grand
Prix. Tom was dead before the
car had come to rest.

Career record

■ *42 Grands Prix, no wins
(best result – 3rd, Austrian*

GP 1975, Brazilian GP 1976)

■ *No championship title (best result – 10th overall 1975)*

DAVID PURLEY

Nationality: **British**

Born: **1945**

Died: **1985**

"Purls" will forever be remembered for his efforts to save the life of Roger Williamson trapped in his burning vehicle in the Dutch Grand Prix of 1973, for which he was awarded the George Medal for his bravery. He had a brief Grand Prix career, starting in 1973, when he hired a private March with little success in terms of results. He then dropped back to a successful Formula Two season in 1974, and then an excellent two years of Formula 5000 before returning to Formula One in 1977, racing his own Lec chassis. He led the Belgian Grand Prix briefly during a sequence of pit stops, but then his front-line racing career ended with a horrific head-on crash into a wall in practice for the British Grand Prix, which he was lucky to survive. Having proved that he had recovered well enough to drive a Formula One car again, he turned to aerobatics to seek his dangerous thrills, and was killed when his Pitts Special crashed off the Sussex coast in 1985.

Career record

■ *7 Grands Prix, no wins (best result – 9th, Italian GP 1973)*

■ *No championship title*

R

HECTOR REBAQUE

Nationality: **Mexican**

Born: **1956**

Hector entered Formula One with a Hesketh in 1977, before fielding Lotus 78s in 1978, with little success. A run of poor results in a Lotus 79 in 1979 led him to commission his own chassis, which appeared only at the last three events of the year. Hector joined Brabham alongside Nelson Piquet in place of Ricardo Zunino for the second half of the season, and benefited from the team's excellent car with a few top-six places in 1981. He raced briefly in Indycars in 1982 before retiring.

Career record

■ *41 Grands Prix, no wins (best result – 4th, San Marino GP 1981, German GP 1981, Dutch GP 1981)*

■ *No championship title (best result – 9th overall 1981)*

BRIAN REDMAN

Nationality: **British**

Born: **1937**

A top-line sports car driver, Brian had a low-key Grand Prix career, which he ended prematurely because he did not like the high-pressure atmosphere in Formula One. Making his debut with a Cooper in 1968, he had to withdraw after three races when he broke his arm in a crash at Spa, but he returned sporadically until 1974, in between a succession of superb performances for Ferrari and Porsche in sports car events, in which he continued to compete until the early 1990s.

Career record
■ *12 Grands Prix, no wins (best result – 3rd, Spanish GP 1968)*
■ *No championship title (best result – 12th overall 1972)*

CLAY REGAZZONI
Nationality: **Swiss**
Born: **1939**

Gianclaudio, also known as Clay, became one of Formula One's most respected performers – and also one of its saddest stories. He made his Grand Prix debut for Ferrari midway through a successful Formula Two season in 1970, and proved himself to be an accomplished driver straightaway.

Not only did he take an excellent fourth place on his debut, in Britain, and follow it with a second place in Austria, but he assured himself of a place forever in the hearts of Ferrari fans when he won the Italian Grand Prix. Clay stayed with the Italian team for another two seasons, before being dropped for 1973, only to return in 1974 alongside Niki Lauda. He proved the perfect foil for the Austrian, coming close to winning the World Championship in 1974, and supporting Lauda ably for another two years, before he was replaced by Carlos Reutemann for 1977. Two years in the comparative wilderness with Ensign and Shadow were followed by a splendid return to the limelight in 1979 with Williams – indeed he gave the team its first Grand Prix win, at Silverstone, before again being replaced by

CLAY REGAZZONI
After a career including five wins, a horrific accident left him partially confined to a wheelchair.

Reutemann and returning to Ensign. However, in his fourth race of 1980, the car's throttle jammed open along the flat-out Shoreline Drive at Long Beach, and he careered down an escape road and into a concrete wall at unabated speed. He suffered severe spinal injuries which have kept him partially confined to a wheelchair ever since. His love of the sport, though, remains, and he is a commentator on Swiss television.

Career record

■ *132 Grands Prix, 5 wins (Italian GP 1971, German GP 1974, Italian GP 1975, US West GP 1976, British GP 1979)*

■ *No championship title (best result – 2nd overall 1974)*

CARLOS REUTEMANN

Nationality: **Argentinian**

Born: **1942**

Carlos was a supremely talented racing driver, who at his best was untouchable, but he could just as easily turn in a performance of overwhelming mediocrity as he could reduce a field of the best drivers in the world to bit players. Never was this more apparent than at the end of 1981 when, poised on the brink of the World Championship and after clinching pole position in brilliant style, he faded badly to eighth place in a race in which he only had to place ahead of Nelson Piquet – who finished the race semi-conscious in fifth place – to take the title. Carlos made a

sensational Formula One debut in 1972, after placing second to Ronnie Peterson in the European Formula Two Trophy in 1971, putting his Brabham on pole position before finishing seventh. The following season saw him establish himself as a consistent top-liner, and he started 1974 in brilliant style, leading the first two races until problems intervened, and winning the third (the South African Grand Prix), before his form tailed off until August, when he recovered to win the Austrian Grand Prix from Denny Hulme in brilliant style. Two more up-and-down seasons followed before he joined Ferrari for 1977,

where he was overshadowed by Niki Lauda (but still won in Brazil), and 1978, when he was back to his best alongside Gilles Villeneuve. Reutemann took four wins that year, only two less than world champion Mario Andretti in the dominant Lotus 79. A switch to Lotus for 1979 proved ill-judged, but the move to Williams in 1980 was not. He ably backed up Alan Jones to the title that first year, before mounting his own challenge in 1981. For most of the year it looked a certainty that he would tie up the championship well before the end of the season, but then came the almost inevitable slump. He returned in 1982, took an excellent second place in the first race, in South Africa, and then quit after the second. He is now a leading figure in Argentinian politics, and since 1991 has been the governor of the country's largest province, Santa Fé.

Career record

- 146 Grands Prix, 12 wins (South African GP 1974, Austrian GP 1974, US GP 1974, German GP 1975, Brazilian GP 1977, Brazilian GP 1978, US West GP 1978, British GP 1978, US East GP 1978, Monaco GP 1980, Brazilian GP 1981, Belgian GP 1981)
- No championship title (best result – 2nd overall 1981)

CARLOS REUTEMANN *Winner of 12 Grands Prix, the Brazilian was never World Champion, but did finish second overall for Williams in 1981.*

PETER REVSON

Nationality: **American**

Born: **1939**

Died: **1974**

After a brief fling with Formula One in 1964, the heir to the Revlon cosmetic fortunes returned to race in sports cars in the USA until good performances in Indycars attracted the attention of the Formula One fraternity. He guested in a Tyrrell at the US Grand Prix in 1971 (retiring on the first lap with a clutch problem) before signing up for Yardley McLaren for the following two years. He soon proved to be a reliable points scorer with a pace that surprised many. When the McLaren M23 came on stream in 1973, he took an excellent first victory in the British Grand Prix, grabbing the initiative in the wet early stages and heading an intense four-car battle (along with Peterson, Hulme and Hunt) towards the end. Another win followed in the confused and wet Canadian race. He left McLaren after he was offered only a third car in 1974 and switched to Shadow. Sadly, however, he was killed in testing for the South African Grand Prix at Kyalami when the front suspension failed and the car collided against the barriers.

Career record

■ 30 Grands Prix, 2 wins (British GP 1973, Canadian GP 1973)

■ No championship title (best result – 5th overall 1972 and 1973)

JOCHEN RINDT

Nationality: **Austrian**

Born: **1941**

Died: **1970**

Jochen's incredible car control enabled him to dominate Formula Two throughout the 1960s, but the Austrian found success in Formula One much harder to come by. He made a brief Grand Prix debut in 1964, before returning full-time in 1965 with Cooper, where he performed with enthusiasm, but little success, until 1967. A move to Brabham looked to be a shrewd one, given that the team had won the last two World Championships, but its new Repco engine was a failure, and he had only two third places to show for two years in the team when he joined Lotus in 1969. After feeling secure with the engineering standards at Brabham, Jochen did not trust Lotus boss Colin Chapman to anything like the same extent, and a broken rear wing, when he was heading for his first victory at Silverstone, did little to bolster his confidence. Nevertheless, the Rindt/Chapman relationship did eventually gel, and he took his first win in the US Grand Prix at the end of 1969. Another win followed in the venerable Lotus 49 at Monaco in 1970, before Chapman unveiled the sleek Lotus 72. The car took Jochen to four consecutive victories in the summer of 1970, but although he was clearly on course for the World Championship, he felt increasingly unsafe after the deaths of

his friends Piers Courage and Bruce McLaren. Tragically, in practice for the Italian Grand Prix at Monza, his fears were realized, and he was killed after crashing under braking for the Parabolica, thus becoming motor racing's only posthumous World Champion.

Career record
■ *60 Grands Prix, 6 wins (US GP 1969, Monaco GP 1970, Dutch GP 1970, French GP 1970, British GP 1970, German GP 1970)*
■ *World Champion 1970*

PEDRO RODRIGUEZ
Nationality: Mexican
Born: **1940**
Died: **1971**

Pedro and his younger brother Ricardo were indulged with high-performance cars from an early age by their wealthy father, and first came to the notice of the European racing fraternity in a Ferrari at Le Mans in 1960, where they almost won. But while Ricardo shot straight into the works Ferrari Formula One team, Pedro's career needed a long time to take off, before he finally got a full-time drive with Cooper in 1967. Thanks to his car's reliability and to heavy attrition he won his first race for the team, switching to BRM in 1968, where his spirited driving lifted the team's morale after the death of Mike Spence at Indianapolis. He had a part-time role in Formula One in 1969, before returning to BRM in 1970, where he took one of the all-time classic victories at Belgium, beating off race-long pressure from Chris Amon's March. This eccentric, who went everywhere with his famous deerstalker hat and a

PEDRO RODRIGUEZ
A leading sports car driver who made it to the top of the podium twice during his Grand Prix career.

bottle of Tabasco sauce for use at the world's finest restaurants, was now at the top of his game. He was acknowledged as a wet weather ace, and had also established himself as the world's leading sports car driver. Halfway through 1971, which looked set to offer Pedro even more success, he accepted an offer to drive in an insignificant Interserie race in Germany. While he was dicing for the lead, a slower car edged him into the wall and his Ferrari burst into flames. The Mexican died shortly after he was extricated from the wreck.

Career record
■ *55 Grands Prix, 2 wins (South African GP 1967, Belgian GP 1970)*
■ *No championship title (best result – 6th overall 1967 and 1968)*

RICARDO RODRIGUEZ
Nationality: Mexican
Born: 1942
Died: 1962
Thought by many to have even more talent than his brother Pedro, Ricardo qualified an astonishing second on the grid at his first Grand Prix, at Monza, when he was just 19 years old. Ferrari signed him for 1962, but he did not drive in every race. Angry that Ferrari did not enter the non-championship Mexican Grand Prix – his home race – Ricardo drove Rob Walker's Lotus instead and, trying to snatch back pole, he went into the Peraltada corner too fast, ran out of road on the exit and was killed.

Career record
■ *5 Grands Prix, no wins (best result – 4th, Belgian GP 1962)*
■ *No championship title (best result – 12th overall 1962)*

KEKE ROSBERG
Nationality: Finnish
Born: 1948
Success in Formula One was a long time coming for this outspoken Finn, and most of his wins came in tricky conditions. He rose to Formula One in 1978 after starring in Formula Two, and won the 1978 International Trophy at Silverstone in streaming conditions. Until 1982, though, when Williams signed him to replace Alan Jones, he was never given top-rate equipment. Keke made the most of his chance, scoring his first Grand Prix win en route to the world title. In 1983, Williams lagged behind the turbo cars, but Keke took an inspired win at Monaco. Though Williams had the Honda turbo in 1984, its FW09 was unable to match the pace of the McLarens, and Keke had to make do with an inspired win at scorching Dallas when most of his rivals had either collapsed with heat exhaustion or crashed out on the crumbling track. By the end of the year he had decided he would retire after a further two years. Two wins followed in 1985 for Williams, and then he switched to

McLaren for his final year, where he was surprised by the pace of team-mate Alain Prost. "I thought I was the fastest driver in the world," he said, "until I came here." There were no wins, but he retired while leading his last race, the Australian Grand Prix. Keke did return to the sport, though, first with Peugeot in sports cars, then with Mercedes, and subsequently with Opel in touring cars.

Career record
- ■ *114 Grands Prix, 5 wins (Swiss GP 1982, Monaco GP 1983, Dallas GP 1984, US GP 1985, Australian GP 1985)*
- ■ *World Champion 1982*

LOUIS ROSIER

Nationality:	**French**
Born:	**1905**
Died:	**1956**

Louis's career was disrupted by

KEKE ROSBERG

The Finn may have won only once in 1982, but it was enough to win the world title.

the Second World War, but he won some non-championship Grands Prix for Talbot. When the first-ever World Championship started in 1950, his Talbot played second fiddle to Alfa Romeo, but Louis picked up some points and won the Le Mans 24 Hours. He also won the 1951 non-championship Dutch and Bordeaux Grands Prix, racing in Ferraris and then Maseratis, until he was killed in a crash at Montlhery.

Career record

- 38 Grands Prix, no wins (best result – 3rd, Swiss GP 1950, Belgian GP 1950)
- No championship title (best result – 4th overall 1950)

RICARDO ROSSET
Nationality: **Brazilian**
Born: **1968**

Ricardo was not thought to be special when he raced in British Formula Three in 1993, but he won a race in 1994, then won first time out in Formula 3000, finishing runner-up to team-mate Vincenzo Sospiri. He moved to Formula One in 1996, but struggled as the number two at Arrows. It got worse in 1997 with Lola pulling out after the first round, and he then struggled with the declining Tyrrell team through 1998.

Career record

- 26 Grands Prix, no wins (best result –8th, Hungarian GP 1996, Canadian GP 1998)
- No championship title

S

LUÍS PÉREZ SALA
Nationality: **Spanish**
Born: **1959**

Success in Formula 3000 was never matched by his form in Formula One. Luís took two wins in F3000 in both 1986 and 1987, was second to Stefano Modena in the championship in the latter year, and looked quite promising when he stepped up to Formula One with Minardi in 1988. But when Pierluigi Martini joined the team he was over-shadowed. He has now turned his attention to racing in the Spanish Touring Car Championship.

Career record

- 26 Grands Prix, no wins (best result – 6th, British GP 1989)
- No championship title (best result – 26th overall 1989)

ELISEO SALAZAR
Nationality: **Chilean**
Born: **1954**

Most famous for being kicked and punched live on television by Nelson Piquet after the two had collided in the 1982 German Grand Prix, Eliseo showed well in Formula Three and the British Formula One series before joining struggling March and then Ensign in 1981. Success did not come any easier with ATS in 1982 when he was overshadowed by team-mate Manfred Winkelhock and, after a few brief appearances with the RAM team in 1983, he was out of a drive. Eliseo moved to race in Indycars in the 1990s.

Career record
- 24 Grands Prix, no wins (best result – 5th, San Marino GP 1982)
- No championship title (best result – 18th overall 1981)

MIKA SALO
Nationality: **Finnish**
Born: **1966**

Like his two compatriots, JJ Lehto and Mika Hakkinen, Mika Salo was European Formula Ford champion. He caught up with Hakkinen in British Formula Three, and the pair jousted for the 1990 crown, with Hakkinen just scraping home. With Formula 3000 teams lining up to sign Salo, he was found guilty of drink-driving, and was effectively banished to Japan, where he stayed until 1994, racing in Formula 3000, when he joined the dying Lotus team for the last two races. He did enough to impress Tyrrell to sign him for the 1995 season and shocked everyone by running third in the opening race. A couple of fifth places in 1995 were repeated in 1996. Talked of as a Ferrari driver in 1997, Mika stayed with Tyrrell, but then moved to Arrows for 1998 and was let down by a weak engine. A stand-in for BAR and Ferrari in 1999, he even handed victory at Hockenheim to Ferrari team-

mate Eddie Irvine. Scored six points for Sauber in 2000 and now heads the Toyota team for 2002.

Career record
- 93 Grands Prix, no wins (best result – 2nd, German GP 1999)
- No championship title (best result – 10th overall 1999)

ROY SALVADORI
Nationality: **British**
Born: **1922**

In a Formula One career spanning ten years, Roy was perpetually overshadowed by his fellow-countrymen. But he was a splendid driver, especially in sports cars, and his finest hour came with a victory in the 1959 Le Mans 24 Hours for Aston Martin. Concentrating on sports cars in the mid-1950s, when he was a member of the factory Aston Martin team, Roy hit the Grand Prix frontline with Cooper in 1957. He then switched to Aston Martin's unsuccessful Grand Prix assault just as Cooper became the team to beat in Formula One. Roy later drove a privately entered Cooper, almost winning the 1961 US Grand Prix, before retiring from Formula One in 1962 and from sports car racing a couple of years later.

Career record
- 47 Grands Prix, no wins (best result – 2nd, German GP 1958)
- No championship title (best result – 4th overall 1958)

LUDOVICO SCARFIOTTI
The Italian had sporadic success with Ferrari that included a home victory at Monza in 1966.

LUDOVICO SCARFIOTTI
Nationality: Italian
Born: 1933
Died: 1968

The nephew of Fiat boss, Gianni Agnelli, Ludovico assured himself of immortality in the annals of Italian motor racing when he won the 1966 Italian Grand Prix for Ferrari. A master at hillclimbs, Ludovico made his Formula One debut in the 1963 Dutch Grand Prix a fortnight after winning Le Mans with Lorenzo Bandini. After sporadic appearances for Ferrari in the next couple of years, Ludovico was expected to appear full-time in 1967 following the Monza win, but was dropped in favour of Chris Amon. But when Bandini was killed and Ferrari team-mate Mike Parkes badly injured, he almost gave up. He returned in 1968 with Cooper, but was killed when he crashed in a hill climb in Germany.

Career record
- *10 Grands Prix, 1 win (Italian GP 1966)*
- *No championship title (best result – 10th overall 1966)*

IAN SCHECKTER
Nationality: South African
Born: 1947

Elder brother of Jody, Ian Scheckter made his Grand Prix debut in the 1974 South African Grand Prix, and competed sporadically until landing a full season with a works Rothmans March in 1977. But it was a disaster and Ian quit at the end of the year. On his return to South Africa he won the Formula Atlantic title twice.

Career record
- 18 Grands Prix, no wins
  (best result – 10th, Dutch GP
  1977)
- No championship title

JODY SCHECKTER
Nationality: **South African**
Born: **1950**

Jody burst on to the Formula One scene amid recriminations and controversy, but retired eight years later a respected elder statesman. In 1971, he raced in Formula Ford in Britain for the first time, and cut such a swathe through it and Formula Three that he was racing in the US Grand Prix car by the end of 1972. But, despite his dazzling progress – he was in the works McLaren team in 1973, and led the French race, in only his third Grand Prix – there were demands that he be banned after he had caused a multiple pile-up that stopped the British Grand Prix two weeks later. Jody moved to Tyrrell for 1974, replacing the retired Jackie Stewart, and began to lose his wildness and his rough edge, taking two wins and third place in the World Championship. The following year was not so successful, but he made the six-wheel P34 a serious proposition in 1976, and again finished third in the title race. He risked switching to the new Wolf team in 1977, but it paid off with three victories and a runner-up spot in the World Championship. However, after a poor year in 1978, he moved to Ferrari with the express intention of becoming World Champion. He shrugged off the shock of being beaten by team-mate Gilles Villeneuve in the new 312T4's first two races, and knuckled down to a season of consistency and reliability – and three victories. And, although Villeneuve was often quicker than Jody, it was Jody's regular scoring that ensured a narrow victory in the World Championship, secured by a triumph at Monza with Villeneuve dutifully trailing him. With the title under his belt, 1980 was a disaster. The new Ferrari 312T5 was hopelessly off the pace and Jody, bemused and demoralized, decided to retire, safe, at the end of the season. He now watches over the career of his son Tomas.

Career record
- 112 Grands Prix, 10 wins
  (Swedish GP 1974, British
  GP 1974, South African GP
  1975, Swedish GP 1976,
  Argentinian GP 1977,
  Monaco GP 1977, Canadian
  GP 1977, Belgian GP 1979,
  Monaco GP 1979, Italian
  GP 1979)
- World Champion 1979

HARRY SCHELL
Nationality: **American**
Born: **1921**
Died: **1960**

Harry began to make his mark in Formula One in 1953 when he joined the Gordini team, and was even more impressive in 1954, driving for Maserati. He was employed by both Vanwall

JODY SCHECKTER
Consistent points-scoring brought him and Ferrari the world title in 1979.

and Maserati in 1955 and gave the first showing of Vanwall's potential in 1956 when he snapped at the heels of the Ferraris in the French Grand Prix. Harry was employed as support for Juan Manuel Fangio at Maserati in 1957, before moving to BRM in 1958, taking a career-best second place in the Dutch Grand Prix. He was driving a private Cooper when he crashed and died in the wet in practice for the Silverstone International Trophy in 1960.

Career record

- 56 Grands Prix, no wins (best result – 2nd, Dutch GP 1958)
- No championship title (best result – 5th overall 1958)

TIM SCHENKEN
Nationality: **Australian**
Born: **1942**

After a successful career in the junior categories, Tim was signed to partner Graham Hill at Brabham in 1971, and overshadowed the former World Champion for most of the year. A move to Surtees in 1972 proved to be a mistake and ended his chances of landing a top Formula One drive. He drove the uncompetitive Trojan in 1974 before concentrating on sports cars and retired in 1977. He then formed a company for building racing cars with racer Howden Ganley.

Career record

- 34 Grands Prix, no wins (best result – 3rd, Austrian

GP 1971)
■ No *championship title (14th overall 1971)*

MICHAEL SCHUMACHER
Nationality: **German**
Born: **1969**

Michael exploded into Formula One in Belgium in 1991 after serving a brilliant apprenticeship in Formula Three and qualified seventh, way ahead of Jordan team leader, Andrea de Cesaris. Following a bitter legal battle, he switched to Benetton for the next race. In his first full season, 1992, his Benetton was outpaced by the Williams, but he proved that not only was he blindingly quick – like when taking second place to Nigel Mansell in the soaking Spanish Grand Prix – he was consistent as well. He visited the podium no fewer than eight times, including victory in the wet/dry Belgian Grand Prix. He continued in the same vein in 1993. Although Williams, this time with Alain Prost, was once again the class of the field, Prost was occasionally overshadowed by Ayrton Senna in a McLaren, which had the same Ford engine as Michael's Benetton. The German took a superb victory in Portugal. At the beginning of 1994, Michael and Benetton surprised everyone by proving faster than Senna and his Williams and, after Senna's death, Michael looked to be unassailable as he headed to his first world title. But he and Benetton were almost swamped by allegations of cheating, with disqualifications and bans, and Michael beat Damon Hill to the title by a single point after a controversial collision in the final race in Australia. Michael then stormed to the 1995 title, picking up nine wins in his now Renault-powered Benetton. Consistent speed, aided by superior fitness and ace race tactics helped him to beat Coulthard and Hill when their Williams looked quicker. He accepted a huge fee to move to Ferrari for 1996 and dragged his car to three wins it didn't deserve. He managed five more wins in 1997 and lost out at the final round when he drove into Villeneuve. Despite winning in Argentina, Michael couldn't match the McLarens at the start of 1998, but bounced back to win five

more times to take the title race to the final round where he stalled and had to start from the back, handing the title to Hakkinen. A broken leg at Silverstone ruined his 1999 season, but Michael bounced back to win nine times in 2000 and finally gave Ferrari the drivers' title it had been chasing since 1980.

Career record

- 145 Grands Prix, 44 wins (Belgian GP 1992, Portuguese GP 1993, Brazilian GP 1994, Pacific GP 1994, San Marino GP 1994, Monaco GP 1994, Canadian GP 1994, French GP 1994, Hungarian GP 1994, European GP 1994, Brazilian GP 1995, Spanish GP 1995, Monaco GP 1995, French GP 1995, German GP 1995, Belgian GP 1995, European GP 1995, Pacific GP 1995, Japanese GP 1995, Spanish GP 1996, Belgian GP 1996, Italian GP 1996, Monaco GP 1997, Canadian GP 1997, French GP 1997, Belgian GP 1997, Japanese GP 1997, Argentinian GP 1998, Canadian GP 1998, French GP 1998, British GP 1998, Hungarian GP 1998, Italian GP 1998, San Marino GP 1999, Monaco GP 1999, Australian GP 2000, Brazilian GP 2000, San Marino GP 2000, European GP 2000, Canadian GP 2000, Italian GP 2000, US GP 2000, Japanese GP 2000, Malaysian GP 2000)
- World Champion 1994, 1995 and 2000

RALF SCHUMACHER

Nationality: German

Born: 1975

Ralf progressed quickly to Formula Three and his first win helped him to third overall in 1994 behind Jorg Muller and Alex Wurz. Second to Norberto Fontana in 1995, they met again in Japanese Formula 3000 in 1996, and Ralf took the title inthe final round, even though he crashed out. He joined Jordan for 1997 and showed raw speed, but upset the team by knocking team-mate Fisichella out of second in Argentina en route to third. He raced for Jordan in 1998 and peaked with second behind team-mate Damon Hill in Belgium before moving to Williams for 1999. New-found maturity shone through as he scored 11 times in 16 races, peaking with second at Monza. He went even better in 2000, ranking fifth overall, but was given a scare by pace of rookie team-mate, Jenson Button.

Career record

- 66 *Grands Prix, no wins (best result – 2nd, Italian GP 1999, Belgian GP 1998)*
- *No championship title (best result – 5th overall 2000)*

AYRTON SENNA

Nationality: Brazilian

Born: 1960

Died: 1994

Ayrton was a natural talent who won kart races from the moment he started competing at 13. He was Brazilian champion as soon as he was old enough to race in the senior category, lifting the South American titles both in 1977 and 1978. When he came to Britain to race in Formula Ford 1600 in 1981, it took him only until his third race to notch up his first win. He won the 1982 British and European Formula Ford 2000 titles, and then it was up to Formula Three for 1983, winning the final round against Martin Brundle to claim the title and the Formula One tests with McLaren and Williams that came with it. Both teams were impressed, but neither signed Ayrton, leaving him to settle for a ride with Toleman for 1984. In an instant he was going faster than people had expected, and a move to Lotus for 1985 brought his first win, in treacherously wet conditions in the Portuguese Grand Prix. Another win followed in the Belgian Grand Prix and Ayrton ended up fourth overall. He won twice more in 1986 to finish fourth overall again. Then, at Monaco in 1987, Ayrton scored his fifth win, one that was special, and it started his love affair with the circuit. He was to win there on five more occasions. A further win helped him to third overall, but his rate of progress was insufficient, so he joined McLaren in 1988. Eight wins and the title were Ayrton's reward. Second overall behind team-mate Alain Prost in 1989 was followed by his second and third World Championship titles in 1990 and 1991, when he took pole position almost by right.

MICHAEL SCHUMACHER

The German won first time out in Brazil in 1994 on his way to the first of three World Championships.

AYRTON SENNA
Sometimes controversial, often brilliant, his death at the San Marino GP in 1994 shocked the world.

Ayrton may have been handicapped by his equipment in the following years, but he always gave his all. Few will forget his opening lap in the wet of the 1993 Grand Prix of Europe at Donington Park. For 1994, he became part of what many saw as the ultimate partnership with Williams and Renault engines. On pole for the first two races, he failed to score. Then came Imola. Ayrton was in front after a restart and he was being pressured by Michael Schumacher. Starting the second lap, his Williams speared right at Tamburello and hit the wall. A broken suspension part pierced

his helmet and the sport lost its greatest-ever exponent.

Career record

- 161 Grands Prix, 41 wins (Portuguese GP 1985, Belgian GP 1985, Spanish GP 1986, US GP 1986, Monaco GP 1987, US GP 1987, San Marino GP 1988, Canadian GP 1988, US GP 1988, British GP 1988, German GP 1988, Hungarian GP 1988, Belgian GP 1988, Japanese GP 1988, San Marino GP 1989, Monaco GP 1989, Mexican GP 1989, German GP 1989, Belgian GP 1989, Spanish

GP 1989, US GP 1990, Monaco GP 1990, *Canadian GP 1990, German GP 1990, Belgian GP 1990, Italian GP 1990, US GP 1991, Brazilian GP 1991, San Marino GP 1991, Monaco GP 1991, Hungarian GP 1991, Belgian GP 1991, Australian GP 1991, Monaco GP 1992, Hungarian GP 1992, Italian GP 1992, Brazilian GP 1993, European GP 1993, Monaco GP 1993, Japanese GP 1993, Australian GP 1993)*

- *World Champion 1988, 1990 and 1991*

JOHNNY SERVOZ-GAVIN

Nationality: **French**

Born: **1942**

After proving wild in Formula Two, he was given a Formula One break in 1968 when an accident to Jackie Stewart saw him drafted into Ken Tyrrell's Matra team at Monaco. He qualified second and led, before thumping a barrier on the first lap. Returning for Monza, he came second, and was kept on by Matra for 1969, winning the Formula Two title. He was signed as Stewart's team-mate for Tyrrell for 1970, but after failing to qualify at Monaco he retired, citing an eye injury from a road accident.

Career record

- *12 Grands Prix, no wins (best result – 2nd, Italian GP 1968)*
- *No championship title (best result – 13th overall 1968)*

JO SIFFERT

Nationality: **Swiss**

Born: **1936**

Died: **1971**

Jo began his Formula One career in 1962, but despite picking up several top-six finishes, success eluded him until 1968. The reason for this change of fortune was that, in his second year with Rob Walker's team, he had front-line equipment in the form of a Lotus 49. Jo duly won the British Grand Prix and was made an offer to join Ferrari for 1970. However, Porsche, for whom he raced in sports cars, was determined to hang on to him and paid for a season in a works March. This proved a disaster and he was delighted to join BRM alongside Pedro Rodriguez for 1971. After Rodriguez was killed in mid-summer, Jo buoyed the team's spirits with a superb win in Austria, only to die in a non-championship race at Brands Hatch.

Career record

- *96 Grands Prix, 2 wins (British GP 1968, Austrian GP 1971)*
- *No championship title (best result – 4th overall 1971)*

RAYMOND SOMMER

Nationality: **French**

Born: **1906**

Died: **1950**

Raymond was a key figure of the inter-war period of racing, especially in sports cars, winning Le Mans in 1931–32, first with Luigi Chinetti and then with the legendary Tazio Nuvolari. Eschewing driving for teams in Formula One because of the constraints they put on him, Raymond delighted in taking on the mighty Ferrari and Mercedes teams and beating them as often as possible. After the war he consolidated his reputation for no-holds-barred racing with an excellent fourth place at Monaco in 1950 in a Formula Two Ferrari, before being killed in a non-championship race at Cadours towards the end of the year.

Career record
- 5 Grands Prix, no wins (best result – 4th, Monaco GP 1950)
- No championship title (best result – 13th overall 1950)

MIKE SPENCE
Nationality: **British**
Born: **1936**
Died: **1968**

Mike began his Formula One career as Jim Clark's team-mate at Lotus and, although he was overshadowed by the great Scot, often ran competitively in his two years at Lotus peaking with third place in Mexico in 1965. Mike switched to a semi-works BRM drive in 1966, before being promoted to the full works team in 1967, under the shadow of another great Scot, Jackie Stewart. That year he also raced the radical Chaparral sports car with some success. After competitive showings in non-championship races early in 1968, he seemed

on the threshold of Grand Prix success, but died of head injuries following a crash at Indianapolis where, ironically, he was replacing Clark, who had been killed the previous month in a Formula Two race at Hockenheim.

Career record
- 36 Grands Prix, no wins (best result – 3rd, Mexican GP 1965)
- No championship title (best result – 8th overall 1965)

JACKIE STEWART
Nationality: **British**
Born: **1939**

Jackie was close to becoming a top-line marksman when he failed to qualify to represent Britain in the 1960 Olympic Games. Perhaps it was the disappointment of this that spurred him to follow his older brother, Jimmy, into racing. Whatever the reason, his early races with the Ecurie Ecosse team demonstrated that he was a bit special at the wheel. Ken Tyrrell spotted him and placed him in his Formula Three car. Wins soon followed, and he was pressed to sign for Lotus for 1965, but opted not to line up alongside established compatriot Jim Clark and joined BRM instead. Jackie then triumphed in only his eighth outing – the Italian Grand Prix – finishing the year third overall behind Clark and BRM teammate, Graham Hill. Still with BRM, Jackie kicked off his 1966 campaign in the best pos-

JACKIE STEWART
Three-time World Champion and team owner, the Scot fought hard to change the safety of the sport.

sible style, winning at Monaco. But the BRM was not to prove as competitive again as the Brabham team took control. Jackie did not win another race until the Dutch Grand Prix in 1968, by which time he was reunited with Tyrrell, driving a Matra to two further wins. Their second year was even more successful, with Jackie winning six races and the title. Then, in 1970, the Matra was replaced by a March, but Jackie could not live with Jochen Rindt's Lotus or the Ferraris. Tyrrell fielded Jackie and team-mate François Cevert in a self-built chassis in 1971 and Jackie went on to win six times. The following year yielded four more, but he was beaten to the title by Lotus driver Emerson Fittipaldi. Then, in 1973, he'd won five races when he reached the American Grand Prix, but Cevert crashed fatally in qualifying, and Jackie elected to hang up his helmet with immediate effect. His record tally of 27 Grand Prix wins from 99 starts was to stand until it was overhauled by Prost in the 1987 Portuguese Grand Prix, his 118th Grand Prix. Jackie has increased his input into the sport since his retirement. He combined forces in 1997 with elder son Paul – who had run a highly successful team in Formula 3000 and Formula Three – to enter the Stewart

Grand Prix team in Formula One with Ford power and drivers Rubens Barrichello and Jan Magnussen.

Career record

- 99 *Grands Prix, 27 wins (Italian GP 1965, Monaco GP 1966, Dutch GP 1968, German GP 1968, US GP 1968, South African GP 1969, Spanish GP 1969, Dutch GP 1969, French GP 1969, British GP 1969, Italian GP 1969, Spanish GP 1970, Spanish GP 1971, Monaco GP 1971, French GP 1971, British GP 1971, German GP 1971, Canadian GP 1971, Argentinian GP 1972, French GP 1972, Canadian GP 1972, US GP 1972, South African GP 1973, Belgian GP 1973, Monaco GP 1973, Dutch GP 1973, German GP 1973)*
- *World Champion 1969, 1971 and 1973*

ROLF STOMMELEN
Nationality: **German**
Born: **1943**
Died: **1983**

After making his name taming the Porsche 917 sports car, Rolf entered Formula One with the Brabham team in 1970. He showed great promise with four top-six finishes, but seasons with Surtees and then the ugly Eifelland March all but destroyed his Formula One career. An occasional drive with Brabham in 1974 provided a lifeline, and he was offered a drive with the Hill team for 1975, only to be injured in a crash at the Spanish Grand Prix, when his car flew into the crowd and killed four spectators. When Rolf returned later in the year, he was off-form and was mainly away from Formula One until spending a season as an also-ran with Arrows in 1978, after which he returned to sports cars. He was killed in a crash at Riverside in California in 1983.

Career record

- 54 *Grands Prix, no wins (best result – 3rd, Austrian GP 1970)*
- *No championship title (best result – 11th overall 1970)*

PHILIPPE STREIFF
Nationality: **French**
Born: **1955**

This tall, serious-minded Frenchman made his debut with a Renault in the 1984 Portuguese Grand Prix. Halfway through 1985, he replaced the accident-prone Andrea de Cesaris at Ligier, where he scored an excellent third place at the end-of-year Australian Grand Prix at Adelaide. Philippe's first full year came with Tyrrell in 1986, and he spent two seasons with the British team, where he was generally outpaced by his team-mates. A move to the tiny AGS team in 1988 revitalized him, and he impressed with a number of excellent performances, including a superb showing in qualifying at the San Marino Grand Prix. Streiff was to stay with AGS in 1989, but a heavy crash in testing for the Brazilian Grand Prix left him in a wheelchair.

Career record
- 54 Grands Prix, no wins (best result – 3rd Australian GP 1985)
- No championship title (best result – 13th overall 1986)

HANS-JOACHIM STUCK
Nationality: German
Born: 1951

The son of pre-war ace Hans Stuck, Hans Jr's natural talent rarely seemed to find full expression in Formula One. Already a touring car ace when he made his Grand Prix debut in 1974 with March, he proved somewhat inconsistent in the following three years. When Carlos Pace was killed early in 1977, Hans replaced him in the Brabham line-up, and scored superb third places at the German and Austrian Grands Prix. He proceeded to lead the end-of-season US Grand Prix only to slide off in the soaking conditions. He drove for Shadow in 1978 and ATS in 1979, but rarely featured prominently, before moving to a very successful career in sports cars and touring cars that continues into 2001.

Career record
- 74 Grands Prix, no wins (best result – 3rd, German GP 1977, Austrian GP 1977)
- No championship title (best result – 11th overall 1977)

MARC SURER
Nationality: Swiss
Born: 1952

Promoted to Formula One after winning the 1979 European Formula Two title, Marc raced three times with Ensign in 1979, before moving to ATS in 1980 and badly damaging his ankles in a crash at the South African Grand Prix. In 1982, when he was driving for Arrows, he crashed in testing again, but once fit, he drove for Arrows until the end of 1984, earning admiration for his often skilled performances. Marc was finally given the chance to show his ability when he replaced François Hesnault in a Brabham-BMW alongside Nelson Piquet in 1985, before moving back to Arrows in 1986. His career ended when he crashed a Ford RS200 rally car heavily. His co-driver was killed and Surer himself was badly burned. After managing BMW's touring car programme, he is now a commentator.

Career record
- 82 Grands Prix, no wins (best result – 4th, Brazilian GP 1981, Italian GP 1985)
- No championship title (best result – 13th overall 1985)

JOHN SURTEES
Nationality: British
Born: 1934

The only man to have won the World Championship in both motorcyles and cars, John was one of four drivers who domi-

JOHN SURTEES

The motorcycle and Formula One World Champion before his penultimate race for Ferrari, the 1966 Monaco GP.

nated Formula One in the mid-1960s. Having won seven World Motorcycle Championships, John showed such talent when he tried his hand at Formula Junior in 1960 that Lotus boss, Colin Chapman, invited him to drive for his Grand Prix team when the races did not clash with his motorcycle commitments. John did not disappoint, finishing second in the British Grand Prix and taking pole in Portugal, where he dominated until damaging a radiator against straw bales. A move to Ferrari for 1963 was the kick-start for success, and he took his first win at the Nurburgring. In 1964, he secured two more wins and

snatched the world title at a nail-biting last race, in which the destiny of the championship first slipped from Clark's hands, then from Hill's before finally falling into John's grasp. His 1965 season was disrupted when he had a heavy crash in a Lola CanAm car, but his doggedness and determination pulled him through and he returned to Ferrari for 1966. He always excelled on the classic road circuits, and Spa 1966 was no exception, John taking a superb victory in the Belgian Grand Prix after an intense battle with Jochen Rindt. But that was followed by a falling-out with team manager Eugenio Dragoni, which caused a split with Ferrari. John drove for Cooper until the end of the season, winning the final race, before spending a difficult couple of years developing Honda's challenge, which included a victory in the 1967 Italian Grand Prix. He signed for BRM for 1969, but it was a trying year, made worse by medical complications which were a long-term effect of the CanAm crash. By now he had made up his mind to start his own team, where he would not need to compromise his ideas on the technical approach to racing. But the team was not a success. After a promising couple of years with John driving, he retired in 1972. The outfit struggled on until the end of 1978 when it ceased competing, a decision hastened by the onset of more medical problems for John.

Career record
- 111 Grands Prix, 6 wins (German GP 1963, German GP 1964, Italian GP 1964, Belgian GP 1966, Mexican GP 1966, Italian GP 1967)
- World Champion 1964

AGURI SUZUKI
Nationality: **Japanese**
Born: **1960**

Aguri is Japan's most successful Grand Prix driver. After winning the Japanese Formula 3000 title in 1988, a dreadful first year in Formula One in 1989, in which he failed to qualify for Zakspeed, was erased by some superb drives for Larrousse in 1990, including a finish that brought him to the podium at his home Grand Prix. But a financially strapped season with Larrousse did nothing to help his reputation, which was damaged further by two years with Footwork, when he was outpaced by Michele Alboreto and Derek Warwick. He signed a contract to race with Ligier in 1995, albeit sharing the drive with Martin Brundle who proved faster.

Career record
- 64 Grands Prix, no wins (best result – 3rd, Japanese GP 1990)
- No championship title (best result – 10th overall 1990)

TORA TAKAGI
Nationality: **Japanese**
Born: **1974**

Formula Nippon champion in 1997, Toranosuke was blindingly fast in his first year with Tyrrell in 1998, but he crashed too much. A move to Arrows for 1999 produced a seventh place, but he stepped back to Formula Nippon in 2000 to rediscover his form. He won almost every race to be champion and has signed to race for Toyota in Indycars in 2001.

Career record
- 32 Grands Prix, no wins (best result – 7th, Australian GP 2000)
- No championship title

PATRICK TAMBAY

Nationality: **French**

Born: **1949**

After success in Formula Two, Patrick made his Grand Prix debut for Ensign, at the same time as Gilles Villeneuve made his for McLaren. Villeneuve was to become a close friend, but McLaren preferred to run Patrick in 1978, while Villeneuve went to Ferrari. Patrick came off worse, as McLaren slumped into a period of uncompetitiveness. He was replaced by Alain Prost and went to the USA and won the CanAm title. He returned to Formula One in 1981 with Theodore then Ligier, but was dropped at the end of the season. At the beginning of 1982 he announced his retirement from Formula One, but was recalled by Ferrari to be Didier Pironi's team-mate after Villeneuve's death. He shone immediately, winning the German Grand Prix before taking an emotional win at the 1983 San Marino Grand Prix. He challenged for the World Championship that year, but was dropped by Ferrari at the end of it, and in subsequent spells with Renault and the Haas-Lola teams this gentle and immensely popular man never had a car worthy of his considerable talent.

Career record

- ■ *114 Grands Prix, 2 wins (German GP 1982, San Marino GP 1983)*
- ■ *No championship title (best result – 4th overall 1983)*

PATRICK TAMBAY

The Frenchman rounds the Loews Hairpin at Monaco in 1984. His career had peaked previously with Ferrari with two wins.

GABRIELE TARQUINI
Nationality: **Italian**
Born: **1962**

Hugely underrated, Gabriele never had a Formula One car that came close to justifying his ability. He caused a sensation in 1985 when, as reigning World Karting Champion, he went straight to Formula 3000 and became a front-runner. Yet it wasn't until 1988 that he got to Formula One with Coloni. Drafted in at AGS to replace the injured Philippe Streiff in 1989, Gabriele scored a point at Mexico, but AGS slipped ever further down the grid over the next two years. Drove for Fondmetal in 1992, but success was thwarted by financial problems, and the team dropped out of Formula One, taking Gabriele with it. He has since made a reputation for himself in touring cars, winning the British title in 1994 for Alfa Romeo.

Career record
■ *38 Grands Prix, no wins (best result – 6th, Mexican GP 1989)*
■ *No championship title (best result – 26th overall 1989)*

PIERO TARUFFI
Nationality: **Italian**
Born: **1906**
Died: **1989**

Piero was in his forties when the World Championship started in 1950. He finished fifth for Ferrari in 1951 and scored his only Grand Prix win in the 1952 Swiss Grand Prix, then concentrated on sports cars.

Career record
■ *18 Grands Prix, 1 win (Swiss GP 1952)*
■ *No championship title (best result – 3rd overall 1952)*

TREVOR TAYLOR
Nationality: **British**
Born: **1936**

Drafted into the Lotus Formula One team, Trevor was compared to team-mate Jim Clark – and like every other driver of the era he was found wanting. Given a full season in 1962, he came second in the Dutch Grand Prix. A succession of accidents took their toll, then a poor season with BRP finished his career.

Career record

- 27 Grands Prix, no wins (best result – 2nd, Dutch GP 1962)
- No championship title (best result – 10th overall 1962)

MIKE THACKWELL

Nationality: **New Zealander**

Born: **1961**

Became the youngest-ever Grand Prix driver when he started the 1980 Canadian Grand Prix for Tyrrell aged 19, but his career never took off. A Formula Two crash in 1981 stalled his progress, but he fought back to win the 1984 Formula Two crown.

Career record

- 2 Grands Prix, no wins (best result – retired both races)
- No championship title

MAURICE TRINTIGNANT

Nationality: **French**

Born: **1917**

Maurice was a top driver when racing resumed after World War Two. With two Grand Prix wins, he was a factor to be reckoned with and occasionally could put in an excellent drive. When he briefly replaced Stirling Moss in 1962, he was still sprightly enough to show Jim Clark the way at Pau. But it proved to be his last competitive year and he quit in 1964.

Career record

- 82 Grands Prix, 2 wins (Monaco GP 1955, Monaco GP 1958)
- No championship title (best result – 4th overall 1954 and 1955)

JARNO TRULLI

Nationality: **Italian**

Born: **1974**

Benetton boss Flavio Briatore paid for World Kart Champion Trulli to go direct to German Formula Three midway through 1995. Jarno won the final two races and carried on in this vein in 1996, easily becoming champion. Briatore put him into the Minardi line-up for 1997, but his big break came when he subbed for Olivier Panis at Prost and led the Austrian Grand Prix. Stayed on with Prost until the end of 1999, peaking with second in the European Grand Prix in 1999 before joining Jordan. The season was blighted by mechanical failure, but he showed flashes of pure class.

Career record

- 63 Grands Prix, no wins (best result – 2nd, European GP 1999)
- No championship title (best result – 10th overall 2000)

ESTEBAN TUERO

Nationality: **Argentinian**

Born: **1978**

Became one of the youngest-ever Grand Prix drivers when he started the 1998 Brazilian Grand Prix for Minardi aged 19, but it soon became clear that he had come to Formula One before he was ready after rushing through Formula Three and Formula 3000 in Europe and Japan with no noteworthy results.

Career record
- 16 Grands Prix, no wins (best result – 8th, San Marino GP 1998)
- No championship title

JOS VERSTAPPEN
Nationality: **Dutch**
Born: **1972**

After a successful career in karting, Jos shone in the GM Euroseries in 1992 before winning the 1993 German Formula Three title. Snapped up by Benetton for 1994, he was thrown in at the deep end when JJ Lehto broke his neck in testing. Survived a pit fire in Germany, then finished third in Hungary. Driving for Simtek in 1995, Jos qualified mid-grid in Argentina, Imola and Spain, but it all came to nought when Simtek ran out of cash. Struggled with Arrows in 1996 and then with Tyrrell in 1997, before joining the Stewart team midway through 1998 season. Dropped for 1999, he returned with Arrows in 2000 and finished fourth at Monza.

Career record
- 74 Grands Prix, no wins (best result – 3rd, Hungarian GP 1994)
- No championship title (best result – 10th overall 1994)

GILLES VILLENEUVE
Nationality: **Canadian**
Born: **1950**
Died: **1982**

Some thought Gilles personified everything good about motor racing, his natural speed and spectacular style complemented by an open, irreverent character. Others said his flamboyance bordered on the reckless. He dominated the Canadian Formula Atlantic scene, and wiped the floor at an invitation race at Trois-Rivières at the end of 1976 that included World Champion James Hunt. That

GILLES VILLENEUVE
The Canadian started Formula One with a bang, running on the pace of the leaders in a two-year-old car in his first Grand Prix in 1977.

led to a drive with McLaren in the 1977 British Grand Prix, where he stunned everybody by running on the pace of the leaders in a two-year-old car. Unfathomably, McLaren did not take up an option on his services, but Ferrari signed him to replace Lauda at the end of 1977. Gilles stayed with Ferrari until the end of his career. He scored his first win, at home in the Canadian Grand Prix, in 1978, and would have been World Champion in 1979, when he won three Grands Prix, had he not honourably stood by team orders at the Italian Grand Prix and sat behind team-mate Jody Scheckter, who took the title instead. There followed two years in hugely inferior cars (although he had two opportunistic wins in 1981) until in 1982 he finally had the equipment to win consistently. But, after having victory stolen from under his nose by team-mate Didier Pironi as he was cruising to the flag in the San Marino Grand Prix, Gilles was plunged into turmoil. He pledged never to speak to Pironi again, and two weeks later, he crashed fatally while practising for the Belgian Grand Prix.

Career record

■ 67 Grands Prix, 6 wins (Canadian GP 1978, South African GP 1979, US West GP 1979, US East GP 1979, Monaco GP 1981, Spanish GP 1981)
■ No championship title (best result – 2nd overall 1979)

JACQUES VILLENEUVE
Nationality: **Canadian**
Born: **1971**

Jacques wasn't interested in racing when his father Gilles was alive, but he took it up and spent three years in Italian Formula Three, ranking sixth overall in 1991. Second in the Japanese series in 1992, he ranked third in North American Toyota Atlantic in 1993. Indycar Rookie of the Year in 1994, when he was second in the Indy 500, he won the title in 1995, with four wins including the Indy 500. Moving to Formula One with Williams for 1996, Jacques won four times and chased team-mate Damon Hill all the way to the final round. He was champion in 1997, with seven wins, surviving an assault by Schumacher at the final round. His title defence in 1998 was ruined by a poor Williams and he ranked fifth. Jacques raced for the new BAR team in 1999, but failed to score as mechanical failures wrecked his year. Jacques starred with some amazing starts for BAR in 2000, collecting four fourths to rank seventh overall.

Career record

■ 82 Grands Prix, 11 wins (European GP 1996, British GP 1996, Hungarian GP 1996, Portuguese GP 1996, Brazilian GP 1997, Argentinian GP 1997, Spanish GP 1997, British GP 1997, Hungarian GP 1997, Austrian GP 1997, Luxembourg GP 1997)
■ World Champion 1997

LUIGI VILLORESI

Nationality: Italian

Born: 1909

A successful Grand Prix driver before the Second World War, Luigi was marginally past his peak by the time the World Championship was founded, although he was still quick enough to win the 1949 Dutch Grand Prix. After years with Maserati and Alfa Romeo, Luigi had moved to Ferrari in 1949 to encourage the career of his young friend Alberto Ascari, whom he recognized as having a far greater talent than his own. Luigi pulled out of Formula One temporarily after Ascari's death in 1955, returning in 1956 for Maserati, only to crash badly at the non-cham-

JACQUES VILLENEUVE
Will be looking for both the car and the form that took him to the 1997 title.

pionship Rome Grand Prix and retire.

Career record

- *31 Grands Prix, no wins (best result – 2nd, Argentinian GP 1953, Belgian GP 1953)*
- *No championship title (best result – 5th overall 1951 and 1953)*

WOLFGANG VON TRIPS

Nationality: **German**

Born: **1928**

Died: **1961**

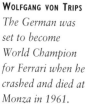

WOLFGANG VON TRIPS
The German was set to become World Champion for Ferrari when he crashed and died at Monza in 1961.

Until Michael Schumacher won the World Championship in 1994, von Trips was Germany's most successful Grand Prix driver. Always quick, he shrugged off the reputation as a crasher he had garnered in his early career, when he rejoined Ferrari in 1960. A number of top-six placings that year were followed by a determined assault on the World Championship in 1961. Two wins (at the Dutch and British Grands Prix) and two second places from six races had him bang on target as he arrived at Monza for the Italian Grand Prix. But after taking pole, he made a poor start and, trying to protect his position on the first lap, collided with Jim Clark. His car crashed into the crowd, killing 14 spectators, and von Trips also died, leaving team-mate Phil Hill to clinch a bitter world title.

Career record

- *27 Grands Prix, 2 wins (Dutch GP 1961, British GP 1961)*
- *No championship title (best result – 2nd overall 1961)*

W

DEREK WARWICK
Nationality: **British**
Born: **1954**

It seems inconceivable that the talented Derek could spend ten years in Formula One and still end his career without a Grand Prix win. Regarded as a better British prospect than Nigel Mansell in the early stages of his career, he appeared to have success in his grasp when he signed to replace Alain Prost at Renault in 1984. But the French team went into a terminal decline and, when he was blocked from joining Lotus in 1986 by Ayrton Senna, he temporarily left Formula One, only to return, for Brabham, after the death of Elio de Angelis. After three promising, but fruitless, years with Arrows, then an even worse one at Lotus, Derek quit Formula One for success in sports cars – in which he was World Champion in 1991 – before returning for another fruitless year with Footwork in 1993. But still the cards did not fall for him, and in 1994 Formula One passed him by. He has now turned to the British Touring Car Championship to seek success.

Career record
■ *147 Grands Prix, no wins (best result – 2nd Belgian GP 1984, British GP 1984)*
■ *No championship title (best result – 7th overall 1984 and 1988)*

JOHN WATSON
Out comes the champagne as the Irishman celebrates what turned out to be his last-ever Grand Prix victory at Long Beach in 1983.

JOHN WATSON
Nationality: **British**
Born: **1946**

On his day, John could drive quite superbly, but those days did not come as often as he would have liked. After a slow rise through the single-seater echelons, he broke into Formula One in 1973, and drove for a number of middle-ranking teams until getting his break with Penske in mid-1975. He took a splendid victory for the team in the 1976 Austrian Grand Prix, and was signed to Brabham for the 1977–78 seasons, when a number of good results failed to translate into wins. He then spent a frustrating couple of seasons with McLaren, before being the first beneficiary of the arrival of John Barnard and Ron Dennis in 1981. He was a World Championship contender when Niki Lauda returned from retirement in 1982 and, although somewhat overshadowed by the Austrian in 1983, John still managed a brilliant victory in that year's Long Beach Grand Prix. But the sacking of Prost by Renault in 1983 was the death knell for John's career. Prost took his McLaren drive, and he was unable to find a seat for 1984. A brief return in 1985 was disappointing, and he enjoyed success in sports cars before setting up his own racing school. He is now a television commentator.

Career record
- 152 Grands Prix, 5 wins (Austrian GP 1976, British GP 1981, Belgian GP 1982, Detroit GP 1982, US West GP 1983)
- No championship title (best result – 2nd overall 1982)

KARL WENDLINGER
Nationality: **Austrian**
Born: **1968**

Winner of the 1989 German Formula Three title, he joined the Mercedes sports car junior team in 1990 then impressed enormously for the underfinanced March team in 1992, before joining Sauber for 1993. A crash at Monaco in 1994 left him in a coma for 19 days, and took Formula One to the political brink after the deaths of Ayrton Senna and Roland Ratzenberger two weeks earlier. He made his racing comeback

for Sauber in 1995, but was not up to the task and was dropped after four races, with just a 13th place to show for his efforts. With Jean-Christophe Boullion also disappointing, Karl was brought back for the last two races, but again failed to impress and he headed for a career in touring cars.

Career record
- 41 Grands Prix, no wins (best result – 4th, Canadian GP 1992, Italian GP 1993, San Marino GP 1994)
- No championship title (best result – 11th overall 1993)

KEN WHARTON
Nationality: **British**
Born: **1916**
Died: **1957**

Ken made his Grand Prix debut in an old-fashioned Frazer-Nash at the 1952 Swiss Grand Prix and finished fourth, but that was to be his best result. A consistent finisher through 1953 and 1954, he called it a day in Formula One after an unproductive year for Vanwall in 1956, in which he received burns in an accident in the International Trophy at Silverstone. Wharton was then killed in a crash in a Ferrari sports car in New Zealand in 1957.

Career record
- 15 Grands Prix, no wins (best result – 4th, Swiss GP 1952)
- No championship title (best result – 13th overall 1952)

PETER WHITEHEAD

Nationality: **British**

Born: **1914**

Died: **1958**

This wealthy businessman was robbed of victory in the 1949 French Grand Prix before problems with the gearbox dropped him to third, and raced on in Formula One, netting a couple of top-ten places in Ferraris, until the end of 1952, by which time he was finding success in sports car events. Thereafter, he raced in Formula One only in the British Grand Prix, and pulled out in 1954. He was killed when his half-brother Graham crashed the car in which both were competing in the 1958 Tour de France.

Career record

■ *10 Grands Prix, no wins (best result – 3rd, French GP 1950)*

■ *No championship title (best result – 9th overall 1950)*

ROGER WILLIAMSON

Nationality: **British**

Born: **1948**

Died: **1973**

A protégé of successful Midlands businessman and racing enthusiast, Tom Wheatcroft, who is the owner of the Donington Park circuit, Roger was a frequent race-winner in Formula Three and Formula Two. Wheatcroft wanted to fund him in a full season of Formula One in 1974, and they dipped their toes in the water in 1973 with a March. But Roger was taken out of the British Grand Prix in a multiple-shunt on the first lap. And then at Zandvoort a suspension failure caused him to crash. The car came to rest upside down and on fire and, apart from David

PETER WHITEHEAD
One of Britain's earliest Formula One drivers, seen here crossing the finishing line in the 1950 Italian GP.

when he qualified fifth. A good drive in a Porsche sports car provided him with some welcome success, but he was killed in an accident at the Mosport Park 1,000km race in 1985.

Career record
- *47 Grands Prix, no wins (best result – 5th, Brazilian GP 1982)*
- *No championship title (best result – 22nd overall 1982)*

ALEXANDER WURZ

Nationality: **Austrian**

Born: **1974**

The third generation of an Austrian racing family, Alex was the German Formula Ford champion in 1992, then runner-up in German Formula Three in 1994. He then raced in the International Touring Car series in 1996, when he also won the Le Mans 24 Hours. Test driver for Benetton in 1997, he got his Formula One break when Gerhard Berger was ill and finished third on his third outing. Had a spectacular year with Benetton in 1998, but struggled in 1999 and 2000 as the team favoured his teammate, Italian Giancarlo Fisichella. He has signed as McLaren's test driver for the 2001 season, hoping to bounce back in 2002.

Career record
- *52 Grands Prix, no wins (best result – 3rd, British GP 1997)*
- *No championship title (best result – 8th overall 1998)*

Purley, no one tried to rescue him. As the marshals stood by, Roger burned to death in front of millions of television viewers.

Career record
- *2 Grands Prix, no wins (retired from both races)*
- *No championship title*

MANFRED WINKELHOCK

Nationality: **German**

Born: **1952**

Died: **1985**

Manfred was backed by BMW as he rose racing's ladder. He spent most of his Formula One career with ATS and RAM, rarely enjoying the chance to shine, but his reflexes and bravery were used to good effect at the Detroit Grand Prix in 1982,

Z

No *championship title (best result – 20th overall 1993)*

ALESSANDRO ZANARDI

Nationality: **Italian**

Born: **1966**

Although he lost the Formula 3000 title to the more consistent Christian Fittipaldi, Alessandro had made his Formula One debut by the end of the year, filling the seat vacated at Jordan by Michael Schumacher and then became Benetton test driver in 1992. He raced for Lotus in 1993 and was lucky to survive a huge accident at Spa, after which he was replaced by Pedro Lamy. He won his seat back in 1994, but the team was short of money and he had no drive in 1995. He moved to Indycars, to be runner-up in 1996 and then champion in 1997 and 1998. However, his Formula One return with Williams in 1999 was a disaster, producing no points.

Career record

- 41 *Grands Prix, no wins (best result – 6th, Brazilian GP 1993)*

RICARDO ZONTA

Nationality: **Brazilian**

Born: **1976**

Ricardo won the South American Formula Three crown in 1995. This helped him land a Formula 3000 ride for 1996 and he rounded out the year with a pair of wins. He duly won the title in 1997. Mercedes signed him for 1998 and he won the FIA GT title for them, as well as testing for McLaren. A Formula One ride for BAR produced no points, but he progressed in 2000, although tension with Jacques Villeneuve led to his dismissal. Test driver for Jordan in 2001, Ricardo is looking for a race seat in 2002.

Career record

- 29 *Grands Prix, no wins (best result – 6th, Australian GP 2000, Italian GP 2000, US GP 2000)*
- No *championship title (best result – 14th overall 2000)*

RICARDO ZONTA

Points-scoring drives for the Brazilian in 2000 were not enough to save his seat at BAR for the 2001 season.

THE TEAMS

ALTHOUGH IT IS DRIVERS WHO RECEIVE THE LAURELS, THEY INVARIABLY PAY TRIB-
ute to the crew in the pits and the technical experts, without whom no team can
succeed. Grand Prix racing began with rich individuals only behind the wheel.
Indeed, the very early road races often saw these gentlemen pedalled by their
chauffeurs. But, inevitably, things changed as racing became more competitive and
cars more hybrid.

Alfa Romeo won most of the early laurels, to be replaced by Auto Union and
Mercedes-Benz. By the late 1950s, with Ferrari, Maserati and Mercedes at the head
of the game, the force of the owner/engineer was beginning to be felt, with British

brains pushing Formula One technology on at a startling pace. And it was in the 1960s that individual teams truly formed their own identity. Later dubbed "the garagistes", these teams popped up, literally from lockups under the railway arches. And so teams such as Lotus, Brabham and McLaren came to the forefront.

Teams have come and gone ever since, often according to the prevalent economic climate and occasionally because the team owner had been disgraced. As we enter the sport's 52nd season, however, only one of the original teams remain — the world's favourite team, Ferrari. From the biggest to the smallest, here's a list of those who have tried their hand in Formula One.

FORMULA ONE STALWARTS *Only the Ferrari team has entered every year of the World Championship.*

ALFA ROMEO

ALFA ROMEO WAS AN EVOCATIVE MOTOR SPORTING NAME of the 1920s and 1930s, and was also prominent after the Second World War. The name is an emotive one, but the company last won a Grand Prix in 1951.

Country of origin:	Italy
Date of foundation:	1909
Active years in Formula One:	1950–85
Constructors' Cup victories:	None

Alfa Romeo entered the Grand Prix arena in 1924. One of the most brilliant designers of the age was Vittorio Jano. After 12 years with Fiat, one of the most successful makes from the sport's early days, Jano was lured to Alfa Romeo in 1923 and his P2 became the standard setter for the next two years. Antonio Ascari won the car's first race, at Cremona and, so crushing was the Italian superiority in the 1925 Belgian Grand Prix at Spa, that Jano actually laid out a quality lunch in the pits and called his drivers in to partake while mechanics polished the cars. The team then continued with their display!

Their fortunes changed when Ascari was killed in the French Grand Prix at Montlhery, but Alfa Romeo still took the manufacturers' championship title and added a laurel wreath to its distinctive badge.

The Tipo B

Another Jano great was the Alfa Tipo B which was fielded in 1932. Between then and 1934, it won every Grand Prix for which it was entered, driven by the likes of Rudolf Caracciola and the great Tazio Nuvolari, whom many rate as the greatest

driver ever. In 1933, Alfa Romeo was nationalized and officially withdrew from the sport, although Ferrari continued to field the cars on a semi-works basis.

Even against the might of the emerging German marques like Mercedes and Auto Union, Nuvolari managed some great feats with the Tipo B, none better than his win in the 1935 German Grand Prix.

Alfa took full control of its racing programme again in 1938, but the war intervened. Put off by the German dominance of Grand Prix racing in the late 1930s, Gioacchino Columbo designed an Alfa Romeo Tipo 158 for the smaller voiturette class in 1939. It was hidden in a cheese factory while the Germans occupied Italy, but under the new, pragmatic, post-war regulations it automatically became a Grand Prix car and dominated the scene for the remainder of the 1940s. Alfa Romeo enjoyed a string of 26 unbroken wins.

By 1951, some 13 years after it was designed, the supercharged car, now in 159 guise, took Juan Manuel Fangio to his first world title in the final race of the season, the Spanish

Grand Prix, in a shoot-out against the Ferraris of Alberto Ascari, Froilan Gonzalez and Piero Taruffi. It was the car's last race and Alfa Romeo then concentrated on sports car racing.

The Brabham-Alfa

In the mid-1970s their flat-12 sportscar engine started to attract the interest of the Formula One brigade, who were watching Ferrari dominate the proceedings with an engine of similar configuration. Former Ferrari engineer, Carlo Chiti, was responsible for the engines, and he did a deal with Bernie Ecclestone to supply them to the Brabham team.

Autodelta was Chiti's company and the organization which conducted Alfa's racing programme. The Brabham-Alfas started to show good form and, despite a strong union movement that was opposed to rich man's sport, Alfa Romeo was not slow to recognize the possible benefits of its own programme. In 1979 Bruno Giacomelli debuted the ugly-looking Tipo 177 in the Belgian Grand Prix at Zolder.

As Brabham reverted to Ford power, the new Alfa V12 was put into a new Tipo 179 chassis and, with Giacomelli joined by Patrick Depailler for 1980, the outlook was healthier. Sadly, though, Depailler was killed in testing at Hockenheim and, although Giacomelli led the US Grand Prix at Watkins Glen before the car expired, Alfa Romeo was not destined to enjoy the success of its heyday. Andrea de Cesaris led the Belgian Grand Prix at Spa in 1982, but the marque did not win another Grand Prix before quitting again.

ON A SWISS ROLL
Giuseppe Farina marches to victory in Alfa Romeo's glory days at the 1950 Swiss Grand Prix at Bremgarten.

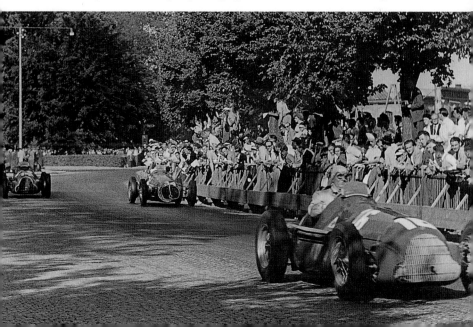

ARROWS

ARROWS WAS FORMED NEARLY 20 YEARS AGO, BUT HAS yet to score a Grand Prix win. Ironically, its second race, the South African Grand Prix of 1978, is the nearest it has come, when emerging Italian, Riccardo Patrese, led convincingly until his engine died.

Country of origin:	GB
Date of foundation:	1977
Active years in Formula One:	from 1978
Constructors' Cup victories:	None

Arrows was established in controversial circumstances when key members of the Shadow team broke away. Shadow had been sponsored by the Italian, Franco Ambrosio, later imprisoned on charges of financial irregularity. Ambrosio became the "AR" of the Arrows name and the other initials belonged to current financial director Alan Rees, former Grand Prix driver and now managing director Jackie Oliver, and designers Dave Wass and Tony Southgate.

Swede Gunnar Nilsson was to lead the team, but developed stomach cancer and died less than a year later. Arrows opted for Patrese who, in his early days, was quick but wild.

Legal problems

After preparing its car in just 60 days and having a good start to the season, Arrows hit trouble. Shadow believed that Arrows' car was a copy of the new Shadow design to which it owned the rights. The High Court ruled in favour of Shadow and told Arrows that it could not race its car.

Arrows had to build a replacement, which it managed to do even more quickly than it had the original, and continued without missing a race. Then, in the Italian Grand Prix, Ronnie Peterson was killed after his Lotus was involved in a multiple starting-line accident. After a witch-hunt by some of the top names, including Niki Lauda and James Hunt, Patrese was held responsible and banned from the US Grand Prix.

Early Arrows cars raced in the distinctive gold livery of the Warsteiner beer company, and the 1979 car, the futuristic-looking A2 "buzz bomb", was much discussed. It was not successful and the team reverted to more conventional thinking.

As racing developed in the 1980s, it was no longer sufficient to bolt on a customer Ford Cosworth V8 and go racing. A manufacturer link became increasingly important to cope with turbocharged engines from BMW, Renault and Ferrari. When BMW pulled out officially, its powerful, four-cylinder turbo engines were renamed Megatrons and were used to good effect by Arrows.

The deal with Footwork

As the 1980s drew to a close,

the Japanese Footwork corporation broke into Formula One striking a deal with Jackie Oliver. The team was renamed Footwork and it looked as though the injection of Japanese funding could move the team to the forefront, especially when a deal for Porsche engines was signed.

Alan Jenkins was design chief by now after a spell at McLaren where the team had swept the board with the Porsche-built TAG turbo engines. Any hopes of a repeat were quickly dispelled when the first 12-cylinder engine (effectively two sixes joined together) arrived. Where-as a typical unit might have weighed 145–150 kilos, the new Porsche weighed 210! Jenkins remembers it as one of the most depressing days of his life.

The Porsche association came to a rapid end, but Footwork soldiered on with Japanese Mugen engines with driver Aguri Suzuki alongside Michele Alboreto and then Derek Warwick.

For 1994 Jenkins designed the neat FA15 for a customer Ford. But new regulations after early-season fatalities spoiled the cars. Footwork boss, Wataru Ohashi, reduced his involvement and the team reverted to being Arrows.

An unspectacular 1996 season masked Tom Walkinshaw's arrival as team owner. His signings for 1997 included Damon Hill, Bridgestone tyres and Yamaha engines. But their form was weak, even though Hill led until the final lap of the Hungarian Grand Prix before falling to second. For 1998, the team chose to build its own engines, with Mika Salo replacing Hill alongside Pedro Diniz, but engines were the team's downfall and Diniz quit. Pedro de la Rosa scored on his debut in 1999, but that was the only point he scored all year. With welcome financial backing from Orange and using Supertec engines for 2000, Arrows made clear progress, with de la Rosa twice running third and Verstappen finishing fourth at Monza.

THE CLOSEST YET

Damon Hill acknowledges the applause after leading for most of the way in the 1997 Hungarian Grand Prix for Arrows, before succumbing to gearbox problems on the final lap.

BAR (formerly Tyrrell)

BAR, OR BRITISH AMERICAN RACING TO GIVE THE TEAM its full name, entered the Formula One World Championship trail in 1999, having had a season of running the affairs of the Tyrrell team.

Country of origin:	GB
Date of foundation:	1998
Active years in Formula One:	from 1999
Constructors' Cup victories:	None

However, there should be no mistaking the two enterprises, for BAR is an all-new team coming into the sport amid a blaze of publicity, while Tyrrell was a 30-year-old team working its way through its final season. Their tie-up was simply one of convenience, with British American Tobacco having put up the money for the team's founder Craig Pollock to buy the Tyrrell team and thus a guaranteed entry for the World Championship.

Tobacco backing

Having gained experience by guiding his former charge and pupil Jacques Villeneuve through the sport's junior categories and onto the big stage with Williams in 1996, Pollock was anxious to form his own team rather then be involved on the periphery of others. Pollock joined forces with world-beating chassis manufacturer Reynard and British American Tobacco, with the multinational tobacco company providing the financial backing for the bold sporting enterprise.

An ultra-modern headquarters was built in Brackley, right in the heart of South-East England's Formula One belt.

And, from early in 1998, the team leaders set about recruiting their employees, raiding all the top teams for personnel as they built the team from the ground up.

While Adrian Reynard heads the technical side, Malcolm Oastler – already successful in designing Reynard Indycar and Formula 3000 chassis – is his chief sidekick, supported by engineer Jock Clear who is one of a host of employees poached from Williams. But Clear was always going to move across to BAR once his charge Villeneuve announced that he too was leaving Williams after three seasons in order to be reunited with Pollock at his new team.

A champion number two

The team signed Ricardo Zonta as its second driver, arriving with an impressive pedigree, having been Formula 3000 champion in 1997 and then the FIA GT Champion for Mercedes in 1998.

For its first season, in 1999 BAR joined Williams and Benetton in running Renault-based Mecachrome engines, but these and numerous teething problems meant that Reynard's incredibly proud boast that his cars have won the first race every time they have moved up to a more senior formula, including their graduations to Formula Three, Formula 3000 and then Indy Cars, was not to be continued. To have done so in Formula One would have required a miracle, especially with McLaren and Ferrari so far ahead of everyone else. BAR would have expected at least to gather some points. Yet, at the end of their first year, they had none.

The same line-up was kept for 2000, but importantly, Pollock had convinced Honda to supply works engines. The return was immediate, with both drivers scoring in the opening round, with Villeneuve and Zonta finishing fourth and sixth respectively.

More point-scoring drives followed, including three more fourth places at Magny-Cours, the A-1 Ring and Indianapolis for Villeneuve. Zonta got in on the act again, too, with two more sixth places at Monza and Indianapolis. But the Brazilian knew by then that he was on the way out of the team, especially after he'd tipped Villeneuve out of the German Grand Prix when trying to pass him... Their combined efforts had propelled BAR up the order to finish equal on points with Benetton, but they had to settle for fifth place on countback in the Constructors' Cup as Benetton had managed a best result of second (Giancarlo Fisichella in Brazil) to BAR's best of fourth.

Battles for control of the team are never far beneath the surface at BAR, with Pollock and Reynard seemingly possessing different aims.

NEW KIDS ON THE BLOCK
Jacques Villeneuve during BAR's first Grand Prix at Melbourne in 1999.

BENETTON

WITH HIS BASE IN TREVISO, NORTHERN ITALY,
Luciano Benetton built a chain of shops selling
colourful clothing with a young appeal. He saw
Formula One as the ideal way of promoting them.

Country of origin:	Italy/GB
Date of foundation:	1986
Active years in Formula One:	from 1986
Constructors' Cup victories:	1995

In the early 1980s the company sponsored Tyrrell, Alfa Romeo and the Toleman teams, which Benetton then bought in 1986 and fielded the cars as Benettons.

A name to be reckoned with
With turbocharged BMW engines, they were tremendously powerful and Gerhard Berger took their first victory in Mexico. Benetton really began to emerge in the late 1980s. In 1989, they had Italian Alessandro Nannini as lead driver and signed Johnny Herbert as his team-mate. Team boss Peter Collins had given Herbert the chance, but when Flavio Briatore took over as kingpin in the Benetton organization both Collins and Herbert were soon shown the door. Briatore replaced Herbert with Emanuele Pirro, not the most inspired of moves, but Nannini finished the year with a win in the controversial Japanese Grand Prix after Senna was disqualified.

In 1990, the team signed three times world champion Nelson Piquet, then in the twilight of his Formula One career. Piquet turned in some fine performances and, as before, Benetton picked up the pieces in

Japan when Senna and Prost collided.

But Benetton's future was shaped by the events of 1991 when a youthful Michael Schumacher burst onto the scene. Already a German Formula Three Champion and Macau winner, Michael was also a member of the Mercedes sports car junior team when he made his Formula One debut in a Jordan at Spa. He stunned the regulars by qualifying seventh.

Benetton had seen enough. After some ugly scenes at Monza, the team managed to prise Schumacher away from Jordan and sign him to a long-term contract. Engineering director, Tom Walkinshaw, had been responsible for running the Jaguar sports car programme and he had had first-hand experience of Schumacher's ability.

Schumacher dazzles
The German was brilliant from the start. He outpaced Piquet immediately and regularly brought the car home in the points. Benetton realized that it had a future champion on its books and Briatore instigated a building programme for a new technical facility in Cotswold

country, bringing the operation together under one roof. In 1992, Schumacher was unable to go for the championship because Williams had mastered active suspension first, allowing Nigel Mansell and Riccardo Patrese to finish one-two in the title race. Schumacher, though, scored a wonderfully judged first Grand Prix win at Spa.

In 1993, Benetton made great strides towards closing the gap with Williams after the introduction of a semi-automatic gearbox and active suspension. But Schumacher did not have traction control until Monaco, where he led, but it was too late to stop Prost and Williams.

However, 1994 was the year. The Benetton B194 was the first chassis to see daylight from the "big four" teams and Ford had done a tremendous job with the Zetec-R V8. Schumacher won the first two races of the year and, when Senna was killed in the Williams at Imola, he was left as Formula One's top gun.

Benetton endured suggestions of illegality, then Schumacher suffered a two-race ban for ignoring a black flag at

Silverstone and was thrown out on a technicality at Spa. He went to the Adelaide finale with a single-point advantage over Damon Hill and the title was decided when the pair collided.

In 1995, Benetton won the valued Constructors' Cup for the first time as Schumacher won nine Grands Prix, retaining his world championship, and Johnny Herbert won two.

Jean Alesi and Gerhard Berger failed to win for Benetton in 1996, and Briatore was furious with Alesi for crashing at the final race to hand Ferrari second in the Constructors' Cup. Berger took a single win in Germany in 1997, but the old guard were replaced in 1998 by Giancarlo Fisichella and Alex Wurz, with rally team boss David Richards at the helm until Rocco Benetton – son of the company owner – took over late in the season.

This line-up stayed the same through 1999 and 2000, albeit with Briatore returning in 2000, but no more wins were scored and the team is hoping that Renault engines in 2001 will improve its fortunes.

RISING STAR

Michael Schumacher drives the Benetton B193B at Portugal in 1993.

BRABHAM

JACK BRABHAM IS THE ONLY DRIVER TO WIN THE WORLD
Championship in a car bearing his own name.

Country of origin:	GB
Date of foundation:	1961
Active years in Formula One:	1962–92
Constructors' Cup victories:	1966–67

Brabham won back-to-back titles for Cooper in 1959–60, but returned home to Australia and struck up a business partnership with Ron Tauranac, an aircraft engineer.

They came to England and set up Motor Racing Developments. The cars were known as MRDs until someone pointed out that, if said rapidly in French, it sounded like something dogs did on the pavement. So, Brabham, never a publicity-seeking man, allowed his own name to be used.

QUICK AS A FLASH
Dan Gurney powers the Brabham BT7 to victory at Rouen in 1965.

In 1963, the Brabham Racing Organization was formed, using cars built by MRD. It won its first Grands Prix in 1964, when Dan Gurney was first past the flag in both the French and Mexican Grands Prix.

Years of triumph

Lotus dominated in 1965, but for the following year there was a new 3-litre formula in Formula One and Brabham had an engine built by the Australian Repco company. With it, Brabham became the first driver to score a win in a car bearing his own name, at the French Grand Prix, and went on to win his third World Championship.

The following season saw the introduction of the Cosworth DFV. The new engine won first time out in Jim

Clark's Lotus, but consistency allowed Denny Hulme to win a second successive championship for Brabham.

Then the team missed out. Brabham managed to sign upcoming Austrian Jochen Rindt for 1968 and there is no doubt that, if the engines had been up to it, Rindt could have prolonged the success. But the new four-cam Repco was neither quick nor reliable. Rindt left for Lotus at the end of the season.

After Jackie Stewart and Matra dominated in 1969, Brabham, now 44, decided that 1970 would be his final year. Tauranac produced his first monocoque Brabham, the BT33, and Jack won the opening race in South Africa. He should also have won in Monaco, but allowed himself to be pressured into a mistake at the last hairpin by a charging Rindt.

Then Lotus upped the ante with its new Type 72. After outdriving Rindt at Brands Hatch, Brabham ran out of fuel on the last lap and that was the end of his challenge that year. Rindt then became the sport's only posthumous champion after an accident at Monza, and Brabham returned to Australia.

After struggling on in 1971, with Graham Hill and Tim Schenken, Tauranac sold the company to Bernie Ecclestone. One of Tauranac's design assistants, South African Gordon Murray, then became responsible for the Brabhams which, instead of taking over an "EM" (Ecclestone/Murray) tag, continued as BTs. Murray's distinctive BT44 was one of the prettiest Formula One cars ever built and won three races in 1974 with Carlos Reutemann at the helm.

Fading glory

Ferrari domination with flat-12 engines caused Ecclestone to turn to Alfa Romeo for a similar unit, but, despite signing Niki Lauda from Ferrari, the team could not win another championship. Lotus was pioneering aerodynamic wing cars and ground effect and, to counter the suction effect, Murray built a BT46B with a huge fan on the back which sucked the car on to the track. Lauda immediately blew the Lotuses away in the Swedish Grand Prix. It was brilliant, but was rapidly banned.

Nelson Piquet joined the team at the end of 1978 and became a great favourite after Lauda retired the following year. Nelson won World Championships for Brabham in 1981 and 1983. But the Brazilian left at the end of 1985 and Brabham rapidly declined. Elio de Angelis was killed testing the lay-down BT55 and at the end of 1987 and Ecclestone withdrew Brabham from the championship.

The team returned in 1989 after being sold to a Swiss financier who ended up in jail for massive fraud. Its ownership then became even murkier and, although the team raced until 1992, it was an embarrassment to its former self before finally disappearing altogether.

BRM

BRM ROOTS GO BACK TO 1947 WHEN THE BRITISH Motor Racing Research Trust was formed with the idea of building a British challenger to break the Italian stranglehold.

Country of origin: GB
Date of foundation: 1947
Active years in Formula One: 1951–77
Constructors' Cup victories: 1962

The man behind it was Raymond Mays, who was the first to bring commercial support to motor racing when he persuaded companies to back his English Racing Automobiles (ERA) efforts in the 1920s and 1930s. BRM (British Racing Motors) was a similar idea.

The original BRM team was a co-operative and the plan was to build a two-stage supercharged engine producing 600 brake horsepower. Unfortunately, when the car made its debut in the non-championship International Trophy at Silverstone, it was a disaster. With Raymond Sommer driving, the car qualified on the back of the grid and broke a drive-shaft on the line. Spectators threw coins at it as it was pushed off.

The research trust lasted until 1952, when Sir Alfred Owen of the Owen Organization took over BRM. No great progress was made until the 1960s, as Cooper and Lotus overtook BRM in the effort to establish Britain at the forefront of the international racing scene.

Year of victory

BRM went into 1962 with just one Grand Prix victory to its name – the Dutch Grand Prix of 1959 with Jo Bonnier – and an ultimatum from Owen to win the championship or else. Peter Berthon, part of BRM since the start, was no longer on the scene and Tony Rudd, a former Rolls Royce apprentice who had worked for Merlin engines, took over as chief engineer and team manager, doing much work on the new BRM V8 engine.

Graham Hill showed the car's potential by winning the first heat of the Brussels Grand Prix in its debut race and then beat Jim Clark's Lotus by a nose length in the International Trophy at Silverstone. He went on to score his first Grand Prix win in the opening round of the championship.

Hill won again in the German Grand Prix and then finished one-two for BRM with Richie Ginther at Monza. He was now embroiled in a championship battle with Clark's Lotus which went right down to the wire in South Africa. Clark took off into the lead with Hill second, but an engine problem put him out and Hill won the World Championship for BRM in the Type P57.

Clark dominated in 1963, but BRM came back with its first monocoque car, the P261, the following year. Hill won two Grands Prix and was only prevented from taking a second championship by John Surtees' Ferrari in the final race of the season, where Hill's BRM was clobbered by Surtees' young Ferrari team-mate, Lorenzo Bandini. Hill reputedly sent Bandini a "Learn to Drive" manual for Christmas.

New technical developments

For the new 3-litre formula of 1966, Rudd developed the H16 engine, which was effectively two V8s mounted on top of each other with the cylinder banks opened out to lie horizontally. It was not a success, despite best efforts over the next two years, and was replaced by a conventional V12 in 1968.

By this time the BRM chassis was a little long in the tooth.

Talented young designer Tony Southgate now joined the organization and designed the P153 and P160 chassis, which put BRM back into the winner's circle when Pedro Rodriguez won a close battle with Chris Amon in the 1970 Belgian Grand Prix at Spa.

The emerging young Niki Lauda turned in some promising drives to launch his career with BRM in 1973, but at the end of the following year the Owen Organization withdrew its support. Louis Stanley tried to keep the team afloat, but it all fell apart in 1977. The new P207 was late and, when it did arrive, neither Conny Andersson nor Teddy Pilette could qualify it and Rotary Watches withdrew their sponsorship.

Their last championship appearance was from Larry Perkins in the 1977 South African Grand Prix, where he finished the race 15th, and last.

BACK ON THE PODIUM
Pedro Rodriguez took BRM to their first race win since 1966 (and also their last) with an inspired drive at Belgium in the 1970 BRM P153.

COOPER

COOPER WAS RESPONSIBLE FOR THE SWITCH TO REAR-engined cars in Formula One, a move which won back-to-back world titles for Jack Brabham in 1959 and 1960.

Country of origin: GB
Date of foundation: 1946
Active years in Formula One: 1950–69
Constructors' Cup victories: 1959–60

It all began when Charles Cooper, a racing mechanic before the war, built son John a 500cc motorcycle-engined racing car. Using a chain-driven JAP engine, the car had to have the power unit close to the driven rear axle, with the cockpit in front.

The cars were very successful and the Cooper Car Company was established to build more. Their 500cc Formula Three cars quickly began to dominate, but there were doubts about whether the same principles could be successfully applied with more potent machinery. People were mindful of the difficult rear-engined Auto Unions.

Mid-engined cars

Cooper concentrated on other projects before returning to the mid-engined concept. An experimental Cooper was run by Jack Brabham in the 1955 British Grand Prix, equipped with a 2-litre six-cylinder Bristol engine. A new 1500cc Formula Two class was due for introduction in 1957 and Cooper geared up for it by putting a Climax engine in the back of a developed version of its earlier chain-driven Formula Three cars. During 1957, enlarged versions

of the cars made a few Grand Prix appearances and clearly outhandled the bigger front-engined machinery, but they were too underpowered to do serious damage.

For 1958 Rob Walker, heir to the Johnny Walker whisky fortune, ordered a new engine from Coventry Climax for a Cooper and recruited Stirling Moss. Moss beat the Ferraris in Argentina in his blue Cooper T45, fooling the Ferraris into thinking he would need a tyre stop, but driving cautiously so that he made the finish without one, although his rubber was worn through to the carcass. It was the first World Championship win by both a rear-engined and privately entered car.

Moss reverted to a Vanwall thereafter, but Maurice Trintignant won in Monte Carlo aboard the Cooper. The cars were still underpowered, but clearly the rear-engined concept had merit, although Vanwall recovered and won the Constructors' Cup.

The successful years

By 1959 Vanwall had withdrawn from Formula One and Jack Brabham, working closely with John Cooper, helped to develop the T51. Coventry-Climax produced a 2.5-litre engine, giving Cooper competitive engines for the first time. Brabham won both the Monaco and British Grands Prix and his championship win was sealed when team-mate Bruce McLaren became the youngest winner of a Grand Prix, aged 22, at Sebring.

The US Grand Prix was new on the calendar that year and Moss had given himself a second successive shot at the title in the last race of the year by winning the previous two races in Rob Walker's private Cooper. He took off into the lead at Sebring but retired with a common gearbox failure, leaving the championship to either Brabham or Tony Brooks, who could win for Ferrari if he took the race with Brabham failing to score.

Brabham led, but ran out of petrol on the final lap, leaving McLaren to beat Trintignant, with Brooks third. New champion Brabham pushed his Cooper across the line in fourth place.

New Coopers were built for 1960 and, after McLaren won the opening race, Brabham scored five consecutive wins to make sure of back-to-back championship wins. Cooper's pioneering development was overtaken by more sophisticated designs from Ferrari, BRM and Lotus over the following seasons. Cooper came back with a monocoque chassis in 1966, but Maserati and then BRM engines were not competitive. Also, John Cooper had been seriously injured driving an experimental Mini Cooper. The marque disappeared from Formula One at the end of 1968.

CHAMPION'S CAR
Jack Brabham drives the Cooper T51 during his 1959 title-winning season.

EAGLE

AMERICAN RACING GREAT DAN GURNEY BROUGHT EAGLE
to the Formula One World Championship in the mid-1960s and soon made a huge impact with his attractive dark blue cars.

Country of origin:	USA
Date of foundation:	1964
Active years in Formula One:	1966–68
Constructors' Cup victories:	None

ALL-AMERICAN
Dan Gurney in the Eagle T1G at Monaco in 1968.

The Eagle story started when Gurney and fellow American racing legend, Carroll Shelby, formed the All-American Racers team in 1965. The focus of this was not Formula One, but the chance of achieving glory in the Indianapolis 500.

Backed by the Goodyear Tyre Company, they were out to try and overturn the domination of Indy Car racing by rivals Firestone.

Shelby moved on to pastures new in 1966 and Gurney found his thoughts wandering

back to Formula One. And so a parallel company was formed in England: Anglo-American Racers. Gurney was armed with experience from a Formula One career that dated back to 1959 when he made his debut with Ferrari before racing for BRM, Porsche and then Brabham. Gurney then pushed ahead and entered the World Championship.

The first Eagle Formula One campaign was hampered by its engines. The undersized and underpowered stop-gap Coventry Climax four-cylinder unit was no match for the dominant Repco V8s used by Gurney's previous team: Brabham. Gurney slipped from fourth overall in 1965 to 12th.

On the up

Eagle's second season of Formula One was a marked improvement and it yielded not only victory in the non-championship Race of Champions at Brands Hatch, but also its first Grand Prix win in the Belgian Grand Prix. This meant that he had echoed the feat of former employer Brabham by winning a Grand Prix in a car he'd built himself and he improved his ranking to eighth overall in the driver's standings and took the Eagle team to seventh in the Constructors' Cup.

Gurney contested only five Grands Prix in 1968, again with Weslake power, before packing the project away, angered by the car's deteriorating level of competitiveness.

Then, once armed with a McLaren, he showed that the problem had been with the car, and not with him, as he qualified at the front end of the grid once more.

While all this was going on, the Eagle chassis continued to race on the Indy Car scene, and Gurney was delighted to finish second in the 1968 Indy 500, beaten by Bobby Unser who was also driving an Eagle. Gurney went on to take his car to two Indy Car wins that season. He was second again in the 1969 Indy 500 and third in 1970. Eagles went on to win the Indy 500 in 1973 and 1975 in the hands of Gordon Johncock and Bobby Unser respectively. While Unser also won the Indy Car Championship for Eagle in 1968 and again in 1974.

Focus on America

In addition to Indy Car racing, Gurney's All-American Racers concern also entered Eagles in the North American Formula 5000 Championship. But the American arm's real success came when it turned its attentions to sports car racing. Backed by Toyota, Gurney built an Eagle that was a race winner in the 1990 American IMSA series. Further successes followed with the team taking titles in 1992 and 1993. More recently, the Eagle name has re-emerged in Indy Car racing, but after a thin season with its own chassis in 1996, All-American Racers reverted to using proprietary chassis from Reynard in 1997.

FERRARI

AFTER FIELDING SEMI-WORKS ALFA ROMEOS BEFORE World War Two, Ferrari later emerged as a force in his own right, carrying the fight to the Alfa 159s with the Ferrari 375 in 1951. Ferrari lost narrowly to Alfa in the final race of the season.

Country of origin:	Italy
Date of foundation:	1946
Active years in Formula One:	from 1950
Constructors' Cup victories:	1961, 1964, 1975–77, 1979, 1982–83, 1999–2000

The FIA then ran its championship races to 2-litre regulations, but Ferrari was prepared and Alberto Ascari dominated in 1952–53. Ferrari then fell behind Maserati and Lancia when 2.5-litre regulations were introduced and, in 1957, failed to win a single race for the first time.

Arrival of the Tipo 146

The Tipo 146 put Ferrari back on the map in 1958, the car being christened Dino, after Enzo Ferrari's son, who had worked with Vittorio on the new engine. Many believe Stirling Moss was the rightful champion that year, but the crown fell to Mike Hawthorn and Ferrari in the last race at Morocco.

After the mid-engined Coopers had dominated in 1959–60, Ferrari was back in 1961, fully prepared for new 1.5-litre regulations with the Tipo 156 "shark-nose". The cars dominated but, as he stood on the brink of the title, Wolfgang von Trips was killed in the Italian Grand Prix at Monza after a clash with Jim Clark. Von Trips team-mate, American Phil Hill, went on to clinch the championship for Ferrari.

John Surtees took another title for Ferrari in 1964, becoming the only man to win World Championships on both two wheels and four, but the new 3-litre regulations which came into effect in 1966 saw Ferrari struggling to match Ford's DFV, which was introduced at the Dutch Grand Prix in 1967.

The dominant years

Although Jackie Ickx enjoyed some success in 1970, it was not until 1974 that Ferrari looked like genuine championship contenders again. Niki Lauda was quick but inexperienced, losing out to McLaren and Emerson Fittipaldi. Lauda made amends by taking the flat-12 312T (transversal) to the championship the following year, and would have retained his title in 1976 had it not been for his near-fatal accident at Nurburgring. He lost out to James Hunt by a single point, but regained the crown with great consistency in 1977.

In 1979, Jody Scheckter beat spectacular young Ferrari team-mate Gilles Villeneuve to the championship with the ugly Ferrari 312T4, but the following season's T5 was a disaster as everybody began to master ground effect aerodynamics.

By now, 1.5-litre turbocharged engines were taking over from 3-litre normally aspirated ones and Ferrari produced the agricultural 126C. But Villeneuve scored remarkable wins with it at both Monaco and Jarama.

Ferrari employed British designer Harvey Postlethwaite and the 1982 Ferrari 126C2 was the class of the field. But Villeneuve was killed in practice at Zolder and Didier Pironi was injured in a career-ending crash at Hockenheim.

Michele Alboreto was competitive in 1985 and Alain Prost won five races in 1990, losing only to Senna in controversial circumstances in Japan.

The arrival of Michael Schumacher in 1996 was not met with delight by the tifosi. However, the way that he galvanized the team earned their undying respect. That he came within a whisker of winning the 1997 title made them like him more, even though the way he barged Jacques Villeneuve at the final race saddened them. But, his herculean efforts to overhaul McLaren's Mika Hakkinen in 1998 made them love him for ever.

Schumacher looked for revenge in 1999, but his challenge was scuppered by a broken leg at Silverstone. However, team-mate Eddie Irvine took over, supported by stand-in Mika Salo, and took the title race to the final round before he lost out to Hakkinen. Ferrari moved up a gear in 2000 and Schumacher won nine times to become champion, with Rubens Barrichello winning once.

THE PRANCING HORSE
Eddie Irvine drives the Ferrari F310B at Monaco in 1997.

FORTI

GUIDO FORTI IS ONE OF THE BEST KNOWN FACES IN
Italian motor racing circles, having run his extremely successful Forti Corse team for decades in both the Italian
Formula Three Championship and later in Formula 3000
as well.

Country of origin:	Italy
Date of foundation:	1975
Active years in Formula One:	1995–96
Constructors' Cup victories:	None

Forti ran Renzo Zorzi in Formula Three in 1975, taking the glory by winning the prestigious invitation race at Monaco. Thereafter, the likes of Teo Fabi and Oscar Larrauri raced for him, and then Franco Forini. Enrico Bertaggia, Emanuele Naspetti and Gianni Morbidelli won the Italian title for him in 1985, 1987, 1988 and 1989 respectively.

Forti took the team into Formula 3000 in the category's third season, in 1987, with Nicola Larini and Nicola Tesini as the drivers. Trouble was, he chose to run Dallara's 3087 chassis and these proved to be the worst ever to come from this otherwise respected marque. Not too surprisingly, they failed to notch up a single point between them.

Matters failed to improve when the team fielded four drivers, including Bertaggia, first in Dallaras and later in Lolas, again without points. But it all came together in 1989 when Claudio Langes was entered in a Lola and finished second at Enna-Pergusa. And now the team was really on its way and Morbidelli ranked fifth overall thanks to taking victory at

Enna-Pergusa with third places at Pau and Nogaro.

The team carried on winning in 1991, with Naspetti producing a string of four straight wins mid-season at Enna-Pergusa, Hockenheim, Brands Hatch and Spa-Francorchamps in his Reynard. This wasn't good enough for the title, though, as Christian Fittipaldi and Alessandro Zinardi had scored heavily in the earlier races and outpointed him.

Forti kept on winning in Formula 3000 in 1992, with Naspetti at the top of the pile at Pau and then Andrea Montermini winning at Spa-Francorchamps and Albacete to end the year as runner-up to Luca Badoer.

For 1993, Monegasque driver Olivier Beretta and Brazilian Pedro Diniz joined the line-up. While Beretta impressed by winning first time out, he failed to win again and ended the season ranked sixth overall. Not so much was expected from his team-mate, as Diniz hadn't shone in the junior formulae. But he brought with him a healthy budget, and, despite failing to score a point, stayed on for 1994. Fourth place in the penultimate race at Estoril was his best result, with team-mate Hideki Noda claiming third place at Enna-Pergusa, but what was important was that the Diniz family had released the money to finance the team's graduation to Formula One.

And so Forti Corse arrived on the big stage in 1995, with a pair of cars for Diniz and the experienced Roberto Moreno, a driver who never seemed to miss out if there was a struggling team to drive for. Giorgio Stirano designed the Ford-powered FG01 chassis, but they had nothing to shout about as they were miles off the pace of the dominant Williams and Benettons. However, from a sponsor's point of view, they received far more coverage for having their names on the overweight cars' yellow flanks than they would have if they had taken their money to a midfield team as the Fortis were spotted being lapped several times per race.

The cars did improve through the season, with Diniz getting all the development parts before Moreno did and thus scoring all the new team's best results, finishing four times in the top ten, with seventh place in the final race, the Australian Grand Prix, his best showing.

However, Diniz moved on to Ligier in 1996, leaving the door open for Badoer and Montermini to fill the two seats. But George Ryton's tidier FG03 design was never given much of a chance as the team's financial health went into terminal decline mid-season when the promised backing from the Shannon Group failed to materialize, with the green and white cars getting no further than the pit garages at Hockenheim as Cosworth refused to supply them with any engines due to a backlog of unpaid bills. And so with no money looking likely to arrive to remedy the situation, the Italian courts made the Forti team close its doors that August.

FLEETING FORTUNES
Pedro Diniz in the 1995 Forti FG01.

HESKETH

LORD ALEXANDER HESKETH WAS A LARGER-THAN-LIFE extrovert who enjoyed a considerable inheritance and had a good time spending it. Always a racing enthusiast, he was a friend of Anthony "Bubbles" Horsley, who was having little success in Formula Three in the 1970s.

Country of origin:	GB
Date of foundation:	1972
Active years in Formula One:	1973–78
Constructors' Cup victories:	None

At the same time, James Hunt was trying to make a name for himself. James was quick but down on his luck, having just been fired by the March works team when he met Horsley in Belgium. They came to an arrangement for James to drive a Formula Three car, with backing from the good Lord.

For 1973, Hesketh bought a Formula Two Surtees, but James shunted it in testing and the good Lord decided he might as well go the whole hog and rented a Formula One Surtees. Hunt was third in the Race of Champions at Brands Hatch and Hesketh decided it was time to forget about the junior ranks. He ordered a new March and managed to persuade one of March's young brains, Harvey Postlethwaite, to design a brand-new car, working from Hesketh's Easton Neston estate.

Hunt immediately showed great promise: he scored his first point in the French Grand Prix; he was fourth after a stirring drive at Silverstone; and capped the year with a fabulous second place behind Lotus's Ronnie Peterson at Watkins Glen in the US Grand Prix.

A touch of class

In that first year Hesketh Racing was looked on with something approaching scorn by the Establishment. They partied everywhere, taking butlers, champagne and Rolls Royces. But all this belied latent talent, and their results showed that they had to be taken seriously.

Jackie Stewart's retirement created the chance for a new order to establish itself and Hunt was one of those at the forefront. Postlethwaite's Hesketh 308 was ready for the International Trophy at Silverstone in 1974 and James scored a tremendously popular

win. With their teddy bear mascot, Hesketh Racing was catching the public imagination.

The 1974 season continued Hesketh's promise, but the Ferraris emerged as the cars to beat, even though the title eventually went to Fittipaldi's McLaren. Hunt again finished the year with a tremendous drive at Watkins Glen.

The speed was clearly there and at Zandvoort in 1975 the team achieved a fantastic first and only win. In a wet/dry race Hunt made an early change to slicks and managed to hold off Lauda's Ferrari for the rest of the race, crossing the line with both fists punching the air.

Financial problems

Hesketh had always run its cars without commercial backing, but even the Lord did not have bottomless pockets and 1976 was looking a bit dubious. Hunt was now in demand and, when Fittipaldi unexpectedly left McLaren to set up his own

operation with backing from the Brazilian sugar corporation, Hunt was given his seat and went on to win the 1976 championship after an epic battle with Lauda.

Hesketh called a halt and the cars were sold off to Frank Williams, who had just gone into what was to prove an ill-advised partnership with Walter Wolf, a Canadian oil millionaire. Thus, Postlethwaite's 308C became the Wolf-Williams.

Horsley kept Hesketh Racing ticking over for a couple of seasons using updated versions of the old car, with paying drivers, and engineer Frank Dernie penned the 308E. Without a driver of Hunt's calibre on the books, however, the motivation of the early days was gone and Hesketh Racing wound down, concentrating on servicing customer Cosworth engines for a time. One of the great chapters of classic British racing romanticism was at an end.

A TEAM LIKE NO OTHER
James Hunt shows his skills in the 1974 Hesketh 308.

HONDA

HONDA GREW RAPIDLY AFTER WORLD WAR TWO, ESTAB-
lishing itself in the motorcycle field before making the
decision to enter Formula One in 1964. The man with
the responsibility for this was development engineer
Yoshio Nakamura.

Country of origin:	Japan
Date of foundation:	1962
Active years in Formula One:	1964–68
Constructors' Cup victories:	None

The first Honda Formula One car, the RA 271, using a 60-degree transverse V12 1.5-litre engine, appeared in the German Grand Prix, driven by American Ronnie Bucknum. Bucknum had never driven a single-seater before and retired with four laps to go when the steering failed while he ran 11th. He then held down fifth at Monza before an overheating engine put him out.

Japanese success

Honda recruited Richie Ginther in 1965 to partner Bucknum and the RA272 chassis showed promise on the quicker circuits. Reliability, unfortunately, was poor, but there was a sweetener at the end of the year. In the Mexican Grand Prix, held at altitude, Ginther led from start to finish for the first Japanese win in the history of Formula One.

Sadly for Honda, Formula One was to have new 3-litre engine rules for 1966. Suspicions that the Japanese would pull out at the end of their second season proved unfounded. Spurred by the Mexican success, Soichiro Honda gave the go-ahead for a new car, equipped with a V12 engine. The unit was powerful but overweight and the Honda weighed in at more than 200 kilos over the limit.

For the following season Nakamura persuaded John Surtees, the only man to have won world championships on both two wheels and four, to join the team. Surtees had seen what Honda could do in motorcycling and figured that it would only be a matter of time before they achieved a similar level of success in Formula One.

The RA273 was still badly overweight and Surtees's best result was third in South Africa. At Monza, though, a new chassis, the RA300, appeared. Lola had been involved in the construction of the car, which still used the V12 Honda engine. It was built at Surtees's factory and became known as "the Hondola".

That 1967 Italian Grand Prix has become one of the most talked about races. Dan Gurney led it before his clutch failed and then Jim Clark took over until he had a puncture which cost him a whole lap. He rejoined a lap down, but slip-streamed past the leaders and

began the task of making up the lost ground. Incredibly, he managed it and went past Brabham and into the lead of the race with a few laps to go. Then he ran out of fuel on the last lap! Clark's drive somewhat overshadowed everything else, but Brabham was left to race wheel-to-wheel with Surtees, who went inside at the Parabolica on the final lap to score a debut win for the new car.

Weight problems

The 1968 season saw the emphasis on solving Honda's perennial weight problem. The new RA301 chassis was developed with the input of Lola's Eric Broadley and his team, but the car was not ready in time, a situation that was not eased by the need for Anglo-Japanese communication. Honda was also behind on its development of the V12 engine. The Japanese produced an entirely Honda-built RA302, with an air-cooled V8 engine, but Surtees did not like the way the car handled and refused to drive it.

Honda took on French driver Jo Schlesser, who lost control of the car early in his Formula One debut in the French Grand Prix at Rouen. The Honda speared off the road with a full fuel load and Schlesser died as the car, equipped with magnesium wheels, burned out. Surtees, in the RA301, was second in the same race to Jackie Ickx's Ferrari.

At the end of the season Honda pulled out of Formula One and did not return until the early 1980s, and then only as an engine supplier.

Massive investment reaped reward and the company won successive world championships with McLaren between 1988 and 1991. Honda made a full return in 2000, supplying engines for the BAR team, and it's doubling up for 2001 by supplying Jordan, too.

PLENTY OF PROMISE
Richie Ginther in the 1965 Honda RA272, a car which showed its potential on the quicker circuits.

JAGUAR (formerly Stewart)

JACKIE STEWART AND SIR JACK BRABHAM WON THREE Formula One World Championships apiece. And they both formed their own Grand Prix teams. But here the similarity between the Scot and the Australian ends.

Country of origin:	GB
Date of foundation:	1997
Active years in Formula One:	from 1997
Constructors' Cup victories:	None

For "Black Jack" started his own team when he was still a racer, indeed clinching his final crown in one of his own cars, back in 1966.

While Jackie waited from when he hung up his helmet at the end of 1973 until 1997 to take the plunge, and Formula One has come a long, long way in the interim. But Stewart was ready for this, as he has spent this period as a successful businessman, commentator and ambassador for a cluster of multinational companies.

Professional approach

The main tenet in Stewart's life is that if you do something, you do it properly. And no-one is more meticulous than Jackie Stewart. Indeed, he was effectively the first professional Formula One driver. Not because he was the first to be paid for his services, but because he was the first to embrace practices and principals that we see today as being "professional".

Renowned for his meticulous approach, his new team was one of the slickest in the paddock as it strived to make its mark.

It would not be entirely correct to say that Stewart Grand Prix was formed from scratch, for Jackie and elder son Paul have been running Paul Stewart Racing since 1987, moving up very successfully through the ranks from Formula Ford via Formula Three and Formula 3000, fielding the likes of David Coulthard, Gil de Ferran and Jan Magnussen, the first of whom has already recorded victories on the Formula One circuit.

The vital ingredient

For the team's maiden season, it had a tidy chassis penned by former Footwork designer Alan Jenkins, power from Ford's best V10 engine, promisingly competitive tyres from Bridgestone and fine young drivers in Rubens Barrichello and Magnussen. However, they didn't come together as Stewart would have wished.

High points included Barrichello finding a new lease of life after rather losing the plot at Jordan and stunning everyone by qualifying fifth in Argentina. The flip-side of this was that Magnussen seemed to suffer all the team's misfortune.

The team was given hope by the way that its Bridgestones appeared to have an advantage over the teams racing on Goodyears whenever it was wet. And so it proved in Monaco, when Barrichello drove an inspired race to not only finish for the first time, but to finish second. The wet track became wetter still as the Stewarts cried their eyes out.

Success in Formula One is not a one-year project, though, and the Stewarts are well aware of this. But one only has to compare their approach to entering the big time and Lola's flawed bid that also kicked off at the 1997 Australian Grand Prix to see that you have to arrive with everything in place.

To start beating the established teams is another matter altogether, and the early races of the 1998 season showed that the corner had yet to be turned. Anxious for progress, Magnussen was shown the door

after scoring for the first time in Canada. Barrichello was fifth that day, as he had been in Spain. Replacement Jos Verstappen failed to do any better and it became clear that much work would have to be done to push the team up the grid in 1999, with Johnny Herbert being signed in place of Verstappen for just this purpose. Progress was made, and it all came together when Herbert and Barrichello were first and third in a wet/dry race at the Nurburgring.

The team was then sold to Ford and rebranded as Jaguar for the 2000 season. Eddie Irvine joined from Ferrari, but neither he nor Herbert could do much with the car, peaking with Irvine's drive to fourth place at Monaco – one of only two points-scoring drives all season.

A Troubled Year
Eddie Irvine finished in the points only twice in 2000 for the rebranded Jaguar team.

JORDAN

IRISHMAN EDDIE JORDAN TYPIFIES THE BRAND OF wheeling and dealing team owners who are almost as much a part of racing as the cars.

Country of origin:	GB
Date of foundation:	1981
Active years in Formula One:	from 1991
Constructors' Cup victories:	None

A journalist countryman of Jordan's was responsible for the idea that Eddie had not so much kissed the blarney stone as swallowed it!

Jordan was a Formula Atlantic champion in Ireland and a promising Formula Three driver before he decided to set up Eddie Jordan Racing in 1981. With Martin Brundle in 1983, he came very close to taking the British Formula Three Championship after a season-long battle with Ayrton Senna.

Jordan claimed the Formula Three Championship in 1987 with Johnny Herbert driving. Moving up into Formula 3000 the partnership continued, but Herbert was seriously hurt in a crash at Brands Hatch in 1988.

Jordan has always fancied himself as something of a talent spotter and, after Jean Alesi had been through a tough Formula 3000 year in 1988, Eddie offered the Frenchman a drive in his Camel-sponsored team in 1989. Alesi repaid him by winning the Formula 3000 championship in fine style, putting both his and Jordan's Grand Prix aspirations on a firmer footing.

Into Formula One

Jordan expanded from his Silverstone industrial unit to new premises across the road from Britain's Grand Prix circuit and formed Jordan Grand Prix. He took the plunge into Formula One in 1991, when Gary Anderson designed the attractive 191, which turned out to be one of the cars of the year. In fact, some Jordan opportunism surrounds the car's designation. It was originally dubbed the Jordan 911, but Porsche objected to the use of a type number to which it owned the rights. He allegedly complained that Porsche was putting him to big expense in demanding he change to the 191 and reprint all his promotional material. In typical style, he ended up with a Porsche 911 out of the deal!

Bertrand Gachot and Andrea de Cesaris were Jordan's drivers, but the season was disrupted when Gachot sprayed CS gas in a taxi driver's face, ending up in jail. In his place, Jordan gave Michael Schumacher his debut at Spa. Sadly, Jordan could not hang on to him and he was spirited away to Benetton before the next race.

Jordan had Ford HB engines in 1991 and the new team was regularly embarrassing Benetton, the Ford works team. With no

guarantee of works engines in 1992, Jordan did a deal with Yamaha, but the Yamaha V12 was a disaster and the two companies parted ways after one year.

Improving fortunes

In 1993, Jordan used Brian Hart's new V10 engine and signed Rubens Barrichello, the youngest driver in Formula One. The Brazilian showed himself to be at home almost immediately, equalling Jordan's best fourth place result.

Ivan Capelli, Thierry Boutsen, Marco Apicella and Emanuele Naspetti all drove the second car before Eddie Irvine did a tremendous job to score a point on his debut with Jordan in Japan.

For 1994 Jordan kept his pairing of promising young drivers, although Irvine made something of a bad boy reputation for himself, earning a three-race ban for an incident he allegedly caused in Brazil.

Barrichello finished sixth in the championship, earning the team's first podium in the Pacific Grand Prix at Aida and finishing fourth four times. He also scored the team's first pole in wet/dry conditions at Spa.

Jordan stood out behind Formula One's "big four" – Williams, Ferrari, Benetton and McLaren – and his company earned itself a three-year works engine deal with Peugeot.

Promising in qualifying in 1995, Jordan should have profited, but their reliability was poor. Jordan signed Giancarlo Fisichella and Ralf Schumacher for 1997, peaking with the Italian finishing second at Spa. Damon Hill replaced Fisichella for 1998 and gave Jordan its first win, at Spa, helping the team to a career-best fourth in the Constructors' Cup.

The team advanced to third overall in 1999, with Frentzen winning at both Magny-Cours and Monza, but it slipped to sixth in 2000 as Frentzen and Jarno Trulli suffered from poor reliability after running behind the Ferraris and McLarens.

LANCIA

VINCENZO LANCIA WAS ONE OF THE CHARISMATIC EARLY racing pioneers. Born in 1881, the son of a soup manufacturer, he was an apprentice to the Ceirano brothers, whose firm became Fiat. He was chosen as their test driver and then raced in some of the sport's earliest events. In one he was flying the Italian flag admirably when a holed radiator eliminated his Fiat. Lancia wept bitterly.

Country of origin:	Italy
Date of foundation:	1906
Active years in Formula One:	1954–55
Constructors' Cup victories:	None

In 1906 he founded his own company to build touring cars and racing cars, although he continued to drive for Fiat. Gianni Lancia took over the company from his father and decided to return to motor racing in 1954. After two years racing to Formula Two rules, the World Championship was run to a new Formula One for 2.5-litre cars.

The great D50
Lancia recruited highly respected designer Vittorio Jano to build a car, which did not appear until late in the season. It also had the dominant Mercedes W196 to contend with. Although the W196 was renowned for its high-level technology, Jano's Lancia D50 was in fact more novel. The engine was positioned diagonally in the chassis, allowing the propshaft to pass through the cockpit without going under the driver's seat. This meant that the car could be built closer to the ground, which was better for the handling.

The D50 was Lancia's first Grand Prix car and it utilized an ultralight chassis of small diameter tubes, while the engine block and crankcase were stressed. Fuel and oil were carried in special side pontoons between the wheels on each side. The trend at the time was for rear tanks behind the axle line. As the fuel load changed on the Lancia, the variable weight was actually between the wheels and so did not have such a marked effect on the handling. Another positive spin-off was a cleaning up of the turbulent area between the wheels. Tipping the scales at just 620 kilos, the D50 was one of the lightest contenders.

The Lancia drivers were Alberto Ascari and Luigi Villoresi, who were loaned to Maserati while the D50 was finished. It finally made its debut in the Spanish Grand Prix of 1954, where Ascari was fastest in practice and showed everyone a clean pair of heels until he retired after nine laps with clutch failure.

Brief success

Things looked highly promising for 1955, although Mercedes had signed Moss to back up Fangio and the pair made for formidable opposition. Fangio won the opening Grand Prix in tremendous heat in his native Argentina, but the D50s won minor races with Ascari in Naples and Turin.

Lancia ran Ascari, Villoresi, Castellotti and Louis Chiron – at the age of 56 – in the Monaco Grand Prix. Moss and Fangio took an early lead, but had engine trouble and retired, leaving Ascari in front until he made a big error and landed himself in the harbour. He was rescued from drowning but, back on the track, Castellotti was beaten by Trintignant's Ferrari. Just four days later Ascari was killed testing a Ferrari at Monza. Like his father Antonio 30 years before him, Alberto was killed on the 26th of the month and was driving in a borrowed helmet.

Ascari's accident was inexplicable, some people feeling that he was still affected by his Monaco accident, but both Villoresi and Gianni Lancia were deeply upset. Lancia decided not to continue and the D50 raced as a Lancia just once more, when Castellotti entered one privately in Belgium.

In addition to his feelings for Ascari, Lancia was also having to cope with the fact that his company was in financial trouble. He sold Lancia and handed over the D50s to Enzo Ferrari, complete with all his spares, designer Jano and Castellotti. There was also a five-year Fiat subsidy arranged. That was Lancia's last appearance in Formula One.

LAST TIME OUT
Formula One's first champion, Alberto Ascari, in action at Monaco in his Lancia D50 in 1955. This would be his last-ever race – he was killed when testing four days later.

LARROUSSE

GERARD LARROUSSE, A STAR IN RALLYING IN THE 1960s and then in sports car racing in the 1970s, ran Lola chassis for five years in Formula One before cars bearing his own name hit the World Championship trail in 1992.

Country of origin:	France
Date of foundation:	1986
Active years in Formula One:	1992–94
Constructors' Cup victories:	None

To understand Larrousse's motivation to move into Formula One, one must first comprehend the competitive force that drove him through his driving career. It was clearly strong when he was a frontrunning rally driver for Alpine-Renault and then Porsche. He then transferred his skills to circuit racing, finishing second in the Le Mans 24 Hours in a Porsche shared with Hans Herrmann in 1969. He then won the Sebring 12 Hours and Nurburgring 1,000kms for Porsche in 1971. Moving to Matra in 1973, he won the Le Mans 24 Hours partnered by Henri Pescarolo and again the following year, a season in which he also won the European 2-litre sports car title with an Alpine-Renault. He even found time that year to sample Formula One, driving a Scuderia Finotto Brabham in the Belgian Grand Prix at Spa-Francorchamps. He then contested the entire Formula Two season in 1975, winning at Hockenheim.

PRECIOUS POINTS
Philippe Alliot took the Larrousse LH93 to fifth place in the 1993 San Marino Grand Prix.

Going it alone

An important event happened at the end of that season, when 35-year-old Larrousse was offerd the job of running Renault's competitions department. He accepted and immediately hung up his helmet.

After working on the company's embryonic Formula One project, Larrousse then moved on to Ligier.

This experience left Larrousse anxious to start his own team, and he duly entered the World Championship in 1987 as the Larrousse Calmels team with a Ford Cosworth-powered Lola chassis for Philippe Alliot, entering a second Lola for Yannick Dalmas. Alliot finished sixth on three occasions with Dalmas sealing the season with fifth place in Australia.

Back in 1988, again with the same chassis, the Larrousse Calmels team failed to score a single point. After Didier Calmels withdrew his backing for 1989 the team re-emerged as Equipe Larrousse, again with Lolas, but this time with Lamborghini engines. Alliot raced to just one point, finishing sixth at Jerez, while Dalmas was a frequent non-qualifier and left the team mid-season, replaced by Eric Bernard and then Michele Alboreto, neither of whom scored any points.

With backing from Japan, the team was known as Espo Larrousse F1 in 1990, with Bernard joined by Aguri Suzuki, their Lolas again Lambourghini-powered. And Bernard gave the team a huge boost by finishing fourth in the British Grand Prix, only to be outdone in the penultimate race when Suzuki finished third in the Japanese Grand Prix to leave the team a highly commendable sixth overall in the Constructors' Cup.

Tough times ahead

The team stayed together for 1991, albeit back with Ford power and had a much harder time of things, with each driver scoring only a point apiece.

So, for 1992, Larrousse took the major jump and built his own chassis. Designed by Robin Herd, the LC92 was effective, but its Lamborghini engine wasn't the best out there and the drivers Bertrand Gachot and the sponsorship-bearing Ukyo Katayama were in the points just once, with Gachot sixth at Monaco.

Alliot rejoined Larrousse in 1993, patnered by Erik Comas and they collected a fifth and a sixth place respectively.

Ford power was reintroduced in 1994 as Comas stayed for a second season and was joined by Olivier Beretta who stood down mid-season to be replaced by a string of drivers who brought much-needed financial backing. However, the Larrousse team never really did more than make up the numbers, and the two points Comas collected for a brace of sixth places were the team's last as it folded when its plans to enter the 1995 World Championship with a pair of cars for Christophe Bouchut and Eric Helary bit the dust.

LOLA

IT REMAINS ONE OF THE MYSTERIES OF POST-WAR motor racing that Lola has never cracked Formula One. From the day that marque founder Eric Broadley built his first sports racing car in 1957, Lola has built more racing cars than anyone else.

Country of origin:	GB
Date of foundation:	1957
Active years in Formula One:	1962–63, 1967, 1974–75, 1987–91, 1993, 1997
Constructors' Cup victories:	None

Yet, try and try again, it has never made the grade in the sport's highest echelon.

Its first attempt at Formula One was in 1962 when it built cars for the Bowmaker team. Quick from the outset, John Surtees put his car on pole for the Dutch Grand Prix, the first race of the season. A season of solid points-scoring drives followed, with a pair of second places in the British and German Grands Prix the highlights as the former motorcycle world champion placed fourth overall in the season's rankings. Team-mate Roy Salvadori, on the other hand, failed to score a single point and dropped out of Formula One. While Surtees moved on to Ferrari for 1963, team boss Reg Parnell kept the cars but ran them without success.

Different partners

Lola then built the T130 chassis for Honda in 1967 and Surtees won the Italian Grand Prix. But the record books credit this solely to Honda. Lola was asked to build cars for Graham Hill's team in 1974 and continued into 1975 until Hill's own cars were ready. Then in 1985

and 1986, the grids were graced by Beatrice-Lolas, but these had no Lola involvement, save for the fact that Lola's American importer, Carl Haas, was behind the team. In 1987, Lola was back, this time building cars for Larrousse, and the project soldiered through five seasons, peaking with sixth in the Constructors' Cup in 1990. The final "part-Lola" project was in 1993 when chassis were built for the Scuderia Italia team and, despite Ferrari engines, often failed to qualify, even with Michele Alboreto at the wheel.

So, when Broadley reached his mid-60s, he decided he ought to get cracking if he wanted to see Lola have a stand-alone shot at Formula One. But it lasted for only the opening race of 1997, indeed only to the end of the day before the race, as both cars were a league away from qualifying in Australia. Lola were not surprised when drivers Vincenzo Sospiri and Ricardo Rosset failed to qualify in Melbourne. Indeed, no-one had expected them to, such was the team's lack of testing. But the margin by which they missed the target was vast – their faster car was 11 seconds off pole – and it seemed a miracle was needed to get the cars on the grid in Brazil three weeks later.

Broken promises

Not only were the cars slow, but the money was tight. Indeed, the project looked set from the outset to be an abject failure as it had been given the green light in November 1996, only because Lola had pulled off a sponsorship coup and landed the Mastercard credit card company, even though there were just three months left to build a car. And, as was shown, this was not enough time. Amazingly, the T97/30 never even saw the inside of a wind tunnel, something that is *de rigueur* in Formula One.

With its backing being dependent on performance, without sufficient secondary support in place to tide the team over, Broadley told the team to return from Brazil before they had even reached the track. Regrouping failed to work and plans to rejoin the series for the fourth round, at Imola, came to naught. Then rescue attempts failed and it died on its feet, sending the team crashing into liquidation with debts of around £6 million.

With up to half of this owed to Lola Cars, the Formula One project had put the parent company into a perilous position, particularly as its core Indycar market had dwindled markedly in 1997. Lola Cars at least had the Indy Lights and Formula 3000 market to fall back on, in which it builds all the chassis. But margins are not great in this market and so there was a sharp intake of breath at the end of May when Lola Cars also went into administration while the financial mess was sorted out.

LIFE IN THE SLOW LANE
A lack of testing meant that it was no surprise when Riccaro Rosset failed to qualify his Lola T97/30 for the 1997 Australian Grand Prix (he was 11 seconds off the pace).

LOTUS

LOTUS FOUNDER, THE LATE COLIN CHAPMAN, HAS MANY times been dubbed a genius. Chapman was an enthusiastic member of the 750 Motor Club who took to building his own cars, calling them Lotuses. He founded the Lotus Engineering Company in 1952 with some money borrowed from his wife to be, Hazel.

Country of origin:	GB
Date of foundation:	1952
Active Years in Formula One:	1958–94
Constructors' Cup victories:	1963, 1965, 1968, 1970, 1972–73, 1978

Chapman started by building lightweight sports cars before constructing his first single-seater, the Type 12, in 1957, aimed at the new Formula Two category. The more sophisticated Lotus 16 was run in Formula One in 1959, but proved to be too fragile.

Chapman followed the mid-engined concept and built the brilliant Lotus 18 for 1960, Stirling Moss giving the marque its first Grand Prix win in a Rob Walker-entered car at Monaco.

POWER PLAY

Jim Clark powers the Lotus 49 to victory in the 1967 US Grand Prix at Watkins Glen.

Lotus triumphant

Lotus really made its name in the 1960s with legendary Scot Jim Clark. Ferrari had been ready for the new 1.5-litre Formula One regulations in 1961, but the British constructors were forced to use stopgap Formula Two Climax engines. Despite that, Stirling Moss scored that historic win at Monaco against Richie Ginther's "shark-nose" Ferrari.

In 1962, Chapman introduced the Lotus 25 monocoque chassis at the Dutch Grand Prix, following trends in aircraft design. Clark was unfortunate to lose the championship to Graham Hill's BRM, but he

made amends the following year. With the car in updated Lotus 33 form, Clark won his second title for Chapman in 1965, also winning the Indianapolis 500 in the same year.

Jack Brabham's Repco-engined Brabhams were the class of the field in 1966, but, with exclusive use of the new Cosworth DFV in 1967, Lotus hit back hard with the 49. Tragically, Clark died in a Formula Two race at Hockenheim in April 1968, the first time that Lotus had run in Gold Leaf colours. Chapman was devastated, but Graham Hill provided a tonic by winning the next two Grands Prix and going on to take the championship.

Chapman managed to replace Clark with the fiery young Jochen Rindt, regarded as the quickest driver in Formula One. The Austrian dominated most of the 1970 season in the brilliant Lotus 72, but died in practice at Monza when a brake shaft broke. Rindt became the sport's first, and only, posthumous champion.

New technology

Emerson Fittipaldi took over and won another title with the 72 two years later, but Lotus then lost its way until 1977, when it reaped the reward of developing ground effect principles. Simply stated, venturi tunnels on each side of a slim chassis created a vacuum and sucked the car on to the track.

Mario Andretti won four times with the Lotus 78 in 1977, but could not stop Lauda's consistent Ferrari taking the title. However, in 1978 the refined Lotus 78 was dominant in the hands of Andretti and Ronnie Peterson. Tragically, Andretti's moment of triumph was soured by Peterson's death as a result of injuries sustained in a multiple pile-up at the start of the Italian Grand Prix.

Continuing his reputation for innovative design, Chapman came out with the twin-chassis Lotus 88, but it was banned by the authorities, leaving a seething Chapman threatening to finish with the sport. It was he who gave Nigel Mansell his Grand Prix break, but in later years Chapman's name was to be tarnished by reports of the De Lorean fraud. Under pressure, in 1982 he succumbed to a heart attack.

Lotus has never been the same without him. The team enjoyed limited success in the mid-1980s, but even with turbo engines from Renault and Honda and Ayrton Senna in the cockpit, they could do no more than win the occasional race.

Former manager Peter Collins bought his way into the team in 1990, but on September 11, 1994, he had to give up the unequal financial struggle and place the company in administration. It was acquired by David Hunt, brother of 1976 World Champion James, but then it folded.

MARCH

THE IDEA OF A GROUP OF ENTHUSIASTS BANDING together to set up a Formula One team at the same time as selling customer cars, employing the reigning world champion and taking pole position at their first race seems ludicrous. But that is exactly what March did.

Country of origin:	GB
Date of foundation:	1969
Active years in Formula One:	1970–77, 1981–82, 1987–92
Constructors' Cup victories:	None

The four founding members were current FIA president Max Mosley, Alan Rees, Graham Coaker and Robin Herd. Herd was a highly regarded young designer who had worked at McLaren and designed the still-born Cosworth four-wheel drive car. They got together in 1969 and moved into a small factory in Bicester.

Jackie Stewart had just won the World Championship in a Matra. The French company was determined to use its own V12 engines in 1970 and neither Stewart nor Ken Tyrrell wanted that. Instead, they were faced with the prospect of finding an alternative chassis.

Opportunity knocks
Enter March. Jumping at the opportunity to grab the reigning champion after attempts to lure Jochen Rindt from Lotus had failed, they ended up fielding a works team as well as selling customer cars in Formula One. There were four March 701s on the grid in South Africa.

They also built customer cars for Formula Two, Formula Three and Formula 5000. The works drivers were Chris Amon

and Jo Siffert, with backing coming from STP and a spare car provided for Mario Andretti in selected races.

The 701s were hurriedly built, but that did not stop Amon from winning first time out in the Silverstone International Trophy. Stewart then won the Race of Champions at Brands Hatch and started from pole at Kyalami, with Amon alongside him. But in the race, Jack Brabham's BT33 won convincingly, while Amon retired and Stewart finished third.

Stewart won in Spain, but soon the heavy 701 was struggling, especially against the new Lotus 72. At the end of the year Stewart left to drive the first Tyrrell.

March signed promising young Swede Ronnie Peterson and Herd came up with the distinctive 711, featuring the famous "dinner plate" front wing. Peterson was highly competitive with the car and, although Stewart was the dominant force for Tyrrell, Ronnie placed second no fewer than six times and ended the season as championship runner-up.

Herd then embarked on the innovative 721X, which fea-

tured a gearbox mounted between the engine and the axle in the interests of improved handling. March took no notice when an inexperienced Niki Lauda told them the car was hopeless, and it required Peterson considerably longer to come to the same conclusion. March then scrabbled together a replacement 721G, based on its Formula Two car. The "G" designation was an in-house joke, standing for Guinness Book of Records, a reflection on how quickly it was thrown together!

Money problems

For 1973 March lost Peterson to Lotus and, always under both financial and customer time pressure, adopted the policy of fielding beefed-up Formula Two cars in Grands Prix, generally with pay drivers at the wheel. Although Stewart had won that second race in Spain in 1970, the first "works" victory did not come until 1975

in Austria, when Vittorio Brambilla, "The Monza Gorilla", won a rain-shortened race. He threw both arms into the air and shunted on the slowing down lap.

Peterson returned in 1976 and won the Italian Grand Prix in the 761 before leaving for Tyrrell. March disappeared from the Formula One scene at the end of the following season, returning a decade later with backing from the Japanese Leyton House concern of Akira Akagi, who would later be prosecuted in Japan for massive fraud.

Ivan Capelli showed flashes of brilliance with Adrian Newey's 881 and CG901 designs, coming second in Portugal in 1988 and second again in France in 1990, this time having led until just before the end, but March disappeared again at the end of the 1992 season, in which it had struggled against a severe shortage of money.

March to Victory
Ronnie Peterson took the March 761 to its final Formula One victory in the 1976 Italian Grand Prix.

MASERATI

THE MASERATI BROTHERS WERE INVOLVED IN EARLY
Italian motor sport before setting up their first business,
making sparking plugs, before the First World War.

Country of origin:	Italy
Date of foundation:	1920s
Active years in Formula One:	1950–60
Constructors' Cup victories:	None

When hostilities ended, Alfieri Maserati raced his own special and then the brothers embarked on building a straight-eight engine for the Diatto Grand Prix car. They bought it to modify it for the 1926 regulations, with Alfieri taking a class win in that year's Targa Florio.

Rivalry with Alfa Romeo

Maserati then did some twin-engined experimentation before building the 8C- 2500 and 2800 chassis. The 8CM was built to take the fight to rival Alfa Romeo's P3 and it was the start of a rivalry between the two marques that would continue until after the Second World War. Baconin Borzacchini was an early Maserati faithful, and was joined in an 8CM by Tazio Nuvolari in 1933.

One of Alfa Romeo's greats was Giuseppe Campari, who had joined Alfa in his teens as a test driver. He was a great music and opera lover and was married to the singer Lina Cavalleri. At Monza, Campari said that he would retire at the end of the meeting. Sadly, he was involved in a tussle with Borzacchini's Maserati, during which they both hit a patch of oil and crashed fatally. Bugatti

driver, Count Czaikowski, hit the same spot and was also killed.

Maserati could not match the German challenge of the mid- and late-1930s and the company was taken over by Cavallieri Adolfo Orsi, with the Maserati brothers remaining as part of the firm. In the early 1940s Maserati moved from Bologna to Modena.

The Maserati 4CLT was a competitive proposition just after World War II, if a little underpowered. The brothers then began work on a sports car before leaving to found Osca. The engine from this car was the basis of a Formula Two car which became eligible for the World Championship when Formula One fell by the wayside in 1952–53. This was a time of Ferrari domination, but Fangio won for Maserati at the Italian Grand Prix.

A promising period

Maserati looked good for the newly introduced 2.5-litre formula of 1954, but once again Mercedes was to launch a major onslaught and spoil the Italian party. Fangio won the first two Grands Prix for Maserati in 1954, while he waited for the Mercedes programme to come on-stream. He was driving the 250F, which was destined to become the best-known Maserati ever.

The 250F proved a very popular car among privateers and was progressively improved, with various weight-saving exercises being carried out. With Mercedes withdrawing, Stirling Moss won two races for Maserati in 1956 (at Monza and Monaco), while Fangio took his fourth world title for Ferrari. The next year Fangio, disgruntled with the politicking at Ferrari, returned to Maserati. He won four races (Argentina, Monaco, France and Germany) to collect his fifth and final title. He did it with one of the most

memorable comeback drives in motor racing history, at the Nurburgring. With one of the hub nuts lost during his pit stop, Fangio rejoined the race about 45 seconds behind the Ferraris of Mike Hawthorn and Peter Collins. On the last lap, he passed both to win by just over three seconds. Afterwards, he said: "I don't ever want to have to drive like that again."

Maserati also gave Fangio his last Grand Prix, at Reims in 1958, although by that time the factory team was no more. Despite a successful 1957, Maserati was in big financial trouble and the 250F continued to race only in private hands until it became outmoded by mid-engined development.

MONACO MAGIC
Stirling Moss led each of the 100 laps in his Maserati 250F (the best-known Maserati ever) to win at Monaco in 1956.

MATRA

IT WAS THE FRENCH MATRA COMPANY THAT HELPED TO take Jackie Stewart to his first World Championship success in 1969. Matra was a big French aerospace concern, whose more lucrative products included guided missiles. They knew all about monocoque construction through their involvement in the aircraft industry and they also had a plastics division.

Country of origin:	France
Date of foundation:	1965
Active years in Formula One:	1966–72
Constructors' Cup victories:	1969

CHAMPIONSHIP CAR
The 1969 Matra MS10 took Jackie Stewart to six wins and the world title.

Matra supplied car bodies to René Bonnet, who was running Formula Junior monocoque cars until he went bankrupt. At that point, Matra executive Jean-Luc Lagardère decided to form Matra Sports to take over where Bonnet had left off. The Matra Formula Three cars were renowned for quality workmanship and when Ken Tyrrell went looking for a chassis, he approached Matra.

Tyrrell had already secured the new Cosworth DFV for 1968 and he had Jackie Stewart signed up, with money and support from Dunlop tyres. After two years of running Matra chassis in Formula Two, Tyrrell went to Formula One with the MS10 in 1968, adding the Matra name to the world championship victory roll at the Dutch Grand Prix. Stewart remained in contention for the championship until the final round in Mexico, where he was pipped by Graham Hill's Lotus, after finishing seventh.

Outside assistance

Matra had funding from Elf and the French government voted an £800,000 grant to Matra to develop its own engine. The French built a V12, which was raced in an MS11 chassis by Jean-Pierre Beltoise. The V12 was not competitive against the Cosworth, however, and for 1969 Beltoise joined Stewart in Tyrrell's DFV-powered team. Matra, meanwhile, concentrated on sports car racing and on developing the V12.

The new Matra MS80 for 1969 was around 15 kilos lighter than the MS10 and it allowed Stewart to dominate the season. After winning in South Africa with the MS10, he gave the MS80 a successful debut in the non-championship Race of Champions at Brands Hatch. He then went to Barcelona, where the Matra team scored a fortunate win when both Lotus 49s suffered failures to the newly introduced high rear wings.

Unfortunately, the Matra broke while Stewart was leading convincingly from pole around the streets of Monaco, but both team and driver were dominant thereafter. The British Grand Prix, one of the all-time great races, featured a tremendous duel between Stewart's Matra and Rindt's Lotus. Mechanical problems hampered Rindt and Stewart took another win.

Monza that year was another epic. The famous track was bereft of chicanes in those days and the Italian Grand Prix was usually a slipstreaming classic.

Stewart had selected a top gear ratio ideal for the sprint to the line out of the last corner. Although Rindt passed him going in to the corner, Stewart led coming out and headed a four-car blanket finish to seal both the race and the World Championship.

A successful year

Although Matra could bathe in the glory of building the championship-winning chassis, it was very much a British success. Both the team and engine manufacturer were based in England and the driver was Scottish.

France had not been properly represented in Formula One since 1957 and for the 1970 season, Matra insisted on using its own V12 engine. Tyrrell and Stewart did not trust the unit and bought a March chassis instead.

Matra's small sports car company had been taken over by Simca and so a Matra Simca MS120 was raced by Beltoise and Henri Pescarolo in 1970, achieving three third places. Chris Amon replaced Beltoise for 1971 and won a non-championship race in Argentina. But over the next two seasons, despite sounding glorious, the cars never won a Grand Prix.

Matra then concentrated on winning the Le Mans 24 Hours and withdrew from Formula One. The V12 engines appeared in a Ligier chassis and Jacques Laffite won the 1977 Swedish Grand Prix with one, but the Matra team never returned.

McLAREN

BRUCE McLAREN IS THE MAN BEHIND THE McLAREN name. Born in Auckland, he won a scholarship to race in Europe in 1958. His results in Formula Two Coopers earned him a place in the Grand Prix team in 1959 and at Hendrick Field near Sebring that year McLaren became the youngest ever Grand Prix winner, aged 22.

Country of origin:	GB
Date of foundation:	1963
Active years in Formula One:	from 1966
Constructors' Cup victories:	1974, 1984–85, 1988–90, 1998

McLaren then formed Bruce McLaren Motor Racing Ltd and constructed his own cars. His first Formula One chassis, the M2B, was designed by Robin Herd and built in 1966. Unfortunately, the first year of the 3-litre engine formula found suitable power units hard to come by and McLaren had to turn to an underpowered Italian Serenissima engine. His first point was scored when he was sixth in the British Grand Prix.

The M7 in action

Before Herd left to join Cosworth, he penned the M7 McLaren, which became a potent weapon when fitted with a Ford Cosworth engine. Bruce gave the car a debut win in the Brands Hatch Race of Champions and the then reigning world champion, Denny Hulme, fought out the 1968 crown down to the final race before losing out to Graham Hill.

In CanAm, the McLarens of Bruce and Denny swept all before them but, on June 2, 1970, Bruce was killed testing an M8 at Goodwood.

The McLaren M19 was a good chassis, but the car that really put McLaren on the map was the M23, with which Hulme and Peter Revson won three races in 1973. In 1974 Emerson Fittipaldi joined from Lotus and won the title after three wins in the first year of backing by Marlboro, a brand that has become synonymous with McLaren.

Fittipaldi lost out to Niki Lauda and Ferrari in 1975 and then left to set up his own Copersucar team. James Hunt replaced him and, after one of Formula One's most dramatic seasons, took the title by a point.

Hunt won three more races as Lauda claimed back the title in 1977, but McLaren seemed overtaken by the ground effect technology which took Formula One on to a new plane.

The years of victory

The foundations of the McLaren steamroller of the 1980s were laid when principal Teddy Mayer sold part of the company to Project Four Formula Two boss, Ron Dennis, who brought meticulous attention to detail and designer John Barnard penned one of the F1 classics, the carbon fibre MP4.

Dennis, who ran a BMW Procar for Niki Lauda in 1979, persuaded the Austrian out of retirement and Niki won at Long Beach and Brands Hatch in 1982. The team struggled with normally aspirated engines against the emerging turbos in 1983, but the debut of a new TAG-badged Porsche V6 turbo was promising.

For 1984 Dennis swooped when Alain Prost suddenly became available. Lauda and Prost dominated the championship, with Alain winning seven races to Niki's five, although the Austrian took the title by half a point. Prost made amends in 1985 and won another title in 1986 despite the Williams-Honda combination of Mansell and Piquet being superior.

Williams delivered in 1987, but for the following year Dennis had the ultimate superteam: Prost, Ayrton Senna and Honda engines. Senna won the first of three titles in four years with McLaren, although Prost left for Ferrari as champion in 1989.

The withdrawal of Honda in 1992 rendered McLaren impotent, but Senna took five wins with Ford power in 1993 before going to Williams.

Ford power gave way to Peugeot for 1994, yielding no wins. A change to Mercedes for 1995 also failed to bring a victory, but Hakkinen came second in Italy and Japan. Their 1996 season was also barren. Then David Coulthard won twice in 1997 and Hakkinen won the season's final race. But this was nothing compared to 1998 when Hakkinen won eight times to be champion, and Coulthard once to be third overall as McLaren won its first Constructors' Cup since 1991. Hakkinen was champion again in 1999, but Ferrari pipped them to the Constructors' Cup. Then Hakkinen lost out to Schumacher in 2000 as McLaren again finished second.

MERCEDES

MERCEDES HAS PLAYED A SIGNIFICANT PART IN GRAND Prix history, although in spectacular bursts. The name dates back to the first Grand Prix of 1906, in which three Mercedes competed. The three-pointed star badge signifies engines produced for land, sea and air.

Country of origin:	Germany
Date of foundation:	1906
Active years in Formula One:	1954–55
Constructors' Cup victories:	None

Mercedes in the Nazi era

A great Mercedes onslaught came in the early 1930s, shortly after Adolf Hitler had risen to power. Hitler wanted to use motor sport to prove the superiority of German engineering and had his transport minister grant a large fund for those building Grand Prix cars. It was shared between Mercedes and Auto Union.

The German development went hand in hand with a new 750kg formula and progress was made on the chassis side, with independent suspension on each wheel improving cornering power.

On the Mercedes driving staff for 1934 were Rudolf Caracciola, Manfred von Brauchitsch and Luigi Fagioli. Both Mercedes and Auto Union missed Monaco so that their cars could make a patriotic debut at Avus in front of over 200,000 people and the Führer himself. Mercedes had some engine problems and withdrew rather than risk losing to the Italians.

This disaster was overcome at the Nurburgring a couple of weeks later. Von Brauchitsch and Fagioli led and the Italian was quicker. A German was supposed to win, however, and team manager Alfred Neubauer signalled Fagioli to slow down. This led to a huge row between the two at one of the pit stops, after which Fagioli hounded von Brauchitsch until he decided to park up and let Stuck finish second for Auto Union.

Duel with the Italians

The Germans then suffered an Alfa one-two-three in the French Grand Prix before starting a run of victories which convinced the top Italians that they had to drive for the German teams. Mercedes already had Fagioli, and Achille Varzi signed for Auto Union, where he refused to have Tazio Nuvolari, "the Flying Mantuan", who was acknowledged as the greatest driver of the age. Nuvolari therefore drove an Alfa for Enzo Ferrari.

The German motor sport governing body had suggested a European Drivers' Championship, which was won by Rudolf Caracciola in the Mercedes W25. The Germans were generally dominant but, ironically, the feature of 1935 that will always be remembered is Nuvolari's fantastic drive in

the German Grand Prix at the Nurburgring with an outdated Alfa P3. After applying relentless pressure, Nuvolari won in front of over 300,000 silent Germans as von Brauchitsch's Mercedes blew a tyre on the last lap.

Caracciola and Mercedes suffered at the hands of Auto Union and Bernd Rosemeyer in 1936, but came back strongly the following year with a new racing department under Rudi Uhlenhaut and the superb new W125. Caracciola took his second European championship.

There was a new 3-litre formula for 1938 and Mercedes dominated until the outbreak of World War II, beaten only a couple of times by Auto Union's Type D, now finally in the hands of Nuvolari.

Postwar fortunes

Mercedes did not come back into Grand Prix racing until 1954, with its technically advanced W196, which could be run in either open-wheeler or streamlined format. Once more it was dominant, with Juan Manuel Fangio winning the French, German, Swiss and Italian Grands Prix.

The domination continued in 1955, when Fangio was joined by Stirling Moss, who usually ran shotgun to the great Argentine, now claiming his third world title. Moss, however, scored an emotional win in the British Grand Prix in front of 150,000 people, which second-placed Fangio insists was won on merit. The year also witnessed the Le Mans tragedy: 80 spectators and Pierre Levegh perished when the Frenchman's Mercedes went into the crowd. Mercedes withdrew at the end of the year. They have never returned as a constructor.

After supplying engines to Sauber in 1993 and 1994, Mercedes signed a five-year engine supply deal with McLaren, which began in 1995 and has which brought two driver's titles for Mika Hakkinen.

MASTER AND PUPIL
Both in a Mercedes-Benz W196, Fangio leads Moss in the 1955 British GP at Aintree. The order would be reversed by the end of the race, but Fangio would go on to win the title.

MINARDI

THE MINARDI GRAND PRIX TEAM IS A MODERN-DAY DAVID in among the Goliaths. Giancarlo Minardi knows he will perhaps never be an Enzo Ferrari, but his little team are true racers and have a special place in the hearts of most Grand Prix enthusiasts.

Country of origin:	Italy
Date of foundation:	1972
Active years in Formula One:	from 1985
Constructors' Cup victories:	None

Minardi was born in 1947 and owned a Fiat dealership in Faenza. From 1974 he began running cars in Formula Two, with a Chevron chassis and a Ferrari V6 engine. He has close ties with Maranello and fielded an ex-works Formula One Ferrari in Scuderia Everest colours in 1976.

Minardi became a constructor in his own right in 1980, building an attractive Formula Two chassis driven by Alessandro Nannini.

Minardi enters the field

Minardi moved into Formula One in 1985, entering a single car for Pierluigi Martini, taking part in the first two races of the season with a Ford Cosworth engine. By this time, however, a turbo was a prerequisite in Formula One, with the TAG Porsche V6 doing all the winning in the hands of Alain Prost and Niki Lauda at McLaren.

At the San Marino Grand Prix, Minardi started to use a Motori Moderni turbo engine, but found that it was woefully uncompetitive. The unfortunate Martini was roundly panned and said to be out of his depth because there was no second car

to compare him with. In fact, the lack of competitiveness was the fault of the equipment.

For 1986, Martini lost his place and went to contest the Formula 3000 category, introduced in 1985. In his place came the two-car, all-Italian line-up of Andrea de Cesaris and old Minardi Formula Two driver, Nannini. They fared little better.

Minardi plugged on with the Motori Moderni turbos in 1987, this time with Spanish journeyman Adrian Campos in place of de Cesaris. Again, there were no points and the cars were makeweights.

Minardi reverted to Ford Cosworth power in 1988 and took Martini back into the fold, alongside another, more

promising Spaniard, Luis Sala. Martini scored the team's first point when he was sixth of the nine finishers after 63 laps of the streets of Detroit.

Some successes

In 1989, Minardi made it into the championship top ten, an important step for a small team because it confers long-distance freight benefits. Minardi was delighted when both Martini and Sala finished in the points at Silverstone. Then, at Estoril, Martini was fifth again and made a little piece of history for the Faenza team by leading the race for a lap... He was also sixth in Adelaide.

For 1990 Martini was partnered by Paolo Barilla and then Gianni Morbidelli, but there were no more points, although the 1991 season looked positive when Minardi struck a deal with Ferrari for V12 engines. The results were not as spectacular as the team had hoped, but they did manage to finish seventh in the manufacturers' series. Portugal was the happy hunting ground for the team again when Martini achieved its best result with fourth place, just ten seconds behind Alesi's third-placed Ferrari.

The Ferrari engines were replaced by Lamborghini V12s in 1992 and Christian Fittipaldi joined Gianni Morbidelli to score the team's only point of the season at Suzuka.

Customer Ford HB engines saw many steady performances from the team through 1993 and 1994, when Martini was back, partnered by Michele Alboreto. A big blow was the loss of a Mugen Honda engine deal to Ligier at the start of 1995. But since then the team has continued in its usual position at the rear of the grid, albeit unearthing talents such as Giancarlo Fisichella and Jarno Trulli along the way.

The cruellest fortune struck Luca Badoer when his car broke when he was heading for fourth place at the Nurburgring in 1999, but Marc Gene made amends by claiming sixth that same day. Neither Gene nor Gaston Mazzacane could match this feat in 2000, and the majority of the team has been sold to sports network PSN.

SEVENTH HEAVEN
Six points took the Ferrari-powered Minardi M191 to seventh in the Constructors' Cup in 1991 – their best effort to date.

PACIFIC

KEITH WIGGINS PROVED HOW DIFFICULT IT IS TO break into Formula One in the 1990s when he tried to move a level up after running highly successful teams in the junior categories.

Country of origin:	GB
Date of foundation:	1984
Active years in Formula One:	1994–95
Constructors' Cup victories:	None

Pacific had an enviable pedigree. The team was started in late 1984 and in its first season, with Marlboro support, took Bertrand Gachot to the RAC British Formula Ford 1600 title, against the likes of Damon Hill, Johnny Herbert and Mark Blundell.

Moving up to Formula Ford 2000, Gachot won the British championship again the following year, with Finnish driver J.J. Lehto continuing the tradition in 1987. The team pursued its policy of moving up the ladder in 1988, when it attacked Formula Three, the domain of highly professional specialist teams such as West Surrey Racing. Again, Pacific rapidly got to grips with the task with Lehto winning the British Formula Three title at the first attempt.

In 1989, Pacific jumped straight into Formula 3000 for a third successive year with the Finn, this time partnered by Eddie Irvine. With the Mugen engine in Europe for the first time, it seemed as though success could almost be taken for granted, but Pacific came up against strong, highly organized opposition in the form of Eddie Jordan Racing, with Jean Alesi and Martin Donnelly driving.

Minor triumphs

Lehto then made the move to Formula One, while the Pacific Formula 3000 team did not make much progress with Stephane Proulx driving. In 1991, though, it all came right. Christian Fittipaldi fought out a season-long duel with fellow Reynard runner Alessandro Zanardi, taking the title in the final round at Nogaro. Pacific had now won the championship in every formula it had contested and Wiggins started to plan for the move up to Formula One.

Reynard had originally intended its own Formula One team, but when there was no works engine deal forthcoming, plans foundered. Key members of the Reynard design team, such as Rory Byrne, rejoined Benetton and Pacific took on the remnants of the Reynard project with former Zakspeed engineer Paul Brown in charge of development.

Lack of finance

Other aspects of the project such as the aerodynamic data had been sold off elsewhere, however, and then Wiggins had to shelve his plans for 1993 because of a lack of finance.

However, he committed himself to action in 1994, forming Pacific Grand Prix to run the PR01 and hiring Gachot again, alongside wealthy Frenchman Paul Belmondo, son of the film star, Jean-Paul. A deal was done to run Ilmor V10 engines.

The season was a disaster, however, and the team never finished a race. The car proved to have no rigidity and, with a lack of initial data, the team had very little to work on. There were also a number of problems with the engines and, after the Canadian Grand Prix at Montreal, Pacific failed to make the grid again.

The team would have preferred to abandon 1994 and concentrate on the design of the new PR02 for 1995, but the championship regulations demand appearance at every race or substantial penalties, which could include the cancellation of the team's championship entry.

Behind the scenes, however, Pacific was working away at securing backing from a Japanese entrepreneur. They had also employed an experienced aerodynamicist and had Frank Coppuck and Geoff Aldridge working on the new car. A customer engine deal was agreed with Cosworth.

The PR02 was a far better car, and went reasonably with Andrea Montermini at the wheel, but a lack of funds saw the drivers restricted to minimal running in the free sessions. By mid-season Gachot stood down so that rent-a-drivers could have a go. And it was downhill to oblivion from there. The team closed its doors after the final race of 1995.

ROAD TO NOWHERE
Andrea Montermini drives the 1995 Pacific PR02, but the team would close its doors at the end of the season.

PENSKE

ROGER PENSKE RUNS WHAT MANY EXPERTS ACKNOWL-
edge as the best racing team in the world. Interestingly,
however, his business interests in the USA have caused
him to concentrate on domestic racing programmes since
having a foray into the Formula One world in the 1970s.

Country of origin:	USA
Date of foundation:	1966
Active years in Formula One:	1974–76
Constructors' Cup victories:	None

Penske has won the Indianapolis 500 a record nine times. A measure of the dominance that he has achieved in America was graphically illustrated in 1994 when his Marlboro-backed cars finished one-two-three in the Indycar World Series. Al Unser Jr took the title, admirably backed up by twice-world champion Emerson Fittipaldi and young Canadian Paul Tracy, who took the opportunity to test a Benetton Formula One car at the end of the 1994 season.

A successful businessman

Penske is entirely self-made, starting off as a tin salesman and building the Penske Corporation into a huge conglomerate. He has a seat on the board of Philip Morris, whose Marlboro brand backs his Indycars, and he is now involved with the Mercedes motor sport programme. Mercedes is a major stakeholder in Penske's successful Detroit Diesel company and Roger himself owns 25 per cent of Ilmor Engineering, which will prepare the Mercedes engines for the three-pointed star's new five-year agreement with McLaren.

Penske was a promising driver in his own right, but hung up his helmet at the age of 28 to concentrate on business. Starting his own team, he struck up a hugely successful partnership with experienced American ace, Mark Donohue.

In 1971, Penske rented a McLaren M19 and Donohue drove it to third place in the wet Canadian Grand Prix. Penske then started to think about a full Grand Prix effort. He bought a factory at Poole, in Dorset, and recruited Geoff Ferris, who had learned his trade with Ron Tauranac at Brabham, to design him a car.

The first car appeared in late 1974, with the testing done by Donohue, who had retired. The project sparked his enthusiasm, however, and Mark agreed to commit to a full Grand Prix programme with Penske in 1975.

Entry into Formula One

With First National City Bank support and a Cosworth engine, Penske hardly set the world on fire and, midway through the season, replaced the PC1 with a March 751. In practice at the Osterreichring, Donohue suf-

fered a deflating tyre and flew off the road, hitting television station scaffolding. Although at first he appeared to have escaped with a headache, he fell into a coma and died from his injuries.

Penske signed John Watson and, with Ferris's elegant new PC4, the combination started to run at the front in 1976. By mid-season Watson was challenging for a win which, somewhat ironically, came at the Osterreichring exactly a year after Donohue's death there.

Formula One was enjoying its epic Hunt versus Lauda season and Watson's sudden intrusion was something that Hunt could have done without, as Niki lay in a Mannheim hospital trying to recover from his

Nurburgring accident. Watson also battled hard with Hunt's McLaren at Zandvoort before retiring.

At the end of 1976 First National City Bank defected to Tyrrell, attracted by the exposure potential to be generated by the Tyrrell six-wheeler. Penske decided to halt his Formula One campaign and concentrate on the Indycar scene.

Despite the occasional rumour, Penske has never returned to Formula One. In 1994, however, his closeness to Mercedes, through both business and personal friendships, convinced many that he would play an active role in the McLaren-Mercedes link. This has yet to happen, though.

NOT IN THE SCRIPT
John Watson made an unlikely challenge for the world title in the 1976 Penske PC4, scoring an emotional victory in Austria.

PROST (formerly Ligier)

GUY LIGIER IS A FORMER BUTCHER'S ASSISTANT WHO was a top rugby player in his native France and made his fortune in the road construction industry, his company being responsible for building many French autoroutes.

Country of origin:	France
Date of foundation:	1997
Active years in Formula One:	from 1997
Constructors' Cup victories:	None

Always a motor racing enthusiast, Ligier drove Cooper-Maserati and Brabham-Repco Formula One cars in the mid-1960s and then teamed up with his long-standing friend Jo Schlesser to drive a pair of Formula Two McLarens in 1968.

Ligier was appalled by Schlesser's death in a fiery accident aboard the new air-cooled Honda in the French Grand Prix at Rouen. He withdrew from driving and ran a GT programme with a car designed by Frenchman Michel Tetu. Ligier races his cars with the "JS" model designation in Schlesser's memory.

In 1975 Ligier achieved second place in the Le Mans 24 Hours, with backing from the Gitanes cigarette company, which was keen to move up to Formula One.

Ligier founds his company

France was lacking a national Formula One effort after the withdrawal of Matra Sports and talented French design engineer Gérard Ducarouge joined Ligier from Matra. The first Formula One Ligier, the JS5, arrived on the scene in 1976 and was a distinctive car.

Ducarouge persuaded Matra to develop its V12 engine to give the Ligier project more of a Gallic flavour. Jacques Laffite, dominant in Formula Two, was taken on as driver.

The JS5 had a distinctive high airbox which earned the car its "teapot" nickname. Laffite qualified it on pole for the Italian Grand Prix.

Laffite won the Swedish Grand Prix at Anderstorp in 1977 in the JS7, and this was the first win by a French driver in a French car with a French engine since the modern-day World Championship began in 1950.

The Swedish win was fortunate and it could never be said that the Ligiers looked set to dominate. But all that changed in 1979 when the team switched to Ford engines and built the ground effect JS11 with its distinctive aerodynamic kick-ups.

Ground effect cars were something of a black art. The Lotus 79 had worked superbly in 1978, but the Ligier's JS11 was suddenly the class of the field in 1979. Nobody at Ligier really knew why, but Laffite won the two opening races of the season. Team-mate Patrick

Depailler took another victory in Spain, then broke his legs in a hang-gliding accident and was replaced by Jacky Ickx. With the Williams taking over as the best car, Ligier could not maintain its early form. For 1980 Ligier signed Didier Pironi, who won in Belgium and drove one for the 1995 season.

Panis didn't drive as well in 1995, but peaked with a lucky second in the season's final race, at Adelaide. Martin Brundle did a far better job, but had to share the other car with the Japanese Aguri Suzuki.

Panis won in the wet at

of the races of the year at Brands Hatch. That, though, was the team's zenith.

Prost shows an interest

Talk of a tie-up between Ligier and Alain Prost in 1992 came to nothing and Ligier moved into the background after selling out to Cyril de Rouvre.

Ligier looked shaky at the start of 1994, but Benetton's Flavio Briatore bought it, and 1993 Formula 3000 champion Olivier Panis had a fine debut season in which he finished 15 of the 16 races. But Ligier never managed to capitalize on a three-year deal for Renault's V10s, and changed to Mugens

Monaco in 1996, but it was all-change for 1997, with Prost taking control and renaming the team eponymously. Panis broke his legs in Montreal, but the team was cheered when stand-in Jarno Trulli led in Austria. However, 1998 was a disaster and they scored just one point through Trulli. The Italian again saved the team in 1999, claiming a surprise second at the Nurburgring in the European Grand Prix. Trulli moved to Jordan for the 2000 season and was replaced by the experienced Jean Alesi, but Prost was at loggerheads with the engine supplier Peugeot and the team went nowhere.

A NEW DAWN
Olivier Panis showed good early-season form in the 1997 Prost JS45, before breaking both legs in Canada.

RENAULT

MARQUES SUCH AS FERRARI AND ALFA ROMEO HAVE long racing histories, constant in the case of Ferrari. But for Renault the decision to enter the World Championship in 1977 was risky, especially with a 1.5-litre turbocharged engine against 3-litre normally aspirated opposition.

Country of origin:	France
Date of foundation:	1898
Active years in Formula One:	1977–85
Constructors' Cup victories:	None

Formula One was the domain of British manufacturers which used customer engines and gearboxes. For a company the size of Renault to do less than win would be disastrous.

Since 3-litre engines were introduced in 1966, an equivalence formula existed which allowed a 1.5-litre turbo engine. It was never regarded as a feasible proposition, but Renault gained a lot of turbo experience in sports car racing.

The Renault RS01 appeared at the British Grand Prix in 1977, with Jean-Pierre Jabouille at the wheel. Initially, the Formula One project was hampered by split resources with the sports car programme and the preoccupation with winning the Le Mans 24 Hours. Once that was achieved in 1978, the Formula One project became much more serious.

Appearance of the RS10

In 1979, Renault introduced the RS10 ground effect cars at Monte Carlo and Jabouille scored a popular first win in the French Grand Prix at Dijon, a race that was also memorable for a crazy last-lap tussle between Villeneuve's Ferrari and Arnoux in the second Renault.

The Renault turbos were devastatingly effective in the high altitude of Kyalami, where the normally-aspirated cars were left gasping for breath. Arnoux won in South Africa and Brazil in 1980 and it was soon obvious that turbocharging was the way to go.

But Renault had a head start and for 1981 it signed the brilliant young Alain Prost. Immediately the Frenchman was competitive and won three races, including his home Grand Prix, but lost out to Nelson Piquet's Cosworth-powered Brabham in the championship.

By 1982, BMW and Ferrari had turbo engines up and running and were rapidly closing the gap with Renault. The Ferraris looked probable champions, but Villeneuve was killed in a qualifying accident at Zolder and team-mate Didier Pironi ended his career when he smashed his legs after colliding with Prost's Renault in poor visibility at Hockenheim. Keke Rosberg wound up as champion with a single victory. This was the last time that a normal-

ly aspirated car would get the better of the turbos.

An unlucky year

The 1983 season looked to be Renault's year. Prost had three wins and a 14-point lead in the championship when the circus got to Austria, but he warned that Piquet and the Brabham-BMW had overtaken the Renault team's level of development.

The championship went right down to the wire at Kyalami, with Renault sending many staff and journalists along in anticipation of Prost's crowning glory. But Prost was out early on and Piquet's Brabham stroked home to the championship, cruising to third place as he let team-mate Riccardo Patrese come through to take the win.

Prost spoke out and said what he thought, promptly getting his marching orders as a result. Ironically, he went to McLaren and enjoyed the best years of his career.

Renault took on Derek Warwick and Patrick Tambay for 1984. Warwick led in Brazil, but he tangled with Lauda and retired with suspension problems. With rival engines now just as good, Renault was facing a tough time and there were no more wins as McLaren's MP4 dominated the scene, ironically with Prost at the helm.

After another struggling season when its drivers dubbed their chassis "tow-car of the year", Renault quit Formula One.

The company continued as an engine supplier from 1986 and began its association with Williams in 1989. Nigel Mansell and Alain Prost took drivers' titles in 1992–93, while Williams won the Constructors' Cup three years in a row before Renault pulled out at the end of 1997. It is returning for 2001 in conjunction with Benetton.

TURBOCHARGED
Rene Arnoux won two of the first three races in 1980 with Renault RE20 before his season tailed off.

SAUBER

PETER SAUBER'S FIRST RACING EXPERIENCE WAS ABOARD a VW Beetle, but he started building his own cars in 1970. Sauber finished second in the 2-litre class at Le Mans in 1978, but he became better known when he built the Sauber C6 for the new Group C sports car category.

Country of origin:	Switzerland
Date of foundation:	1970
Active years in Formula One:	from 1993
Constructors' Cup victories:	None

Sauber entered his first Mercedes-powered car in 1985 and his team went on to set new standards in sports car racing. At first, the team entered chassis with Mader engines, but as the cars became the class of the field, so Mercedes invested more and became an official entrant. In 1989, the Sauber-Mercedes won both Le Mans and the World Sports Car series.

Going Formula One

Formula One was the next logical step. But in November 1991 Mercedes announced that it would not be making the move into Grand Prix racing. It did, however, promise financial and technical support for Sauber. Designer Harvey Postlethwaite had already left Tyrrell to draw the new Sauber C12, but when he heard that Mercedes was not coming in behind it, he quit. Sports car designer Leo Ress and former McLaren man Steve Nichols were then responsible for development.

Sauber himself designed the company's state-of-the-art factory. The building is four stories high with a showpiece elevator capable of lifting a 40ft truck to any part of the factory.

Much wind tunnel work was done before the car's introduction in 1993. The car showed immediate pace, but lacked much of the electronic technology, such as active ride, which was now a prerequisite in Formula One.

Sauber chose JJ Lehto and Karl Wendlinger as his first-year drivers. Lehto arrived on the recommendation of Nichols, who had worked with him at Ferrari, and Wendlinger had been part of the Mercedes Junior Team in sports cars, with Schumacher and Heinz-Harald Frentzen.

Early success

The team made a stunning debut in the 1993 South African Grand Prix when Lehto qualified sixth and finished fifth, the first time that a new team had scored points in its first Grand Prix since Jody Scheckter won the 1977 Argentinian Grand Prix for Wolf. But it had come into the season with a lot of testing under its belt and was thus well prepared, although they struggled as other teams got up to speed.

There were strained relations between the drivers after they

collided at Monaco, but there were some solid performances. Lehto was fourth at Imola, with Wendlinger getting a similar result at Monza.

For 1994 Lehto lost his seat to Frentzen, who immediately proved one of the revelations of the season. Frentzen qualified fifth on his Formula One debut in Brazil and then finished fifth in the Pacific Grand Prix at the new TI circuit in Japan.

But then things started to go wrong for Sauber. The team suffered a big blow when Wendlinger crashed in practice at Monaco: he lost the car under braking for the harbour front chicane. He went into a coma and his life hung in the balance for some time. Happily, he made a complete recovery and was testing again before the end of the year, after Andrea de Cesaris had deputised.

There were also sponsorship problems and then Mercedes announced its move to a new five-year deal with McLaren, and the end of its association with Sauber. However, Ford, having lost Benetton to Renault, then agreed to a works deal for 1995.

Despite Frentzen's best efforts, which peaked with a third place in the Italian Grand Prix, Sauber improved to seventh overall in 1995, bumping Tyrrell down the order.

Then came the news that Stewart Grand Prix would take over the works Ford engines in 1997. But, in a move that shocked everyone, Sauber landed 1996-spec Ferrari engines for 1997, rebadged as Petronas units in deference to the team's chief sponsor. No wins came their way, despite the best efforts of Johnny Herbert, with third in Hungary their best showing. And, despite the mercurial talent of Jean Alesi in 1998 and 1999, then Mika Salo in 2000, still the team optimistically awaits that first win.

SLOW PROGRESS
Heinz-Harald Frentzen took the 1995 Sauber C14 to third at Monza, but that was as good as it got.

SHADOW

SHADOW BOSS DON NICHOLS WAS FIRST ACTIVE ON THE
sports car scene in America. Jackie Oliver drove a Shadow
CanAm car in 1971 and Nichols persuaded Universal Oil
Products (UOP) to back the team.

Country of origin:	USA
Date of foundation:	1968
Active years in Formula One:	1973–80
Constructors' Cup victories:	None

Oliver regularly ran at the front with the black-painted cars in 1972, when Shadow announced its plan to go to Formula One the following year.

Nichols recruited former BRM designer Tony Southgate, with Oliver and veteran American sports car ace, George Follmer, to drive. Kit cars were supplied to Graham Hill's newly established team.

Nichols set up a British base for his team in Northampton after Southgate had built the first car in the garage of his Lincolnshire home. The Cosworth-powered DN1 was not spectacular, but ran in the top half of the field regularly.

Success and tragedy
Oliver drove only the CanAm cars in 1974, winning the championship against thin opposition, while rapid Frenchman Jean-Pierre Jarier and American Peter Revson were drafted into the Formula One team. Things looked promising until Revson was killed in a pre-season testing accident at Kyalami. Brian Redman raced briefly before handing over to Welsh hot-shot Tom Pryce.

As young drivers fought to establish themselves in the post-Stewart era, it was evident that Shadow had two of the quickest, even if the car's reliability was not all that it might have been.

Pryce won the Race of Champions for Shadow at the beginning of 1975 and Jarier sometimes got very close to the qualifying pace of Niki Lauda's dominant Ferrari. Still, solid results did not come and the team struggled when UOP withdrew its support at the end of the year.

Oliver had now hung up his helmet and was the team's main sponsorship sourcer. The DN5 had become a little long in the tooth, but Southgate's new DN8 looked highly promising. The only problem was that Southgate himself had been lured to Lotus temporarily before returning to Shadow.

Main backing was now coming from Tabatip cigarillos, but Italian financier Franco Ambrosio also became involved, until he was jailed on charges of financial irregularity.

A poor year
Shadow started 1977 with Pryce and Italian Renzo Zorzi, who had sprung a surprise in the previous year's Monaco Formula Three race. But at

CASTING NO SHADOW
Alan Jones recorded the team's first success in his Shadow DN8 at the 1977 Austrian Grand Prix, beating the dominant Niki Lauda into second place.

Kyalami tragedy struck. Zorzi stopped on the far side of the main straight, just after a hump in the track. There was no problem and he was getting himself out and trying to extricate his helmet oxygen supply when a young marshal ran across the track to stand by in case of fire. Pryce crested the brow, killed the marshal instantly and died when he was hit by the fire extinguisher.

Alan Jones replaced Pryce and brought a partial sweetener to a sad year with the team's one and only win. Niki Lauda was on the way to taking his title back after his Nurburgring accident of the year before, when the circus arrived at his home Osterreichring track. In a wet/dry race, Jones outdrove the Austrian and beat the Ferrari into second place.

Financial problems led to a team split in 1977, with Oliver, Alan Rees and Southgate heading off to form their own Arrows set-up. The Arrows A1, unsurprisingly, bore remarkable similarity to Southgate's unfinished drawings for the Shadow DN9. Nichols took legal action and got a decision in his favour from the High Court which led to Arrows having to build a new car. Meanwhile, John Baldwin finished the DN9 and Shadow continued in the hands of Hans Stuck and Clay Regazzoni.

The team went into 1979 with the young Elio de Angelis/Jan Lammers pairing and then in 1980 with Geoff Lees and David Kennedy. It finally collapsed after failing to qualify for the French Grand Prix in 1980.

SIMTEK

SIMTEK GRAND PRIX WAS ONE OF TWO TEAMS NEW TO the Grand Prix scene in 1994. Team boss Nick Wirth, at 28, was the youngest team owner in Formula One and was the design and engineering force behind Simtek.

Country of origin:	GB
Date of foundation:	1989
Active years in Formula One:	1994–95
Constructors' Cup victories:	None

Clients included some of the motor industry's major manufacturers and, before Wirth's direct involvement as a team owner, the FIA itself.

No longer is Grand Prix racing possible with an off-the-shelf customer chassis, engine and gearbox. Teams have to build their own cars, even if the work is contracted out. And, in the 1990s, so sophisticated and expensive are the materials that it is not so much a case of entering a sport as beginning a manufacturing industry.

Whereas a budget for a leading Grand Prix team will be well over £20 million, not including free works engines, a new team like Simtek will operate on something much closer to £5 million. There will be no specialized test team, no 200-plus employees and no fancy hotels.

David Brabham joins

Wirth went into the challenge with his eyes open and recruited David Brabham, youngest son of triple world champion Sir Jack, to drive. Brabham Sr had shares in Simtek and, although 30 years had gone by since he was a constructor/driver, he brought valuable experience.

Sadly, the fledgling team suffered Grand Prix racing's first fatality at an event for 12 years when Roland Ratzenberger crashed on the flat-out approach to Imola's Tosa corner. The likeable Austrian had done a deal for five races with Simtek, achieving his lifetime ambition of making it to Formula One.

The team's telemetry showed that Ratzenberger had left the circuit on the lap before his fatal crash, probably weakening the front wing assembly in the process. The nose section flew off the car as it reached maximum speed and thus maximum down load on the straight, caus-

ing the Simtek to spear straight on.

In the past it was customary for a team to withdraw its other entry in the event of a fatality to one of its drivers. But Brabham, looking around and seeing the desperation, particularly among the older members of the team, decided that in order to lift spirits and keep the team together, he should carry on.

Italian Andrea Montermini drove for Simtek at the Spanish Grand Prix in Barcelona and was also involved in a sickening crash in practice. Happily, he escaped with a slight ankle injury, but, with another damaged monocoque, the team was under enormous pressure.

Seeing the year out

Frenchman Jean-Marc Gounon was then signed as partner to Brabham and actually achieved the S941's best finish of the season when he was ninth in his home Grand Prix at Magny-Cours. Brabham, meanwhile, was tenth in Barcelona and brought the car to the finish six times. He was also involved in a couple of controversial incidents with Jean Alesi's Ferrari, when the Frenchman was lapping him.

Gounon's Simtek deal took him as far as Portugal and then the team ran Italian Domenico Schiattarella at Jerez and Adelaide, with Japanese driver Taki Inoue at Suzuka.

With the 1995 season fast approaching, the team suffered a blow when Brabham decided to accept a BMW ride in the British Touring Car Championship.

Simtek started 1995 with a bang, the S951 flying in the hands of Dutchman Jos Verstappen; he qualified it 14th in Argentina. But refinements were too frequent, and the team folded at Monaco when a sponsorship deal collapsed and the money ran out. Wirth then moved on to work with the Benetton team.

A Short Stint in F1
David Brabham in the 1994 Simtek S941. The team only lasted for two years.

SURTEES

JOHN SURTEES IS THE ONLY MAN TO HAVE WON WORLD Championships on two wheels and four. Surtees had his first experience of four wheels in one of Ken Tyrrell's Formula Two Coopers before joining Ferrari in 1963. He took a close World Championship for the Scuderia in 1964, but left suddenly in the middle of 1966.

Country of origin:	GB
Date of foundation:	1966
Active years in Formula One:	1970–78
Constructors' Cup victories:	None

Wide-ranging interests

Surtees did not restrict his racing to Formula One and was an active sports car driver for Ferrari as well, setting up his own small team in association with Lola's Eric Broadley.

Surtees had a huge accident in a Lola CanAm car at Mosport in 1965 when suspension failure pitched him off the track. He was seriously injured, but fought back to fitness and broke the lap record at the Ferrari test track when he returned to the team.

Ferrari team boss, Eugenio Dragoni, was not convinced about his recovery, however, and was also a mentor of Ferrari's second driver, Lorenzo Bandini, whom Surtees usually shaded without much ado. Despite being favourite to take

TWO WHEELS TO FOUR
Mike Hailwood took the Surtees TS9B to second place at Monza in 1972 – a car entered by fellow motorcycle champion John Surtees.

the championship and winning at Spa in the teeming rain, Surtees and Dragoni had one run-in too many and John left immediately to join the Cooper-Maserati team.

For the following two seasons he drove for Honda and then had a year with BRM before deciding to build his own car.

The first Surtees Grand Prix car made its debut in the British Grand Prix at Brands Hatch, where Surtees ran seventh before retiring. He scored his first points as a Formula One constructor with the TS7 when he finished fifth in the Canadian Grand Prix. His first win came in the non-championship Oulton Park Gold Cup.

The next TS9 followed for 1971, with Rolf Stommelen joining Surtees in his last full season as a driver. For 1972, Surtees concentrated on running his team for motorcycle-racing buddy Mike Hailwood and Tim Schenken. Hailwood had made a promising debut for the team the previous year, when he had come second in the Italian Grand Prix.

Fade-out at Monza

Surtees's last Grand Prix was at Monza in 1972 when he debuted the new TS14. Hailwood led the Race of Champions at Brands Hatch with the car in 1973 until he crashed heavily after a mechanical failure. He was joined thereafter by promising Brazilian Carlos Pace, who finished on the podium in Austria.

The 1974 season was grim. Jochen Mass and Pace started the year, but Carlos soon left and later in the year Derek Bell and Jean-Pierre Jabouille drove. The team was operating on a shoestring and both cars failed to qualify at Monza. Austrian Helmut Koinigg drove a TS16 in the Canadian Grand Prix, finishing ninth, but was killed in a slow-speed accident next time out at Watkins Glen.

John Watson drove for Team Surtees in 1975 before joining Penske. Surtees then did a deal leading to what his cars were probably most famous for: racing in Durex livery. Alan Jones was the first driver and, ironically, the TS19 proved much more competitive than most of the chassis that had gone before. It led to a very public withdrawal of the BBC TV's cameras from the pre-season non-championship British races.

The TS19s did not actually achieve much in the form of hard results and Vittorio Brambilla was driving one when he was injured in the multiple accident at the start of the 1978 Italian Grand Prix.

René Arnoux looked the most promising driver to try the new TS20 and, with ground effects technology taking over, Surtees planned the TS21 with that in mind for 1979. Unfortunately, however, sponsors would not commit to the team and so Surtees decided to bring down the curtain on his team's Formula One participation.

VANWALL

TONY VANDERVELL WAS AN INDUSTRIALIST, RACING FAN and patriot. One of the original backers of the BRM project, he became frustrated at the lack of progress and decided to go his own way.

Country of origin:	GB
Date of foundation:	1949
Active years in Formula One:	1954–60
Constructors' Cup victories:	1958

Vandervell bought a Ferrari 125 in 1949 with the intention of testing it and helping the BRM learning process. The car ran as a Thinwall, a Vandervell trade name.

After a couple of years of Formula Two rules, the World Championship conformed to a new 2.5-litre formula in 1954. Vandervell commissioned John Cooper to construct a new chassis for a 2-litre, four-cylinder engine built by Vandervell and based on four Norton motorcycle engines. This was developed into a full 2.5-litre unit by 1955.

The car became known as a Vanwall for the first time, a combination of Vandervell's name and his Thinwall bearing business. But racing then was dominated by the Mercedes-Benz team and the lone Vanwall was raced by Peter Collins. Harry Schell and Ken Wharton drove in 1955, but there was little to write home about.

Chapman's chassis

In 1956, Vandervell commissioned a new chassis from Colin Chapman. The bodywork was styled by aerodynamicist Frank Costin and the engine produced a respectable 285 brake horse-power. Schell, Maurice Trintignant and Mike Hawthorn were the drivers, but before the Grand Prix season started, Stirling Moss gave the car a winning debut in the International Trophy race at Silverstone.

In the French Grand Prix at Reims Chapman himself was entered by Vanwall, but his brakes locked up in practice and he rammed Hawthorn! The brakes could not be repaired and he did not start the race.

Schell gave the Ferraris a shock in the race, passing both Collins and Castellotti, and getting up alongside race leader Fangio on two occasions.

The 1957 season saw Vanwall emerge as a force to be reckoned with. The team could boast Stirling Moss, along with Tony Brooks and newcomer Stuart Lewis-Evans.

The British Grand Prix at Aintree brought the day Vandervell had been waiting for. Moss qualified on pole, with Jean Behra's Maserati between him and Brooks. Moss took the lead, but Behra hauled him in when the Vanwall started to misfire and Stirling had to pit for attention to an earth lead. Still there was a problem and so Brooks was called in to

hand over his car to Moss, who resumed ninth. He was soon up to fourth, behind Lewis-Evans, Hawthorn and Behra. But the gods were looking after him. Behra's flywheel shattered and Hawthorn punctured a tyre on the debris, allowing Moss to win. It was the first time that a British car had won a major Grand Prix since 1923 and the first victory by a British car and driver in the British Grand Prix.

The little mid-engined Coopers made a sensational start to the 1958 season, with Vanwall not ready for the hastily arranged Argentine Grand Prix. But then Moss won in Holland and Brooks in Belgium. Brooks won again in Germany, a win spoiled by Peter Collins' death in a Ferrari. Moss won in Portugal before Brooks was successful again at Monza.

Constructors' crown

The championship went to the wire in Morocco and was between Moss with three wins and Hawthorn's Ferrari with one, but five second places. Moss won superbly, but teammate Lewis-Evans died as a result of major burns received in an accident. Hawthorn was second, enough to clinch the title. On the way, however, he had gone off, stalled and push-started his car against the flow of traffic. He was disqualified, but Moss said he had seen him pushing the car only on the pavement, which was permitted. Hawthorn was reinstated, costing Moss the title. Sportsmanship was different back then, but at least Vanwall had won the manufacturers' crown.

Vandervell was shaken by the accident to Lewis-Evans and, in poor health, gave up his involvement in 1959. With the rear-engined revolution on the way, a chapter of British racing history was over.

TOP OF THE TREE
Tony Brooks eases his Vanwall to the first of three victories in 1958 (Belgium, Germany and Italy) – enough to bring the team the manufacturer's crown.

WILLIAMS

FRANK WILLIAMS IS PROOF THAT REAL DETERMINATION will triumph over adversity. An amateur driver of talent, he struck up a friendship with Piers Courage and ran a Formula One Brabham BT26 for him in 1969.

Country of origin:	GB
Date of foundation:	1968
Active years in Formula One:	from 1972
Constructors' Cup victories:	1980–81,
1986–87, 1992–93, 1994, 1996, 1997	

A fine second behind Graham Hill in Monaco attracted the attention of De Tomaso and Williams ran their car in 1970, but he was devastated when Courage was killed at Zandvoort.

Williams struggled in the early 1970s, running a selection of paying no-hopers. A liaison with Walter Wolf in 1976 turned sour, but led to Frank founding Williams Grand Prix Engineering with Patrick Head.

Williams invested a lot of time into attracting Saudi Arabian backing and Head's functional FW06 allowed Australian Alan Jones to turn in some fine drives in 1978.

Arrival of the FW07

Head came up with the ground effects FW07 in 1979 and Clay Regazzoni scored the team's first win at Silverstone before Jones went on to dominate the second half of the year. Jones was teamed with Carlos Reutemann in 1980. He won five times and Reutemann once as Jones won the drivers' championship and Williams took the Constructors' Cup. Jones was pipped by Nelson Piquet in 1981.

By 1982 turbo engines were too strong for normally aspirated rivals, but Keke Rosberg managed to give the Ford Cosworth engine its final championship success.

Williams then forged an alliance with Honda. The V6 turbo was brutal and heavy, but constant development meant that by the end of 1985, with Nigel Mansell on board, the Williams-Honda combination was the one to beat.

Rosberg left for McLaren at the wrong time and, although Nelson Piquet and Mansell were the class of the field in 1986, Prost's McLaren stole the title in Adelaide when Mansell suffered an exploding tyre.

Williams suffered an even bigger blow in March 1986 when Frank was paralysed in a car crash on the way back from a test at Paul Ricard.

Piquet was outpaced by Mansell in 1987, but consistency brought his third world title.

The 1988 season was a watershed with normally aspirated Judds, but a deal with Renault brought Williams back as a major strength although, with Riccardo Patrese and Thierry Boutsen on their books, the team lacked a recognized top-line driver until Mansell returned for 1991 after a two-year spell with Ferrari.

Victory for Williams

Patrick Head's FW14 was a superb car and Mansell lost out to Senna's McLaren in 1991 only because of gearbox problems. By 1992 Williams had mastered active suspension and, with the FW14B, Mansell was unbeatable, winning nine races en route to the title.

After a contractual dispute with the team, Mansell left to try his hand on the Indycar circuit. Alain Prost took up where Mansell left off and won the second consecutive drivers' and constructors' double for the Williams FW15 in 1993.

Frank Williams was the man who first gave Ayrton Senna a Formula One test. He had wanted the Brazilian ever since and, in 1994, he got him. Tragically, the great Brazilian died in an FW16 at Imola. Damon Hill then rose in stature and saved a desperately sad year by challenging Michael Schumacher for the drivers' title, losing out only in the final round at Adelaide. Williams,

though, won the constructors' crown again.

It was always going to be harder for Williams in 1995, with Benetton also running with Renault engines. But the team must have expected more than five wins, four for Hill and one for Coulthard, as poor race tactics cost them dear.

The 1996 season was far better, as Hill and Jacques Villeneuve won all but four of the 16 races and Hill lifted the world title. Villeneuve repeated the feat in 1997, but only after a clash with Schumacher at the Jerez finale, while Heinz-Harald Frentzen won just once. But the loss of works Renault engines cost them dear in 1998 as they were outstripped by McLaren and Ferrari, and very nearly by Jordan and Benetton. Ralf Schumacher shone for Williams in 1999, but real progress was made in 2000 when BMW became partners and Ralf and newcomer Jenson Button were impressive all year as Williams rose to third overall.

UNSTOPPABLE
Riccardo Patrese comes through to secure his only win of the 1992 season in his FW14B at Suzuka – team-mate Nigel Mansell won nine races that year and the title.

WOLF

WALTER WOLF WAS AN AUSTRIAN WHO MADE HIS fortune in the oil business in Canada. A lifelong racing enthusiast, he used his new-found wealth to forge an involvement in the sport.

Country of origin:	GB
Date of foundation:	1975
Active years in Formula One:	1977–79

Wolf first appeared on the Formula One scene in 1975 and was courted by Frank Williams who, at that time, was still struggling to make an impression on the sport.

Wolf and Williams struck a deal for 1976, but it soon became apparent that Wolf was an autocrat who did not wish to adopt a mere supporting role. The Hesketh team was winding down, so Wolf took on Harvey Postlethwaite's promising 308C design and the man himself.

An unpromising start

The 1976 season was disastrous. Jackie Ickx was the driver, but he was not impressed with the car and did not gel with Postlethwaite. Williams did not like working for anyone else and decided to cut his links and go his own way with designer Patrick Head.

Wolf had a major reorganization for 1977. He recruited former Lotus team manager Peter Warr to run his team and he signed Jody Scheckter from Tyrrell. Postlethwaite's neat Wolf WR1 chassis looked promising and Scheckter took advantage of some good fortune to win on the car's debut in Argentina.

Good luck he may have had, but the WR1 was a good car and the team was well drilled. Scheckter led a great tussle involving Niki Lauda's Ferrari and Mario Andretti's Lotus in Long Beach, only losing out in the closing stages when a tyre went down.

Lauda had won for the previous two seasons in Monte Carlo, but Scheckter went to the Principality, where he lived, and outdrove the Ferrari to claim his second win.

Scheckter remained in contention for the championship throughout the year, but the crown eventually went to a consistent Lauda. Andretti's Lotus was the class of the field, but the American did not have the best of reliability. One of the places where Scheckter gained by that was Mosport. There he scored an emotional "home" triumph for his team boss.

Triumph of ground effects

The form shown by Andretti and Lotus had served a warning that a ground effects car would be a prerequisite for success in 1978, and so it proved. The Lotus 79s of Andretti and Ronnie Peterson proved to be unbeatable. At Wolf,

Postlethwaite came up with the WR5, but the team could not add to its victory tally, a pair of seconds in Germany and Canada, being their best results.

Scheckter was becoming disgruntled and an offer to join Ferrari was quickly accepted, the South African going on to win the championship the following season. Wolf took on James Hunt who was also disgruntled at McLaren's inability to crack the ground effect concept.

On paper this looked good. Hunt and Postlethwaite, of course, went back to Hesketh's glory days and the new WR7 looked as if it should work. Like the successful Ligier JS11, it had distinctive aerodynamic

kick-ups ahead of the rear wheels and a futuristic shape.

It was a rush to get the car ready in time, however, and the results did not come. Hunt was always aware of his profession's inherent dangers and, with just one finish behind him, he did not want to put his life on the line for a sixth or seventh place. He had the trappings of wealth and announced his sudden retirement mid-season. Wolf then took on the aggressive, young Keke Rosberg, but even the exuberant Finn could do little with the Wolf.

A man used to success, Walter Wolf did not take kindly to being an also-ran and folded his team at the end of its fourth season.

First Time Winner
Jody Scheckter took the Wolf WR1 to victory on its first outing in Argentina in 1977.

THE FAMOUS CIRCUITS

IF A DRIVER CAN HAVE TALENT, A CAR MECHANICAL SUPERIORITY AND A TEAM great organization, can a circuit have class? You bet. Almost to a person, Formula One fans have a favourite circuit. The mighty Spa is considered the ultimate by many; others opt for the Silverstone layout of the early 1970s; while some swear

by Monaco for its unique atmosphere. So what is the difference? A great deal.

When anyone builds a circuit today you will most likely be able to predict how the corners will be laid out and where the main straights will be located — circuits are now designed to be able to contain both the cars and the drivers, whatever happens. It was not always so. From the early races on public roads to the early purpose-built tracks, including the mighty 17-mile-plus Nurburgring, only the Monaco street race remains of the old tracks

A PLACE LIKE NO OTHER *Monaco has retained its curious mix of chic and chicanes over the years.*

ARGENTINIAN GRAND PRIX

THE WORLDWIDE SUCCESS OF JUAN MANUEL FANGIO encouraged the popularity of motor racing in Argentina, and it hosted the first World Championship Grands Prix to be held outside Europe – six years before the first US Grand Prix.

BUENOS AIRES

Circuit distance: 2.647 miles (4.259 kms)
Race distance: 190.571 miles (306.71 kms)
No of laps: 72

OFF THE GRAND PRIX CALENDAR FOR years, this famous track was eventually given the all-clear for a race in 1995 after its ancient pits were replaced. Sadly, the high-speed lay-out was eschewed and a tight, twisty circuit (derivative of the number six) was used instead.

The Buenos Aires track was built with the support of President Juan Perón, who was keen to use both Fangio and the sport as publicity tools. Opened in March 1952, the Autódromo Municipal de la Ciudad de Buenos Aires was located on the southern outskirts of the Argentinian capital and featured more than a dozen track configurations, with long straights linked by twists and turns around the pit and paddock area. The earlier races were run without the twists and turns, and lap speeds were correspondingly high. Yet, whatever the layout, the first corner, an "S" after the main straight, has always been a fearsome stretch of track.

It was flat, but challenging and the view from any of the grandstands was far-reaching – the best vantage point being the one on the old back straight, which also allowed the spectator to see across to the start/finish straight and down to the famous arch at the circuit entrance.

The main hazard in the early days was the crowd, who seemed to have little respect for fast-moving racing cars. As in all South American sporting events, the crowd was always massive and extremely voluble.

The first Argentinian Grand Prix was held in 1953, the fourth year of the championship. Back from plying his trade in Europe, Fangio received a hero's welcome. He had already won the title once, in 1951, and so his popularity at home was enormous. He failed to finish, however, and reigning champion Ascari took the laurels. The race was overshadowed by a terrible accident involving Farina. The Italian star survived, but nine spectators were killed.

Fangio made amends by winning in 1954 (a massive two minutes ahead of Farina) and, indeed, he won three more times in the following three years. It seemed nobody could beat him at home until, in 1958, Moss triumphed in his Cooper, with Fangio fourth. After one more start at the French Grand Prix, Fangio confirmed his retirement. It was no coincidence that there was no race in Argentina the following year, but it was revived in 1960, when Bruce McLaren gave Cooper another win.

Reutemann – rising star

There were no Grands Prix from 1961 to 1970, and it took the discovery of a new local hero to encourage its return. The old Autódromo was pressed back into service for a non-championship race in 1971, won by Chris Amon. But all eyes were on newcomer Carlos Reutemann, who finished third. For 1972 the race was given World Championship status. Reutemann joined Mario Andretti in the history books by taking pole for his first championship Grand Prix, although Jackie Stewart won.

Throughout the 1970s Argentina was established as the venue for the season-opening race, apart from 1976, when political unrest led to its cancellation.

In 1981, there was controversy as Piquet and his "hydraulic suspension" Brabham overcame the new ride-height rules. Reutemann was second, fated never to win at home.

The 1982 event was cancelled and Reutemann, having started the year with Williams, unexpectedly quit racing. Within weeks, Argentina and Britain had gone to war over the Falkland Islands and sport took a back seat.

Argentina became a Grand Prix venue once again in 1995 and saw a fine win for Damon Hill, with the English driver making it two in a row for Williams in 1996. The Williams domination continued with Jacques Villeneuve's victory in 1997 (ahead of Irvine), before Michael Schum-acher won there for Ferrari in 1998 after barging David Coulthard's McLaren out of the way.

BUENOS AIRES
No longer the high-speed circuit of old, the circuit is packed with mainly low-speed corners.

AUSTRALIAN GRAND PRIX

DESPITE THE MYRIAD INTERNATIONAL SUCCESSES OF Jack Brabham and Alan Jones, it was not until 1985 that Australia first hosted a World Championship event. This was in Adelaide, and it became established as one of the most popular events on the Formula One calendar.

MELBOURNE	
Circuit distance: 3.274 miles (5.278 kms)	
Race distance: 189.9 miles (305.6 kms)	
No of laps: 58	

MOVING THE RACE TO MELBOURNE IN 1996 shifted the Australian GP to the start of the Formula One season, thus scuppering Adelaide's traditional end of season party. The new parkland circuit, built around a lake, proved popular with the drivers for its fast-flowing nature.

With the full support of the local government, nothing was left to chance in the planning stages, and over the years the Australian race has often been cited as the best-organized event of the year.

It was also popular with the teams, because it came at the end of a long, hard season, and because the weather was splendid – unless, of course, it was raining...

The Adelaide track, used until 1995, was a temporary one, running partly on public roads in and around the Victoria Park horse racing facility. It was not a typical street circuit in that it was very fast, with long, straight sections punctuated by slow, right-angle turns and some fast kinks – notably the tricky chicane at the first turn, where Michael

MELBOURNE
Although far from straight, the stretch from Turn 10 to Turn 11 is seen by the drivers as a flat-out blast.

Schumacher came to grief in qualifying in 1994. The tight hairpin at the end of the Brabham Straight was a notable overtaking place, and the scene of much action over the years. Like most street circuits, though, there was no run-off area, just unyielding concrete walls.

Spectating was best from the temporary grandstands set up in the park, although hundreds of faces could be spied peering from the surrounding buildings where the track passes the city's fruit and vegetable market.

A memorable start
Rosberg won the inaugural

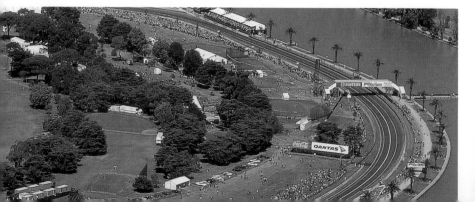

race, which happened to be Lauda's last Grand Prix, but it was really the 1986 event which stands out. Mansell was on course for the world title when his rear tyre blew, and his Williams skated down the escape road in a shower of sparks. Prost won the race, and with it his second title.

After a win for Berger in 1987 and a second success for Prost in 1988, the 1989 race proved a memorable event. Rain had affected qualifying in the past, and for the first time it struck on race day. The Grand Prix was stopped after two laps, and Prost declined to take the restart. With many top drivers crashing, including Senna, Boutsen scored a hard-earned win in his Williams.

The following year, Adelaide had the honour of hosting the 500th Grand Prix, and triple World Champion Piquet won for Benetton after a strong challenge from Mansell. The rain came again in 1991, and the event lasted for just 14 laps before being red-flagged, with Senna adjudged the winner. It was the shortest-ever World Championship event.

Senna was in the news the following year, too, when he and new champion Mansell collided, and Berger scored his second win. Ayrton got revenge with a dominant win in 1993. It was his last race for McLaren and his final Grand Prix win.

The 1994 event was a classic, the first final-round title showdown since 1986. The contest ended when Schumacher and Damon Hill collided in controversial circumstances while fighting for the lead, securing the title for the German. Having started from pole, returnee Mansell scored a surprise win (after Berger had made a mistake.)

Adelaide held the Grand Prix for the last time in 1995, with Damon Hill winning by two laps after all his chief rivals hit trouble, including race leader David Coulthard, who drove into the pit wall.

Melbourne took over for 1996, and a great race was run at the Albert Park venue. Hill won again, but only after new Williams team-mate, Jacques Villeneuve, had to slow down with engine problems at the end. David Coulthard won in 1997 and the McLaren domination continued in 1998 with a controversial one-two – with Mika Hakkinen victorious.

Since then, it has been a Mclaren graveyard, with both Mika Hakkinen and David Coulthard breaking down after just a couple of laps in 1999 to hand a first Grand Prix victory to Eddie Irvine and then doing so again in 2000 to allow Schumacher through to win.

ADELAIDE
The temporary circuit was really a downtown track, as the buildings in the background testify.

AUSTRIAN GRAND PRIX

DESPITE ITS RELATIVELY SMALL POPULATION, AUSTRIA has produced two great World Champions in Jochen Rindt and Niki Lauda, plus Gerhard Berger, one of the most enduring stars of the 1990s.

A-1 RING		
Circuit distance: 2.67 miles (4.297 km)		
Race distance: 186.892 miles (301 km)		
No of laps: 70		

THE REBUILT A-1 RING MAY LACK THE excitement of the former Osterreichring, on which it is built, but the first bend is very tight over a sharp ridge and never fails to produce drama on the opening lap. The second corner, the Reams Kurve, is even tighter and is the ultimate viewing spot on the circuit. The views around the track are fantastic, thanks to its setting on the side of a hill in the styrian region of Austria.

The country also has one of the most spectacular circuits, and it played host to the Austrian Grand Prix from 1970 to 1987, before the race was dropped from the schedule.

The first Austrian Grand Prix was held at the Zeltweg airfield in 1964. Noted for its bumpy surface, the track proved a car breaker, but Lorenzo Bandini's Ferrari survived to win. Being flat and uninteresting, Zeltweg was not a popular venue with the drivers.

After a six-year break, the Formula One circus returned to the Styrian area to find a brand-new venue: the Osterreichring. This new track was set in mountainous countryside and consisted almost entirely of high-speed sweeps making it one of the fastest on the schedule. It was also the most scenic. Indeed, as a spectator venue, it was unrivalled, with those in the know hanging out at the first corner: the mighty Hella Licht Kurve. The cars would approach this up a steep hill, with the right-hand bend at the brow.

Traversing the hillside, the track rounds a right-hander, then climbs to its trickiest corner: the wonderful Bosch Kurve, a never-ending right-hander that tips the track downhill again. A long left-hander brings the track back up to the Rindt Kurve, a double-apex right-hander that leads back on to the pit straight. In some places the barrier is alarmingly close to the trackside, while in others, drivers have the luxury of hundreds of metres of grass before anything solid.

A brief but spectacular history

Rindt was the darling of the crowd at that first event in 1970, but the race was won by Ickx's Ferrari; Jochen would die a few weeks later at Monza. A tradition that the event produces an unusual winner began in 1971, when Siffert won for BRM.

Perhaps the strangest race was in 1975, when heavy rain turned the event into a lottery. Italian veteran Brambilla was in front when the race was curtailed, and he marked his only Grand Prix victory by crashing

A1-Ring
*Rubens
Barrichello
brakes hard for
the Gösser
Kurve in 1998.*

on the slowing-down lap. Sadly, American driver Mark Donohue succumbed to the injuries he sustained when he crashed his Penske March that morning, and a chicane was built at the Hella Licht Kurve to slow the cars down. Penske gained revenge in 1976, when Watson scored his first (and Penske's only) win, while in 1977 Jones scored his maiden win – and the only success for Shadow. The 1978 race was again hit by rain, and Peterson survived the carnage to score his victory. Then, in 1982, the race saw one of the closest finishes ever, when de Angelis held off Rosberg by just 0.05 seconds.

Lauda finally managed to win at home in 1984, during his successful campaign for his third title. Prost won in 1983, 1985 and 1986, while the 1987 event was won by Mansell who headed home his Williams team-mate after the race was started three times due to two huge pile-ups on the narrow grid, and the resulting safety concerns contributed to the demise of the event.

Finances were also part of the equation, and the fact that the track was so far from major towns did not help in an era when corporate entertainment had become so important. However, the race returned to the calendar in 1997 and Jacques Villeneuve's victory (beating off the attentions of both Coulthard and Frentzen) enabled him to put his championship aspirations back on track. Hakkinen then headed Coulthard home in 1998.

He expected to do the same in 1999, but Coulthard tipped him into a spin on the opening lap and the Scot was then out-raced by Ferrari's Eddie Irvine. To prove his superiority at the A1-Ring, though, Hakkinen won as he pleased in 2000, with his team-mate Coulthard finishing second.

BELGIAN GRAND PRIX

THE BELGIAN GRAND PRIX HAS HAD THREE HOMES, but for most people only one matters: Spa-Francorchamps. The charismatic track has had two lives: the first until 1970 and the second, in rebuilt and truncated form, after 1983. It has always been regarded by the drivers as the greatest challenge of the day.

SPA-FRANCORCHAMPS	
Circuit distance: 4.350 miles (6.974 kms)	
Race distance: 191.400 miles (308.00 kms)	
No of laps:	

THE BEST OF TODAY'S GRAND PRIX CIRCUITS by a country mile. This is the one the drivers like to get their teeth into as it climbs and falls, twists and turns through the Ardennes forests. The vicious, uphill Eau Rouge is the one the drivers fear most, with only the brave trying to take it flat-out, but Pouhon and Blanchimont also deserve respect.

ZOLDER
Alain Prost and Rene Arnoux make up the front row for the 1982 Belgian Grand Prix.

Spa was first used in 1924 and joined the World Championship trail right at the very start, in 1950. Set in attractive wooded countryside in the Ardennes hills, it made use of public roads and ran for an incredible 8.76-miles, consisting almost entirely of long straights, punctuated by tricky kinks and, occasionally, a proper corner. Without doubt, the most famous section came at the start of the lap just after the pits – a terrifying downhill plunge followed by Eau Rouge and Raidillon, a left-right-left flick up and over a hill. This really sorted the greats from the ordinary. The track then climbed to the top of the hill at Les Combes and plunged into the valley beyond, with a frighteningly adverse camber as it poured into a long right-hander. The driver had to be flat-out here, or he

would be nowhere. Basically triangular in shape, the circuit then turned sharp right and climbed all the way back through the woods to the hairpin at the top, La Source, before dropping steeply back past the pits for another lap.

Because the track used virtually unprotected public roads, trees, lampposts, road signs and houses were among the "natural" hazards. Perhaps the most terrifying aspect of Spa, however, was the weather. The sun could be shining in the pits while rain poured on one of the far-flung sections. Spa was, in a word, dangerous.

Spa's perilous history

The Belgian Grand Prix ran at Spa from 1950 to 1970, with the exception of three years, and the list of winners shows its propensity for surrendering to the very best. Champions Farina, Ascari and Fangio won there, as did Brabham, Graham

Hill and Surtees. The man who made Spa his second home, though, was Clark who won four times from 1962 to 1965.

The danger was ever present, and in 1960 British youngsters Alan Stacey and Chris Bristow were killed in separate accidents. By 1970, it was clear that the speeds were getting out of hand: Pedro Rodriguez averaged a shade under 150 mph. So a new home was sought, and two were found. Nivelles, a bland new autodrome near Brussels, ran the race in 1972 and 1974 before being dropped. In the intervening year the race was run at Zolder, in the Flemish-speaking part of Belgium, northwest of Liège. This was no Spa, but far preferable to Nivelles. The track broke up badly in 1973, but Zolder became home to the Grand Prix from 1975 to 1982, often providing great races. Tragically, it is best remembered for the accident which claimed the life of Gilles Villeneuve in 1982.

The race returned to Spa in 1983, with the the track shortened to 4.328 miles, cutting out most of the really dangerous road section with a purpose-built link. Some of the old track remained, including the famous La Source hairpin and the Eau Rouge to Raidillon complex. Everybody loved the place and most drivers regarded it as their favourite track.

Like the original track, the new Spa rewarded only the most talented. Senna won five times – including four consecutive wins from 1988 to 1991 – while Prost and Mansell also won. Schumacher took his very first win in 1992, and Hill triumphed in 1993–94, but only after Schumacher was disqualified in 1994. 1995 saw a win for Berger, 1996, Hill, and Schumacher swept all before him in the rain-soaked 1997 race.

The race in 1998 is one that will never be forgotten. Firstly for the mass pile-up on the first lap that involved 13 of the 22 starters. Then for Schumacher throwing away victory by slamming into Coulthard when lapping him as the Scot slowed to let him past. And, finally, for Hill giving Jordan its first-ever Grand Prix win. Things were less dramatic in 1999 once Coulthard had toughed it out with Hakkinen at the start before going clear to win. Hakkinen was on better form in 2000 and, despite losing ground by staying out too long on wet tyres, came through to win.

BRAZILIAN GRAND PRIX

JUST AS JUAN MANUEL FANGIO ENCOURAGED THE popularity of racing in Argentina, the success of Emerson Fittipaldi led to the inauguration of the Brazilian Grand Prix as a World Championship event in 1973 — in São Paulo, Emerson's home town.

INTERLAGOS
Circuit distance: 2.687 miles (4.325 kms)
Race distance: 190.77 miles (307 kms)
No of laps: 71

FAST, BUMPY AND A SHADOW OF ITS FORmer self, this circuit nestles in the heart of São Paulo: the home of the late Ayrton Senna. The fervent atmosphere will never be the same there again. The super-fast first corner has been slowed by a chicane. Watch out for overtaking manoeuvres going into Curva 3 at the end of the back straight.

In fact, the Interlagos track was around even before Fittipaldi was born. Set in the suburbs of São Paulo, running partly around a lake, the circuit had an unusual layout, with a sweeping "outer" section followed by a twisty trail through the infield. That added up to an interesting track of 4.946 miles – one of the longest used in any era. The proximity to the big city meant that it always attracted huge crowds, which had eyes only for Fittipaldi and his compatriots like Carlos Pace. Spectators had a great view, since the track was set in a natural amphitheatre.

Like all circuits in the tropics, Interlagos is bumpy, upsetting the cars in the fast corners. This is no longer such a problem at the first corner, as a chicane has been inserted there to slow the cars down. The diffi

INTERLAGOS
The circuit offers wonderful views. Here the field streams through Pinheirinho in 1995 with the pit straight in the background.

culty is that this funnels the cars into a tight "S", which has led to trouble on the opening lap, as shown by the acrobatics of both Michael Andretti and Gerhard Berger there in 1993.

The track then feeds through a long right-hander on to the back straight before a left-hander that takes the track over a lake and on to another straight. At the end of this there is Curva do Laranja, which takes the track into an uphill section that twists along the top of the hill before feeding into a long, long left-hander on to the pit straight. Combine these twists

with Brazilian heat and the result is a car breaker.

Brazil held a poorly supported non-championship race in 1972. Fittipaldi led but retired, allowing Reutemann to win. In 1973, the race had World Championship status and for the rest of the decade would traditionally follow on from Argentina in a South American double-header.

Fittipaldi pleased his fans by winning in both 1973 and 1974. Then Pace scored his only victory for Brabham in 1975. Ferrari won through Lauda in 1976, and Reutemann took the honours in 1977.

In 1978, the circus moved off to Jacarepagua, near Rio de Janeiro. A typical modern track of two straights and a mixture of slow- and medium-speed constant radius corners, it was well constructed and had a scenic backdrop, but lacked the character of Interlagos. Reutemann won again, while Fittipaldi took second, the best result of his five-year spell with the Fittipaldi team.

Rapid change of venue

The race returned to Interlagos in 1979–80, but from 1981 onwards, it was back at Rio, amid some heavyweight politicking.

Prost always enjoyed Brazil, winning five times in the 1980s, while new local hero, Piquet, triumphed twice. Mansell won his first race for Ferrari in 1989, then cut his hands on the trophy...

That proved to be the last race at Jacarepagua. With domestic politics again clouding the issue, the race moved back to Interlagos in 1990, after a nine-year absence. But the track was very different, modernized, cut back to 2.687 miles and with the fast, challenging "outer" section all but gone. Fittingly, Prost won the first race, and then, in 1991, Senna finally achieved his dream by becoming the fourth local star to win the Brazilian Grand Prix, a feat he repeated in a dramatic wet/dry affair in 1993. Mansell won in 1992.

The 1994 race marked Senna's first start for Williams. Great things were expected, but it didn't work out, and victory went to Schumacher. It was to be Senna's last Brazilian Grand Prix, and the mammoth turnout at his funeral showed the depths of emotion that he had stirred in the public. Hill was dominant there for Williams in awful conditions in 1996, and Villeneuve followed suit in 1997. However, no one could get close to the McLaren duo in 1998 and the same was the case in 1999. Looking for a hat-trick in 2000, Hakkinen's McLaren broke down and Schumacher won for Ferrari.

JACAREPAGUA

If Interlagos in São Paulo is undulating, the Rio circuit is as flat as a pancake.

BRITISH GRAND PRIX

WHILE FRANCE HAS HAD A GRAND PRIX SINCE 1906, Britain's event was a late starter. Despite the fact that the wonderful, banked Brooklands course — a sort of odd-shaped oval — opened for business in 1909, it was not until 1926 that it first hosted a British Grand Prix. However, the two races held there were not great successes, and the idea was dropped.

SILVERSTONE
Circuit distance: 3.142 miles (5.140 kms)
Race distance: 191.662 miles (308.45 kms)
No of laps: 61

THE HOME OF BRITISH MOTOR RACING. Once an airfield, it hosted the first-ever modern-day Grand Prix event in 1950 and has been frequently transformed since then, largely to slow the cars down. The latest change has emasculated the once mighty Stowe corner, but the new-look Becketts esses is one of the most exciting squiggles in motor racing.

In 1937 and 1938, Donington Park hosted two races which were British Grands Prix in all but name, attracting the might of Mercedes and Auto Union to its parkland setting south of Derby. However, the races are mentioned in the history books merely as Donington Grands Prix. Those who attended still remember the spectacle of the powerful German cars surging out of the hairpin and flying over the brows.

The British Grand Prix proper started in 1948 at Silverstone, and the former airfield in Northamptonshire is still the home of the country's premier race, and its fastest. The track has changed substantially during that time and on 17 occasions since it started, the Grand Prix has taken place somewhere other than Silverstone.

The track used in 1948 was a one-off. While using some of the perimeter roads which would become so familiar, it also had two forays up the wide runways and into what is now the infield. But legendary corners such as Copse, Maggots,

Becketts, Chapel, Stowe, Club, Abbey and Woodcote already had their names.

By the time of the first World Championship race in May 1950, only the perimeter roads were in use, and the track had assumed the 2.926-mile shape which would remain until 1975 and, in subtly modified form, until 1990. It was very, very fast, and no corner was more testing or more dramatic than Woodcote, the sweeping right-hander which led on to the what eventually became the pit straight.

That first race was, in fact, the first-ever round of the World Championship, and was held with King George VI and Queen Elizabeth in attendance. Alfa Romeo dominated and Farina, who would take the inaugural title, won the race. It was not until 1955 – and a change of venue was made – that the British Grand Prix had a home winner.

The move to Aintree

The driver was Moss, and the new track was Aintree. The RAC had decided, somewhat controversially, that it should share the Grand Prix between Silverstone and the brand-new three-mile circuit built around the Grand National horse racing course in Liverpool. Aintree had some quick corners, but was a lot slower than Silverstone. Its great advantage was the facilities – the car and four-legged crowds shared the same grandstands.

As in the rest of the 1955 events, Mercedes proved dominant at Aintree, and Moss added to his growing status by leading team-mate Fangio home It was Stirling's first win, but for years afterwards people wondered if Fangio had allowed him to take the home win.

Aintree was to host the Grand Prix five times, alternating with Silverstone in 1955, 1957, 1959 and 1961, and then hanging on to the event for a second consecutive year in 1962. That upset much of the motor sporting establishment, who wholeheartedly supported Silverstone's case.

Silverstone had another new rival, however, in Brands Hatch. From 1964 to 1986 the two circuits would swap, Silverstone taking the race in the odd-numbered years.

Undulating its way through the Kentish countryside, the 2.65-mile track was specially extended for the 1964 British Grand Prix, with a loop into the woods added to the short circuit "bowl", at that time used only for national racing.

Brands was very different from the flat and fast Silverstone. It had some superb and challenging corners, none more popular with fans (and worrying to drivers) than Paddock Bend, the plunging right-hander after the start. In the vicinity of the original, short circuit, it was possible to see much of the track, and that was

SILVERSTONE
The home of British motor racing and where it all began back in 1950.

where most of the fans tended to congregate, leaving the goings-on at tricky (and less accessible) places like Hawthorns and Westfield to their imaginations.

The venue may have been different, but the result was the same. Clark won at Aintree in 1962, Silverstone in 1963 and again at Brands Hatch in 1964. He would win the British Grand Prix twice more.

The Silverstone/Brands Hatch mix was a good compromise, and both circuits proved popular with fans and competitors alike. Both also had a tendency to produce memorable races, especially in the mid-1970s.

The action started at Silverstone in 1973, when Scheckter spun his McLaren at Woodcote and triggered a multiple pile-up at the start of the second lap.

The following year at Brands Hatch Lauda led until pitting with a late puncture, only to find the pit exit blocked by people and an official car. He was later awarded a token fifth place.

BRANDS HATCH
Niki Lauda leads at the Druids hairpin during the 1982 British Grand Prix.

Changes at the major circuits

For 1975, Silverstone made its first important change for 25 years with the addition of a chicane at Woodcote, albeit quite a fast one. That did not prevent drivers taking to the fences at nearly every other corner in a dramatic, rain-hit race, which was forced to a stop, and eventually won by Fittipaldi.

Brands also made modifications for 1976, changing the line at Paddock Bend and modifying the straight behind an expanded pit complex for a new lap of 2.61 miles. The race went down in history thanks to a first-corner accident triggered by the Ferraris of Lauda and Regazzoni, and also involving Hunt. The Briton won the restart, but was later disqualified.

There are other great memories: Hunt battling with Watson in 1977; Reutemann nipping past Lauda in 1978; Regazzoni giving Williams its first win in 1979; Jones beating the flying Ligiers in 1980; Watson avoiding a first-lap skirmish to win for McLaren in 1981; and Warwick hauling his "half-tank" Toleman up to a brief second place in 1982.

Brands Hatch boss, John Webb, managed to secure extra "European Grands Prix" in 1983 and 1985, the second of these giving Mansell his first-ever victory. But the 1986 British Grand Prix proved to be the last at the Kent track. Silverstone secured a long-term deal and, although the final Brands race saw Mansell score

another fine win, a serious accident for Laffite underlined that current cars had outgrown its tight confines.

Silverstone was not immune to safety concerns. For the 1987 race, the 1975 chicane was replaced by a new, much tighter complex well before Woodcote. That year produced one of the best-ever races, as Mansell defeated team-mate Piquet. Mansell was always news, finishing second in the wet in 1988 and again after a puncture in 1989. In 1990, he announced an emotional retirement after his Ferrari's gearbox failed.

For 1991 the track was hugely rebuilt. The original Becketts was replaced by a fast set of esses, while Stowe was slowed to a harder right, followed by a new left-hander called Vale, and a much slower Club. After Abbey there was a completely new section: a fast right-hander at Bridge, followed by double lefts of Priory, and double rights of Luffield.

Mansell won the first race on the new track, followed it up in 1992, and on both occasions the crowd went berserk. With Nigel gone to America the audience shrank in 1993, and those who turned up went home disappointed after Damon Hill's engine blew and Prost won.

Another major rebuild followed in 1994. Copse was reprofiled, with further modifications at Stowe. A slow complex was introduced at Abbey and Priory was also changed. This time the fans got the result they wanted, victory for Hill after Michael Schumacher was penalized for a start procedure irregularity. Herbert won for Benetton in 1995 and Villeneuve for Williams in 1996, before making it two out of two in 1997. Schumacher won in strange circumstances in 1998 when he was allowed to keep victory despite taking a stop/go penalty in the pits after crossing the finish line.

Coulthard has reigned since then, winning in 1999, in the race in which Schumacher broke a leg, and then overpowering Barrichello to win in 2000.

DONINGTON PARK
There was a grand backdrop for the World Championship's only visit here for the European Grand Prix in 1993.

CANADIAN GRAND PRIX

CANADA JOINED THE GRAND PRIX CALENDAR IN 1967 and, apart from absences in 1975 and 1987, has been a regular fixture ever since, with the Canadian fans relying on one family for someone to cheer on: the Villeneuve family, with Jacques following Gilles.

MONTREAL	
Circuit distance: 2.765 miles (4.421 kms)	
Race distance: 190.79 miles (307.05 kms)	
No of laps: 69	

SURROUNDED BY WATER, THIS TRACK IS built on the site of the EXPO pavilions and it's famed for being a car breaker. The track combines high-speed sections with some slow, blind corners and puts stress on the brakes and transmission like no other. Mansell fans will remember the Pits Hairpin, for it was exiting here in 1991 that he waved on the final lap and lost all drive, and with it the race...

The original home of the Canadian Grand Prix was Mosport Park, in eastern Ontario. This magnificent road course undulated through wooded countryside and had some great corners, including the tricky Turn Two, a long left-hander. Moss won the first big event in 1961, while the first World Championship race, in 1967, was won by Brabham.

Canada alternated the Grand Prix between its two major circuits: in 1968 and 1970 the race was run at Mont Tremblant in Quebec. It, too, was a challenging, tree-lined track, but was deemed dangerous even by the lax standards of the time. From 1971 Mosport Park took over.

Usually run as the penultimate event of the season, one of Mosport's most memorable

MONTREAL
The city provides the circuit with a recognizable backdrop.

races was in 1973, when a deluge caused a pace car to be deployed for the first-ever time in Formula One. Revson was declared the winner. Three years later, Hunt scored a superb win as his successful championship bid built up momentum. Then, in 1977, Scheckter gave the Canadian-owned Wolf team its third (and last) victory.

Mosport was always regarded as a dangerous and outdated venue, and for 1978 the race moved to a brand-new home in Montreal. Built on the Ile Notre Dame around the site of Expo '67, it was an unusual track. A cross between a street circuit and a permanent road course, it had lots of fiddly, slow corners and some fast, barrier-lined sections as it ran around the Olympic rowing basin, surrounded by the water of the St Lawrence River on both sides. It was just minutes from down-

town Montreal, and could even be reached by subway. The event proved to be a big hit with the visiting teams.

From the start there is a chicane that catches many out on the opening lap. There is then a kink going into a hairpin that feeds on to a curving section punctuated by a left-right "S" and then a tight left before a more open right that leads the cars on to the back straight. Another chicane follows before a hairpin. Yet another chicane interrupts the flow on the way back to the start. No wonder the track breaks so many cars.

Brief triumph for Villeneuve

The first race produced the dream result: a maiden win for local hero Villeneuve. In 1981 the race was hit by rain. Villeneuve starred, but Jacques Laffite won for Ligier.

The 1982 race was run without Villeneuve, who had been killed at Zolder. The track was renamed in his honour, but sadly Riccardo Paletti died in a crash on the startline.

Oddly, Montreal has rarely provided a memorable lead battle. But the race has the distinction of twice having a "winner" docked a minute for jumping the start. In 1980, Pironi was the culprit, while Berger did the same in 1990. The beneficiaries on each occasion were Jones and Senna.

In 1989, Boutsen secured his first victory. The 1991 event saw one of the strangest finishes ever, when leader Mansell began celebrating a little too early and stalled his Williams. A surprised Piquet swept through to score his last victory.

The following year Mansell crashed over the final chicane. Berger evenged his 1990 nightmare by winning. Prost scored his first, and only, Canadian success in 1993, while Schumacher won in 1994, when a temporary tyre chicane was added in the aftermath of the Imola tragedies. Hill thwarted Villeneuve's hopes of a home win in 1996, and Schumacher spoiled the party in 1997 when the race was marred by Olivier Panis's accident, with the German winning again for Ferrari in 1998 when both the McLarens failed. Schumacher led again in 1999, but Hakkinen harried him into making a mistake – crashing into the wall at the final chicane – and Hakkinen went on to win. Schumacher gained his revenge in 2000 when he won, with team-mate Barrichello sitting dutifully behind.

DUTCH GRAND PRIX

TOGETHER WITH THE ARGENTINIAN, MEXICAN, PORTUGUESE AND South African events, the Dutch Grand Prix is one of several classic races which, sad to say, no longer has a place on the Formula One calendar.

The event was run 30 times between 1952 and 1985, initially in June and latterly in August, and every race took place at the same circuit – Zandvoort. Set in sand dunes just a few hundred yards inland from the North Sea, the resort town of Zandvoort was one of the most popular stops on the schedule for decades. The track itself, opened in 1948, was a clever design which encouraged entertaining racing.

A fast and difficult corner on to the long pit straight was followed by the slow right-hander at Tarzan, where heavy braking was required and overtaking opportunities were frequent.

ZANDVOORT

Nelson Piquet heads a trail of cars through the Rob Slotermakerbocht at the last Dutch GP in 1985.

One of the most famous corners in racing, it was for years the scene of some exciting action, and occasionally, spectacular accidents. The rest of the track was basically a square, with one side interrupted by a chicane and another by an "S" which fed into the fast right-hander on to the long straight down to Tarzan. This loop was later chopped and altered in the name of safety. Sand blowing across the track from the neighbouring dunes always seemed to provide a disconcerting hazard to the drivers.

Triumph and tragedy

The list of Dutch Grand Prix

winners reads like a Who's Who of motor racing's greats. Ascari won the first two races in 1952 and 1953, while the 1955 event saw a victory for Fangio and the mighty Mercedes team. Moss won for Vanwall in 1958 and Jo Bonnier gave BRM its first victory a year later. All the big names triumphed in the 1960s: Brabham, von Trips, Hill, Clark (four times) and Stewart.

Everyone loved Zandvoort and its holiday atmosphere, but in the early 1970s the track hit the headlines for all of the wrong reasons. In 1970, Piers Courage died in a fiery accident with the Williams-entered de Tomaso, and then, three years later, the same fate befell fellow Englishman Roger Williamson, in only his second race with a privately-entered March.

But while concerns about safety were voiced, the race went on. Lauda registered one of his first triumphs in 1974, and, in 1975, Hunt memorably scored his first win for Hesketh. He won again the following year for McLaren after a great battle with Watson. In 1977 Hunt tangled with Andretti, allowing Lauda to win. The 1978 race saw an Andretti/Peterson steamroller performance for Lotus with the American finishing just 0.3 seconds ahead of his team-mate.

The 1979 event is remembered not so much for Jones's victory, but more for the efforts of Villeneuve to drag his three-wheeled Ferrari back to the pits. A year later Daly flipped his Tyrrell at Tarzan, but escaped from the carnage without injury.

The 1983 event was notable for a collision between title contenders Piquet and Prost. Both men were out of the race, and victory went to Arnoux, who had survived a huge first-corner crash in 1982. Prost gained revenge by winning in 1984.

The Formula One circus visited Zandvoort for the last time in 1985, and the race was a classic, Lauda just holding off Prost as he scored his final victory. The track was coming under threat from developers, and suddenly Holland did not seem like a fashionable place to hold a Grand Prix. Indeed, the country had never produced a truly competitive driver, which made it hard to justify keeping the race when other venues were applying for dates.

Shortened and rebuilt, Zandvoort survives as a venue for mainly domestic racing, with the famous Tarzan corner, thankfully, still intact.

FRENCH GRAND PRIX

THE FRENCH GRAND PRIX UNDOUBTEDLY HAS THE finest pedigree of any current motor race. The sport originated in France with the inter-city marathons, like the Paris-Bordeaux-Paris race of 1895, and the very first French Grand Prix was run at Le Mans in 1906.

MAGNY-COURS
Circuit distance: 2.654 miles (4.27 kms)
Race distance: 191.088 miles (307.53 kms)
No of laps: 72

LITTLE-LOVED VENUE FOR ONE OF THE traditional Grands Prix. Uprated from a club circuit at the behest of President Mitterand, it brought income to a rural region, but little in the way of excitement to Formula One fans. The Adelaide hairpin at the end of the back straight is the place to watch. The daft chicane just before the pit entrance is not...

Le Mans was one of 11 venues used until the outbreak of the Second World War, by which time the Grand Prix had found two regular homes in Reims and Montlhery, the banked track outside Paris. Since the Grand Prix joined the World Championship trail in 1950, no fewer than seven tracks have hosted it.

The only circuit used both before and after the war was Reims, which hosted the inaugural championship event in 1950. Dating back to 1925, Reims was a five-mile blast along public roads. It was best known for its long main straight – the Thillois straight – which made every race into a dramatic slipstreamer. Along with Spa, it was one of the fastest of the era. Fangio won in 1950 and 1951, taking over the car of Fagioli on the latter occasion. One of the best battles at Reims was in 1961, when young Baghetti overcame strong pressure to win his first championship race. It was also the scene of tragedy: Italian star Luigi Musso lost his life there in 1958.

New venues
Reims held the Grand Prix 11 times: from 1950 to 1954, in 1956, from 1958 to 1961, in 1963, and finally in 1966, by which time it had come under severe pressure from alternative sites. As early as 1952 the French authorities were indulging in their habit of moving the Grand Prix about. In the early years the only alternative was Rouen-Les-Essarts, which held the race in 1952, 1957, 1962, 1964 and 1968.

Extended to 4.06 miles for 1957, Rouen was another circuit based on public roads, famous for its downhill plunge after the start, which led to the cobbled Nouveau Monde hairpin, before climbing up through the woods again, with several blind corners to keep the drivers on their toes. Fangio's win in 1957 is regarded as one of his best, while Jacky Ickx put in a fine performance to win in the rain in 1968. But that race is best remembered for the death of local veteran, Jo Schlesser, who was making his Formula One debut for Honda. As with many other tracks, a serious accident heralded the end of Rouen as a Grand Prix circuit, although other forms of racing continued.

The mid-1960s was a confusing time for French fans, with four different tracks hosting the race from 1965 to 1968. In 1967, the race was held, for one time only, on the 2.74-mile Le Mans Bugatti circuit, which used the pits and starting line of the 24 hours track, linked by a purpose-built twisty section. The race was boring. Competitors did not like it and neither did the public and Formula One never went back.

With Reims pensioned off, Clermont-Ferrand emerged briefly as its natural heir. The race was first held there in 1965, and returned in 1969, 1970 and, lastly, in 1972. Opened in 1958, Clermont-Ferrand was a magnificent five-mile road course, set in the mountains of the Auvergne. Something of a mini-Nurburg-ring with twists and turns aplenty, it had a curious habit of both inducing car sickness and tiring even the best drivers. It was also known for the loose stones alongside the track, which often led to punctures and, in 1972, cost Austrian Helmut Marko the sight of one eye. That year's race was perhaps the most dramatic ever held at Clermont-Ferrand, as initial leader Amon fought back from a puncture to claim third behind winner Stewart.

After the challenges of Reims, Rouen and Clermont-Ferrand, the French Grand Prix moved to a very different home in 1971. Those dramatic road courses were replaced by a brand-new track at Le Castellet, north of Marseilles. Named after Paul Ricard, the aperitif manufacturer who built it, the track was the first of the bland, modern autodromes which would proliferate over the next two decades.

Teams liked Ricard because the weather and facilities were good, but the drivers were less impressed, although they appreciated the run-off areas and barriers. In contrast to its predecessors, the 3.6-mile track was flat and dull, but it did have one sting in the tail – Signes, a fast, right-hand kink near the end of the long back straight. That and

ROUEN

John Surtees races his Lola through the famous downhill plunge into the Nouveau Monde hairpin in the 1962 French Grand Prix.

MAGNY-COURS

Jacques Villeneuve slams on the brakes into the Adelaide hairpin at the head of the pack in the 1997 French Grand Prix.

the fast section beyond the pits were real tests.

A wide choice

Paul Ricard would become the main home for the Grand Prix for the next 20 years, hosting the race 14 times. However, for much of that period the alternating continued. The new second choice, introduced in 1974, was Dijon-Prenois. Initially, the fast, undulating track ran only 2.044 miles, producing a ridiculous lap time of less than a minute, and consequently a great deal of traffic problems. By the time the race returned in 1977, an extension had been added which brought it up to a more respectable 2.361 miles and, thanks to this sequence of slower corners, the lap time was increased by around 13 seconds.

Dijon hosted the Grand Prix five times, in 1974, 1977, 1979, 1981 and 1984, and had a bonus "Swiss Grand Prix" in 1982. Some memorable races took place, notably in 1979, when Jabouille gave Renault its first win, and Arnoux and Villeneuve battled hard for second. In 1981, a young Alain

Prost scored his maiden win in a race split into two parts by rain.

By the mid-1980s, FISA was demanding that Grands Prix find long-term homes and, with Dijon dropped, Paul Ricard was the sole host between 1985 and 1990. Once regarded as the state of the art in safety, Ricard saw tragedy when Elio de Angelis was killed in testing in 1986, after his wing had failed approaching the fast sequence after the pits.

For that year's race the track was cut back to 2.369 miles, removing the section where de Angelis crashed, halving the back straight and slowing the approach to Signes. In its last years as a Formula One venue Prost was the King of Ricard, winning during 1988–90. The 1989 race is best remembered for a first corner crash which saw Gugelmin somersault over the pack, while in the following year, Gugelmin and Leyton House team-mate Capelli stunned everyone with their pace. The Italian led for 45 laps and eventually finished second.

For 1991 the track was dropped and replaced by the Grand Prix's seventh home since 1950. With support from President François Mitterand, the club circuit of Magny-Cours was transformed, re-emerging as the Circuit de Nevers. It was a typical modern autodrome, full of slow turns and hairpins, but boasting top-class pit and paddock facilities. The 2.654-mile facility did not offer much of a challenge, apart from the relatively fast left/right sequence after the start. The rest of it was very slow, and there was even an unnecessary chicane – right after a hairpin! – that was later removed.

The first race turned out to be quite a good one, with victory going to Mansell after a long battle with Prost's Ferrari. Mansell won again in 1992, a race split by rain. Then Prost added a third for Williams in 1993, pipping Hill. Schumacher won in 1994, but most eyes were on Mansell, making a brief comeback. However, he failed to last the distance. Schumacher won again in 1995, but didn't even reach the start in 1996, after his Ferrari's engine blew up on the parade lap, and Hill took the honours.

Michael Schumacher was in a class of his own in 1997, beating Heinz-Harald Frentzen to the flag, with Eddie Irvine making it a good day for Ferrari by finishing third. And Irvine went one better in 1998 when he followed Schumacher home.

The 1999 Grand Prix was one of the most bizarre as wet qualifying left Barrichello on pole for Stewart. Coulthard soon powered clear for McLaren, but retired. The rain hit hard and, as teams came in to change tyres, Jordan pulled off a coup and put on enough fuel for Frentzen not to make an extra stop, and he duly won ahead of Hakkinen. Coulthard overcame Schumacher to win for McLaren in 2000.

PAUL RICARD
Keke Rosberg lines up on pole for the 1985 French Grand Prix.

GERMAN GRAND PRIX

UNTIL 1976, THE GERMAN GRAND PRIX WAS HELD ON the most remarkable circuit of them all: the old Nurburgring. Since then it has found a second home at Hockenheim.

HOCKENHEIM	
Circuit distance: 4.234 miles (6.822 kms)	
Race distance: 190.53 miles (306.63 kms)	
No of laps: 45	

NO ONE HAS EVER BEEN FOND OF THIS place since it claimed the life of Jim Clark in 1968. It's largely characterless, with a high-speed blast through the forest interrupted by three chicanes at which cars often collide. However, the 'Autodrom' section is impressive, if only for the gargantuan grandstands packed with flag-waving Schumacher fans.

The first German Grand Prix was held at Berlin's Avus track in 1926, and the wet event was blighted by horrific accidents – including one which killed three officials in a timekeepers' box. Safety concerns precipitated a move to the Nurburgring – somewhat ironic, considering the reputation that the circuit was to acquire.

Designed as a means to alleviate local unemployment, work on the 'Ring began in 1925 with full government backing. In its full glory it ran to 17.58 miles, including the Southern circuit "extension". In later years this was excluded and races were held

AVUS

Tony Brooks guides his Ferrari around the banking en route to winning the 1959 German Grand Prix.

on the 14.17-mile Nordschliefe.

The 'Ring was a seemingly endless chain of ups and downs, and twisting left and right curves between the pine trees. Corner names became part of motor racing folklore: Flugplatz, Bergwerk, the Karussel, Pflanzgarten. Much more than Spa-Francorchamps, the 'Ring separated the great from the average, but even the very best drivers took several years to feel fully at home with the hard-to-learn course.

What made the place yet more daunting was the weather. Even in the summer, rain and fog were common, and conditions could change suddenly in the course of the lap.

The German Grand Prix was held at the 'Ring regularly until 1939, when war intervened. Racing resumed in 1949, and Germany joined the World Championship two years later when an estimated 180,000 fans turned up to see Alberto

Ascari win the race for Ferrari.

A venue with a reputation

The early Grands Prix confirmed the 'Ring's dual distinction as both a creator and killer – of racing heroes. Ascari had one of his best races in 1952, recovering from a late pit stop to regain the lead from Farina. In 1957, Fangio drove what he regarded as his best race, coming back from a fuel stop to pass Hawthorn and Collins. But a year later Collins crashed to his death, as had Fangio's protégé, Marimon, in 1954.

In 1959, the 'Ring was temporarily overlooked in favour of Avus, because crowds at the former had fallen. As in 1926, the track was basically a run up and down two sides of a dual carriageway, but since that first race it had been shortened and acquired banking at its north end. Uniquely, the race was run over two heats, Brooks winning, but Grand Prix great Jean Behra lost his life in a supporting sports car race and Formula One never went back.

The 1960 race was held on the 'Ring's short South circuit – and only for Formula Two cars – but for 1961 it was both back in the championship and on the familiar, long track. Moss scored his last (and one of his best) wins.

World Champions Hill, Surtees, Clark, Brabham and Hulme won in the 1960s, but none more comprehensively than Stewart, who mastered dreadful conditions to win the 1968 race by over four minutes.

By the end of the decade pressure from Stewart and his colleagues had encouraged an increased emphasis on safety. In 1970, the year of the last race on the original track, the Nurburgring underwent major modifications. Barriers were installed, the road was widened and reprofiled in places, and run-off areas were created.

While this was going on, the Grand Prix moved to a new venue at Hockenheim, near Heidelberg, built originally as a test track for Mercedes. Sadly, it is best known as the place where Clark lost his life in a Formula Two race in 1968. The

HOCKENHEIM
Crowds pack the grandstands in the circuit's stadium sections.

4.218 miles of Hockenheim consisted of two long blasts into and out of the forest, followed by a twisty section through a stadium, in front of huge grandstands. Since Clark's death, new barriers had improved matters somewhat, and the race was a slipstreamer, won by Jacky Ickx.

For 1971 the Grand Prix moved back to the modified 'Ring, its essential spirit unchanged. Ickx, who had won the last race in 1969 in fine style, was again the pacesetter – but he crashed on the second lap, handing the win to Stewart. The Belgian made amends in 1972.

Despite the modifications the 'Ring remained an anachronism as the cars became quicker, and it was fortunate that no one was hurt in 1975 when much of the field suffered punctures. But the following year the track's tenure as the Grand Prix venue came to an end. Reigning

World Champion Lauda suffered horrific burns when he crashed on the second lap of the race and, while Lauda staged a recovery, the 'Ring did not.

Return to Hockenheim

For 1977 the race moved back to Hockenheim, itself now modernized by chicanes. Appropriately, the first race was won by Lauda. The track was notable for a high attrition rate, the long flat-out blasts proving hard on the engines. In addition, the start and chicanes tended to produce a lot of carnage.

In 1980, Hockenheim was once again the scene of tragedy, veteran Depailler losing his life in a testing crash at the fast Ostkurve, the link between the two long straights.

One of the most memorable races came in 1982, by which time a third chicane had been added at the Ostkurve. Pironi

NURBURGRING
The Dunlop Kehre is the lowest point of the current circuit that replaced the Nordschleife when it opened in 1984.

was injured in wet practice and in the race itself Piquet hit the headlines by trying to punch Salazar after they collided while Piquet was lapping the Chilean. Pironi's team-mate, Tambay, scored an emotional win.

Formula One returned to the 'Ring in 1984, for the European Grand Prix. Built alongside the original, the new 'Ring was a 2.822-mile track with few interesting corners, but with unnecessarily huge run-off areas – built in the name of safety. Prost won. Then, for one time only, the new 'Ring hosted the German Grand Prix in 1985. Like nearly every race ever held at the place, there was a shunt at the first corner chicane, but Alboreto survived it to win for Ferrari ahead of Prost.

Since 1986 the Grand Prix has been back at Hockenheim, which continues to extract a heavy toll on machinery. In

1987, Prost led until a failure with four laps to go, allowing Piquet to win. In 1989, Prost lost sixth gear with two laps to go, letting Senna through. Senna also won in 1988 and 1990, and Mansell in 1991 and 1992, before Prost finally scored his first Hockenheim win in 1993. This time he was lucky; he was given a controversial stop-go penalty, but took the lead when team-mate Hill had a puncture.

The 1994 race was one of the craziest, with almost half the field going off in a series of first-lap incidents. After Schumacher retired, Berger gave Ferrari its first win in four years.

1995 saw two races in Germany, with the Nurburgring making a return to the schedule, after a ten-year absence, to host the European Grand Prix. To the joy of the locals, Schumacher won both. In 1996, it was German success for Williams, with Villeneuve winning at Hockenheim and Hill at the 'Ring. Gerhard Berger completed a dominant weekend by winning the German Grand Prix in 1997 (with the European GP in Portugal). Hakkinen furthered his title aspirations by winning both German events in 1998, and Irvine did his title hopes no harm by winning at Hockenheim in 1999. Meanwhile, Herbert scored an emotional victory for the Stewart team in a bizarre race at the 'Ring. 2000 saw Ferrari success, with Barrichello notching up his first win at Hockenheim and Schumacher victorious at the Nurburgring.

HUNGARIAN GRAND PRIX

IN 1986, FORMULA ONE IMPRESARIO BERNIE ECCLESTONE achieved the impossible by taking Grand Prix racing into the Eastern bloc — well before the thawing of the Cold War. For some time there had been talk of a street race in Moscow, but nothing came of it. However, it did not take long for Ecclestone to persuade the Hungarian authorities to fill the gap.

HUNGARORING	
Circuit distance: 2.465 miles (3.968 kms)	
Race distance: 189.805 miles (305.46 kms)	
No of laps: 77	

A WASTED CHANCE TO MAKE MOTORSPORT catch on as the Iron Curtain was lifted. It has a beautiful setting in a natural amphitheatre, with spectators able to see much of the track from wherever they watch. But the track is too narrow and twisty for anything other than follow-my-leader processions. Watch for drivers going for a tow down the main straight on the run to the only overtaking place: the first corner.

Built in rolling countryside, 12 miles north-east of Budapest, the 2.465-mile Hungaroring is a typical modern autodrome, somewhat lacking in character. Its corners are mostly slow and the track is narrow, limiting overtaking opportunities, which has led to frustration for quicker drivers and sometimes collisions. The first corner – a tight right-hander that drops away on its exit – sees quite a bit of action, but the preceding straight is too short for drivers to be able to get a good run on cars of similar speed.

The track drops down into a valley through a left-hander followed by a right. From the bottom the track climbs up towards a massive bank of spectators, darting right to traverse the face of the hill, then right again, followed by a sequence of twists before climbing up to the level of the pits once more. The last corner is a long right-hander, through which drivers must get close to the car ahead if they are to have any hope of slipstreaming past them on the straight.

For the first three years, the circuit was even slower than it was planned to be, for an extra kink had to be built to avoid an underground spring, discovered during construction. For the 1990 race the problem was solved and the section of track straightened.

A popular venue

The teams enjoy the trip to Hungary – the fine August weather certainly helps – and the local fans are wildly enthusiastic.

There have been some entertaining and close races in Hungary, but thanks to the nature of the track, they have rarely featured much actual overtaking at the front; several years have seen flag-to-flag wins.

That said, the inaugural race saw Piquet beat Senna after they swapped places during a close fight. Piquet won again in

1987 – but only after team-mate Mansell lost certain victory when a wheel nut worked loose with just six laps to go.

Senna was embroiled in another tight battle in 1988, this time with charging McLaren team-mate Prost, but the Frenchman dropped out with wheel bearing failure just as Senna began to feel the pressure.

The 1989 event was one of the more memorable races. Patrese led until his Williams sprang a water leak, leaving Senna in the lead. Mansell rose from 12th on the grid and ducked past the Brazilian in an opportunistic move in traffic.

Senna and Mansell were in the news again in 1990. Boutsen took pole and, against the run of form, led all the way. He came under strong pressure from Nannini, but there was no way past. The following Senna punted Nannini off, but he could not find a way past Boutsen in the closing laps. Meanwhile, Berger had pushed Mansell out of the way.

Senna won in 1991 after Mansell and Patrese used up the brakes on their Williams-Renaults, and Ayrton triumphed yet again in 1992. Despite a puncture Mansell finished second and clinched the world title.

Prost was destined never to win in Hungary, and he blew his last attempt in 1993 by stalling on the warm-up lap. Hill stormed to a great first Grand Prix victory. Schumacher earned Benetton its first Hungarian win in 1994, as Hill gave chase. But Hill went one better in 1995, then was second again in 1996, behind Villeneuve. It was so close for Hill in 1997, but his Arrows hit gearbox problems on the last lap and this handed victory to Villeneuve. Then Schumacher raced to one of the all-time great wins in 1998, outracing the superior McLarens by stopping three times to their two-stop strategy. Hakkinen then led all the way the following year, and made it two on the trot by keeping Michael Schumacher's Ferrari behind him in 2000.

HUNGARORING

Thierry Boutsen in the first Hungarian Grand Prix in 1986.

ITALIAN GRAND PRIX

THE NAME MONZA IS ONE OF THE MOST EVOCATIVE IN motor sport and it reflects a remarkable heritage. Since 1950 the circuit has hosted the Italian Grand Prix every season except one – 1980, when the race was run at Imola.

MONZA
Circuit distance: 3.604 miles (5.800 kms)
Race distance: 191.012 miles (307.40 kms)
No of laps: 53

TO MANY, THIS IS THE SPIRITUAL HOME OF motor racing, its abandoned banked track a reminder of bygone days. It is blessed with long straights and fast corners that make for the best slipstreaming battles. The Lesmo bends are the biggest test, followed by a straight then one of the best chicanes in Formula One.

In fact the history of the famous Autodromo goes right back to 1922, when it was first built. An Italian Grand Prix had been run for the first time at Brescia the year before, but Monza, set in an attractive park near Milan, soon became its rightful home.

A variety of configurations was available in the early days, but much of the track still used today was in place from the start. Monza has always been one of the fastest tracks on the schedule, even after the addition of chicanes in the early 1970s.

The Grand Prix has a wonderful atmosphere and always attracts a massive crowd of loyal Ferrari fans – known as the "tifosi". If their team is not winning, they soon make their feelings known...

The present track is 3.604 miles long. The wide pit straight, which passes the charismatic old grandstands, is curtailed by an absurdly tight double chicane, the Rettifilio, which nearly always produces first-lap drama. The sweeping Curva Grande right-hander is followed by a second chicane, Curva della Roggia, which leads to the legendary double

Lesmo right-handers. Two of the most famous corners in motor racing, they were slightly realigned in 1994 as a result of a safety campaign.

The track then rushes under the old banked circuit (more of that later) to the relatively fast Vialone chicane. Then comes the much-photographed blast down the back straight, followed by the fast Parabolica corner, scene of many dramas over the years. That catapults the cars back on to the main straight.

Before the chicanes were built, the track was virtually a flat-out blast. More than any other, it saw wonderful slipstreaming battles, especially when cars became more "slippery" in the 1960s. However, it was also one of the toughest on machinery, and very often races were decided more by engine longevity than driver skill. It is still a circuit, though, where power and straight-line speed are all-important.

MONZA
Alessandro Nannini reaches the Ascari Chicane in the 1988 Italian Grand Prix.

A remarkable history

Monza has seen some memorable races, but has also had more than its fair share of tragedy. Indeed, in the pre-war races several of the great stars of the day lost their live there. Three top drivers were killed in one event in 1933 alone.

Monza had a place in the very first World Championship calendar in 1950. Like most of the early races, it saw a battle between Alfa Romeo and Ferrari; Farina won for the former.

The first of many dramatic finishes occurred in 1953. It was one of the rare occasions when the lead battle continued to the last lap, and was not compromised by mechanical failure. At the last corner Ascari spun, Farina took to the grass and Marimon hit Ascari. Fangio motored through the mayhem to win.

Ascari was killed testing a sports car at Monza in May 1955, and that year's Grand Prix saw a major change. A banked circuit had been added to the layout, and a long, 6.2-mile course was devised, incorporating both the original track and the two banked corners. The banking was bumpy and unpopular with the drivers, and proved particularly hard on tyres. Fangio won in 1955 (the last Grand Prix for Mercedes) and Moss triumphed in 1956, before the layout was temporarily abandoned. In the latter race Collins handed his car to Fangio and in doing so sacrificed his World Championship hopes to the Argentinian maestro.

Moss's 1956 win started a remarkable run of success for English-speaking drivers, who would win every Italian Grand Prix bar one until 1969. Perhaps the most galling loss for the local fans came in 1957 when Moss won for Vanwall, beating their beloved red cars.

In 1960, the race was, controversially, restored to the

combined road/banked course, and the British teams boycotted the event. Finally, a Ferrari won again. It was the last victory by any front-engined car, and driver Phil Hill was the first American to win a Grand Prix.

Hill clinched the world title at Monza in 1961, but in tragic circumstances after team-mate Wolfgang von Trips and 12 spectators were killed. The race was back on the road course in 1962, and in 1963 an attempt to return to the banked course was abandoned after first practice. The banking was forgotten.

The 1960s races saw some wonderful dicing, but time and again it would be spoiled by leading cars dropping out. In 1965, Jackie Stewart scored his first-ever win, and in 1966 Scarfiotti led home a Ferrari one-two.

In 1969, the race finally delivered the photo finish that had been promised since 1953. In the closing yards Stewart just pulled clear of Rindt, Beltoise and McLaren.

Tragedy returned in 1970 when Rindt lost his life in qualifying. The race again saw a wonderful lead battle, from which Regazzoni emerged to score his first win. The following year brought the most sensational finish of any Grand Prix, as the unrated Gethin led a pack of five cars across the finishing line.

Sweeping changes

Monza was changed forever in 1972 with the introduction of a chicane beyond the pits, and another at Vialone. The days of slipstreaming fights were over, and the first "new" race was

MONZA

Peter Gethin (18) pushes the nose of his BRM forward to pip Peterson (25), Cevert (2), Hailwood (9) and Ganley (at rear) in Formula One's closest-ever finish at Monza in 1971.

won by Fittipaldi, who also clinched the title for Lotus.

Peterson emerged as a Monza specialist, winning in 1973, 1974 and 1976, but the track was also to claim his life. A pile-up in the 1978 race saw him hospitalized with broken legs, and he died from complications the next day.

In 1980, the race moved – for one time only – to Imola (*see* San Marino story). The political problems were solved when Imola earned its own San Marino Grand Prix, and the Italian race returned to its original home in 1981.

Monza was a circuit where the turbo cars could really stretch their legs. In 1986, at the peak of the turbo era, Fabi's BMW-powered Benetton blasted to pole. But remarkably, neither he nor fellow front-row man Prost took up their grid positions after last-minute problems – a unique occurrence in Formula One history.

Three times in the late 1980s Senna lost Monza victories when he seemed to have the race won. In 1987, he went across the grass at the Parabolica, handing Piquet the lead. In 1988, he was leading comfortably when he tangled with back marker Schlesser, allowing Berger to score the last triumph of Enzo Ferrari's lifetime. Then, in 1989, Senna's engine blew with nine laps to go, allowing Prost to win. The Frenchman gave his trophy to the fans in a calculated insult to team boss Ron Dennis.

Senna's luck changed when he won in 1990, but the luckiest man that day was Warwick, who survived a massive first-lap crash at the Parabolica.

The 1991 event was one of the best of recent years, as Senna fought with the Williams-Renault pair of Mansell and Patrese. The Italian retired, Senna was forced to take new tyres and Mansell scored a memorable win. But Senna got his own back the following year when the Williams duo suffered unusual hydraulic pump belt failures, and the Brazilian took advantage.

As in the 1950s Monza continued to exert a mechanical toll. Prost was leading in 1993 when engine failure handed the win to team-mate Hill. He scored a second success in 1994. Since then, Herbert won in 1995, with Michael Schumacher sending the *tifosi* wild in 1996. Coulthard secured his second victory of the year by winning in 1997, but blew up when leading in 1998 and Schumacher passed Hakkinen to head a Ferrari one-two in 1998. Hakkinen crashed out of the lead in 1999, much to the delight of the *tifosi* who'd seen him do the same earlier in the year at Imola – and Frentzen came through to win for Jordan. The 2000 race was marked by a massive first lap crash at the second chicane, with six cars tangling and an airborne wheel killing a marshall. Schumacher went on to win to send the *tifosi* wild as his title challenge gathered pace.

JAPANESE GRAND PRIX

THE JAPANESE GRAND PRIX IS ONE OF THE MOST established events on the calendar as it's held on one of the best circuits and usually plays a key role in the outcome of the World Championship.

SUZUKA	
Circuit distance: 3.644 miles (5.864 kms)	
Race distance: 182.150 miles (293.14 kms)	
No of laps: 50	

TI CIRCUIT	
Circuit distance: 3.643 miles (5.863 kms)	
Race distance: 193.100 miles (310.76 kms)	
No of laps: 53	

A REALLY TOUGH AND TECHNICAL CIRCUIT, it is unusual for the fact that it crosses over itself. The crowds are always enormous and chase everything that looks like a driver with an autograph book. The toughest corner is the 130R at the end of the back straight — it is both very fast and very narrow.

Japan's first involvement in Grand Prix racing was through Honda, which competed from 1964 to 1968. It was not until 1976 that Japan hosted its first Grand Prix. The original venue was Fuji, a charismatic circuit set on the slopes of Mount Fuji. It was notable for having one of the longest straights ever seen in Formula One, linked by a succession of sweeping corners.

The first, rain-soaked race there went down in the history books as the one which gave James Hunt his World Championship after Niki Lauda pulled out. Few remember that Andretti gave Lotus its first win for more than two years. The sun shone in 1977 and Hunt scored his last-ever win, although it was overshadowed by the death of several onlookers after Gilles Villeneuve vaulted over the back of Peterson's Tyrrell. The accident did Fuji's hopes no good at all and, with the Japanese motor industry showing little or no interest in the sport, the Japanese Grand Prix disappeared for a decade.

It came back in 1987, at Suzuka, as a direct result of Honda's successful return to Formula One — as an engine supplier. Honda had owned the Suzuka track since it was opened in 1963, and made a considerable effort to bring the circuit up to scratch. Featuring a unique "figure of eight" layout, the track had a variety of fast and slow corners, including 130R, the heart-in-mouth, flat-out left.

A popular circuit

From the start, the Suzuka circuit was loved by the drivers. However, overtaking was not easy and it was made even more difficult when the chicane before the pits was tightened in 1991, spoiling the main passing opportunity that had been at the end of the main straight.

The first Grand Prix there in 1987 is best remembered for a practice accident which ended Mansell's title hopes, handing

the honours to team-mate Piquet. The race itself was won by Berger's McLaren.

In 1988, Senna's growing status in Japan was confirmed when he won after recovering from a bad start. The following year he and McLaren team-mate Prost famously collided at the chicane when battling for the lead. Senna eventually crossed the line first, but his disqualification handed the win to Alessandro Nannini.

In 1990, Prost (now with Ferrari) and Senna tangled again, going off into the gravel trap at the first corner. Senna claimed the crown and later admitted it had been a premeditated move.

Senna was again at the forefront in 1991, when he led but allowed team-mate Berger to win at the last corner. In 1992, Patrese took advantage of Mansell's retirement to score his final Grand Prix victory.

Senna bounced back to score

SUZUKA

The uphill "S" Curves offer drivers a real challenge and are just one of the reasons why this circuit is such a test of both man and machine.

TI CIRCUIT
The circuit was only visited in 1994 and 1995.

a magnificent win in 1993, dominating a tricky wet/dry race and made the headlines by punching newcomer Eddie Irvine.

The 1994 race was one of the best. Rain struck, and a string of accidents caused a pace car period and then a stoppage. After the restart Hill overcame Schumacher's first-part advantage to score perhaps the hardest-earned win of his career.

Japan earned a second race for the first time in 1995. Dubbed the Pacific Grand Prix, it was held at the narrow TI Circuit in Aida, south of Suzuka. Against expectations the race, won by Schumacher, proved to be an organizational

success, but the lack of overtaking possibilities meant it was not popular with the drivers.

Suzuka hosted the 1996 finale in which Hill won both the race and the championship. Schumacher's victory in 1997 took the championship down to the wire at Jerez. While his stalling on the grid in 1998 made him start the re-started race from the back and made it all the easier for Hakkinen to win and wrap up the title. With Irvine as his title rival the following year, Hakkinen won again to clinch the title. But a narrow defeat by Schumacher in 2000 meant that he had to make do with being runner-up.

MALAYSIAN GRAND PRIX

MALAYSIA
Circuit distance: 3.444 miles (5.542 kms)
Race distance: 192.864 miles (310.352 kms)
No of laps: 56

Malaysia announced in the mid-1990s that it planned to build a circuit to host a round of the Formula One World Championship. But then the economy of South-East Asia crashed and burned and everyone thought that would be the last of their plans, government support or not. However, the fact that the president is a motorsport fan meant that the plans were not scrapped. And, 26 months after a greenfield site near capital Kuala Lumpur's airport was cut, the Sepang circuit was ready.

Designed by former touring car racer Herman Tilke, it is an interesting mixture of corners with two long straights. And, best of all for fans of overtaking, it's wide at all the right places. One of the features of the brand new facilities is the covered grandstand for 30,000 spectators overlooking the start-finish straight and one half of the circuit from one of its banks of seats and the back straight and the other half of the circuit from the other.

The first Malaysian Grand Prix held there in 1999 marked Michael Schumacher's return from a broken leg and he supported team-mate Eddie Irvine, holding of McLaren's Mika Hakkinen so that he could win.

In 2000, Michael Schumacher benefitted from his good deeds of the previous year by changing to a two-stop strategy, after an unusually early stop by leader Coulthard, and emerged in the lead, and was just able to resist Coulthard to the flag.

SEPANG
A grandstand with room for 30,000 spectators offers spectacular viewing as the action unfolds.

MEXICAN GRAND PRIX

THE MEXICAN GRAND PRIX IS UNIQUE IN THAT IT HAS TWICE BEEN A regular Grand Prix fixture and has twice been dumped from the calendar and quickly forgotten.

The race ran in its first form from 1963 to 1970, and had a second lease of life from 1986 to 1992. All the events were held on the Hermanos Rodriguez Circuit in the suburbs of Mexico City. The track shared two characteristics with Italy's Monza. Firstly, it was located in a public park. Secondly, it had a fearsomely fast final corner, leading on to a long pit straight. But, unlike Monza's Parabolica,

Mexico's Peralta was slightly banked, which made it even quicker – and even more apt to catch out the unwary. The first corner now has a chicane to slow it before turning right and going into a left-right flick, a hairpin, then a series of "S" bends on to the back straight and then that final corner...

Mexico City is regularly shaken by earthquakes, and the tremors contributed to a notori-

MEXICO CITY
The Peralta Curve, leading on to the pit straight, provides a wonderful challenge for the drivers.

ously bumpy surface which was often criticized. The other unusual factor was its high altitude, 7,400ft, to which both man and machine had to adapt.

Much of the inspiration for the Grand Prix was provided by brothers Ricardo and Pedro Rodriguez. Ricardo lost his life practising for the inaugural non-championship race in 1962, and the track was subsequently named after him. His brother was in the field for the first official Grand Prix a year later, and soon matured into one of the top stars of the decade.

Clark won the first championship race in 1963, and a year later Mexico was the scene of a dramatic title showdown involving Clark, Surtees and Hill. Gurney won the race, but Surtees took the title. In 1965, Ginther gave Honda its first-ever win. John Surtees won the race for the first time in 1966, ahead of Brabham, both of whom were a lap up on the rest of the field. Jim Clark stormed to an easy win in 1967, and Graham Hill secured the second of his world titles by winning in 1968. Denny Hulme won for McLaren the following year.

Until 1970 the race was firmly established as the season-closer, but that year's race, won by Ickx, was notorious for the lack of crowd control. Drivers raced between human barriers, and it was a miracle that there were no incidents.

The race was dropped from the schedule for 1971. Pedro Rodriguez was killed in June, and with him went any chance

that the Mexican authorities might push for the race to be back on the calendar. Pedro's name was later added to that of his brother in the official title of the circuit.

Grand Prix returns to Mexico

However, 16 years later the financial circumstances were right for FOCA and the race was indeed restored, with the track cut from 3.1 to 2.7 miles and suitably uprated with new (but outdated) pits. The Peralta turn was a wonderful challenge for the modern breed of Formula One cars, but over the years it would be the scene of several huge accidents, many of them on the exit.

Berger earned maiden wins for both himself and the Benetton team in the 1986 event, while Mansell, Prost and Senna won over the next three seasons. The chicane at the end of the pit straight proved a popular passing place.

Prost won again in 1990, but the race is best remembered for a daring move by Mansell on Berger – on the outside at Peralta, ensuring a Ferrari one-two. Mansell was again second in 1991, this time behind Patrese.

The last Mexican Grand Prix was held in 1992. Not surprisingly, the Williams-Renault of Mansell – the best "active" car – rode the bumps to perfection and led all the way. Team-mate Patrese finished second.

The race disappeared from the calendar in 1993, mainly due to finances.

MONACO GRAND PRIX

WITH ITS CASINO AND ROWS OF MILLIONAIRES' yachts bobbing in the harbour, Monaco is still a glamorous locale for the rich and famous, for whom the race is of secondary importance to the socializing.

MONACO	
Circuit distance: 2.068 miles (3.328 kms)	
Race distance: 160.68 miles (258.59 kms)	
No of laps: 78	

EVER AN ANACHRONISM IN MODERN DAY Formula One, yet this harbourside track, nestling in the principality of Monte Carlo, corners more glamour than the rest of the Grands Prix put together. It is incredibly bumpy and narrow, but the cars still hit a heck of a speed as they power out of the tunnel and on to the waterfront And the sight of Formula One cars being flung between the barriers in Casino Square never fails to excite.

Winding its way around the streets of the tiny principality, the track has remained basically unchanged for decades, and much (but not all) of it would be familiar to drivers who raced in the 1950s. The same can not be said for the surroundings, since the skyline of Monaco has been changed by apartment blocks and huge hotels.

From the first corner at Ste Dévote the track blasts up the hill to Casino Square. From there its plunges down to the right-hander at Mirabeau, and then to the tight Loews (formerly Station) hairpin. Portier leads on to the seafront, and the charge through the tunnel to the harbour-side chicane. After that comes the left-hander at Tabac, the Swimming Pool section (which was substantially modified in the early 1970s), then finally the tight right at Rascasse and the pit straight.

Overtaking was never easy at Monaco, but in recent decades it has become virtually impossible. More than anywhere else, it is vital to qualify at the front. However, the attrition rate is often high, and careful driving can earn a midfielder valuable points.

Monaco's racing history

The Grand Prix was first held in 1929, and the pre-war races saw some great battles, with the legendary Nuvolari among the winners. Monaco hosted the second-ever round of the World Championship in 1950 – just a week after the opening race at Silverstone. Ten cars were eliminated in a first-lap crash and Fangio scored a famous win.

There was no race at all in 1951, 1953 and 1954, and the 1952 event was held for only for sports cars and, sadly, Grand Prix star, Luigi Fagioli, was fatally injured.

The World Championship returned in 1955, and Monaco has had a race every year since – no other circuit can match that record (Monza lost the 1980 Italian race to Imola). In that 1955 race the Mercedes effort collapsed, and Trintignant scored a surprise

win. But it is best remembered for Ascari's flight into the harbour. Four days later the double World Champion died in a testing accident.

Moss won in 1956, when the chicane was tightened, but, in 1957, he and fellow Brits Hawthorn and Collins crashed at the chicane. Fangio won again. Then Trintignant scored a second win in 1958 as the opposition faded away, this victory the first for a rear-engined car.

Moss lost out to Brabham in 1959 through axle failure. He won in 1960, but his victory in 1961 was the one for which he is remembered, as in the first race of the 1.5-litre formula his

underpowered Lotus held off the Ferraris of Ginther and Phil Hill.

For most of the 1960s Graham Hill was the undisputed King of Monaco. He won five times in all while, curiously, the great Clark – who scored five British Grand Prix wins and four at Spa – never won at the street circuit.

Hill first shone at Monaco in 1962, leading until his engine failed with just eight laps to go, allowing McLaren to win. Hill soon made amends, winning in 1963, 1964 and 1965. On the first two occasions he was certainly helped by problems for Clark, but Clark missed the third race to attend the Indy

MONACO

Harbourside in the principality with great viewing from the hoards of boats. The event remains the jewel in Formula One's crown.

500. However, that was perhaps Hill's greatest victory, for he had to recover from a trip up the chicane escape road when caught out by a slower car. Hill added further wins in 1968 and 1969.

Stewart scored his first Monaco victory in 1966 (he added two more, in 1971 and 1973), while Hulme scored his first-ever win there in 1967. But that race was spoiled by the death of Lorenzo Bandini, who crashed in flames at the chicane while pressing on in second place.

An exciting decade

The start of the 1970s saw two very memorable races. In 1970, Brabham slid into the barrier at the very last corner, handing victory to the hard-chasing Rindt. Two years later the race was run in torrential rain and, against all odds, plucky Frenchman, Jean-Pierre Beltoise, beat the stars to give BRM its last-ever Grand Prix win.

The 1974 race saw a massive pile-up on the run from Ste Dévote to Casino Square, and in its aftermath Peterson scored a fine win in the old Lotus 72, even overcoming a spin.

Lauda was the master of Monaco in the mid-1970s, winning in 1975 (in the wet) and 1976. In 1977, he lost out to Scheckter's Wolf by less than a second, and in 1978 he set a new lap record as he chased Depailler, the Frenchman scoring his first Grand Prix win.

Another thrilling finish took place in 1979, veteran Regazzoni confirming his return to form as he pursued Scheckter's Ferrari. The 1980 race is remembered more for the start. Daly eliminated three other cars as he bounced high over the pack at Ste Dévote. Reutemann scored a canny win as others hit trouble.

Villeneuve added to his growing reputation by winning the 1981 event in the unloved Ferrari 126CK, while the next year brought one of the most memorable races of recent years. In the closing laps, Prost and Daly both crashed, Pironi and de Cesaris ran out of fuel, and Patrese spun – but resumed to score an amazing success.

A virtuoso performance on a damp track earned a great win for Keke Rosberg in 1983, and in 1984 the rain returned in style. Much of the field fell off the road, including Mansell when leading and amid much controversy the race was stopped prematurely with leader Prost being caught by newcomer Senna, who was in turn being reeled in by fellow rookie Stefan Bellof. Senna would get another chance! Prost won again in 1985 after a battle with Alboreto.

In the biggest change since the introduction of the Swimming Pool corners in the early 1970s, the chicane was completely rebuilt for the 1986 race. It was turned from a high-speed flick into a slow left, right, left. The result was the same, as Prost scored his second win in a row Each race seemed to produce a spectacular crash, and the victim this time was Tambay, who rolled his Haas Lola.

Prost's reign as Monaco's man to beat was almost over. The 1987 race saw Senna pick up his first win with the "active" Lotus, but only after Mansell's Williams-Honda had retired.

The following year Senna was in a class of his own, but with a handful of laps to go, he made one of the most publicized mistakes of his career, hitting the barrier just before the tunnel. Prost nipped through to score his fourth (and last) triumph.

For the next five years Senna reigned supreme, winning each year from 1989 to 1993. More often than not, Mansell was his closest challenger, and Senna won the 1992 race after Nigel made a late stop with a loose wheel. And he won in 1993 only after Prost and Schumacher had encountered problems.

The 1994 Monaco race was the first Grand Prix after Senna's death, and he was missed as Schumacher became the first winner other than Prost and Senna since 1983. There was a surprise first Grand Prix win for Panis in 1996, but Schumacher returned to win the race for the third time in 1997 before Mika Hakkinen controlled the event for McLaren the following year. Schumacher led all the way in 1999, then streaked clear in 2000, with Coulthard bottled up behind Trulli's Jordan. But his rear suspension broke, Trulli retired and Coulthard was the clear winner.

MONACO
Stirling Moss scores Lotus's first win in 1960.

PORTUGUESE GRAND PRIX

PORTUGAL IS A SMALL COUNTRY WHICH HAS NEVER HAD a great Formula One driver, and yet its Grand Prix was a well-supported event right up until the last race there in 1996 and it often produced high drama.

ESTORIL	
Circuit distance: 2.709 miles (4.36 kms)	
Race distance: 192.339 miles (309.54 kms)	
No of laps: 71	

The Portuguese Grand Prix had a brief flourish during 1958–60. In the even years it was held on the Oporto street track – where tramlines and cobblestones were just some of the hazards – and in 1959 it was run at Monsanto, near Lisbon, a tricky parkland venue.

The starting line at Oporto was on the harbourfront and, like the modern Macau track, it combined long straights with twisty bits between buildings. Moss won the first race, while Hawthorn nearly threw away his world title after driving the wrong way after a spin.

Moss was again the class of the field in 1959 in his Cooper. The race was started late to avoid the afternoon heat, and finished after 7pm! Moss, returning from injury, was never really in the hunt in the 1960 Oporto event, which was won by Brabham.

Formula One didn't return for 24 years, this time to a permanent road course near the resort of Estoril. Built in 1972, the 2.70-mile Autodromo do Estoril hosted European Formula Two in the mid-1970s, but had largely been forgotten when it was resurrected and tidied up in 1984.

NOW ONE OF THE OLD-GUARD OF GRAND Prix circuits. And it still retains some character despite changes made in 1994 on safety grounds. Drivers love the challenge and know the track well from winter testing there. The key corner is the long, long last one leading onto the main straight. It's essential to get this right so you can slipstream down the straight to the first corner.

A demanding circuit

Featuring up and down sweeps through barren, rocky terrain, the lap starts with a flowing right-hander that leads almost immediately into a wicked downhill right-hander and a hairpin. Then it's uphill to another hairpin and down the kinked back straight. A long left-hander, a short straight, then an uphill right-hander lead the track into a series of twists before a long, long right-hander on to the pit straight. It is tough on the drivers, but has more overtaking opportunities than most tracks built in recent years.

The 1984 event was held in October and proved to be the championship decider. Prost won the race, but Lauda did just enough to win the title – by half a point! – by keeping his nerve and coming in second ahead of a young Ayrton Senna. The 1985 race was held just seven months later, in April, and Prost was one of several drivers to crash out in torrential conditions. The master on that memorable day was Senna, who collected his first win for Lotus ahead of Ferrari's Alboreto.

After that experiment the race moved to September. Mansell won in 1986 beating Prost, who made amends by triumphing again in 1987 (pressuring Berger into a spin) and again in 1988, beating Capelli in the Leyton House. One of the most controversial races came in 1989, when Mansell was black-flagged after reversing in the pits. He did not respond, and three laps later crashed out of the race with Senna. Berger came through to win.

Nigel was banned from the next event, but the following year he came back and beat Senna at Estoril – a rare good result during his miserable second season with Ferrari. But at the start he had lunged at team-mate Prost, costing them both positions.

Patrese won in 1991, after Mansell lost a wheel leaving the pits! Nigel was later black-flagged, and his title hopes took a major knock. He scored his third success in 1992. That race was notable for a spectacular accident involving Patrese, who nearly hit the pit straight bridge after hitting a slowing Berger.

The 1993 race saw Schumacher score his second-ever win for Benetton after the team's superior pit strategy overcame that of Prost and Williams. This time Berger had a massive accident on the main straight, albeit at the other end – when this

time he was leaving the pits!

In 1994, Hill took full advantage of the absence of a suspended Schumacher by winning ahead of Coulthard, who made amends by winning the following year. The track now had an absurdly slow chicane, corners Nine and Ten, introduced after the Imola tragedies. And it was here that the McLarens collided in 1996 as Villeneuve raced to victory to take the title race to the final round. The race was dropped from the calendar in 1997 when safety modifications hadn't been made. However, it remains a popular testing venue.

ESTORIL
Prost leads Capelli through the circuit's final corner in 1988.

SAN MARINO GRAND PRIX

FOR MANY YEARS GRAND PRIX RACING STUCK TO THE rule which stated that each country was entitled to only one race, although there was a rare exception in 1957, when Italy had events at both Pescara and Monza.

IMOLA	
Circuit distance: 3.042 miles (4.929 kms)	
Race distance: 191.630 miles (308.40 kms)	
No of laps: 63	

A FABULOUS PLACE TO WATCH A GRAND Prix, every grandstand bedecked in banners of Ferrari red, but its memory will always be tainted by the double fatality of Ayrton Senna and Roland Ratzenberger in 1994. Located in beautiful parkland, it has been modified greatly since the accidents, but now has the downhill Acque Minerale restored to its former glory.

In 1976, it was decided that the United States was large enough to deserve East and West coast races, and, in 1984, America actually had three events. In 1982, there was a one-off Swiss Grand Prix at Dijon, and since then Brands Hatch, the Nurburgring, Donington and Jerez have hosted extra races under the "European Grand Prix" banner. Those were usually one-offs, but since 1981 Italy has run two Grands Prix, the second borrowing its title from the little-known principality of San Marino.

The first San Marino Grand Prix was held as a non-championship race in 1979, just a week after the Italian Grand Prix at Monza. The venue was Imola. It was built in the 1950s, but had rarely hosted major events and, like other established circuits emerging suddenly on to the Formula One scene, it had to be substantially rebuilt.

Popular with the drivers, the track was set in attractive wooded countryside and featured wonderful up-and-down sweeps, linked by unloved chicanes. Tamburello, the high-speed left-hander shortly after the pits, was a real test. Following this there was a blast down to Tosa, an uphill right-hander that leads on to the "back" section of the track that dives up and down – albeit with great corners like Acque Minerale chopped by the addition of a chicane – before doubling back with the double-apex left-hander at Rivazza and returning to the pit straight via a double chicane, where Barrichello crashed so dramatically in 1994. The Italian fans loved the place too, and the support of Enzo Ferrari – the track was renamed after his late son Dino – ensured that the race was a success.

Lauda won that first event for Brabham and, after some political manoeuvring, Imola ousted Monza as host of the 1980 Italian Grand Prix. For the following season a suitable compromise was reached, and since then both circuits have held a race each year. San Marino has usually opened the European season.

Piquet won the one-off Italian Grand Prix and triumphed again in the first and very wet pukka San Marino event held the following April.

An eventful era

Imola soon developed a reputation for providing drama. The 1982 event was notable for a boycott by the British-based FOCA teams, and for the start of a feud between winner Pironi and his Ferrari team-mate Villeneuve; the Canadian was killed at Zolder a fortnight later. Exactly a year after the feud started, Villeneuve's replacement, Tambay, scored an emotional win at Imola.

Imola is tough on fuel mileage, which was particularly important in the turbo era. In 1985, Prost ran out on the slowing-down lap – and was disqualified for being underweight.

Mansell won in 1987 after team-mate Piquet survived a massive qualifying accident at Tamburello. In 1989, Berger crashed at the same place. Ferrari's worst day at Imola was in 1991: Prost spun off on the warm-up lap, and team-mate Alesi went off the road three laps later. In 1992, Mansell set a record with his fifth straight win, and, in 1993, Prost scored another win for Williams. However, Imola will always be known for the terrible events of 1994. Roland Ratzenberger died in qualifying and then Senna crashed to his death in the race – at Tamburello. Hill made Williams happier about the place by winning there in 1996, then Heinz-Harald Frentzen recorded his first win in 1997, beating old enemy, Michael Schumacher, to the flag. In 1998, David Coulthard controlled the race for McLaren, then Mika Hakkinen was set to do the same in 1999, but he crashed out of the lead, leaving the way clear for Schumacher to win, which the German duly did again in 2000.

IMOLA
The track sweeps through a verdant setting, but it was also the scene of disaster in 1994 with two fatal accidents.

SOUTH AFRICAN GRAND PRIX

A GRAND PRIX WAS FIRST HELD IN SOUTH AFRICA IN THE 1930S, BUT IT WAS NOT UNTIL 1962 that the country hosted its first World Championship race.

The original venue was the 2.44-mile seaside track at East London. It was the closing race of a competitive season, and in fact practice started on December 26. The race was won by Hill and, with Jim Clark retiring, the moustachioed Englishman secured the drivers' title for himself and the constructors' title for BRM.

The race remained at East London for two more years, but in 1967 it had found a new home at Kyalami, near Johannesburg, and a new role as the season opener. Like so many classic circuits, Kyalami had a long pit straight, preceded by a fast final corner. The undulating 2.54-mile layout included a spectacular downhill run to the tricky first corner, Crowthorne. That led into the Barbecue/Jukskei Kink section, regarded as one of the most dramatic of any Grand Prix venue.

Pedro Rodriguez won in 1967, but privateer John Love nearly caused the biggest upset of all time by leading – until he had to make a late stop for fuel. In 1970, Jack Brabham scored his last Grand Prix victory, while the following year Andretti took his first.

Tragedy struck twice in the 1970s and both times the Shadow team was involved. American star, Peter Revson,

was killed in testing in 1974, and three years later Welshman Tom Pryce lost his life when he struck a marshal who crossed the pit straight during the race. Lauda won that event – his first victory since his horrific Nurburgring crash.

One of the most exciting Kyalami races came in 1978, when Peterson and Depailler battled for the lead over the last few laps, Ronnie eventually winning and reaffirming that he could still do the job.

The 1979 event saw more excitement as Villeneuve put in a fine wet-weather drive, beating team-mate Scheckter (who had won his home race in 1975). Rain struck again in 1981, when the race took place without the "grandee" FISA-aligned teams, and was outside the championship. That did not detract from a fine drive by the Williams pairing of Jones and Reutemann who came home first and second.

A controversial pre-practice drivers' strike is what the 1982 event is best remembered for. The race was eventually won by Prost, who recovered in great style after a puncture. For 1983 the race moved to the end of the season, and Prost lost a last-round title showdown to Piquet, although the Brazilian finished only third.

Prost in top form

Prost was the star in 1984, starting from the back in the spare car and charging through to second, behind team-mate Lauda. The following year Mansell backed up his maiden win at Brands Hatch with a second straight success.

Motor racing had retained links with South Africa far longer than most other international sports, but after the 1985 race the political pressure became so great – particularly in France – that Kyalami was dropped from the calendar.

However, the political climate changed, and in 1992 the race was back, but on a substantially revised Kyalami track. This included sections of the old track, but not the long straight. Indeed, it was barely recognizable to the Formula One teams. Something of a bland, modern autodrome, it was slow and lacked the character of the original.

The first "new" race was won by Mansell, and it was as boring as the revised venue suggested. Fortunately, the 1993 event was rather more exciting, as Prost and Senna put on a spectacular show in the early laps. Prost, in his first race for Williams, came out on top.

That event was a much better advertisement for Kyalami than the previous race, but after a domestic financial wrangle the South African Grand Prix disappeared from the 1994 calendar. If the problems can be overcome, it may return in the future.

KYALAMI
Michael Schumacher at what is now the Goodyear Corner in the 1992 South African Grand Prix.

SPANISH GRAND PRIX

LIKE PORTUGAL, SPAIN HAS NEVER HAD A GREAT Grand Prix driver, although Alfonso de Portago showed some promise before his death in 1957. However, the Spanish Grand Prix has a distinguished history, and has been shared between five different circuits.

CATALUNYA	
Circuit distance:	2.949 miles (4.727 kms)
Race distance:	191.685 miles (308.49 kms)
No of laps:	65

ONE OF THE MODERN CIRCUITS, ALBEIT one with a little more to it than most. Mainly g-forces, actually, and an undulating crown to the track that keeps the cars unsettled. Watch for the chicane that acts as the first corner. Almost every race sees someone beached in the gravel trap there on the opening lap. The last corner is pretty special, too.

In its first incarnation the race was run twice – in 1951 and 1954 – at Pedralbes, a street circuit in the suburbs of Barcelona.

It would be 14 years before Spain was back on the calendar. The race was alternated between two rival venues: Jarama and Montjuich Park. On the outskirts of Madrid, Jarama was one of the first purpose-built autodromes, designed by the man responsible for both Zandvoort and Suzuka.

The 2.11-mile track consisted almost entirely of tight, slow corners and, as such, was perhaps 20 years ahead of its time! In total contrast, Montjuich was a thrilling road circuit, winding up and down through a Barcelona park.

Hill won the first Jarama race in 1968. In the first Montjuich race, both he and team-mate Rindt suffered wing failures and had huge crashes.

Seven years later an uncannily similar fate befell Stommelen who, by coincidence, was driving a Hill-entered car. After crashes had wiped out much of the field, the German was in the

JARAMA
Carlos Reutemann leads down the pit straight in the non-championship 1980 Spanish Grand Prix.

lead when the wing failed. The car cleared a barrier, killing five spectators. Jochen Mass was declared winner of the curtailed event, and from then on the race stayed at Jarama.

There was more controversy in 1976, when Hunt was initially disqualified for being too wide, and in 1980 when, at the heart of the FISA/FOCA dispute, the race went ahead without the FISA "grandee" teams, and was kicked out of the championship. Jarama rarely produced great racing, overtaking being difficult, but that very factor allowed Villeneuve to score a memorable win in 1981, with four cars on his tail!

Jarama was dropped, and it was five years before the Spanish Grand Prix re-emerged at a new track, Jerez, in the far south. The regional government supported the building of the 2.62-mile track, which was composed of hairpins with a couple of blindingly quick turns behind the pits.

Drama at Jerez

The first Jerez race produced a thrilling finish as Senna held off Mansell by the slenderest of margins. However, subsequent events tended to be boring processions, with comfortable wins for Mansell (1987), Prost (1988 and 1990) and Senna (1989). In 1990 Martin Donnelly was hurt in a horrific crash in qualifying at one of the fast kinks.

That did not help to promote Jerez's case, and, by 1991, the race had moved to the Circuit de Catalunya, near Barcelona, which was adjudged better than most, with a long straight followed by hard braking.

The first two races were hit by rain, and both were won by Mansell. In 1991, Nigel and Senna staged a fabulous, if brief, battle for second, running side by side down the straight. Then Nigel was in a class of his own in 1992, while Prost proved to be a dominant winner in 1993.

Hill won in 1994 after Schumacher hit trouble, but the German won at Jerez in the 1995 event. And he won in the wet in 1996. But 1997 saw a Villeneuve double in Spain – and much controversy. There was no race at Jerez in 1998, while the McLarens dominated at Barcelona, with Hakkinen ahead of Coulthard. It has been real McLaren territory since, with Hakkinen winning in both 1999 and 2000.

JEREZ
Michael Schumacher gets the jump on Jacques Villeneuve at the start of the title-deciding European Grand Prix held at the circuit in 1997, although they would not finish in that order.

UNITED STATES GRAND PRIX

THE UNITED STATES CAN LAY CLAIM TO MORE GRAND Prix venues than any other country. No fewer than eight circuits have held World Championship races. One year there were three events in the United States — plus a fourth in Canada! That was in 1982, and yet after 1991 it took another nine years before Formula One returned — to Indianapolis.

INDIANAPOLIS	
Circuit distance: 2.609 miles (4.200 kms)	
Race distance: 190.51 miles (306.6 kms)	
No. of laps: 73	

The first US Grand Prix was held in 1959 at Sebring, the air-field circuit in Florida famous for its bumpy runways and its sports car race. Bruce McLaren won, and Cooper team-mate Brabham took the title. Next year the event moved across the country to Riverside, the dusty Californian road course. This time Moss won, but once again the race was a one-off.

Finally, in 1961, the race found its true home. Watkins Glen, an undulating road course in upstate New York, was the host of the US Grand Prix until 1980. The event was popular with the teams, not least because in pre-FOCA days it paid the most prize money... The most famous section of the track was the dramatic uphill "S" soon after the start. The inaugural event in 1961 was won by Innes Ireland, and for the next six years Clark and Hill shared the victories.

The track was extended for 1971, when Cevert scored his first and only win. Two years later the Frenchman was killed in qualifying at the Glen, and a year after that Austrian rookie, Helmuth Koinigg, lost his life.

Despite the tragedies the race went on. But by 1980, with the turbo era dawning and the cars developing at an astonishing pace, it was clear that the Glen could not keep up. After that year's race, won by Alan Jones, the circus never went back.

LAS VEGAS
Alan Jones gets the jump on team-mate Carlos Reutemann at the start of the 1981 US Grand Prix.

Popularity of street racing

By now street racing had taken a grip. Back in 1976, British promoter Chris Pook introduced the US Grand Prix (West), taking advantage of a dispensation which allowed the States to have two events. The race was held over a challenging round-the-houses course at Long Beach in California (passing the permanently moored Queen Mary cruise liner), noted for a long, curving pit straight, followed by a tight hairpin. Clay Regazzoni was the inaugural winner and the race became a classic, but after 1983 Pook switched to Indycars, no longer willing to pay the fees Formula One demanded.

Others decided they could do a similar job, and in 1981 the Glen was replaced by an event at Las Vegas – held quite literally in the car park of the Caesar's Palace hotel. Jones won, but nobody liked the place and it lasted just two years.

In 1982, Long Beach and Vegas were joined by another street race, in Detroit, home of the US motor industry. That was rather more successful than Vegas, and produced some entertaining races and three wins for Ayrton Senna. It ran until 1988, when it too joined the Indycar trail.

In 1984, Dallas became a Formula One venue – but it was a disaster, the track falling apart in the heat. The race turned into a one-off...

After the loss of Long Beach, Vegas, Dallas and Detroit, Phoenix stepped forward with

yet another downtown event in 1989, despite the presence of a successful Indycar oval just outside town. The race is best remembered for a wonderful fight between Senna and Jean Alesi, who in 1990 produced one of the best televised dices in years.

The US Grand Prix ran three times at Phoenix, but disappeared from the calendar after 1991.

After a raft of rumours, including potential races in Las Vegas and San Francisco, the US Grand Prix was back on the calendar in 2000, this time held at Indianapolis. The track used one of the four banked corners, the start/finish straight – running in the opposite direction to normal – and a twisting loop around the infield. Michael Schumacher was the first to win there for Ferrari.

INDIANAPOLIS
2000 saw a welcome return to the States for Formula One – and where better to host the return than Indianapolis, the home of American motor racing.

CHRONOLOGY OF FORMULA ONE

1950 First FIA Drivers' World
Championship – six European
Grands Prix, plus Indy 500. Alfa
returns with Fangio, Giuseppe
Farina and Luigi Fagioli, and
dominates championship. Farina
pips Fangio for title.

1951 Alfa dominates, but Ferrari
and Froilan Gonzales achieve a
breakthrough at British Grand
Prix. Alfa's Fangio clinches title
from Ferrari's Alberto Ascari at
last race. BRM and Girling intro-
duce disc brakes.

1952 World Championship is run for
2-litre, normally aspirated cars
after Alfa withdrawal. Ferrari
dominates, with Ascari an easy
champion.

1953 Ascari and Ferrari do it again.
Classic duel between Mike
Hawthorn's Ferrari and Fangio's
Maserati at Reims sees first
British win since 1923.

1954 2.5-litre normally aspirated
Formula One is introduced,
luring Mercedes back. Fangio
takes second title after starting
the year with Maserati and ending
it with Mercedes.

1955 Stirling Moss joins Fangio for a
Mercedes steamroller and
Fangio's third title. Ascari dies in
sports car crash at Monza. Tony
Brooks and Connaught take first
all-British Grand Prix win since
1924 at Syracuse. Mercedes withdraws after Le Mans disaster.

1956 Fangio dominates in a Lancia-
Ferrari for title number four.
British challenge strengthens,
with Moss and Peter Collins
both winning Grands Prix.

1957 Fangio moves to Maserati for
fifth title. His four wins include a
classic battle with the Ferraris of
Collins and Hawthorn at the
Nurburgring race. Moss moves to
Vanwall and wins British (with
Brooks), Pescara and Italian
Grands Prix.

1958 Ferrari's Hawthorn becomes
Britain's first World Champion
with single Grand Prix win in
France. Collins, Stuart Lewis-
Evans and Luigi Musso killed in
tragic year. Grieving Hawthorn
dies in road accident. Fangio
retires. Moss takes first rear-
engined Grand Prix victory for
Cooper. Vanwall wins inaugural
Constructors' Cup.

1959 Rear-engined cars take over.
Works Cooper driver, Jack
Brabham, wins title as Moss's pri-
vate Cooper falters. Cooper wins
Constructors' Cup as Vanwall
withdraws and Ferrari struggles.
Lotus makes debut.

1960 Brabham and Cooper do the
double again. Lotus scores its
first win. Ferrari wins Italian
Grand Prix when British teams
boycott bumpy banked track.
Last year for Indy 500 in World
Championship.

1961 Formula One changes to 1.5-litre, normally aspirated engines as sop to Ferrari. Ferrari dominates with V6 Dino. Phil Hill is first US champion, but team-mate Wolfgang von Trips is killed at Monza. Lotus picks up crumbs – Moss wins in Germany, Innes Ireland in USA.

1962 Britain back in control, with Climax and BRM V8s. World Champion Graham Hill (BRM) and Jim Clark (Lotus) are new stars. Moss has career-ending accident at Goodwood. Monocoque Lotus 25 revolutionizes Formula One. Bruce McLaren wins in Monaco in a car bearing own name.

1963 Clark and Lotus win seven out of ten Grands Prix. British white wash as Hill wins twice for BRM and ex-motorcycle World Champion John Surtees once for Ferrari.

1964 British domination continues. Three-way shoot-out at Mexican finale between Surtees' Ferrari, Hill's BRM and Clark's Lotus. Surtees takes title.

1965 Second titles for Lotus and Clark. Clark wins six of ten Grands Prix. Jackie Stewart scores first of 27 wins in Italy, while Honda and Goodyear score their first win with Richie Ginther in Mexico.

1966 Shaky debut season for 3-litre formula. Jack Brabham takes title with Brabham-Repco.

1967 Denny Hulme gives Brabham second consecutive title. Ferrari's Lorenzo Bandini dies at Monaco. Ford Cosworth DFV, the most successful Formula One engine ever, wins on debut at Zandvoort in Clark's Lotus.

1968 Clark, Ludovico Scarfiotti, Mike Spence and Jo Schlesser die in a tragic year. Clark's accident, in a Formula Two race at Hockenheim, seems inexplicable. Hill restores Lotus morale with first DFV-powered title. Wings and aerodynamics take on new significance. Gold Leaf Lotus heralds the age of sponsorship.

1969 Stewart, Tyrrell-run Matras and DFVs dominate, winning six Grands Prix plus drivers' and constructors' titles. Hill scores fifth Monaco win.

1970 Rindt becomes first posthumous World Champion after crashing in practice for Italian Grand Prix. McLaren dies testing his CanAm car. Piers Courage's death adds to another terrible year. Brabham retires. First Formula One March and Tyrrell's self-built car make their debuts.

1971 Stewart takes a second title, giving Tyrrell its first as a constructor. Pedro Rodriguez and Jo Siffert are both killed.

1972 Emerson Fittipaldi and Lotus win title with five victories. Stewart is second after illness. Jo Bonnier dies at Le Mans.

1973 Stewart decides it's his last season – and wins third title. Five more wins give him record 27 victories, beating Fangio's 24. Team-mate François Cevert dies in practice for US Grand Prix.

1974 Fittipaldi wins title after moving to McLaren. Peter Revson dies after crashing in practice in South Africa.

1975 Niki Lauda takes first title as Ferrari revival gathers pace. Mark Donohue dies after accident in Austria. James Hunt and Hesketh win Dutch Grand Prix. Hill and protégé Tony Brise killed in light aircraft accident.

1976 Hunt wins world title with McLaren at rain-soaked Japanese finale. Lauda takes it to wire despite near-fatal accident at the Nurburgring.

1977 Lauda and Ferrari take title, but the Austrian switches to Brabham for 1978. Renault's RS01 brings 1.5-litre turbo engines to Formula One. Lotus 78 introduces ground effect. Tom Pryce killed in freak South African Grand Prix tragedy.

1978 Mario Andretti becomes World Champion as he and team-mate Ronnie Peterson dominate for Lotus. Peterson dies from complications after startline shunt in Italian Grand Prix. Brabham's "fan car" wins Swedish Grand Prix and is banned from further racing.

1979 Ferrari are back. Jody Scheckter takes title ahead of team-mate Villeneuve. Clay Regazzoni takes first win for Williams at Silverstone. Alan Jones follows it up with four more. Jean-Pierre Jabouille and Renault score first win for a turbo-charged engine. Lauda and Hunt both retire from racing.

1980 Jones and Williams win title after fighting off Nelson Piquet's Brabham. FISA/FOCA "war" blights season. Patrick Depailler is killed testing at Hockenheim. Regazzoni is paralysed at Long Beach. Nigel Mansell makes debut.

1981 Piquet and Brabham snatch title from Williams's Carlos Reutemann in Las Vegas finale. Ferrari turbo signals beginning of end for normally aspirated engines. Alain Prost scores first

three of his 51 Grand Prix victories. McLaren's carbon-fibre monocoque revolutionizes Formula One car construction.

1982 Williams's Keke Rosberg emerges as champion with a single victory as Renault unreliability throws the title. Year supplies 11 different winners, including unretired Lauda. Villeneuve and Didier Pironi feud at Imola. Villeneuve dies in practice at Zolder. Pironi suffers career-ending injuries at Hockenheim. Riccardo Paletti dies in Canada.

1983 Piquet wins title number two, courtesy of Brabham and BMW – the first turbo-charged World Champions. Ground effect is banned with introduction of flat bottoms. Michele Alboreto scores DFV's last win.

1984 Lauda takes third title by half a point from team-mate Prost. TAG-powered McLarens win 12 of the 16 Grands Prix. Ayrton Senna stars in rain-soaked Monaco Grand Prix in amazing debut year.

1985 Prost becomes France's first World Champion. Senna scores maiden win in Portugal for Lotus. Mansell breaks duck by winning European Grand Prix at Brands Hatch. Manfred Winkelhock and Stefan Bellof die in sports car accidents. Lauda retires again.

1986 High-speed blow-out for Mansell at Adelaide hands title to McLaren's Prost. Elio de Angelis dies while testing.

1987 Piquet takes third title after diffident season with Williams-Honda. Mansell, with six wins, is thwarted, but his pursuit of Piquet at Silverstone is a high-light. 3.5-litre normally aspirated engines introduced alongside turbos.

1988 McLaren gets Senna and Honda's V6 and dominates year, winning 15 of 16 Grands Prix, with first-time champion Senna winning eight and Prost seven. Ferrari's Gerhard Berger is only other winner. Last season of turbo era.

1989 Title number three for Prost at McLaren. Third consecutive title for Honda, now with 3.5-litre V10. Feud between Prost and team-mate Senna culminates in collision at Japanese Grand Prix. Mansell leads Ferrari revival. Berger escapes fiery Imola crash.

1990 Senna's second title with McLaren and Honda. Prost and Senna collide in Japan again. Prost and Mansell feud at Ferrari. Mansell quits, then signs for Williams. Martin Donnelly serious-ly injured in qualifying at Jerez.

1991 Senna fights off challenge of Mansell, Williams and Renault to take third title. McLaren's seventh drivers' title in eight years; Honda's fifth in a row. Ferrari politics force Prost to quit after first winless season in 11 years. Michael Schumacher makes debut.

1992 Mansell finally wins world title with Williams after dominant year, but quits for Indycars. Renault's first-ever title. Schumacher takes his maiden win at Spa.

1993 Prost returns to take fourth title with Williams. Senna drives race of his career at wet/dry European Grand Prix at Donington. Prost retires. Mansell wins Indycar title at first attempt.

1994 Senna dies in San Marino Grand Prix at Imola after Roland Ratzenberger's death in practice.

Major rule changes brought in as a result. Benetton's Schumacher emerges champion, beating Williams's Damon Hill at Adelaide finale. Mansell returns to Williams for four races, winning the closing round in Australia.

1995 Schumacher versus Hill from the outset in contest marked by sev-eral collisions. Schumacher wraps up title with one race to go. Jean Alesi, Johnny Herbert and David Coulthard all take their first wins, Alesi in his 91st Grand Prix. Benetton lifts Constructors' Championship.

1996 Damon Hill becomes first second generation World Champion. Williams team-mate, Jacques Villeneuve, runs him close Schumacher revives Ferrari, but no one can live with Williams-Renault.

1997 Villeneuve wins seven times to be champion for Williams, surviving a last race assault from title rival Schumacher. Stewart Grand Prix team makes Formula One debut. Panis breaks legs in Canada.

1998 McLaren-Mercedes dominate from the start, but Schumacher, Ferrari and Goodyear combine to take the battle to them, with Hakkinen only winning the title for McLaren at the final round.

1999 Ferrari challenge blunted when Schumacher breaks leg, but Irvine pushes McLaren's Hakkinen all the way to the final round. Sepang and BAR make championship bow.

2000 McLaren and Ferrari do battle again and Schumacher takes the title at the penultimate round. US Grand Prix returns, this time at Indianapolis. Jaguar takes over rebadged Stewart team.

FORMULA ONE RECORDS

Most Grands Prix starts

256	Riccardo Patrese (ITA)
210	Gerhard Berger (AUT)
208	Andrea de Cesaris (ITA)
204	Nelson Piquet (BRA)
199	Alain Prost (FRA)
194	Michele Alboreto (ITA)
187	Nigel Mansell (GBR)
184	Jean Alesi (FRA)
176	Graham Hill (GBR)
175	Jacques Laffite (FRA)
171	Niki Lauda (AUT)
163	Thierry Boutsen (BEL)
162	Johnny Herbert (GBR)
161	Ayrton Senna (BRA)
158	Martin Brundle (GBR)
152	John Watson (GBR)
149	Rene Arnoux (FRA)
147	Derek Warwick (GBR)
146	Carlos Reutemann (ARG)
145	Mika Hakkinen (FIN)
	Michael Schumacher (GER)
144	Emerson Fittipaldi (BRA)
135	Jean-Pierre Jarier (FRA)
132	Eddie Cheever (USA)
	Clay Regazzoni (SUI)
130	Rubens Barrichello (BRA)
128	Mario Andretti (USA)
126	Jack Brabham (AUS)
123	Ronnie Peterson (SWE)
119	Pierluigi Martini (ITA)
116	Jacky Ickx (BEL)
	Damon Hill (GBR)
	Alan Jones (AUS)
114	Heinz-Harald Frentzen (GER)
	Keke Rosberg (FIN)
	Patrick Tambay (FRA)
113	Eddie Irvine (GBR)
112	Denny Hulme (NZL)
	Jody Scheckter (RSA)

Constructors

636	Ferrari

509 McLaren

490 Lotus

428 Williams

418 Tyrrell

394 Brabham

392 Prost

354 Arrows

300 Benetton

254 Minardi

230 March

197 BRM

163 Jordan

132 Osella

129 Cooper

Most wins

51 Alain Prost (FRA)

44 Michael Schumacher (GER)

41 Ayrton Senna (BRA)

31 Nigel Mansell (GBR)

27 Jackie Stewart (GBR)

25 Jim Clark (GBR)

    Niki Lauda (AUT)

24 Juan Manuel Fangio (ARG)

23 Nelson Piquet (BRA)

22 Damon Hill (GBR)

18 Mika Hakkinen (FIN)

16 Stirling Moss (GBR)

14 Jack Brabham (AUS)

    Emerson Fittipaldi (BRA)

    Graham Hill (GBR)

13 Alberto Ascari (ITA)

12 Mario Andretti (USA)

    Alan Jones (AUS)

    Carlos Reutemann (ARG)

11 Jacques Villeneuve (CDN)

10 Gerhard Berger (AUT)

    James Hunt (GBR)

    Ronnie Peterson (SWE)

    Jody Scheckter (RSA)

9 David Coulthard (GBR)

8 Denny Hulme (NZL)

    Jacky Ickx (BEL)

7 Rene Arnoux (FRA)

6 Tony Brooks (GBR)

    Jacques Laffite (FRA)

    Riccardo Patrese (FRA)

    Jochen Rindt (AUT)

    John Surtees (GBR)

    Gilles Villeneuve (CDN)

Constructors

135 Ferrari

130 McLaren

102 Williams

79 Lotus

35 Brabham

27 Benetton

23 Tyrrell

17	BRM
16	Cooper
15	Renault
10	Alfa Romeo
9	Ligier
	Maserati
	Matra
	Mercedes
	Vanwall
3	Jordan
	March
	Wolf
2	Honda
1	Eagle
	Hesketh
	Penske
	Porsche
	Shadow
	Stewart

	Alain Prost (FRA) 1988
	Alain Prost (FRA) 1993
	Ayrton Senna (BRA) 1991
	Jacques Villeneuve (CDN) 1997
6	Mario Andretti (USA) 1978
	Alberto Ascari (ITA) 1952
	Jim Clark (GBR) 1965
	Juan Manuel Fangio (ARG) 1954
	Damon Hill (GBR) 1994
	James Hunt (GBR) 1976
	Nigel Mansell (GBR) 1987
	Michael Schumacher (GER) 1998
	Ayrton Senna (BRA) 1989
	Ayrton Senna (BRA) 1990

In one season

9	Nigel Mansell (GBR) 1992
	Michael Schumacher (GER) 1995
	Michael Schumacher (GER) 2000
8	Mika Hakkinen (FIN) 1998
	Damon Hill (GBR) 1996
	Michael Schumacher (GER) 1994
	Ayrton Senna (BRA) 1988
7	Jim Clark (GBR) 1963
	Alain Prost (FRA) 1984

Constructors

15	McLaren 1988
12	McLaren 1984
	Williams 1996
11	Benetton 1995

10	Ferrari 2000
	McLaren 1989
	Williams 1992
	Williams 1993
9	McLaren 1998
	Williams 1986
	Williams 1987
8	Benetton 1994
	Lotus 1978
	McLaren 1991
	Williams 1997
7	Ferrari 1952
	Ferrari 1953
	Lotus 1963
	Lotus 1973
	McLaren 1999
	McLaren 2000
	Tyrrell 1971
	Williams 1991
	Williams 1994
6	Alfa Romeo 1950
	Alfa Romeo 1951
	Cooper 1960
	Ferrari 1975
	Ferrari 1976
	Ferrari 1979
	Ferrari 1990
	Ferrari 1996
	Ferrari 1998
	Ferrari 1999
	Lotus 1965
	Lotus 1970
	Matra 1969
	McLaren 1976

McLaren 1985
McLaren 1990
Vanwall 1958
Williams 1980

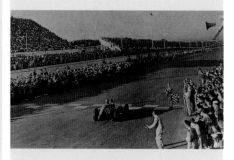

Most consecutive wins

9	Alberto Ascari (ITA) 1952/53
5	Jack Brabham (AUS) 1960
	Jim Clark (GBR) 1965
	Nigel Mansell (GBR) 1992
4	Jack Brabham (AUS) 1966
	Jim Clark (GBR) 1963
	Juan Manuel Fangio (ARG) 1953/54
	Damon Hill (GBR) 1995/96
	Alain Prost (FRA) 1993
	Jochen Rindt (AUT) 1970
	Michael Schumacher (GER) 1994
	Michael Schumacher (GER) 2000
	Ayrton Senna (BRA) 1988
	Ayrton Senna (BRA) 1991

Grand Prix starts without a win

208	Andrea de Cesaris (ITA)
158	Martin Brundle (GBR)
147	Derek Warwick (GBR)

135	Jean-Pierre Jarier (FRA)
132	Eddie Cheever (USA)
119	Pierluigi Martini (ITA)
109	Philippe Alliot (FRA)
99	Pedro Diniz (BRA)
97	Chris Amon (NZL)
95	Ukyo Katayama (JAP)
94	Mika Salo (FIN)
93	Ivan Capelli (ITA)

Most pole positions

65	Ayrton Senna (BRA)
33	Jim Clark (GBR)
	Alain Prost (FRA)
32	Nigel Mansell (GBR)
	Michael Schumacher (GER)
29	Juan Manuel Fangio (ARG)
26	Mika Hakkinen (FIN)
24	Niki Lauda (AUT)
	Nelson Piquet (BRA)
20	Damon Hill (GBR)
18	Mario Andretti (USA)
	Rene Arnoux (FRA)
17	Jackie Stewart (GBR)
16	Stirling Moss (GBR)
14	Alberto Ascari (ITA)
	James Hunt (GBR)
	Ronnie Peterson (SWE)
13	Jack Brabham (AUS)
	Graham Hill (GBR)
	Jacky Ickx (BEL)
	Jacques Villeneuve (CDN)
12	Gerhard Berger (AUT)

10	David Coulthard (GBR)
	Jochen Rindt (AUT)
8	Riccardo Patrese (ITA)
	John Surtees (GBR)

Constructors

137	Ferrari
110	McLaren
108	Williams
107	Lotus
39	Brabham
31	Renault
16	Benetton
14	Tyrrell
12	Alfa Romeo
11	BRM
	Cooper
10	Maserati
9	Ligier
8	Mercedes
7	Vanwall
5	March
4	Matra
3	Shadow

2	Jordan
	Lancia
1	Stewart

In one season

14	Nigel Mansell (GBR) 1992
13	Alain Prost (FRA) 1993
	Ayrton Senna (BRA) 1988
	Ayrton Senna (BRA)1989
11	Mika Hakkinen (FIN) 1999
10	Ayrton Senna (BRA) 1990
	Jacques Villeneuve (CDN) 1997
9	Mika Hakkinen (FIN) 1998
	Damon Hill (GBR) 1996
	Niki Lauda (AUT) 1974
	Niki Lauda (AUT) 1975
	Ronnie Peterson (SWE) 1973
	Nelson Piquet (BRA) 1984
	Michael Schumacher (GER) 2000
8	Mario Andretti (USA) 1978
	James Hunt (GBR) 1976
	Nigel Mansell (GBR) 1987
	Ayrton Senna (BRA) 1986
	Ayrton Senna (BRA) 1991
7	Mario Andretti (USA) 1977
	Jim Clark (GBR) 1963
	Damon Hill (GBR) 1995
	Ayrton Senna (BRA) 1985

Constructors

15	McLaren 1988
	McLaren 1989
	Williams 1992
	Williams 1993

12	Lotus 1978
	McLaren 1990
	McLaren 1998
	Williams 1987
	Williams 1995
	Williams 1996
11	McLaren 1999
	Williams 1997
10	Ferrari 1974
	Ferrari 2000
	Lotus 1973
	McLaren 1991
	Renault 1982
9	Brabham 1984
	Ferrari 1975

Most fastest laps

41	Alain Prost (FRA)
40	Michael Schumacher (GER)
30	Nigel Mansell (GBR)
28	Jim Clark (GBR)
25	Niki Lauda (AUT)
23	Juan Manuel Fangio (ARG)
	Nelson Piquet (BRA)
22	Mika Hakkinen (FIN)
21	Gerhard Berger (AUT)
20	Stirling Moss (GBR)
19	Damon Hill (GBR)

	Ayrton Senna (BRA)
15	Clay Regazzoni (SUI)
	Jackie Stewart (GBR)
14	David Coulthard (GBR)
	Jacky Ickx (BEL)
13	Alberto Ascari (ITA)
	Alan Jones (AUS)
	Riccardo Patrese (ITA)
12	Rene Arnoux (FRA)
	Jack Brabham (AUS)
11	John Surtees (GBR)

Constructors

143	Ferrari
111	Williams
101	McLaren
71	Lotus
40	Brabham
35	Benetton
20	Tyrrell
18	Renault
15	BRM
	Maserati
14	Alfa Romeo
13	Cooper
12	Matra
11	Ligier
9	Mercedes
7	March
6	Vanwall

Most points
(this figure is gross tally, ie. including scores that were later dropped)

798.5	Alain Prost (FRA)
678	Michael Schumacher (GER)
614	Ayrton Senna (BRA)
485.5	Nelson Piquet (BRA)
482	Nigel Mansell (GBR)
420.5	Niki Lauda (AUT)
385	Gerhard Berger (AUT)
383	Mika Hakkinen (FIN)
360	Damon Hill (GBR)
	Jackie Stewart (GBR)
310	Carlos Reutemann (ARG)
294	David Coulthard (GBR)
289	Graham Hill (GBR)
281	Emerson Fittipaldi (BRA)
	Riccardo Patrese (ITA)
277.5	Juan Manuel Fangio (ARG)
274	Jim Clark (GBR)
261	Jack Brabham (AUS)
255	Jody Scheckter (RSA)
248	Denny Hulme (NZL)
236	Jean Alesi (FRA)
228	Jacques Laffite (FRA)

Constructors

2524.5	Ferrari
2480.5	McLaren
2031.5	Williams
1352	Lotus
867.5	Benetton
854	Brabham
617	Tyrrell
439	BRM
420	Prost
333	Cooper

312	Renault
233	Jordan
171.5	March
164	Arrows
155	Matra
90	Sauber
79	Wolf
67.5	Shadow
57	Vanwall

	Ayrton Senna (BRA)
	Jackie Stewart (GBR)
2	Alberto Ascari (ITA)
	Jim Clark (GBR)
	Emerson Fittipaldi (BRA)
	Mika Hakkinen (FIN)
	Graham Hill (GBR)
1	Mario Andretti (USA)
	Giuseppe Farina (ITA)
	Mike Hawthorn (GBR)
	Damon Hill (GBR)
	Phil Hill (USA)
	Denis Hulme (NZL)
	James Hunt (GBR)
	Alan Jones (AUS)
	Nigel Mansell (GBR)
	Jochen Rindt (AUT)
	Keke Rosberg (FIN)
	Jody Scheckter (RSA)
	John Surtees (GBR)
	Jacques Villeneuve (CDN)

Most driver titles

5	Juan Manuel Fangio (ARG)
4	Alain Prost (FRA)
3	Jack Brabham (AUS)
	Niki Lauda (AUT)
	Nelson Piquet (BRA)
	Michael Schumacher (GER)

Most constructors' titles

11	Ferrari
9	Williams
8	McLaren
7	Lotus
2	Brabham
	Cooper
1	Benetton
	BRM
	Matra
	Tyrrell
	Vanwall

INDEX

PICTURE CREDITS

Carlton Books Ltd. would like to thank the following sources for their
kind permission to reproduce the pictures in this book:

Allsport UK Ltd/Michael Cooper, Tony Duffy, Hulton-Deutsch, Clive Mason,
Steve Powell, Pascal Rondeau, Mark Thompson, Vandystadt/Bernard Asset

Diana Burnett
Empics
Hulton Getty
LAT Photographic
Ludvigsen Library Ltd.
©Phipps Photographic
Sporting Pictures